Human Factor in Military Aviation Accidents

Dedications

This book is dedicated to…

To my wife Marta, every time she enters home, our lives are filled with light and joy.

To my sons Santiago, Javier and Jorge, for being for Marta and me our reason to live every day.

To my parents, for teaching me the value of perseverance.

Human Factor in Military Aviation Accidents

A Resume of 31 USAF accidents extracted from Accident Investigation Board (AIB) public reports

Juan Urrutia de Hoyos

This book contains information obtained from the Air Force Magazine public website (http://www.airforcemag.com/Pages/HomePage.aspx).

Disclaimer: The USAF has neither endorsed, sponsored, nor authorized this publication. The views expressed herein are solely those of the Author and do not necessarily represent the views of USAF. The author cannot assume responsibility for the validity of all materials or the consequences of their use.

Cover

The cover is an oil painting made by the author who tries to transmit the affective relationship between the man and the machine.

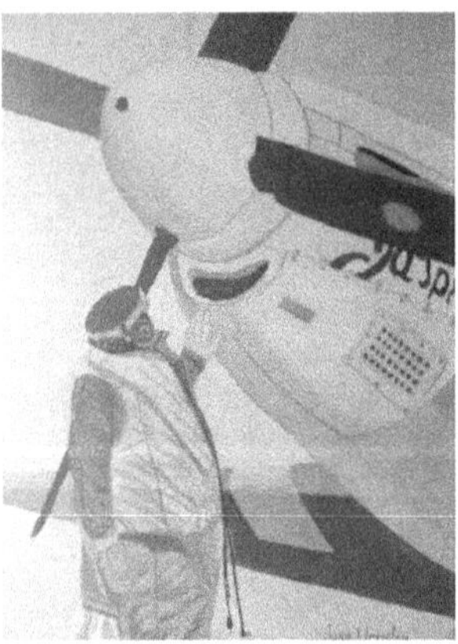

Contents

Acknowledgments

I am grateful to the USAF for making public the reports of these accidents, allowing the aeronautical community to learn from them.

Particular thanks are due to my wife, Marta, for her careful help to prepare the preface and her help with the English translation.

To Luis Gracia, for trusting me and giving me the opportunity to work at Airbus DS Product Safety Department and to encourage me to study the subject of human factors in the military field.

To my colleague Pepe Casado, for his constant support in the activities that I do related to the Human Factor.

Gratitude is also to Lucía Ferraz due to the editorial work and her support in the work of Human Factor in Airbus DS.

I am grateful to all my colleagues in Airbus DS Product and Flight Safety and the rest of the people with whom I have worked, especially to Mr. Chorro, colleague and teacher, both professionally and personally, a great person.

Preface

I will never forget the summer day of August 2001, I was on the beach on vacation with my family and, as always, I went in the morning to buy "churros" (typical Spanish sweet) for breakfast, as well as the newspaper. I was disheartened by the appearance on the front page of the newspaper of a CN-235 from the Spanish company Binter Mediterráneo that had crashed at Málaga airport.

Figure 1: CN-235 accident.

In the photograph, taken from the outside of the plane, you could see the cabin of the plane completely destroyed and inside one of the injured pilots.

At that time, I was responsible for Airbus Military (formerly CASA) Flight Manuals Department. I participated actively in the investigation of this accident. According to the report of the accident, the cause of it was the incorrect application of the emergency procedure Engine Fire by the pilots that led them to switch both engines off when the airplane was at the final approach for landing.

At that time, I wondered how competent pilots could make such errors.

I found the answer by analyzing this accident with some aeronautical engineers from Iberia Spanish Airline that told me it was the typical accident related to Human Factors.

This was the moment when I became interested in Human Factors and has become a passion in my professional life.

During the last 15 years I have been working in the research and application of human factors principles in the design of flight procedures, as well as their application in a company that manufactures airplanes and makes possible the continuous airworthiness of their aircraft.

As Captain Daniel Maurino says, "the discovery of human error should be considered as the starting point of research, and not as the point of arrival that has marked so many previous investigations".

Nowadays is relatively feasible to determine "What" happened in an accident. Knowing what happened in an accident is essential to define and design improvements to the aircraft and its systems, as well as to the operating procedures, but this does not ensure us that this type of accident will occur again.

In order to ensure that the causes of an accident do not lead to similar accidents again, we need to determine the "Why" of the errors made, that is to say, to answer the question of Why were made the errors that caused the accident.

Once it has been concluded that there has been a human error, the question to ask is "Why was the error made?" Have any of the following human factors contributed to the accident?

- Procedural Guidance/Publications

- Overconfidence

- Channelized Attention

- Violation - Lack of Discipline

- Procedural Error

Human Factor in Military Aviation Accidents

-      Misperception of Operational Conditions

-      Spatial Disorientation Unrecognized

-      Supervision-Policy

-      Cognitive Task Oversaturation

-      Task Misprioritization

-      …

Only after determining which factors have contributed to it, human error can be understood and the underlying conditions corrected.

Contemporary thinking considers error as a "symptom of deeper trouble" (Dekker, 2002) within the system. Maurino said human error should be "considered like fever: an indication of illness rather than its cause. It is a marker announcing problems in the architecture of the system" (Maurino, 1997).

A lot of effort has been invested in improving the safety of aircraft systems, their structure, their aerodynamics, their engines, but what effort has been invested in people (Pilots, Controllers, Maintenance Personnel, Safety Culture of the Company)?

It is evident that airplanes have evolved a lot, but what about people? People, in terms of what we define as Human Factors, continue to be similar. To reduce the number of accidents there is no other option than to invest from the first stages of the training of pilots about Human Factors: fatigue, stress, error management, leadership, communication, motivation, crew coordination, automatisms, interruption management, situational awareness, decision making, the safety culture of an operator, and so on.

We all owe a lot to the professionals who investigate aviation accidents as well as to the agencies that publish these accident reports on the internet so that everyone can learn and apply this knowledge.

The objective of this book is to present a summary of military accidents from the point of view of human factors.

In this book it has been resumed 31 public accident reports made by United States Air Force Aircraft Accident Investigation Board (AIB).

I want to thank to the United States Air Force for making these accident reports available for public.

As stated by Ms. Tsongas, U.S. Representative for Massachusetts's 3rd congressional district, during the Tactical Air and Land Forces Subcommittee 115th Congress on Department of Defense Aviation Safety Mishap Review and Oversight Process which was carried out on 13rd June 2018:

"The past few years and the statistics provided by the witnesses show that despite the best efforts of the services, the aviation safety community and others, **military aviation is an inherently risky endeavor. We ask our aviators to train foreign conduct missions in bad weather, at night, at low altitude, and under other high-risk conditions that no civil aviation aircrew would ever even consider attempting to operate under.**"

From the study of these 31 accidents, the most common human factors are the following:

- Channelized Attention
- Procedural Error
- Misperception of Operational Conditions
- Risk Assessment - During Operation
- Procedural Guidance/Publications
- Vision Restricted by Meteorological Conditions
- Breakdown in Visual Scan

The most repetitive Human Factors

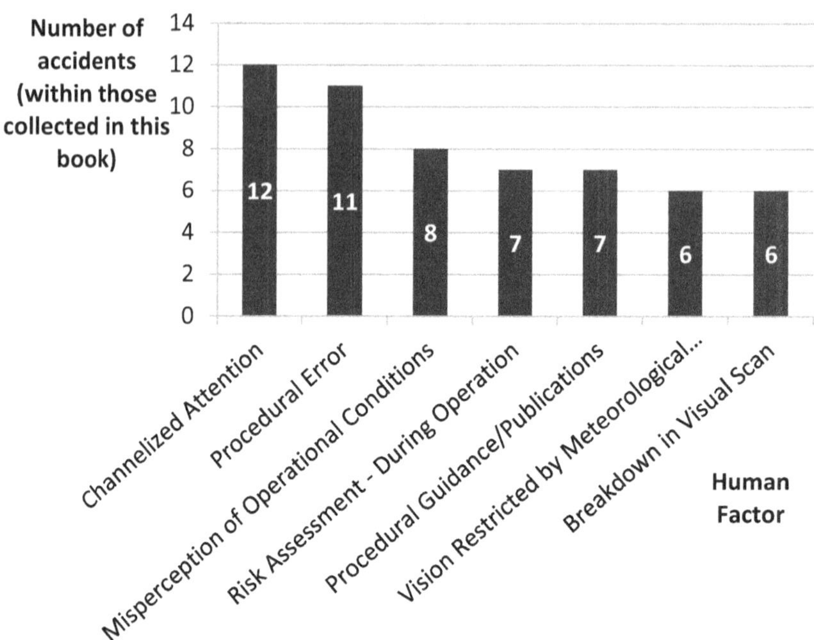

In Chapter 32 a DoD Human Factors Analysis and Classification System HFACS description is included.

Author

From the time I was a boy, I have always been fascinated by airplanes.

My father was a big fan of them and filed many aviation magazines on a shelf above my bed.

When I went to bed I read and reread those magazines, so little by little I got to know and loved the different planes.

I remember the day of my First Holy Communion. My parents offered me either to go to the Theme Park or to go to Barajas Airport in Madrid.

Of course I chose to go to the airport with the consequent anger of my brothers and cousins.

My grandfather worked in an air photography company in the 1920s, it was an extremely dangerous job, he suffered several accidents, the worst of which is the one we can see in the following picture. In this accident he lost the vision of one eye, but over the years he fell in the subway and miraculously he recovered the vision of his eye.

Figure 2: Author Grandfather´s airplane accident.

My grandmother's brother was a pilot in the early years of the Spanish Air Force, throughout his life he suffered six air accidents.

Here we can see two photographs of both of them.

Figure 3: Author grandmother's brother airplane accidents.

When I was a boy I liked to watch these photographs in the family album and I think all this contributed to dedicate my best efforts to study how to avoid air accidents. I guess this is why I currently work in the flight safety area.

There was another photograph that impacted on my life. It was the explosion of the Shuttle Challenger. At that time, I was in second year of my degree on Aeronautical Engineer. I thought that in the future, after finishing my university degree, I shall work to reduce this type of accidents.

Figure 4: Explosion of the Shuttle Challenger

During the years I was studying my aeronautical engineer degree, I become an ultralight pilot to know the operative point of view of aviation.

I started working in Airbus Training Department where I understood the close relationship between training and flight safety.

A well designed Training Need Analysis, Courses for pilots and engineers, Training Aids, Simulators, having competent and well trained Instructors are essentials things for ensuring flight safety.

After 10 years, I changed my job position to the engineering department, where I worked 15 years as head of the flight manuals department.

During these years, I also learned the importance of well designed, validated and certified flight procedures included in the Flight Manual and Flight Crew Operation Manual, well designed and ergonomic cockpit, simple, reliable and easy to operate and maintenance airplane systems, accurate calculation of airplane performances, well designed and executed flight test plan and so on.

With all this, I had a clear idea of what safety meant for an aeronautical engineer working on an aircraft design company.

Figure 5: Author

But when I really felt what flight safety stands for, was the first time I flew alone in the airplane of the flight school where I learned how to fly.

This is how I understood what means to put your life in the hands of other people involved in the safe operation of your aircraft, with the confidence that each one of them was going to do their job correctly.

But something changed definitely my professional life, when the accident of the CN 235 of Binter Mediterráneo occurred. Since then I began to study everything related to the human factor and how this knowledge could be implemented in the flight procedures of our company.

And it became a passion for me …

1 M-28 Afghanistan crash landing

Figure 6: M-28 (Source: U.S. AIB report).

The United States Air Force Aircraft Accident Investigation Board (AIB) describes in their report that:

At 0939 hours Zulu time on 18 December 2011, an M-28, Tail Number 08-0319, departed Kandahar Air Base, Afghanistan on a mission to pick up four passengers at Qalat, Afghanistan, transport them to Walan Rabat short takeoff and landing zone, transport two additional personnel from Walan Rabat back to Qalat, then return to Kandahar Air Base. The mishap aircraft and crew were assigned or attached to the 318th Special Operations Squadron, 27th Special Operations Wing at Cannon Air Force Base, New Mexico, and were deployed to the 318th

Expeditionary Special Operations Squadron (ESOS) at Kandahar Air Base, Afghanistan.

After an uneventful stop at Qalat to onload four passengers and their bags, the mishap crew flew a 20-minute leg to Walan Rabat. Surface winds at Walan Rabat were 190 degrees at 14 knots gusting to 17 knots, 30 degrees off a direct tailwind for runway 34. Because the landing zone has a three percent upslope for runway 34, and a 1,500-foot mountain exists 1½ miles to the north, the pilot elected to land with a tailwind on runway 34, the preferred landing direction.

According to the AIB report, Walan Rabat Landing Zone is a 1,756-foot long, 31-foot wide, semi-prepared dirt strip with poorly defined boundaries. The landing zone was marked with AMP-3 markings, commonly called a "box-and-one" with colored panels. The mishap pilot consulted a wind component chart and incorrectly calculated the tailwind component, mistakenly believing it was within the allowable limit for landing the M-28. The pilot flew a shallow 2½-3 degree approach due to the upsloping landing zone. At approximately 1,000 feet short of the landing zone, the mishap pilot visually acquired the AMP-3 markings and landed the mishap aircraft. After a firmer than normal landing, the aircraft veered to the right and departed the prepared surface.

The nose gear encountered uneven terrain and collapsed, causing the mishap aircraft to flip tailover-nose. The mishap crew and passengers then egressed the aircraft through the copilot's window. According to the report, there were no serious injuries to crew or passengers, the mishap aircraft was destroyed and there were no civilian casualties.

Figure 7: Mishap aircraft (Source: U.S. AIB report).

Accident cause

The AIB president found no clear and convincing evidence of the primary cause of the accident.

According to the report, he determined by a preponderance of evidence that the Landing Zone Condition, Cross-Monitoring Performance, Task/Mission-in-Progress Re-planning, Landing with an Excessive Tailwind, and Aircraft Engine Anomalies substantially contributed to the mishap, ultimately causing the mishap aircraft to veer off the prepared surface into rough terrain, resulting in the collapse of the nose landing gear and destruction of the aircraft.

The report said: The 318 ESOS builds individual mission crews based on experience levels and operations tempo. The mishap crew (MC) consisted of an AF (Air Force) major, the mishap pilot (MP), an AF captain, the mishap copilot (MCP), and an AF staff sergeant, the mishap loadmaster (MLM). All three aircrew members were current and qualified in the M-28 mission, and all were assigned or attached to the 318 SOS.

The MP and MCP had not flown together prior to the mishap flight. The MP was also the 318 ESOS deployed squadron commander, had been in country for 22 days, and had flown twice on his current rotation. He was on his second OEF deployment with the 318 ESOS. The MCP and MLM had been deployed for 85 days.

Accident summary

The report continued explaining how was performed the Planning/Briefing.

The pre-mission brief also included an in-depth route study of the objective areas. Emphasis on this mission was placed on Walan Rabat STOL LZ, since this was the most challenging landing zone and was unfamiliar to the MC.

At 7 minutes, 25 seconds before touchdown, the MC contacted the LZ controller, and AF combat controller (CCT). The CCT called surface winds at 190 degrees at 14 knots, gusting to 17; there was no ceiling and visibility was unrestricted. At this point, the MP expressed surprise at the direction of the wind, noting that it was only 30 degrees from a direct tailwind for the final approach. The MP directed the MCP to check the chart to determine the tailwind component. The MCP explained that his wind chart was in his pubs bag in the back of the aircraft, but commented "tailwind component, that's 30 degrees off...it's going to be about half...8 to 9...is that right? The MP then referenced his own chart to determine the crosswind and tailwind components.

Per Airplane Flight Manual (AFM) PZL M28, the "maximum demonstrated tailwind velocity" for landing is 8 knots. This is generally recognized by the M-28 community as the maximum allowable tailwind component for landing. The MP misread the wind chart believing he would have an 8 knot tailwind and a 12 knot crosswind. He should have computed an 8 knot crosswind and a 12 knot steady state tailwind. This tailwind component would have been well past the maximum allowable 8 knots.

According to the report, the MP elected to continue the approach and landing at Walan Rabat STOL LZ, runway 34. The MP briefly discussed and rejected landing on runway 16 due to the high terrain north of the LZ and 3 percent down-sloping runway.

The MCP initially identified the landing zone environment at greater than 6 miles out as the MA approached course centerline from left to right. The MA intercepted course centerline at 5 miles out, but the pilot had not yet positively identified the landing zone.

The MP initially identified the LZ environment inside of 3.5 miles out and set up to fly a 2-3 degree glide slope on final. Inside 1.5 miles, the MCP noted that the approach was "...still drug in looking." The MP acknowledged the shallow approach with "Yep, this one will be drug in".

At 13 seconds prior to landing, both MP and MCP stated "negative box" meaning they did not see the AMP-3 landing zone markings.

At 6 seconds prior to landing, both MP and MCP stated "got the zone".

At 5 seconds prior to landing, the MP stated "Coming back to centerline".

Shortly after, the cockpit voice recorder records the sounds of the aircraft landing for 5 seconds followed by a loud yell from an unidentified crewmember as the recording ends.

Impact

The report added the Landing/Impact as follows:

After an initial firm landing, the MA veered to the right. Approximately 3 seconds after landing, the nose dipped and the right wing dropped as the landing gear collapsed. The impact of the nose caused the MA to summersault forward, tail-over-nose, coming to rest upside down, just off the right edge of the LZ at approximately midfield.

The AIB report explains the Search and Rescue (SAR):

An United States Air Force (USAF) HH-60 rescue helicopter was dispatched to recover the MC from the site of the accident. The helicopter landed near the Walan Rabat STOL LZ and onloaded the MC. Upon departure, the HH-60 crashed as well.

The MCP was thrown from the aircraft during the crash and was partially pinned underneath some of the wreckage. He experienced minor injuries. The other mishap crewmembers experienced no significant injuries from the helicopter crash.

The report includes an Engines Evaluations and Analyses, it is as follows:

An analysis of the FDR data during landing indicates the presence of asymmetric thrust pushing the aircraft to the right. At touchdown, the aircraft was producing forward thrust from the lefthand engine and within one second of touchdown was producing reverse thrust from the righthand engine, which would cause the aircraft to veer to the right.

Additionally, the FDR data for TQLH and TQRH indicates that both subject engines experienced over torque conditions during the mishap sortie per the PZL M28 AFM.

Another anomaly identified from the FDR data is "torque droop" during power reductions. When power was reduced on both engines simultaneously, the torque on the right-hand engine would droop 10-20% lower than the left-hand engine.

The report includes a Propellers Evaluations and Analyses, it is as follows:

The subject propellers were investigated at the Hartzell Propeller Inc. factory. The investigation concluded that both propellers had blade damage consistent with rotation while at low or moderate power at the time of impact.

Human factors analysis

According to the report, the board evaluated human factors relevant to the mishap using the analysis and classification system model established by the Department of Defense (DoD) Human Factors Analysis and Classification System (HFACS) guide, implemented by Air Force Instruction 91-204.

The report defines five relevant factors that may have contributed to the mishap.

1. Risk Assessment - Formal

Risk Assessment – Formal is a factor when supervision does not adequately evaluate the risks associated with a mission or when pre-mission risk assessment tools or risk assessment programs are inadequate.

The MP and unit supervision failed to accurately assess the risks involved with an unfamiliar landing zone as the ORM (Operational Risk Management) worksheet was marked as low risk for LZs. Additionally, the MP failed to assess the impact of a forecasted tailwind at Walan Rabat LZ during pre-mission ORM.

2. Excessive Motivation to Succeed

Excessive Motivation to Succeed is a factor when the individual is preoccupied with success to the exclusion of other mission factors leading to an unsafe situation.

The MP and MCP focused on the landing at Walan Rabat to the exclusion of eliminating the uncertainty regarding the cross and tail-wind components of the prevailing winds at the LZ.

3. Cross-Monitoring Performance

Cross-Monitoring Performance is a factor when crew or team members failed to monitor, assist or back-up each other's actions and decisions.

When it appeared that the winds at Walan Rabat were not what the Mishap Crew expected, and from the testimony, there was some confusion regarding the cross and tail wind components, the MCP was unable to verify the Mission Pilot's computations due to his not having his wind chart on his knee board. He had left it in his helmet bag.

4. Mission Planning

Mission planning is a factor when an individual, crew or team failed to complete all preparatory tasks associated with planning the mission, resulting in an unsafe situation.

In the preflight mission brief, the MP was under the impression that the winds at Walan Rabat were variable at 5 knots, when in fact, that was the wind factor at Qalat. Recognizing the winds at Walan Rabat being 190/14G17 would have alerted the Mishap Crew to the possibility of out of limit winds at the destination, and allowed them to develop appropriate alternative procedures to deal with them.

5. Task/Mission-in-Progress Re-Planning

Task/mission-in-progress re-planning is a factor when crew or team members fail to adequately reassess changes in their dynamic environment during mission execution and change their mission plan accordingly to ensure adequate management of risk.

When the wind conditions at Walan Rabat were realized, the Mishap Crew failed to accurately assess the cross and tail wind components of the winds, and based on this miscalculation, prosecuted a landing with an out of limits tail wind component.

6. Aircraft Engine Anomalies

The flight data recorder (FDR) indicates an approximate 12-second over-torque of 107.06% on the right-hand engine during initial takeoff on from Kandahar. The M-28 has an audible warning tone for an engine over-torque. The tone starts when either engine's torque exceeds 100% and extinguishes when both engines' torques are below 100%. However, there was no audible tone on the CVR. The FDR indicates another over-torque on the takeoff from Qalat. The right-hand engine shows 107.06% torque for 1-2 seconds and the left-hand engine shows 106.86% torque for 1-2 seconds. The second set of over-torques did have an associated audible warning tone on the CVR.

Another anomaly identified from the FDR is "torque droop" during power reductions. When power was reduced on both engines simultaneously, the torque on the right-hand engine would droop 10-20% lower than the left-hand engine. The droop would last 5-10 seconds at which point the torques of both engines would re-synchronize.

During the portions of flight where the Power Control Levels (PCLs) are typically matched-up and moved simultaneously (takeoff roll and approach to landing) the right-hand engine torque readings are approximately 5% lower than the left-hand engine. This condition will give the aircraft more thrust on the left side, pushing the aircraft to the right. It is common in any case, neither engine was producing much power during that time.

The report says that the board indicated that asymmetric thrust was present at and shortly after landing, which would facilitate the aircraft veering to the right.

7. Violating Safe Landing Criteria

AFSOC M-28 crews are conditioned to think of the "maximum demonstrated wind velocity" of 8 knots on the tail as an operational limit that is not to be exceeded.

Because of confusion in the cockpit, the MP erroneously read an 8-knot tailwind component from the allowable wind component chart. The correct reading was 12 knots. In effect, the MC violated regulatory guidance by landing with 50 percent more tailwind component than allowed by the Aircraft Flight Manual.

As a result of the investigation, AIB concluded that: No clear and convincing evidence of the primary cause of the accident.

AIB determined by a preponderance of evidence that the Landing Zone Condition, Task Mission-in-Progress Replanning, Cross-Monitoring Performance, Landing with an Excessive Tailwind, and Aircraft Engine Anomalies substantially contributed to the mishap, ultimately causing the mishap aircraft to veer off the prepared surface into rough terrain, resulting in the collapse of the nose landing gear and destruction of the aircraft.

2 A-10 C Lapse in Flight Discipline

Figure 8: A-10C (Source: U.S. AIB report).

The United States Air Force Aircraft Accident Investigation Board (AIB) describes in their report that:

On 22 May 2013 at approximately 1548 central daylight time, the mishap aircraft (MA), an A-10C, tail number (T/N) 79-0164, assigned to the 442nd Fighter Wing, Whiteman Air Force Base (AFB), Missouri, impacted two cables during a low altitude training mission over Stockton Lake, Missouri, approximately 70 miles south of Whiteman AFB.

Neither the mishap pilot (MP) nor any civilians near the mishap site were injured. The MA sustained extensive damage to the right horizontal stabilizer, vertical tail and rudder; the left wingtip; and weapons and suspension equipment mounted under the left wing.

Accident cause

The board president found clear and convincing evidence that the cause of the mishap was the MP's poor judgment and lapse in flight discipline resulting in violation of flight rules and operating procedures relating to minimum altitudes.

Additionally, the board president found by a preponderance of the evidence that the following factors substantially contributed to the mishap:

(1) the MP channelized his attention on the boat and did not see the cables he ultimately impacted;

(2) the MP's complacency led to lack of response to altitude advisories; and

(3) the MFL did not confirm that the MP saw the cables nor direct the MP to climb in the absence of that confirmation, contrary to widely utilized techniques.

Accident summary

According to the report, the mishap flight (MF) was planned, briefed and flown as a local two-ship low-altitude surface attack tactics mission. The planned flow of the mission was to depart Whiteman AFB under visual flight rules, complete air-to-air refueling in the Truman A and B Military Operating Areas (MOA), conduct low altitude tactical navigation (LATN) training in the LATN East area at 300 feet above ground level (AGL), execute simulated Maverick attacks in the Truman C MOA, and return to Whiteman AFB.

The MF departed the Truman MOA and flew south toward Stockton Lake to conduct LATN. As the flight flew over the southeast branch of the lake, the MP descended below the approved minimum altitude of 300 feet AGL and maneuvered toward a boat that was traveling southeast on the lake.

According to the AIB report the MF lead (MFL) advice to the MP that he was approaching to the power lines that cross the lake:

The MF lead (MFL) called on the radio that the flight was approaching power lines that cross the lake. The MP acknowledged the call but did not call "contact" on the obstruction as he continued his descent. At approximately 140 feet AGL, the MA impacted two protective cables that run above the power lines crossing the lake.

The MP called "knock-it-off" and began a climb as the MFL rejoined with the MP. The MP stated to the MFL that he "hit those power lines". The MFL examined the visible damage to the MA. The flight coordinated and completed checklist procedures for structural damage, controllability, and hydraulic failure, as the right hydraulic system eventually failed due to a cut hydraulic line in the leading edge of the right horizontal stabilizer. The flight coordinated the recovery plan with the supervisor of flying and declared an emergency with Whiteman AFB tower. The MP safely recovered the MA out of a straight-in approach. The MP shut down at the end of runway after landing, and the MA was towed to the parking ramp.

The AIB determined the probable cause of the accident was:

"... the MP's poor judgment and lapse in flight discipline resulting in violation of flight rules and operating procedures relating to minimum altitudes."

According to the report , the board president found that the following factors substantially contributed to the accident:

(1) the MP channelized his attention on the boat and did not see the cables he ultimately impacted;

(2) the MP's complacency led to lack of response to altitude advisories; and

(3) the MFL did not confirm that the MP saw the cables nor direct the MP to climb in the absence of that confirmation, contrary to widely utilized techniques."

The AIB explains that the mishap mission, was planned as a local two-ship low altitude surface attack tactics (SAT) continuation training (CT) mission. The purpose of the mission was to improve the proficiency of the Mishap Flight Lead (MFL) and MP in air-to-air refueling (AAR), low altitude operations down to 300 feet above ground level (AGL), and Maverick air-to-surface missile employment. No special emphasis was placed on training rules or operating procedures that applied to low altitude operations and obstacle avoidance because the MFL had selected a route that avoided obstacles that would be a factor to the flight at 300 feet.

During the briefing, MP did not say anything about his intention to flight above the boat:

According to the MFL, the MP was attentive and focused in the briefing and did not indicate any lack of understanding of the overall mission plan prior to stepping to the aircraft. The flight proceeded to the southeastern branch of Stockton Lake in southwest Missouri.

Before flying over the lake, the flight was flowing as planned:

Approximately 7 minutes prior to the mishap, the flight was established at 300 feet AGL. From that time to the mishap, the flight flew over mildly rolling terrain before reaching the lake shoreline. En route to the lake, the MFL made a radio call identifying a tower 2 miles southeast of the formation, which the MP acknowledged by calling "contact," indicating he saw the tower the MFL had called out.

This is the normal procedure, to answer to the radio call saying "contact" when the pilot sees the object above terrain.

The MA started to descend to the lake, in spite of multiples alert from the aircraft alerting system the MP followed with his intention to fly over the boat, as describe in the report:

The MP experienced 52 audible "ALTITUDE, ALTITUDE" alerts from the aircraft voice messaging system over those 7 minutes, indicating his altitude was below the 300 feet AGL advisory altitude he had set. Throughout this sequence, his altitude indicated as low as 120 feet AGL. The MP did not appear to react to any of those alerts by maneuvering the aircraft vertically to correct the deviation or stop the altitude advisories.

According to the report, the attitude of the MP was not appropriate:

The MP was also whistling in the intercom throughout this sequence.

As the flight reached the southeast corner of the lake, the MP executed a turn from south to west utilizing approximately 80° right bank and the nose dropped to 6° of dive. The predictive ground collision avoidance system (PGCAS) generated a "PULL UP, PULL UP" audio warning and a "break X" in the HUD. The PGCAS warning is designed to alert the pilot that the aircraft will descend to less than 90 feet AGL on its current trajectory unless an aggressive, wings-level climb is initiated. The MP did not appear to react to these indications and continued to turn and descend toward two boats he saw on the water.

The MP continued the flight in spite of the warnings of the MFL.

The MFL made a radio call that the flight was approaching power lines that cross the lake, to which the MP responded "2," indicating he heard the MFL's radio call but not necessarily that he had the obstruction in sight, contrary to the MFL's assumption. The MFL did not confirm that the MP had the cables in sight when the MP responded "2," which is the normal technique of every other pilot interviewed.

According to the report, six seconds later, the MP flew at 130 feet above the water nearly directly over the first boat traveling northwest on the lake.

The MP climbed slightly and acquired the second boat traveling southeast on the lake toward him. The MP maneuvered his aircraft in a shallow, left-turning descent to point in the direction of the boat.

At 140 feet AGL, 3° of descent, approximately 10° left bank, heading 283°, and 299 knots indicated airspeed (KIAS), the MA impacted and severed two cables that spanned the lake.

Figure 9: Severed cable at mishap site (Source: U.S. AIB report).

The MP called "knock-it-off' on the radio and the MFL rejoined with the MP.

The MP stated on the radio that he "hit those power lines".

The MFL did a visual check of the MA, and noted that the Maverick air-to-ground and Air Intercept Missile-9 (AIM-9) air-to-air missiles were damaged, as well as the suspension equipment under the left wing and the left wing tip. The Bomb Dummy Unit-33 (BDU-33) on the center station of the left Triple Ejection Rack (TER) was twisted, but all training munitions were still on the MA. On the right side of the MA, the MFL noted there was damage to the leading edge of the right horizontal stabilizer and base of the right vertical stabilizer.

Figure 10: MA with visible damage to rudder cap and horizontal stabilizer (Source: U.S. AIB report).

Despite the visible damage, the MP maintained control of the MA and returned to base with no further events.

He also observed the MA was leaking some unknown fluid. The flight turned toward Whiteman AFB and coordinated their recovery plan with the Supervisor of Flying (SOF). The MP completed the structural damage and controllability checklists.

According to the report, the MA has a left and right hydraulic system for primary and back-up control. The left system was intact. However, the cable struck the leading edge of the right horizontal stabilizer, removing a portion of the leading edge, and damaging the right system hydraulic line to the right rudder. The break in the line compromised the right hydraulic system to the point that the MP attempted to isolate it to prevent total hydraulic failure.

With the right system failure, the MP had no control of the slats, speed brakes, and air-refueling door.

The MP had control of the MA to land safely back at Whiteman AFB. Due to the break in the hydraulic line, the right system was depleted of fluid, and the MP completed the hydraulic system failure checklist.

The MA had normal braking available because the left hydraulic system was intact. The MP pulled the emergency brake handle in accordance with the controllability check checklist to provide a minimum of five brake applications. The brake system did not sustain any damage and operated normally on recovery of the aircraft.

Figure 11: Damage to BDU-33, TGM-65 Maverick, AIM-9, DRA (Source: U.S. AIB report).

Figure 12: Damage to right vertical and horizontal stabilizer and right rudder cap (Source: U.S. AIB report).

The MP coordinated for an emergency landing on Runway 01 at Whiteman AFB, he flew an uneventful straight-in approach, taxied clear of the runway, and shut the aircraft down after post flight end of runway and engine shutdown procedures were completed.

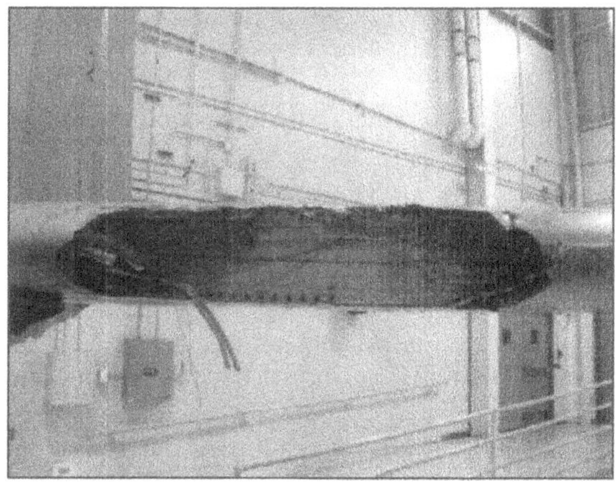

Figure 13: Severed/damaged hydraulic, electrical (lighting), avionics, and manual flight control lines (Source: U.S. AIB report):

Figure 14: Damage to right rudder bottom cap and hinge (Source: U.S. AIB report).

The AIB describes in their report about the MP lifestyle:

The MP was not available for questioning. Therefore, the AIB was only able to use information gathered from interviews of other squadron members. None of the witnesses interviewed disclosed information indicating that the MP had demonstrated any behavior, stress, distraction or unusual habits in the days leading up to the mishap that would have contributed to the mishap.

There is no evidence that any behavior, stress, distractions or unusual habits displayed by the MFL contributed to the mishap. Neither witness testimonies nor the 72-hour history of the MFL revealed evidence of abnormal behaviors that contributed to the mishap.

Human factors analysis

According to the report, the investigation of human factors was carried out using the AFI 91-204, Attachment 5, Department of Defense Human Factors Analysis and Classification System (DOD HFACS).

Two human factors were identified as causal to this mishap: risk assessment-during operation and lack of discipline.

Three factors were identified as substantially contributing: channelized attention, complacency, and challenge and reply.

Applying this method the Human Factors applicable in this accident are the following:

1. Risk Assessment - During Operation

Risk Assessment - During Operation is a factor when the individual fails to adequately evaluate the risks associated with a particular course of action and this faulty evaluation leads to inappropriate decision and subsequent unsafe situation. This failure occurs in real-time when formal risk-assessment procedures are not possible.

The MP's response to the MFL's radio call identifying the cables, along with the MP's call after the mishap that he "hit those power lines," indicate he was aware that the cables were in the vicinity and were a factor to the MF.

He did not call "contact" as he had done previously during the LATN. The lack of a "contact" call indicated he did not see the cables. Failure to appropriately address the risk the cables posed to the flight and the people on the boat led to an inappropriate decision to continue his maneuver to make a low altitude pass over the boat. This created an unsafe situation and was causal to the mishap.

2. Violation - Lack of Discipline

Violation - Lack of Discipline is a factor when an individual, crew or team intentionally violates procedures or policies without cause or need. These violations are unusual or isolated to specific individuals rather than larger groups. There is no evidence of these violations being condoned by leadership. These violations may also be referred to as "exceptional violations."

According to the report, interviews with eleven 303 FS pilots who know and have flown with the MP indicate that he does not regularly violate flight rules or operating procedures. The MP knows the rules and normally adheres to them. In this case, the MP intentionally and unnecessarily maneuvered his aircraft in violation of flight rules and operating procedures contained in AFI 11-202, Volume 3; AFI 11-2A-I0C, Volume 3; and AFI II-2AOA-I0V3/442 FW Supplement 1.

While it seems to be anomalous for the MP, the lack of discipline demonstrated by his attempt to do a low pass over the boat in violation of these directives created an unsafe situation and was causal to the mishap.

3. Channelized Attention

Channelized Attention is a factor when the individual is focusing all conscious attention on a limited number of environmental cues to the exclusion of others of a subjectively equal or higher or more immediate priority, leading to an unsafe situation. It may be described as a tight focus of attention that leads to the exclusion of comprehensive situational information.

According to the report, the MP was clearly focused on flying over the boats on the lake. This focus caused him to exclude information being made available to him through MFL radio calls and auditory and visual advisories from the aircraft. It also prevented him from considering the highest priority task at the time-gaining visual contact with the cables.

By channelizing his attention on the boat in the vicinity of the cables, the MP allowed an unsafe situation to develop, substantially contributing to the mishap.

4. Complacency

Complacency is a factor when the individual's state of reduced conscious attention due to an attitude of overconfidence, under motivation or the sense that others "have the situation under control" leads to an unsafe situation.

According to the report, while it is not unusual to have occasional altitude alerts when operating at low altitude over rolling terrain, the MP experienced 52 altitude alerts and one ground collision warning in the 7 minutes prior to the mishap.

According to the report, the MP's lack of response to these advisories, along with the fact that he was audibly whistling over the intercom throughout that period, demonstrated the MP's overconfidence during low altitude operations and MP demonstrated a high level of comfort flying at low altitude, which resulted in the MP's complacency during low altitude operations. His overconfidence resulted in reduced attention to the threat posed by the cables in the mishap area. This behavior continued up to impact with the cables. Complacency substantially contributed to the mishap.

5. Challenge and Reply

Challenge and reply is a factor when communications did not include supportive feedback or acknowledgement to ensure that personnel correctly understand announcements or directives.

According to the report, Eleven 303 FS pilots were asked to explain the squadron standard for identification and avoidance of obstacles during low altitude operations. All but the MFL adhere to the same technique. The MFL stated that, depending on whom he was flying with, he did not necessarily expect to hear his wingman call "contact" to indicate that the wingman had a declared obstacle in sight.

The MFL said that with a more experienced wingman, like the MP, a response of "2" would be sufficient to indicate that he heard the call identifying the obstacle and had the obstacle in sight.

Only a "no joy" call would be definitively interpreted by the MFL that the wingman did not see the obstacle. In that case, the wingman would need amplifying information to locate the obstacle, or a directive call to maneuver to avoid it.

In the case of the MF, the MP responded "2" when the MFL called out the cables over the lake, but the MP did not have them in sight, contrary to the MFL's assumption. The MFL did not confirm that the MP had the cables in sight when the MP responded "2," which is the normal technique of every other pilot interviewed.

A no-notice review of 7 HUD videos conducted by the board during the investigation revealed that in all cases when an obstacle was encountered, communication continued until all flight members called "contact" with the obstruction. That communication is not directed or procedural, nor is it written in the squadron standards.

However, it appears to be the accepted, and perhaps the expected, flow of communications in this situation. Had the MFL utilized this accepted/expected technique, he may have gotten the MP's attention and prevented the impact with the cables.

According to the report, the Lack of the accepted/expected challenge and reply technique substantially contributed to the mishap.

3 CV-22 Afghanistan crash formation taking off

Figure 15: CV-22B (Source: U.S. AIB report).

The United States Air Force Aircraft Accident Investigation Board (AIB) describes in their report that:

On 11 Oct 11. at 19:53 Zulu (Z) time, the Mishap Aircraft (MA), a CV-22B, tail number (TIN) 08-0037, departing Kandahar Air Base (KAF), Afghanistan, operated by the 8th Special Operations Squadron, sustained damage to the right proprotor hub and proprotor gearbox when the aircraft maneuvered to avoid collision with another aircraft in its formation immediately upon takeoff and impacted the ground . The aircraft was assigned to the 20th Special Operations Squadron, 27th Special Operations Wing. Cannon Air Force Base. New Mexico.

 No deaths and one minor injury resulted from the mishap.

According to the AIB report, the MA was the third aircraft in a three aircraft formation supporting a nighttime mission.

The formation was taxi complete and cleared for takeoff by tower.

As the formation commenced with takeoff the Mishap Copilot (MCO) performing the takeoff applied takeoff power and became airborne prior to Chalk 2 (Chk2), who was located 150 to 200 feet in front of the MA.

The takeoff procedure was a formation 75 degree short takeoff (75 STO) which was understood to include a spacing delay between aircraft.

According to the AIB report, lack of clarity on the formation 75 STO procedures regarding aircraft spacing, coupled with shortening the six second power push to less than three seconds, contributed to the MCO responding to forward motion from Chk2 with an anticipatory response and taking off out of sequence prior to Chk2.

The out of sequence takeoff by the MA caused the mishap pilots to assess a risk of collision between the two aircraft. The MCO tried to arrest his forward motion and avoid overtaking Chk2 by pulling back on the cyclic control stick and pulling the thrust control lever (TCL) back to idle.

This reduced aircraft power and pitched the aircraft nose up. These control inputs produced a high sink rate prompting the MCO and Mishap Pilot (MP) to rapidly apply full power. The MA had only achieved approximately 13 feet (ft) in altitude as measured by the MA's radar altimeter and was unable to arrest the sink rate before impacting the ground at 525 ft per minute.

According to the AIB report, the MA impacted first on the ramp then pitched forward onto the main landing gear and finally the nose gear before immediately becoming airborne again. The movement of the TCL from idle to full power in six-tenths of a second in conjunction with striking the ground and the rapid application of three and one-half inches of aft cyclic caused excessive flapping of the rotor blades resulting in damage to the proprotor hub and proprotor gearbox.

Accident cause

The Accident Investigation Board (AIB) President determined by clear and convincing evidence the causes of the mishap were:

1) The MCO's failure to maintain formation discipline during takeoff and

2) The MCO's aggressive application of control inputs after prematurely becoming airborne in conjunction with impacting the ground.

Additionally the AIB President found by a preponderance of the evidence the non-standardized procedures for executing a formation 75 STO substantially contributed to the mishap.

Accident summary

The AIB report includes as Summary of Accident:

The MA taxied out of parking onto the taxiway heading 230 degrees approximately 150-200 ft behind and 25 ft to the right of Chk2. The MA was the third of three aircraft in the formation. Chk2 had a white landing light on the position lights on steady dim and the proprotor tip lights set to NVG bottom (bottom of blade tips illuminated only if wearing NVGs). The Chalk 1 Formation Lead Aircraft Commander (C1FL) contacted the local control tower for permission to takeoff. The control tower cleared the formation for takeoff. The formation lead aircraft initiated its takeoff roll.

The AIB explains that both Chk2 pilots stated that prior to the formation lead taking off the Chalk 2 Copilot (C2CP) released the brakes and began a slow forward roll in anticipation of takeoff. The Chalk 2 Aircraft Commander (C2AC) told the C2CP to stop, that the takeoff was to be a 75 STD, and to wait until the formation lead aircraft was airborne to begin the takeoff sequence. The Chalk 1 Aircraft Commander (C1AC) told Chalk 2 Copilot (C2CP) to stop forward roll because he wanted to avoid miscuing the MA. C2CP then applied the brakes and came to a complete stop. The C2CP testified that he had in fact been initiating his takeoff sequence early when he was stopped by the C1AC. However it cannot be determined with the Vibration Structural life and Engine Diagnostic Data (VSLED) precisely when this event occurred.

The report continued explaining, the MCO saw formation lead begin the takeoff roll. At this point the MCO perceived Chk2 to be rolling forward. The MCO then looked to the right to clear his immediate area of hazards and then looked forward at Chk2. The MCO then released the brakes and applied takeoff power.

At the time of power application the MA was at 0.69 kts. Formation lead lifted off and was at full power two and four-tenths of a second after Thrust Control Lever (TCL) push. The C2CP began applying power. Chk2 had 6.68 kts at the time the TCL was moved from eight-tenths of an inch toward full power. The MA became airborne nine-tenths of a second earlier than when Chk2 became airborne and was at full power two and four-tenths of a second after initial power application. Due to the out of sequence takeoff the MA was airborne before and closing on Chk2. At this time the MP told the MCO to abort the takeoff by stating "Whoa, Whoa, Whoa". The MCO then exercised aggressive control inputs to arrest forward motion and avoid what he perceived as risk of collision with Chk2.

According to the AIB report, CV-22 technical guidance warns against both rapid power increases to arrest descent and rapid or excessive application of aft stick during and after liftoff as possibly leading to high flapping conditions:

1) "Rapid or excessive application of aft stick during and after liftoff may result in high flapping".
2) "A rapid power increase to arrest a descent in CONV can lead to both undesired pitch-up and a FLAPPING CRITICAL caution. Slower TCL increases (i.e. full power over 4 to 5 seconds) may reduce the pitch-up and flapping severity".
3) "Damage to the rotor due to high flapping can occur in two ways. Very high flapping causes damage when there is hard contact near the hub. When (sic) total flapping at the transient napping limit the FLAPPING CRITICAL caution will post. This flapping level is indicative of potential contact damage in the rotor hub area. The resulting damage is typically cosmetic in nature; however severe impacts could result in more

significant damage. Flapping stop contact is typically associated with aggressive maneuvering particularly between 75 degrees and 60 degrees nacelle or in low speed VTOL mode flight with high relative wind components".

Each of the above emphasis items occurred as the MCO applied control inputs.

According to the report, to arrest forward motion, the MCO simultaneously pulled back on the cyclic control stick and pulled the TCL from full takeoff power (four inches of TCL travel) back to idle power (zero inches of TCL travel). The combination of these two control inputs caused the MA to pitch approximately 10 degrees nose up and develop a high sink rate from an altitude of approximately 13 ft. Both the MCO and MP responded to the sink rate by pushing the TCL from idle to full power (zero inches to four inches) in six-tenths of a second. After reapplying full TCL power the MCO then continued to apply an cyclic moving from two inches of aft cyclic to three and one-half inches of aft cyclic keeping the aircraft in a nose high attitude.

As the report details, it should be noted that the TCL moves to six inches but there is no additional power produced by pushing the TCL from four inches to six inches. Data shows the pilots pushed the TCL to six inches however, once the TCL was moved to four inches, no additional power was gained by continuing the TCL push to six inches.

The MA could not arrest the descent in time to avoid impacting the ground. Chk2 lifted off the ground and was at full power two and six-tenths of a second after initial TCL input. The Chk2 Flight Engineer Tail Scanner (C2T) stated that he witnessed the MA impact the ground as his aircraft (Chk2) was taking off.

All three aircraft applied full takeoff power in less than three seconds which is counter to technical data that calls for a power push of about six seconds.

Impact

The report describes the Impact as follows:

The MA impacted taxiway 23 foxtrot. The MA impacted ramp first then on the main landing gear and finally the nose landing gear. The aircraft was configured with the landing gear down and locked nacelle angle at 75 degrees and interim power active.

The aircraft had a vertical velocity of 525 ft. per minute upon impact. The right hand flapping sensor registered a Flapping Critical caution. A Flapping Critical caution alerts the aircrew that the proprotor system has exceeded the flapping limit (vertical movement of the proprotor blades) and may be damaged.

Since the TCL was at full power on impact the MA bounced and became airborne again. During the impact the MCO continued to apply aft cyclic increasing his pull to three and eight-tenths of an inch aft cyclic.

The MCO regained control of the MA and flew a left downwind pattern while the MP and MS (Mishap Flight Engineer, Seat) ran the Flapping Critical checklist procedure. The MP radioed CIFL (Chalk I Formation Lead Aircraft Commander) that the MA had to land for maintenance issues and would be breaking out of the formation.

The MA proceeded back to taxiway 23 foxtrot and landed from a hover.

After landing the MA taxied to parking and shutdown.

Human factors analysis

According to the AIB report, the board evaluated human factors relevant to the mishap using the analysis and classification system model established by the Department of Defense (DoD) Human Factors Analysis and Classification System (HFACS) guide, implemented by Air Force Instruction 91-204.

The report defines ten relevant factors that may have contributed to the mishap.

1. Procedural Error

Procedural error is a factor when a procedure is accomplished in the wrong sequence or using the wrong technique or when the wrong control or switch is used.

According to the report, in this mishap the MCO committed procedural error by initiating takeoff of the MA prior to the takeoff Chk2. Several witnesses including the MCO stated that the MCO failed to execute the proper formation takeoff procedure by taking off too early. Furthermore, when comparing the weight on wheels data of MA and Chk2 it is easily recognized that the MA broke ground when Chk2 was still on the ground. This was procedurally incorrect and created an unsafe situation.

It was briefed by the C1FL and understood by all the pilots that the takeoff procedure on 11 Oct 11 would be a formation 75 STO. The 75 5TO was understood as including a delay between aircraft when in formation. Furthermore despite any objective time delay between two aircraft, the ultimate responsibility of a pilot is to ensure that the Flight path is cleared and safe prior to takeoff. The MCO failed to ensure adequate spacing; therefore. He committed procedural error and created an unsafe situation.

2. Necessary Action - Rushed

Necessary Action - Rushed is a factor when the individual takes the necessary action as dictated by the situation but performs these actions too quickly and the rush in taking action leads to an unsafe situation.

According to the report, the evidence in this mishap shows that the MCO rushed a necessary action in two instances:

a) The first instance was when the MCO rushed the takeoff procedure resulting in the MA taking off before Chk2. The mishap launch occurred very quickly. MA's takeoff speed was 0.69 kts whereas Chk2 and formation lead had approximately 6.68 kts and 7 kts. Respectively at similar points in their takeoff profile. This suggests the MA takeoff was rushed because MCO applied takeoff power more rapidly after releasing the brakes when compared with the other aircraft in the formation. The weight on wheels data which shows the MA airborne prior to Chk2 also supports the takeoff being rushed. By rushing takeoff power and accelerating the launch the MCO failed to maintain formation discipline,

b) The second instance was when the MCO rushed control inputs to correct his position after takeoff. Once the MA became prematurely airborne, the MCO assessed the need to arrest his forward motion by simultaneously pulling back on the cyclic and pulling the TCL to zero which produced a high sink rate. This prompted the MCO to then apply full power to arrest the sink rate. During this three and two-tenths of a second timeframe the MCO moved the TCL from full power to zero and back to full power. The rushed control inputs resulted in the aircraft impacting the ground and damaging the proprotor system.

3. Over-control/ Under-control

Over-control/Under-control is a factor when an individual responds inappropriately to conditions by either over-controlling or under-controlling (the aircraft/vehicle/system). The error may be a result of preconditions or a temporary failure of coordination.

According to the report, the human factor of "Over-control/Under-control" was a factor in the mishap.

Over-control occurred when the MCO reduced the TCL from full power to zero in an attempt to arrest his forward motion. This excessive reduction in the TCL resulted in the aircraft entering a sink rate due to lack of power from an altitude of 13 ft. At 13 ft, the aircraft was unable to recover from the descent before impacting the ground. Similarly the MCO over-controlled the aircraft when he reapplied power and pulled back the cyclic in response to the sink rate.

Both of these actions were cautioned against in aircraft technical data. Hence the pilot's over-control in response to the out of sequence takeoff followed by over-control in response to the self-induced sink rate were causal to the mishap.

4. Response Set

Response Set is a factor when the individual has a cognitive or mental framework of expectations that predispose them to a certain course of action regardless of other cues.

According to the report, this human factor occurred when the MCO took off prematurely after seeing Chk2 roll forward. The MCO's response set was to initiate takeoff power almost immediately after Chk2 started takeoff. Per the MCO he initiated takeoff because he interpreted the roll of Chk2 to be the start of Chk2's takeoff.

The MCO's response set was conditioned to immediately initiate takeoff when he saw the aircraft in front of him initiate takeoff.

5. Expectancy

Expectancy is a factor when the individual expects to perceive a certain reality and those expectations are strong enough to create a false perception of the expectation.

According to the report, as discussed in the human factor Response Set, the MCO expected Chk2 to be airborne a few seconds after he visually perceived Chk2 to begin moving forward. Because the MCO expected the forward roll of Chk2 to immediately result in takeoff the MCO initiated takeoff before verifying that Chk2 had actually become airborne.

6. Misperception of Operational Conditions

Misperception of Operational Conditions is a factor when an individual misperceives or misjudges altitude, separation, speed, closure rate, road/sea conditions, aircraft/vehicle location within the performance envelope or other operational conditions and this leads to an unsafe situation.

According to the report, Misperception of Operational Conditions occurred in this case because the MCO stated he visually perceived Chk2 to be further ahead of its actual distance; thus he misjudged separation and closure rate. Based on the misperception of Chk2's movement and distance between Chk2 and the MA, the MCO initiated takeoff out of sequence and created an unsafe situation.

7. Risk Assessment - During Operation

Risk Assessment - During Operation is a factor when the individual fails to adequately evaluate the risks associated with a particular course of action and this faulty evaluation leads to inappropriate decision and subsequent unsafe situation. This failure occurs in real-time when formal risk-assessment procedures are not possible.

According to the report, by initiating takeoff before Chk2 took off the MCO failed to evaluate the risk of inadequate spacing between the MA and Chk2 resulting in an unsafe situation.

8. Error due to Misperception

Error due to Misperception is a factor when an individual acts or fails to act based on an illusion misperception or disorientation state and this act or failure to act creates an unsafe situation.

According to the report, the MCO stated he visually perceived Chk2 to have advanced farther in his takeoff roll than what was later determined to be the actual distance. He also stated he perceived the rear wheels of Chk2 to rotate uncompress and the aircraft begin to lift; however Chk2 had no actually taken off. The MCO misperceived the timing of Chk2' s takeoff based on observed forward motion. From the MCO's experience Chk2's forward roll would have resulted in Chk2 being airborne in seconds giving the MA a clear flight path. Based on this misperception, the MCO committed an error by initiating takeoff out of sequence.

9. Supervision - Discipline Enforcement (Supervisory act of omission)

Supervision - Discipline Enforcement is a factor when unit (organizational) and operating rules have not been enforced by the normally constituted authority.

According to the report, while there was published guidance of a formation 75 STO the understanding implementation and execution techniques varied amongst the pilots. Strict adherence to a specific procedure was not an emphasis item because it had never been highlighted as a problem in the past. Additionally formation takeoffs and aircraft separation in a 75 STO was not a per se pilot evaluation item. Therefore, because the takeoffs were not practiced with a standardized delay the topic had never been highlighted for command interest nor specifically required to be evaluated. The result was a lack of disciplined enforcement for the formation 75 STO procedure.

10. Procedural Guidance/Publications

Procedural Guidance/Publications is a factor when written direction checklists. Graphic depictions, tables, charts or other published guidance is inadequate, misleading or inappropriate and this creates an unsafe situation.

According to the report, in the two years preceding the mishap the MU (Mishap Unit) SOP (Standard Operating Procedures) were rescinded and replaced with guidance that was less specific regarding takeoff procedures from prepared surfaces.

Also, other published guidance, the relevant CV-22 technical order, did not specifically define the procedures for a formation 75 STO departure. As such, the published guidance at the time of the mishap was less specific than years prior and inadequate in providing the specific requirements for formation departure procedures.

4 C-130J-30 Afghanistan Overrun

Figure 16: C-130J (Source: USAF AIB report).

The United States Air Force Aircraft Accident Investigation Board (AIB) describes in their report that:

On 19 May 2013, at approximately 1420 local, a C-130J, T/N 04-3144, assigned to the 41st Airlift Squadron, 19th Airlift Wing, Little Rock AFB, Arkansas, ran off the end of a runway at FOB Shank, Northeast, Afghanistan, struck a ditch which collapsed the nose gear and eventually ripped the right main landing gear from the fuselage. The right outboard engine struck the ground, pressurized fuel and oil lines were broken, fluid was sprayed over the cracked engine casing, and the right wing caught fire. The mishap aircraft (MA) came to full stop approximately 544 feet (ft) off the end of the paved runway surface.

The MA was on an Aero-Medical Evacuation (AE) mission and included five active duty C-130J crewmembers from the 772nd Expeditionary Airlift Squadron (19th Airlift Wing deployed), Kandahar Air Base (AB), Afghanistan.

Additionally, the MA had aboard six AE crewmembers from the 651st Expeditionary Aeromedical Evacuation Squadron.

The mishap sortie happened on the third of five planned legs that day to an airfield that was at 6,809 ft Mean Sea Level (MSL) and experiencing winds varying from 200 to 250 degrees gusting from 6 to 28 knots. On the second attempted landing, the MA touched down approximately 1,500 ft down the runway but was 27 knots indicated airspeed (KIAS) faster than computed touchdown landing speed leading to the aircraft going off the end of the runway at approximately 49 KIAS.

Accident cause

The Accident Investigation Board (AIB) president found, by clear and convincing evidence, that the causes of the accident were poor Crew Resource Management (CRM) and mishap pilot one's (MP1) late power reduction causing a 27 KIAS fast touchdown at a high altitude airfield (6,809 ft MSL).

Additionally, the AIB President found by the preponderance of evidence that each of the following factors substantially contributed to the mishap:

1) Channelized Attention;

2) Risk Assessment;

3) Delayed Necessary Action;

4) Response Set;

5) Procedural Error.

There were no fatalities, significant injuries or damage to civilian property.

Figure 17: FOB Shank (OASH) airport (Source: US AIB report).

The FOB Shank (OASH) airport is described in the report as follow:

FOB Shank (OASH) is located approximately 40 miles South of Kabul, Afghanistan. Runway 34 Right/16 Left is primary and is 6,827 ft long by 90 ft wide. Field elevation is 6,809 ft. When landing Runway 34 Right, there is a 1.5 degree down slope coupled with a "W" gradient effect consisting of two pronounced "hills."

According to the report, to operate in this airport is necessary:

Due to the mountainous terrain and the potential for visual illusions while on final and on the ground, AMC (Air Mobility Command) declared this a special Pilot in Command (PIC) airfield. This requires one pilot on the crew to have operated to or from the airfield in the past 12 calendar months.

The Mission is described in the report as:

The MC was alerted for a routine Afghanistan AE mission to transport patients from Kandahar AB, to Camp Bastion, to FOB Salerno, to FOB Shank, deliver them to Bagram AB and return to Kandahar AB upon mission completion.

The Mission Crew consisted of:

Mishap Pilot 1 (MP1), Mishap Pilot 2 (MP2), Mishap Pilot 3 (MP3), Mishap Loadmaster 1 (MLM1) and Mishap Loadmaster 2 (MLM2).

MP1 was the aircraft commander all day and was seated in the left pilot seat on the flight deck.

The aircraft commander is the one responsible for the safe accomplishment of the tasked mission.

MP2 was the copilot and was seated in the right seat on the flight deck.

MP3 was an extra pilot and occupied the seat located between MP1 and MP2, immediately aft of the center flight deck console.

MLM1 was seated at the right paratroop door in the aft section of the cargo compartment.

 MLM2 was seated at the left paratroop door in the aft cargo compartment.

Normally the C-130J has a combat crew composition of two pilots and two loadmasters. The usual four-person hard crew, which included MP1, MP3, MLM1 and MLM2, had an additional pilot on 19 May 2013, MP2.

According to the report, the MC was aware that the meteo was going to be a factor:

The Mission planning was normal and during the mission brief, the MC took note that gusty winds would be a factor of concern for the mission.

Accident summary

According to the report, the Summary of Accident is the following:

At approximately 0925Z, the MA departed FOB Salerno for FOB Shank . At 0942Z, the reported weather conditions at FOB Shank were 5,000 meters of visibility with dust and haze, temperature 29 degrees Celsius, altimeter setting at 30.04, with winds 240 degrees at 18 knots gusting to 26 knots.

Initially, MP2 was planned to fly the approach and complete the landing, but due to the high crosswinds reported by Air Traffic Control (Tower), MP1 decided to make the landing itself.

A first landing attempt was made, MP1 decided to make it with a flap position of 100%, this selection is called Maximum Landing Effort.

The report explains that a Maximum Effort Landing is a 100% flap landing flown at slower speeds than a normal 100% flap landing and results in shorter landing distances.

After executing an approach to runway 34R, the MC determined they were too high and too fast, so a go-around was initiated. A go-around is an approach to landing that is aborted before or after touchdown. Following the go-around, the MC requested and was approved a right overhead (right traffic pattern) in order to reattempt the landing.

While the MA was on a 160 degree heading (downwind leg), tower reported winds 250 degrees at 23 gusting to 28 knots, a straight crosswind. MP2 later testifies that the HUD indicated a quartering tailwind for final, but does not verbalize the indication.

This is important because it shows at this point a lack of CRM in terms of communication because if it had been noted to the MP1 at best this would have noticed the existence of tailwind.

MP1 makes a key decision:

Shortly thereafter, prior to turning right (base leg), MP1 decided to fly a 50% flap approach due to the high crosswinds.

Although 100% flap approaches are the normal landing configuration for a C-130J, 50% flap approaches improve roll control in high crosswind conditions. Landing with flaps set at 50% is carried out in a similar fashion to a 100% flap landing, however longer landing distances are required.

But the MC did not compute if with this flaps selection, runway was enough to land.

Before landing the crew had another chance to be aware about the tailwind at that time and that could make the runway was not long enough to land:

Just after the MA turns base leg, tower broadcasts new winds to another aircraft within the air traffic control area. Those winds were reported as 230 degrees at 19 gusting to 28 knots. This report created a tailwind component of approximately 10 knots, but there is no evidence that the crew took note of the reported wind shift.

Additionally, the aircraft's flight data recorder showed the MA experienced an approximate 17-knot tailwind component at touchdown.

The approach could not be considered stabilized as stated in the report:

As the MA turned for landing, MP1 overshot the extended centerline of the runway and had to correct back in order to line-up with the runway (final approach). When the MA was established on final approach, the aircraft was approximately 5 miles from the runway.

Once established on final, MP2 testified everything looked good except the MA was not slowing and was approximately 20 KIAS too fast. Note, KIAS is airspeed as reported to the pilots on the primary airspeed indication system. Just prior to touchdown MP2 stated, "100 ft, you're fast." No reference to how fast was verbalized.

There is also a lack of assertiveness on the part of the MP2 by not warning the MP1 that the approach was not within computed values and proposing a Go around.

At this point the MA speed was 148 KIAS (169 knots true airspeed and 187 knots ground speed) and made initial touchdown with the aft main landing gear only, 27 KIAS faster than the computed touchdown speed of 121 KIAS. Touchdown was light, approximately 1,500 ft past the approach end of the runway, slightly long, with 5,500 ft of runway remaining.

With crew-entered winds of 250 degrees at 23 gusting to 28 knots, the computed landing distance for a 50% flap landing, was 5,147 ft. The crew-entered runway distance available, was 6,827 ft. The MC concluded that they had enough available runway distance to land.

The MP1 takes too long (12 seconds) to apply brakes:

After the main landing gear touched down, MP1 held the nose wheel up for approximately four seconds and delayed maximum antiskid braking for approximately eight seconds after the nose wheel came down.

MP2 stated "four board," indicating that the aircraft was about to pass the marker that designates 4,000 ft to go before the end of the runway. The aircraft's nose tire was on the ground at this time.

An Advisory Caution and Warning System (ACAWS) alert for Anti-Skid Fail occurs. The MC did not notice the caution.

The report as we shall see further shows that this failure did not leave without all the braking power to the airplane, it was not a factor in the accident.

The MA was traveling at 140 KIAS, 160 KTAS, with a ground speed of 169 knots.

MP1 stated, "alright, brakes" and began applying full anti-skid braking and power reversing. At that point, the MA had approximately 2,200 ft to go to the end of the paved runway surface (including the 300 ft overrun). Almost immediately after braking and moving the power levers into full reverse, the MA experienced a directional control problem abruptly veering to the left side of the runway coming close to the edge. MP1 uses differential braking (full right brakes) with minor nose wheel steering to regain control of the aircraft and stop it from diverging even more. The MA started to correct back towards the runway centerline with approximately 1000 ft of paved runway surface remaining and was traveling 97 KIAS, 111 KTAS, and 131 knots ground speed. At that time, MP1 began to use maximum brake pedal deflection in order to stop the MA before it departed the paved runway surface. Note, MP1 stated that the brakes did not feel normal and did not slow the aircraft as expected.MP1 states "going of everybody hold on" to the crew.

Impact

The report describes the impact as follows:

The MA departed the paved runway surface traveling at approximately 49 KIAS, and 69 knots ground speed. It traveled approximately 440 ft before it struck a ditch, which collapsed the nose gear and ripped the right main landing gear from the fuselage. The right outboard engine struck the ground, and pressurized fuel and oil lines broke, fluid sprayed over the cracked engine casing and the right wing caught fire. The aircraft came to a complete stop approximately 544 ft past the end of the paved runway surface.

Figure 18: Photo of the MA at the crash site (Source: US AIB report).

Figure 19: Photo of the MA at the crash site (Source: US AIB report).

According to the report, the emergency evacuation was performed as follows:

After the MA came to a complete stop, the MC, AE crew and two ambulatory patients quickly egressed the aircraft through the flight deck overhead escape hatch.

Evacuation through the flight deck hatch was necessitated by the fire on the right wing, extensive damage, loss of electric power, and spinning propellers on the left wing. MP3 was the first out of the aircraft in order to help individuals down from the fuselage.

MLM2 was the last out of the aircraft and ensured 100% accountability. Upon exit, all individuals rallied 600 ft off the nose of the aircraft to take another head count and to get everyone to a safe distance due to the aircraft being equipped with hazardous flares on board .

Search and Rescue (SAR) was conducted as follows:

Immediately following the accident, the airfield control tower contacted Crash-Fire-Rescue, the Task Force Battle Captain, and base Command Post. Crash-Fire-Rescue arrived on the scene within minutes and the crew was reported safe and accounted for. There were no fatalities or significant injuries reported.

The AIB report explains that Anti-Skid Control Unit was functional and would have provided anti-skid protection.

The AIB report discusses the operation of the braking system as follows:

MP1 stated that the brakes did not feel normal and did not slow the aircraft as expected.

The brakes were examined and were found to be in serviceable condition.

There was an anti-skid fail caution. The anti-skid components were tested and found to be serviceable. A couple of factors could be the reason for what the MC experienced. If you put too much energy into the brakes and the brakes heat up, several things can occur. You could have brake fires. You could melt fuse plugs. Also, brake performance degrades as the brakes get hotter – this is called brake fade. There is not always visible indications of brake fade or clear signs that the brakes were over temped (over heated).

The AIB report includes the research conducted in the C-130J-30 Weapon Systems Trainer (WST) simulator:

The AIB Pilot Member flew approximately 30 approaches and landings in a C-130J-30 Weapon Systems Trainer (WST) simulator. The simulator's software was designed to replicate FOB Shank runway 34R and the flight characteristics of a C-130J-30 aircraft. During the tests, the AIB Pilot Member flew different landing scenarios to recreate and to help identify causal and contributing factors relevant to the mishap.

These factors included:

1) a landing touchdown speed 27 KIAS faster than intended;
2) a delay of 12 seconds from touchdown to actuating brakes;
3) a unreported tailwind component of 14 knots;
4) asymmetric reversing of engines causing a directional control problem that results in the aircraft veering left.

According to the AIB report the Results were as follows:

Under all the above landing scenarios, when touching down 27 KIAS fast, the aircraft went off the end of the runway.

Additionally, in recreation of the exact mishap scenario, a safe go-around could have been executed all the way up to the point where MP1 initiated breaks and reverse (approximately 2000 ft remaining). The MA was at 139 KIAS (168 knots ground speed, 160 KTAS) at that point. In simulation, a go-around was able to pass over the end of the runway at 150 ft.

The AIB report considers that the Weather was a factor in this mishap, but not substantially. Weather advisory was in effect for FOB Shank Air Traffic Control tower was winds from 250 degrees at 23 knots gusting to 28 knots, visibility was 5000 meters with dust and haze.

The AIB report says that the mission was operating within acceptable weather standards. Nothing was noted for the day of the mission other than the weather shift with gusty winds. Wind never exceeded a crosswind component of 28 kts, which is within the MA's crosswind landing limitation.

Human factors analysis

The investigator highlight that the Human Factors substantially contributed to this mishap.

AFI 91-204, Safety Investigations and Reports, Attachment 5, contains the Department of Defense Human Factors Analysis and Classification System, which lists potential human factors that can play a role in mishaps. It is designed for use by members of an investigation board in order to accurately capture the complex layers of human error in context with the individual and mishap or event.

According to the report, the analysis below lists the human factors directly involved in this mishap with their definitions.

1. Channelized Attention

Channelized Attention is a factor when the individual is focusing all conscious attention on a limited number of environmental cues to the exclusion of others of a subjectively equal or higher or more immediate priority, leading to an unsafe situation. Channelized attention may be described as a tight focus of attention that leads to the exclusion of comprehensive situational information.

According to the report, MC, particularly MP1, was consumed with landing the aircraft under difficult conditions. These conditions included high gusting crosswinds, a tailwind, high outside air temperature and high-pressure altitude.

On two occasion, MP1 verbalized difficulty with crosswinds. Unfortunately, due to channelized attention on crosswinds, MP1 failed to acknowledge/heed the "fast" call of MP2 on short final thus leading to a touchdown that was 27 KIAS faster than computed touchdown landing speed.

Additionally, MP1 did not recognize that the winds had shifted to include a 17 knot tailwind. This tailwind increased the aircraft's ground speed on touchdown further complicating the MA's landing solution.

Both the high ground speed and true airspeed drove the MC to fixate on technical-order limitations with the nose landing gear and power-lever transition, which delayed their braking, and power reversing, thus invalidating the aircrafts computed landing performance.

Furthermore, this fixation drew their attention away from the approaching end of the runway and considerations of alternative actions such as performing a go-around. In fact, just before MP1 chose to begin braking and reversing, the aircraft was traveling at 139 KIAS (168 GS) with approximately 2,000 ft remaining. At that moment, the MA was at a safe speed to execute a go around for another attempt.

2. Risk Assessment – During Operation

Risk assessment during operations is a factor when the individual fails to adequately evaluate the risks associated with a particular course of action and this faulty evaluation leads to inappropriate decision and subsequent unsafe situation. This failure occurs in real-time when formal risk assessment procedures are not possible.

According to the report, T.O. 1C-130J-1 states that special high speed landing procedures are required if the temperature is greater than +15 degrees Celsius and the landing field elevation is greater than 2,000 ft MSL.

Under these conditions, the crew should determine the maximum indicated airspeed for transition from FLT IDLE to high speed GND IDLE. Additionally, they should reference the Maximum Landing Weight Permitted by Power Lever Transition Limits chart.

According to the report, and this is an important point, the rush to land the aircraft on the second attempt lead to a truncated Before Landing brief and did not allow the MC to properly reference these high speed-landing concerns.

Therefore, risk associated with landing the MA increased without proper consideration.

The MC failed to assess or appreciate the risks associated with a 50% flap landing at a high altitude airfield. A 50% flap landing dictates higher landing speeds which result in longer landing distances and less time to safely stop the aircraft. Landing at a higher altitude airfield with a higher temperature compounds the landing solution further by necessitating even higher landing speeds and longer landing distances.

One of the core curricula of Cockpit/Crew Resource Management (CRM) found in AFI 11-290 is Risk Management (RM). RM includes risk assessment, the risk management processes/tools, breakdowns in judgment and flight discipline, problem-solving, evaluation of hazards, and control measures.

The MC missed several opportunities where CRM could have help advert this accident. Examples of those opportunities include: When MP1 asked if FOB Shank was "landing Runway 34R" and tower took it as a request for 34R. This strengthened the MC's idea that Runway 34R was the preferred runway when in fact it may not have been.

It continued with poor coordination of the go-around when MP1 moved the flaps on his own and MP1's quick report to MP2's challenge of the aircraft's low altitude on downwind.

Furthermore, MP2's lack of verbalization of the expected tailwind on final and the distraction with animals on short final did not help with situational awareness of the crew.

The late notice to change to a 50% flap landing led to a truncated Before Landing Brief by MP1 and left no time for the MC to check critical/required information. This was evident when MP3 relayed the total runway length instead of the required landing distance upon MP1's query.

The fact that no one challenged that "68" was the same distance as the runway itself shows how risk assessment had fallen off the MC's scope.

It further progressed with the poor verbiage used by MP3 and MP2 to help guide the aircraft around the final turn causing it to overshoot final, or the lack of inputting a computer aided turning radius called a "white line" into the navigation system to help MP1 navigate around the turn himself.

Additionally, MP2's "Fast" call on short final without the 20 KIAS deviation included did not alarm the crew to a potential problem. This could have informed the MC that they were traveling much faster than normal and may have alerted them to the need to go-around or immediately start using full braking when on the ground. The lack of a go-around call coupled with the delayed braking shows the crew was truly not aware of the risk they had placed the aircraft and themselves in.

3. Necessary Action – Delayed

Necessary action delayed is a factor when the individual selects a course of action but elects to delay execution of the actions and the delay leads to an unsafe situation.

According to the report, MP1 and MP2 recognized the need to slow the aircraft down, but due to competing interests, they delayed doing so. Because of the increased ground speed on touchdown, MP1 kept the nose wheel up due to technical-order limitations. This delayed the MC's ability to apply brakes early on in their ground roll.

Additionally, because of the high true airspeed on touchdown, MP1 delayed bringing the aircraft throttles into GND IDLE and full reverse due to concern of a propeller over speed. The fact that MP1 delayed putting the nose wheel down for approximately four seconds and full anti-skid braking for another eight seconds only ensured that the MA would depart the paved runway surface at a high speed.

When the MC experienced a directional control problem upon reversing the power at a high true airspeed, it necessitated the crew to use differential braking in order to keep the aircraft on the runway, which further reduced their ability to reach full anti-skid braking in time to stop the aircraft before the end of the paved surface.

4. Response Set

Response set is a factor when the individual has a cognitive or mental framework of expectations that predispose them to a certain course of action regardless of other cues.

According to the report, even after the MA reached a three point taxi attitude (nose wheel and main landing gear on the ground), MP1 failed to apply full anti-skid braking on the aircraft until approximately 2,000 ft remaining on the runway. This contradicts the basic landing distance assumptions of T.O. 1C-130(C)J-1-1 that are predicated on a one second allowance for distance traveled during transition from touchdown to taxi attitude and maximum anti-skid braking with power achieved upon reaching that three point attitude. The fact that MP1 delayed anti-skid braking and only partially used braking early in the landing sequence suggests he was not aware of his high speed and perhaps motivated to delay braking because of a recent experience of losing a tire on landing.

The MC (with the exclusion of MP2) were recently involved in a landing that led to a loss of a tire. Due to this recent event and concern for negative feedback, MP1 may have been motivated to delay breaking early in the landing sequence.

Additionally, the MC's experience with landing lightweight aircraft on airfields at approximately sea level (0 ft MSL) would have led them to believe that 2,000 ft of remaining runway would have given them plenty of time and space to stop the aircraft. Unfortunately, a lightweight landing at 27 KIAS faster than computed touchdown speed on a high altitude airfield (6,809 ft) with a 17 KIAS tailwind far exceeded the capability of the aircraft to stop in the remaining paved.

Therefore:

MP1's experience with normal landing speeds at lower altitudes may have led MP1 to believe that 2,000 ft of remaining runway was plenty of space to stop the aircraft. However, MP1 did not account for the higher airfield altitude and the additional increased touchdown speed at the time that MA had 2,000 ft of runway remaining.

5. Procedural Error

Procedural Error is a factor when a procedure is accomplished in the wrong sequence or using the wrong technique or when the wrong control or switch is used. This also captures errors in navigation, calculation or operation of automated systems.

The main landing gear tires have a limiting speed of 174 knots ground speed. The nose wheel has a limiting speed of 139 knots ground speed. The aircraft flight data recorder shows the aircraft main landing gear touching down at 187 knots ground speed, and the nose gear touching down at 180 knots ground speed.

Both speeds exceed the T.O. C-130J-1 limitations for main landing gear and nose wheel landing gear.

In order to validate TOLD calculations, aircrews must follow certain assumptions. These assumptions include:

a) A one-second allowance for distance traveled during transition from touchdown to taxi attitude;
b) Maximum anti-skid breaking (brakes at ambient temperature) and power selection achieved upon reaching taxi attitude. Taxi attitude is when all wheels are on the ground. Following main landing gear touchdown, MP1 held the nose wheel off the ground for approximately four seconds in order to attempt to slow below the nose wheel limiting speed. After nose wheel touchdown, MP1 delayed going to maximum anti-skid braking for another eight seconds. In total, there was a delay of 12 seconds from initial touchdown to full anti-skid braking. Delays in lowering the nose and initiating full anti-skid braking invalidated the computed landing data for the MA.

T.O. 1C-130J-1 states that the safe condition to move power levers below FLT IDLE is when the weight of the aircraft is on all three gear and the KTAS is below 145. The MA landed at 170 KTAS and recognized they could not immediately select reverse power due to this limitation. However, data from the aircraft flight data recorder shows MP1 selected reverse power while the aircraft was still traveling at 160 KTAS, well above the 145 limitation. Furthermore, the data recording shows that the power levers went straight from FLT IDLE to full reverse, with no pause at GND IDLE.

The T.O. 1C-130J-1 directs pilots to pause momentarily with power levers in GND IDLE to check for symmetric power. If symmetric power is confirmed by BETA indications, the pilot can then use reverse. Failure to identify an asymmetric problem before max reversing could result in directional control difficulties. As cautioned, the MA experienced a directional control problem following reversing the power without first checking for BETA indications at GND IDLE. The right outboard propeller (number four) delayed going into reverse for approximately two seconds. At this time the MA abruptly veered to the left of the runway coming close to the edge of the paved surface.

In summary:

Recognizing that the aircraft was traveling too fast to touch down the main landing gear should have alerted the MC for the need to perform a go-around instead of landing. The need to delay placing the nose landing gear down or delay selecting reverse power because the speed was too great should have alerted the crew for the need to perform a go-around. Finally, the fact that their actions totally invalidated their computed TOLD should have alerted them to the need for a go-around. As it was, there was only one valid procedural option for the MC once they touched down 27 KIAS fast, that was to execute a go-around. Procedural error clearly contributed to the destruction of the MA.

5 C-130 crash wildland firefighting operations

Figure 20: C-130H3 (Source: US AIB report).

The United States Air Force Aircraft Accident Investigation Board (AIB) describes in their report that:

On 1 July 2012, at approximately 1738 Local time, a C-130H3, Tail Number 93-1458, assigned to the 145th Airlift Wing, North Carolina Air National Guard, Charlotte Douglas International Airport (KCLT), Charlotte, North Carolina, crashed on public land managed by the United States Forest Service (USFS), while conducting wildland firefighting operations near Edgemont, South Dakota.

At the time of the mishap all members of the Mishap Crew (MC) were assigned or attached to the 156th Airlift Squadron, based at KCLT.

The Mishap Crew (MC) consisted of Mishap Pilot 1 (MP1), Mishap Pilot 2 (MP2), Mishap Navigator (MN), Mishap Flight Engineer (ME), Mishap Loadmaster 1 (ML1) and Mishap Loadmaster 2 (ML2).

For the mishap sortie, MP1 was the aircraft commander and pilot flying in the left seat. MP2 was in the right seat as the instructor pilot. MN occupied the navigator station on the right side of the flight deck behind MP2. ME was seated in the flight engineer seat located between MP1 and MP2, immediately aft of the center flight console. ML1 and ML2 were seated on the Modular Airborne Fire Fighting System (MAFFS) unit, near the right paratroop door. ML1 occupied the aft MAFFS control station seat and ML2 occupied the forward MAFFS observer station seat.

MP1, MP2, MN and ME died in the mishap. ML1 and ML2 survived the mishap, but suffered significant injuries. The mishap aircraft (MA) and a USFS-owned MAFFS unit were destroyed.

Accident cause

The Accident Investigation Board (AIB) president found by clear and convincing evidence the cause of the mishap was MP1, MP2, MN and ME's inadequate assessment of operational conditions, resulting in the MA impacting the ground after flying into a microburst.

Additionally, the AIB president found by the preponderance of evidence, the failure of the White Draw Fire Lead Plane aircrew and Air Attack aircrew to communicate critical operational information; and conflicting operational guidance concerning thunderstorm avoidance, substantially contributed to the mishap.

Accident summary

The AIB investigators say in his report that the Mission was:

By 28 June 2012, all eight MAFFS-equipped C-130 aircraft were requested for activation due to increased wildland fire activity in the Rocky Mountain Region and were directed to Peterson AFB, Colorado (KCOS).

The AIB explains that the Planning and Preflight was as following:

1 July 2012 at approximately 0800L, the MC met in their hotel lobby and drove to KCOS. After arriving at KCOS, all participating aircrews, including the MC, attended a MAFFS mission briefing. The mission briefing consisted of safety, local and regional weather, fire outlook and Notices to Airmen.

The AIB details the accident as follows:

After performing two drops and a landing to refuel, MA finally entered the area to make two drops.

The AIB report describes the area "...had been actively burning for three days and was 10 percent contained. The fire had consumed nearly 3,000 acres of grassland and timber. Steep terrain and forecast winds combined to create a high risk that the fire would rapidly spread and endanger nearby structures and utilities".

A lead plane was nominated, call sign Lead Bravo 5 (Lead B-5). Lead B-5, a Beechcraft King Air C90 twin-engine turboprop aircraft.

After MN made contact, Lead B-5 directed the MN to divert the MA to the White Draw Fire. The MN contacted Lead B-5 and received updated fire area coordinates and radio frequency information. As the MA approached the White Draw Fire Traffic Area (FTA) from the southwest, the MC agreed to take a wide berth around the thunderstorm to the southeast of the fire.

The MA entered the White Draw FTA and both MP2 and MP1 made visual contact with Lead B-5. A third aircraft (Air Attack), a Beechcraft King Air C90 twin-engine turboprop, entered the White Draw FTA while descending to 7,000 ft Mean Sea Level (MSL) due to "more than moderate turbulence". Upon arrival at the FTA, Air Tactical Group Supervisor (ATGS) assumed the duties of the White Draw Fire Air Tactical Group Supervisor. ATGS duties were to manage air and ground firefighting assets in and around the FTA.

Lead B-5 executed a "show me" run while the MC observed from a higher altitude. A show me run is a standard maneuver executed by the lead plane in preparation for a retardant drop. The show me run aids Modular Airborne Fire Fighting System (MAFFS) aircrew in identifying the retardant drop path and potential hazards, as well as, establish an escape route.

After observing the show me run, MP1 gave a One Minute Advisory in preparation for the first of two planned drops on the White Draw Fire. One minute later, MP1 positioned the MA approximately one-half mile behind Lead B-5 in a loose formation while the MC verbally reviewed retardant drop and escape parameters.

The MC configured and slowed the MA to drop parameters of flaps 100 percent and 120 knots indicated airspeed (KIAS). Approaching the initial drop, MP1 had difficulty maintaining desired airspeed despite maximum power and the MA slowed to approximately 110 KIAS. MP1 directed MP2 to reposition the flaps from 100 percent to 70 percent. MP2 immediately repositioned the flaps to 70 percent and the MC made no additional comments regarding low airspeed during the drop. The MC successfully completed the first drop precisely on target and repositioned the flaps to 50 percent during the escape maneuver.

While positioning for the second and final drop, the MC critiqued the first drop and MP1 decided the final drop would be accomplished with 70 percent flaps. ME commented on an increase in surface winds and fire growth. The MA had descended to the assigned altitude of 4,500 ft MSL, and MP2 verbalized flaps were positioned to 70 percent, in preparation for the final drop.

Unbeknown to the MC, at about this time, the crew of Air Attack again experienced severe turbulence. Air Attack was approximately one mile from the MA and at an altitude of approximately 7,000 ft MSL.

At this point, Lead B-5 hit a "bad sinker", meaning the bottom dropped out from underneath the aircraft; this caused the airplane to rapidly lose altitude and airspeed. MP2 verbalized seeing Lead B-5 get "backed up". Air Tactical Pilot (ATP) struggled to maintain control of Lead B-5, at one point coming within 10 ft of the ground. ATP radioed to the MC, "I got to go around."

A call for a go around is most commonly heard regarding misalignments for drops rather than urgent situations. One second later, MP2 stated, "Yeah. Let's go around, out of this". MP2 instructed MP1 to "Keep going. Get us some".

Thirteen seconds after announcing the go-around, ATP radioed the MC to "Dump your load when you can". Three seconds later, MP1 called "E-dump, e-dump".

An "e-dump" is an emergency release of remaining retardant executed by the copilot or loadmaster, which will increase aircraft performance by decreasing aircraft gross weight. MP2 confirmed the e-dump. One second later, ME stated, "attitude" indicating concern for the MA orientation.

The final MC intercom transmissions are as follows:

MP2 stated, "Bring some power."

MP1 stated, "Power's in."

MP2 stated, "Power"

Unknown stated, "Power"

MP1 stated, "Power's in."

ME stated, "Blee..."

MP2 stated, "We're going in."

ME stated, "Bleed's closed."

MP1 stated, "Hold on, Crew."

Then the MA impacted with trees.

Impact

During the impact sequence, the number four propeller forcibly removed the right paratroop door, creating the presumed egress point of ML1 and ML2. Due to extensive damage and fire in the center fuselage, it is highly unlikely ML1 and ML2 were able egress anywhere other than through the right paratroop door opening. ML1 and ML2 have no memory of egressing the MA.

Human factors analysis

A DoD taxonomy was developed to identify hazards and risks, called DoD Human Factors Analysis and Classification System (DoD-HFACS), referenced in Attachment

5 of AFI 91-204, Safety Investigations and Reports, 24 September 2008. The relevant human factors are discussed below.

MP1, MP2, MN and ME died in the mishap. ML1 and ML2 survived but have varying recollection of the mishap events. Human factors are extrapolated from CVR data, witness testimony, radar logs, and reconstruction of the accident through a simulator. There is a certain level of uncertainty inherent in the human factors cited below.

1. Risk Assessment – During Operation

Risk Assessment – During Operation is a factor when the individual fails to adequately evaluate the risks associated with a particular course of action and this faulty evaluation leads to an inappropriate decision and subsequent unsafe situation. This failure occurs in real-time when formal risk-assessment procedures are not possible.

The report said that despite multiple objective indicators of deteriorating operational conditions, MP1, MP2, MN and ME inadequately assessed the sum of the individual cues in time to successfully abort the mishap drop.

As the MA approached the FTA, MP1, MP2, MN and ME recognized and avoided the nearby thunderstorm. While loitering, MP2 and ME commented on lightning and the thunderstorm within 10 NM. During the "show me" run, MP1 and MP2 noticed "a little bit of rain."

A "show me" run aids MAFFS aircrew in identifying the retardant drop path, potential hazards and establishing an escape route. At the same time, the aircrew of Air Attack, ATGS and AA3, relayed they were experiencing "more than moderate" turbulence and descended from 9,500 to 7,000 ft above mean sea level (MSL), to avoid the turbulence. On the first retardant drop, the MA approached the drop 10 knots slower than planned, the aircraft was sluggish to respond despite the use of full power, after the drop MP1 commented, he "didn't like how that felt."

All indications seem clear that the conditions were not the safest to continue with the mission nonetheless the MC continued with the drop.

While maneuvering for the mishap drop, ME commented the sky was "getting darker," and "you can see that fire a lot better now."

About a minute later, turning to the final drop heading, ME, commenting on the fire stated, "looks like that thing got bigger." MP2, referring to storm activity stated, "that thing is moving into the fire." The ME also noticed the surface winds had "picked up" and the fire was blazing. As the MA lined up for the mishap drop behind Lead B-5, MP2 saw Lead B-5 get "all backed up," and ATP simultaneously announced "I got to go around." In response, MP2 immediately commanded a go around "out of this." ATP called the "go around" because he hit a "bad sinker," and rapidly lost altitude and airspeed, at one point coming within 10 ft of impacting the ground.

Approximately 13 seconds after ATP's go around call, ATP stated, "Dump your load when you can" and MP2 immediately complied. MP1 and MP2 applied full power, ME closed the bleeds, but the MA continued to descend. As the MA dropped below radar coverage, it was observed in an extremely nose high attitude, indicating MP1 was attempting to avoid impact. At that point, despite the mishap crew's best efforts and the use of aircraft maximum power, the MA crashed.

The approaching thunderstorm created a phenomenon known as a dry microburst. A dry microburst is a severe localized wind, blasting down from a thunderstorm that most commonly occur in semiarid regions. While a dry microburst is a unique weather phenomenon, there were multiple objective cues of the deteriorating operational conditions for MP1, MP2, MN and ME to recognize the unsafe situation and abort the mishap drop.

Prior to the mishap drop, MP1, MP2, MN and ME acknowledged the approaching thunderstorm, witnessed lightning, heard Air Attack report "more than moderate" turbulence. Additionally, on the first retardant drop, after dropping 10 knots below targeted speed, the MA responded sluggishly despite the use of maximum power. Finally, as the MA approached the mishap drop, MP1, MP2, MN and ME acknowledged darker skies, increased surface winds and fire activity, and MP2 saw Lead B-5 get "backed up" and rapidly lose altitude.

For all this the AIB report concludes that MP1, MP2, MN and ME inadequately assessed the sum of the individual cues in time to successfully abort the mishap drop.

2. Response Set

Response Set is a factor when the individual has a cognitive or mental framework of expectations that predispose them to a certain course of action regardless of other cues.

According to report, as the second drop was planned to occur less than five minutes after the first successful drop, it is highly probable the MC continued preparing for the second drop with the expectation that the operational conditions would remain similar, despite deteriorating weather conditions. MAFFS aircrew members attested that a call for a go around is most commonly heard regarding misalignments for drops rather than urgent situations. It is possible that ATP's call for a go around while meant to abort the mishap drop, was not interpreted by the MC as significantly urgent, based on their prior experience.

3. Communicating Critical Information

Communicating Critical Information is a factor when known critical information was not provided to appropriate individuals in an accurate or timely manner.

According to report, as Air Attack approached the White Draw FTA, AA3 observed virga beneath the clouds and experienced severe turbulence. However, when relaying this information over the FTA frequency, the crew of Air Attack did not report the virga and only described the turbulence as "more than moderate".

Prior to ATP calling the go around, ATGS witnessed the White Draw Fire "sheeting" and "running hard," and "the smoke was laying down," indicating extremely strong surface winds. Additionally, Air Attack encountered sudden updrafts and downdrafts with airspeed fluctuations between 20 to 40 knots, which forced the aircraft into bank angles of approximately 90 degrees.

The primary responsibility of the Air Attack crewmembers, AA3 and ATGS, was to circle at the top of the FTA and manage the incident airspace by controlling air traffic. As such, AA3 and ATGS were in the best position to ascertain and relay operational conditions however, they did not report the virga, sheeting fire, drastically increased surface winds and severe turbulence.

The primary mission of the lead plane pilot in a FTA is to ensure the safe, efficient and effective use of air tankers in the management of wildland fires. Just prior to the mishap, Lead B-5 experienced a severe and sudden loss of altitude. However, other than ATP stating, "I got to go around" the crew of Lead B-5 did not report critical information regarding the severe conditions encountered. For the 12 seconds after announcing the go around, ATP struggled to recover the aircraft. After recovering, ATP calmly advised the MC to "drop your load when you can".

The aircrew of Lead B-5 again failed to communicate critical information regarding the severe conditions they had encountered.

For all that the AIB report concludes that known critical information was not provided to appropriate individuals in an accurate or timely manner.

4. Limited Total Experience

Limited Total Experience is a factor when a supervisor selects an individual who has performed a maneuver, or participated in a specific scenario, infrequently or rarely.

According to report, the overall flying experience of the MC was high. However, MP1 had limited experience as a MAFFS aircraft commander and MN was participating in his first MAFFS mission. MP1 was a current and qualified Senior Pilot with over 1,900 total C-130 hours, however prior to the day of the mishap he had accomplished only seven drops as a MAFFS copilot and zero drops as a MAFFS aircraft commander. MN was a current and qualified Senior Navigator with over 2,200 total C-130 hours, however as this was MN's first MAFFS mission, he had participated in zero MAFFS drops prior to the day of the mishap.

5. Procedural Guidance/Publications

Procedural Guidance/Publications is a factor when written direction, checklists, graphic depictions, tables, charts or other published guidance is inadequate, misleading or inappropriate and thus creates an unsafe situation.

According to report,

(a) Conflicting guidance applicable to weather avoidance AFI 11-2C-130, Volume 3, C-130 Operations Procedures, 23 April 2012, paragraph 6.21.3.1.3, directs avoidance of thunderstorms:

"by five nautical miles for tactical low-level operations below flight level 23,000 ft MSL, provided the outside air temperature is at or above 0° Celsius at flight altitude. Avoid gusts fronts and winds preceding a rapidly moving thunderstorm."

Additionally AFI 11-2C-130, Volume 3, paragraph 6.21.3.1.4 cautions,

" Aircraft damage may occur up to 20 NMs from any thunderstorms. Aircrews must familiarize themselves with information on thunderstorm development and hazards."

Memorandum from NGB/A3 dated, 20 July 10 states:

"Weather Avoidance: until bonding measures are accomplished, the MAFFS II nozzle assembly creates an increased risk of lightning strikes. Avoid thunderstorms by at least 25 NM when any portion of the MAFFS II unit extends outside the aircraft."

The MA was operating well within 10 NM of a thunderstorm when the mishap occurred. However, because the MA was equipped with the nozzle assembly unit outside the aircraft, the MC should have avoided all thunderstorms within 25 NM IAW the NGB/A3 memorandum.

Post-mishap, multiple aircrew members from the mishap unit were uncertain which guidance was controlling on 1 July 2012. Witness accounts also varied regarding the emphasis provided to the NGB memorandum. These varying accounts indicated a lack of understanding as to what guidance controlled during live MAFFS operations on 1 July 2012.

(b) Unsafe Pre-Slowdown Checklist

The C-130H MAFFS Operations Cockpit Crew Checklist, Page 2, Pre-Slowdown Checklist, Item 8 states:

"GCAS/GPWS Circuit Breaker(s) – Pulled (On Some Airplanes)".

Accomplishing this step at this time during the drop sequence is considered unsafe. Pulling this circuit breaker disables the Traffic Collision Avoidance System which is critical regarding situational awareness of all aircraft in the area, including the lead plane. In practice, pulling this circuit breaker is delayed until the MAFFS pilot has visually acquired the lead plane. This last item had no direct effect on the mishap, but is significant in regards to aircraft safety.

6. Organizational Training Issues/Programs

Organizational Training Issues/Programs are a factor when one-time or initial training programs, upgrade programs, transition programs or other training that is conducted outside the local unit is inadequate or unavailable and this creates an unsafe situation.

According to report, IAW Forest Service Instruction (FSI) 12-001, MAFFS Operating Plan, 24 February 2012, paragraph 2.5.1.1, requires MAFFS flight crews attend a training exercise with USFS personnel at home station on a biennial basis. However, FSI 12-001 also requires annual currency, which can be regained by dropping at least three retardant loads on a live fire.

Prior to FY2012, annual MAFFS refresher training was done as a mass training event with all four MAFFS units. The training rotated annually varying geographical locations throughout the US. As of 2012, annual training guidelines for MAFFS squadrons directed, local training at each of the four MAFFS unit.

Local training did not include different terrain conditions, density altitudes and congested pit operations, all of which are essential components in order to comprehend what live MAFFS operations entail. Additionally, all four MAFFS units were not integrated in order to provide a more realistic learning environment for new and seasoned MAFFS crewmembers.

6 F-16C Afghanistan controlled flight into terrain

Figure 21: F-16C (Source: US AIB report).

The United States Air Force Aircraft Accident Investigation Board (AIB) describes in their report that:

On 3 April 2013 at 23:10:06L the mishap aircraft (MA), an F-16C, tail number 00-0219, deployed with the 77th Expeditionary Fighter Squadron to Bagram Airfield (BAF), Afghanistan impacted a mountainside 10 nautical miles southeast of BAF. The mishap flight was a combat mission in support of ground forces assigned in the United States Central Command's Area of Responsibility. The crash occurred in an unpopulated area. The MA was destroyed. The mishap pilot (MP) did not attempt to eject from his aircraft and was fatally injured. United States air and ground forces recovered the remains of the MP. The mishap caused neither civilian injuries nor damage to civilian property.

According to report, the MA took off from BAF on 3 April 2013 at 19:06:47L and flew the entire sortie at night. The MP was the flight lead of a two ship of F-16Cs tasked to provide close air support in eastern Afghanistan. Upon completion of the mission, the MP directed the Mishap Wingman (MW) to a two nautical mile trail position. The MP then contacted air traffic control and requested a visual flight rules recovery, whereby the MP assumed responsibility for traffic and terrain avoidance.

BAF was reporting a broken cloud layer and light rain. While maneuvering to land, the MP descended below the minimum safe altitude into a mountainous area, which was visually obscured by weather conditions. Prior to impact, the MA provided low altitude warnings, however the MP did not take timely corrective action.

Accident cause

The Accident Investigation Board President found by clear and convincing evidence the cause of the mishap was the MP's failure to perceive mountainous terrain directly in his flight path while flying below the minimum safe altitude using visual flight rules in instrument meteorological conditions (i.e., clouds) resulting in controlled flight into terrain.

Accident summary

The AIB report explains:

The MF taxied on time and departed BAF at 19:06:47L. The MF departed using Visual Flight Rules (VFR) via a standard tactical departure. In accordance with AFMAN 11-217, Volume 2, paragraph 1.1.2.1, VFR is defined as a set of rules governing the conduct of flight clear of clouds. Takeoff, departure and the tactical portion of the sortie were uneventful. No munitions were expended and no enemy contact was reported.

At 22:58:01L, 68 NM from BAF, MP began to Return to Base (RTB) at an appropriate VFR altitude of 18,500 feet MSL. The MP directed the MW into a 2 NM trail formation. The MF remained in this formation until the mishap occurred. The MP cleared the MW to remove his NVGs at his discretion. However, the MW stated he kept his Night Vision Goggles (NVGs is on throughout the recovery).

The MP cleared the MW off frequency to check out with the Control and Reporting Center, obtain the current BAF Automatic Terminal Information Service (ATIS) weather broadcast, and report maintenance codes back to squadron operations. In accordance with AFMAN 11-217, Volume 3, paragraph 1.2.6, ATIS is a voice communication capability able to broadcast weather information. At the same time, the MP initiated contact with Kabul Approach Control and requested a VFR straight-in to runway 03. Kabul Approach approved the MF direct to BAF VFR. During this exchange, the MW was on a different radio frequency completing his assigned duties and did not hear this communication.

At 36 NM from BAF, Kabul Approach contacted the MP and asked him to repeat his approach request. The MP again requested a visual straight-in runway 03 at BAF. Kabul Approach acknowledged the straight-in request, and approved the MP VFR altitude at his discretion. The MW was still on a different radio frequency and therefore he assumed the MF had been granted an IFR clearance to BAF. The MW stated, using NVGs, he could see the MF approaching IMC conditions at 16,000 feet MSL and sporadic lightning ahead of the MF .

At 32 NM from BAF, the MP radioed the MW that he was beginning a shallow descent and began a five degree nose low descent. The MP utilized maximum afterburner (AB) and idle power with speed brakes in order to burn down fuel. The MW acknowledged and replied he had the current ATIS. The MW then relayed the ATIS to the MP as "Tango, runway three, it's wet. Winds are 220 at 5.

We got scattered ceilings at 4000 and 5000, light rain and 3022". In accordance with Air Force Handbook 11-203, Volume 2, paragraph 2.2.5, cloud bases in the terminal area are expressed in feet above ground level (AGL).

The AIB report notes that the BAF ATIS stated:

Bagram Tower information Tango 1755Z, wind estimated 320/5, visibility unrestricted, light rain shower, scattered 4000, scattered 5500, broken ceiling 7000, broken 8500, temperature 11, dew point 3, altimeter 3022, expect ILS approach, runway three in use, wet runway, wind advisory, winds forecast greater than 15 knots, less than 25 knots, lightning watch, lightning potential within 5 miles of the airport. Runway closure is scheduled between 2200Z and 0100Z.

The AIB report indicates that the MP was requested to advise on initial contact you have Tango.

Twenty-one NM from BAF, the MP asked the MW, "Where are the clouds?" The MW responded with, "5000, 7000 broken 10,000".

The MP entered IMC descending through 16,000 feet MSL at 21 NM from BAF.

As the MW entered IMC, the MW asked the MP what altitude they were cleared to. The MW assumed the MP had already received an IFR clearance. The MW stated his assumption was based on the MP's briefed ILS recovery plan and the fact they entered IMC. The MP replied with a broken radio call stating the MF is "vis, uh, our discretion". The MW stated this was the first indication his IFR recovery assumption was incorrect.

At 17 NM from BAF, Kabul Approach directed the MF to continue its VFR descent. The MW stated this was his second indication the MF may not have been on an IFR clearance. He was still unclear if the MF was VFR or IFR.

At 16 NM from BAF, the MP received the first audible altitude warning from the MA. The warning was generated from the MA's line-in-the-sky (LIS) system, and is designed to alert the MP one time when descending through a pre-set altitude, in this case 15,000 feet MSL. At 23:08:31L, 14 NM from BAF, the MW received the same warning.

The AIB report adds that the MP descended through 14,200 MSL, the published MSA.

At 13 NM from BAF, Kabul Approach directed the MF to BAF Tower frequency.

Immediately following this communication, the MP told the MW he was attempting to intercept a 10 NM final. The MP checked the MF in on BAF Tower frequency and contacted BAF Tower. The MW testified he became concerned the MF was on a VFR clearance.

The MW "knew something was not right" and was waiting for radio availability to query the MP.

At 12 NM from BAF, BAF Tower requested the MF proceed to a five mile straight-in final with an altitude restriction of at or below 6,000 feet MSL at 2 NM Distance Measuring Equipment (DME). In accordance with AFI 11-217, Volume 1, paragraph 4.5, DME is the distance from the airport navigational aid. The MP acknowledges BAF Tower's request and again repeats his intent to intercep

t a 10 NM final approach.

At 11 NM from BAF, the MP received the second audible altitude warning. This warning was from the MA's altitude low (ALOW) system, which was set at the squadron standard of 1,800 feet AGL. Anytime the MA's AGL altitude descended below 1,800 feet AGL, the MA emitted "altitude, altitude". Over the next six seconds, the MP received this warning two additional times. This warning was re-voiced as the MA flew over uneven, mountainous terrain despite a constant descent.

At 10 NM from BAF, the MW asked the MP if he was still in the weather. The MP replied that he was, and asked if the MW was also in the weather. The MW replied yes, and began to shallow his descent profile because he was concerned about terrain. Hereafter the MA's Predictive Ground Collision Avoidance System (PGCAS) emitted a "pull up, pull up" audible alert while flashing an "X" in the MA's head-up display (HUD) and both multi-function displays (MFDs).

The AIB report clarifies the predictive feature of PGCAS was not available at the time of the mishap because the MA was off the digital terrain database. The non-predictive portion of PGCAS provided the warning when the radar altimeter detected an AGL altitude less than the selected minimum terrain clearance (MTC), which was set to 450 feet AGL.

The MP selected military power (maximum Afterburner) and pulsed the control stick, resulting in a modest two degree nose high climb, simultaneously MA impacted the mountainside.

The MW averaged 1,560 feet higher than the MP throughout the descent. At the time of the MA impact, the MW observed a bright flash through his NVG and could see a "tinge of red" from underneath his NVG. Having seen this visual cue coupled with his terrain clearance concerns and uncertainty of the type of clearance, the

MW selected military power and immediately executed a nose high climb. The MW avoided the mountain by 1,540 feet AGL.

Impact

The AIB report describes the Impact as follows:

The MA impacted mountainous terrain at 23:10:06L 10 NM southeast of BAF. At the time of the impact, the MA had the same configuration as it did upon takeoff, with 4,700 pounds of fuel remaining. Upon impact, the MA's flight conditions were: altitude 8,760 feet MSL; two degree climb; 1,800 feet per minute positive vertical velocity; 244 knots calibrated airspeed; maximum Afterburner (AB); and 1.8 G's.

Human factors analysis

AFI 91-204, Attachment 5, contains the Department of Defense Human Factors Analysis and Classification System which lists potential human factors that can play a role in aircraft mishaps.

As a result of the investigation, AIB concluded that the Applicable Human Factors are the followings:

1. Risk Assessment – During Operations

In accordance with AFI 91-204, Attachment 5, "Risk Assessment – During Operation" is a factor when the individual fails to adequately evaluate the risks associated with a particular course of action and this faulty evaluation leads to an inappropriate decision and subsequent unsafe situation. This failure occurs in real-time when formal risk-assessment procedures are not possible.

According to the report, following the tactical portion of the mission, the MF began to RTB, the MP made radio contact with Kabul Approach Control while the MW was simultaneously monitoring another radio frequency to check out with the tactical control agency, obtain ATIS information, and call in aircraft codes to squadron operations. The MP requested a VFR recovery from Kabul Approach.

Kabul Approach approved the VFR request. Then Kabul Approach clarified with the MP as to his intentions for landing. MP requested a visual straight-in for runway 03 at Bagram. Approach answered, "Roger, VFR altitude is your discretion". This approval is consistent with standard Kabul Approach procedures.

After receiving the current weather and seeing a 16,000 foot MSL undercast, the MP elected to operate under VFR in IMC. The MW testified that through the NVGs he could see the cloud they were flying into and it was definite cloud penetration. The MP descended below the published MSA.

The MP operated under VFR in IMC in the terminal area for 2 minutes 44 seconds and below the published MSA for 1 minute 49 seconds without taking corrective action.

The AIB report concluded that the MP likely failed to adequately evaluate the risks associated with flying VFR in IMC and below the MSA and subsequent unsafe situation.

2. Caution/Warning Ignored

In accordance with AFI 91-204, Attachment 5, "Caution/Warning Ignored" is a factor when a caution or warning is perceived and understood by an individual but is ignored by the individual leading to an unsafe situation.

According to the report, the MA systems warned the MP of low altitude conditions, 23 seconds before impact. Within six seconds, the MA alerted the MP two additional times, yet the MP continued to descend. These low altitude warnings would not have been present if the MA remained above MSA. Four seconds prior to impact, the MP received a "pull up, pull up" warning and a large, flashing "X" symbol mnemonic in the HUD and both MFDs. At this point, data indicates the MP did perceive this final warning since he applied aft pressure.

The AIB report concludes that despite the severity of this warning however, the MP only pulsed the control stick with 2.0 to 17.5 pounds of aft pressure instead of applying full aft pressure.

3. Vision Restricted by Meteorological Conditions

In accordance with AFI 91-204, Attachment 5, "Vision Restricted by Meteorological Conditions" is a factor when weather, haze, or darkness restricted the vision of an individual to a point where normal duties were affected.

According to the report, the mishap occurred with a waning crescent moon that was 38% visible. The MW stated the weather from 20 to 30 NM from BAF was enough to "get your attention and look for ice." Further, he said, "There's no way you're getting back VFR maintaining any kind of VFR cloud clearance getting back". The AIB report then explains that the darkness and weather conditions limited the MP's ability to see the mountainous terrain.

The AIB was unable to determine if the MP was using NVGs at the time of impact; however, the MW stated that during previous sorties, the MP would notify the MW once he had taken them off in accordance with Air Force procedures. As the MW had not received this call during the mishap sortie, it was likely the MP was still using NVGs. When using NVGs in weather, there is a significant increase in scintillation (often referred to as "sparkles"). This scintillation would have further restricted the MP's ability to see both inside and outside the cockpit and caused a distraction.

The MW asked the MP if he was still in the weather to which the MP responded "affirm," then asked the MW if he was as well. The MP was IMC and would have been unable to see the mountain prior to impact.

4. Negative Transfer

In accordance with AFI 91-204, Attachment 5, "Negative Transfer" is a factor when an individual reverts to a highly learned behavior used in a previous system or situation and that response is inappropriate or degrades mission performance.

According to the report, the MP and MW spent the first five months of their deployment flying out of KAF. The area around KAF had very little elevated terrain. Four days before the MF, the MP's squadron moved to BAF, which has high terrain. The MF was only the MP's second sortie flown out of BAF. As the MP flew

40 night approaches into KAF, and only one prior night approach into BAF, it is possible he reverted to a mental model of flat terrain.

Figure 22: KAF (minimal terrain) (Source: US AIB report).

Figure 23: BAF (mountainous terrain) (Source: US AIB report).

Evidence shows an additional negative transfer occurred. While operating outside of a terminal area during tactical portions of any sortie, pilots flew under VFR due to the limitations of the airspace system in Afghanistan. Throughout the deployment, MSQ pilots routinely flew in IMC, above the MSA, while under VFR as this was necessary to complete their combat requirements.

These requirements included cruising en-route, air-to-air refueling, and tactical holding.

According to the report, the negative transfer of this learned behavior likely contributed to the MP inappropriately entering and remaining IMC in the terminal area while under VFR.

5. Expectancy

In accordance with AFI 91-204, Attachment 5, "Expectancy" is a factor when an individual expects to perceive a certain reality and those expectations are strong enough to create a false perception of the expectation.

According to the report, the MW assumed the MP was on an approved IFR approach as the MF began descending through clouds. The MW switched frequencies to obtain ATIS and did not hear the MP's request and Kabul Approach's approval for a VFR recovery.

The MW further expected an IFR approach for the following reasons:

- In the mission brief prior to flight, the MP briefed the MF would recover IFR to an ILS absent "glorious" weather;

- AFI 11-202, Volume 3, ACC Supplement, paragraph 8.1.4, states: "Pilots shall fly under IFR if operating fixed-wing aircraft at night, unless the mission cannot be flown under IFR;" and

- The MW assumed the MP would not descend into IMC without an IFR clearance.

According to the report, the MW's expectations for an IFR recovery were strong enough to create a false perception that the MF would actually recover IFR. Therefore, the MW disregarded the initial indications the MF was on a VFR recovery. By the time the MW realized the flight was operating VFR in IMC and started to query the MP, it was too late.

7 T6A, Texan II severe engine damage

Figure 24: T-6A (Source: USAF photo by MSgt. David Richards).

The United States Air Force Aircraft Accident Investigation Board (AIB) describes in their report that:

On 24 September 2010, a T-6A, Tail Number 08-3925, assigned to the 84th Flying Training Squadron, 47th Flying Training Wing, Laughlin Air Force Base (LAFB) Texas, crashed after the engine suffered severe damage during an airstart attempt. The crash occurred at 1115 local Central Daylight Time on a ranch 20 miles east of LAFB. The mishap aircraft (MA) was destroyed following aircrew ejection. The

Mishap Student Pilot (MSP) suffered a significant back injury as well as minor injuries and the Mishap Instructor Pilot (MIP) suffered minor injuries.

The mishap occurred during a Joint Specialized Undergraduate Pilot Training formation sortie for the MSP who occupied the front cockpit. Upon return to base, approximately 57 minutes into the sortie and 4,900 feet above ground level (AGL), the MSP executed a straight-ahead rejoin with too much speed. The MIP assumed control of the aircraft, inadvertently raised the engine cut-off gate handle, and pulled the [throttle] Power Control Lever (PCL) into the OFF position.

The MIP immediately pushed the PCL above IDLE where the engine recovered to normal operation. However, due to misperception of engine status, the M1P shut down the functioning engine again. The MIP did not correctly execute appropriate restart procedures, which led to an unsuccessful airstart.

Following engine shutdown for the third time, the MIP applied the correct Immediate Airstart procedures until he incorrectly advanced the PCL above IDLE while the engine was still in a sub-idle condition. This forced excessive fuel to the engine, which led to an extreme heat condition severely damaging the engine and rendering it unrecoverable.

The following five airstart attempts were unsuccessful due to this engine damage. The mishap crew (MC) missed the opportunity to make a forced landing at a suitable alrfield, and the MIP initiated ejection at 580 feet AGL. The MA was destroyed.

The MA impacted a field, causing incidental damage to a barbed wire fence on private property.

Accident cause

The Accident Investigation Board President (AIBP) found by clear and convincing evidence, the cause of this mishap was pilot error. The MIP induced severe engine damage due to inadvertent shutdown of a normal engine followed by procedural errors to restart the engine. In addition, the MC missed the opportunity to attempt a forced landing at a suitable airfield. The AIBP also found by a preponderance of the evidence that the mishap crew's channelized attention on the engine, delayed the decision to reach a suitable airfield.

Accident summary

The AIB report describes the accident as follows:

The MA departed the Military Operating Area (MOA) on the wing in the fighting wing position. The flight was cleared the Rio-One Procedure and was instructed to cross the OTULE waypoint at 6,000 ft mean sea level (MSL). The lead aircraft initiated a descent to 6,000 ft MSL and directed the MA to take spacing for a straight-ahead rejoin on a 1200 heading.

On the first rejoin attempt, the MSP failed to recognize the rapidly closing range between the two aircraft, causing the MIP to take control of the aircraft and dissipate the excess closure. The MIP repositioned the MA to lead's six o'clock position. After a brief discussion on proper rejoin procedures and recognition of closure rates, the MIP transferred aircraft control back to the MSP for a second rejoin attempt.

Level at 6,000 ft MSL, the MSP executed the second straight-ahead rejoin as the MIP placed his left hand and right elbow on the respective canopy rail. The MSP again gained excessive closure during the rejoin and was slow to correct. As the MIP assumed control of the MA, he lowered his left hand from the canopy rail to the throttle power control lever (PCL). The MIP placed his palm on the top of the PCL and his hand continued moving down. The MIP inadvertently pulled up on the engine cut-off gate handle with his fingers as his hand was pulling back. The PCL moved through the cut-off gate to the OFF position, thus shutting down a functioning engine.

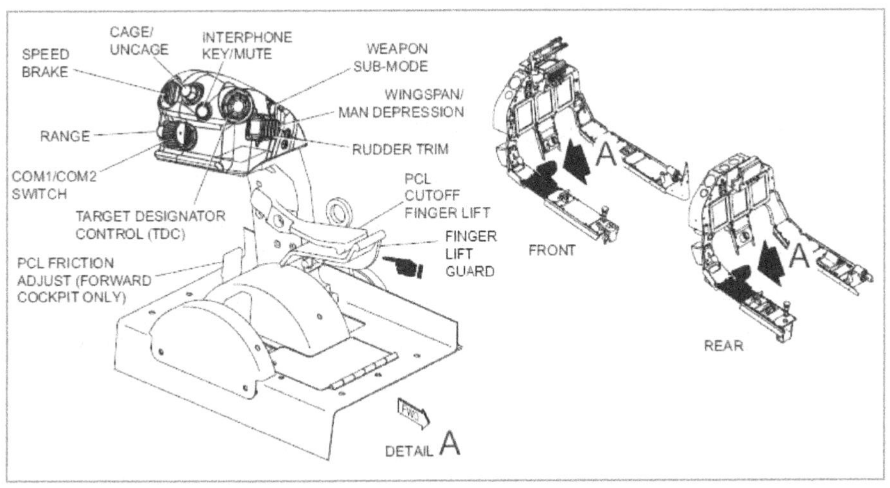

Figure 25: Power Control Lever (PCL) T-6A

The AIB report explains with detail that, it is typical for an instructor to fly with hands in what is described as a "defensive position" particularly during critical phases of flight. Examples of critical phases of flight include, but are not limited to, rejoins, close formation, takeoffs, and landings. The defensive position refers to the instructor positioning his hands just behind or shadowing the stick and PCL in case of a dangerous situation developing. The MIP did not have his hands in a defensive position just prior to assuming control of the MA. The MC felt a deceleration of the MA and the MSP noted the propeller slowing down.

The MIP immediately recognized the PCL was back farther than the normal IDLE position and reactively pushed the PCL back up through IDLE (**it is the first airstart attempt**).

Acquisition Recording System (IDARS) shows engine instruments recovered when the PCL was pushed up above the IDLE position. The MIP failed to recognize the recovered engine and subsequently brought the PCL back to the OFF position.

During the mishap, there were **eight times** that the PCL was moved to OFF and back to IDLE or above. For the purposes of this report, each of these instances are referred to as an airstart attempt regardless of whether appropriate procedures were applied or not.

The MIP initiated a shallow climb to the left to maneuver away from the lead aircraft. Upon seeing this, the lead aircraft attempted to establish communication with the MA. The lead aircraft received no response, noted the MA's propeller slowed, and began to reposition to follow the MA. The chase aircraft (previously the lead aircraft) attempted to establish contact with the MA several times during the mishap, none of which received a response. The chase aircraft declared an inflight emergency (IFE) for the MA with radar approach control (RAPCON).

Slowing through 150 Knots Indicated Airspeed (KIAS), the MIP attempted a **second airstart** by initiating the Immediate Airstart (PMU Norm) BOLDFACE procedure as the engine decelerated through 27% N1. N1 is the speed of the gas generator section of the engine, expressed as a percentage with 104% representing maximum rated speed. However, the MIP incorrectly applied the BOLDFACE procedure by failing to activate the starter switch resulting in an unsuccessful airstart.

The MIP directed the MSP to find the closest airfield. The MSP found the nearest airfield in the GPS, and then the MIP directed the MSP to find Wizard (LAFB auxiliary field).

The MIP assumed control of the aircraft to find Wizard and then transferred aircraft control back to the MSP and focused on airstarts. The MIP recalled making a left 90° turn toward Wizard (the start of a 280° turn), yet Wizard was in the opposite direction. No mention or attempt to reach the two closer airfields was made for the remainder of the mishap.

The AIB report does not explain why the crew made the decision to fly to Wizard airport instead of flying to any of the two nearest airports, it is only assumed that the Instructor was sure he would be able to restart the engine.

Approximately 47 seconds after the PCL was inadvertently placed in OFF, the MIP attempted the **third airstart**. The MIP applied the BOLDFACE procedure at 120 KIAS. T-6 procedural guidance states the airstart envelope is 125 to 200 KIAS from sea level to 15,000 ft. While airstarts may be attempted at any airspeed and altitude, airstart attempts outside of the airstart envelope may be unsuccessful or result in engine overtemperature.

All engine airstart indications appeared normal, however passing 37% N1, the MIP incorrectly advanced the PCL past the midrange position in an attempt to expedite the airstart resulting in excessive fuel flow to the engine. The checklist for Immediate Airstart (PMU Norm) states that if an airstart is successful:

PCL .... As required after N1 reaches IDLE RPM (approximately 67% N1)

This increase of fuel flow, from 80 pounds per hour (PPH) to 260 PPH, overtemped the engine as Interstage Turbine Temperature (ITT) climbed through 1200° Celsius (C).

The report indicates that the ITT remained off the scale for the remainder of the mishap.

The increase in temperature in the compressor turbine section resulted in catastrophic engine damage. N1 continued to climb to a peak of 47% during this airstart where it began to decrease as the compressor turbine section of the engine failed.

Data indicated that from this moment on, any attempt to restart the engine would be ineffective since it was catastrophic damaged.

As the airstart progressed, the MA slowed to 103 KIAS. The MSP notified the MIP of the slow airspeed. The MIP noted the propeller begin to slow and engine instruments winding back. The MIP placed the PCL to the OFF position and lowered the MA's nose to accelerate. The MIP transferred aircraft control of the stick and rudder to the MSP while the MIP maintained control of the PCL and starter switch to continue airstart attempts.

The AIB report shows how pilots exchanged responsibility for flying the plane without a specific plan. According to the basic principles of CRM the allocation of tasks was not done correctly.

The MA proceeded on a 150° heading at 6,000 ft MSL (4,900 ft AGL) with two emergency airfields in front of the aircraft. Anacancho, a 6,000 ft runway, was approximately eight miles away. Spofford/Frontier, a 4,200 ft runway, was slightly farther.

In the MA's configuration at 125 KIAS, the MA can glide two nautical miles (nm) for every 1,000 ft AGL with no wind and without attempting airstarts. At 5,000 ft AGL and 125 KIAS the T-6A can glide ten miles. This put both airfields within gliding range if the MIP had attempted to reach an emergency airfield.

Following the **third airstart**, the MA began a left 280° turn effectively taking the MA off profile for an emergency airfield, thus eliminating the possibility of successfully recovering the aircraft if the engine did not restart. As the MA began the left 280° turn at 115 KIAS, the MSP accelerated to 125 KIAS.

What it has no explanation in the AIB report is how being this two airports at sufficient distance to be able to make an emergency landing in both of them the crew did not it.

The report then explains in detail the following attempts made by the MIP to start the engine.

The MIP attempted a **fourth airstart** by applying the proper procedures. During the airstart, N1 climbed to a peak of approximately 27% and then stagnated while airspeed varied from 120-135 KIAS. With no increase of N1 for approximately 20 seconds the MIP terminated the airstart by placing the PCL in the OFF position.

The **fifth airstart** was initiated at 130 KIAS and airspeed varied from 120 to 130 KIAS during the airstart, After starter switch activation and as N1 passed 15%, the MIP incorrectly advanced the PCL past the IDLE position. The PCL varied from approximately 30% to MAX during the airstart. Once N1 reached 26% it stagnated and after no upward trend for six seconds, the MIP terminated the airstart.

The MSP notified the MIP the MA was descending through 3,000 ft MSL (1,900 ft AGL) which is 100 ft below the recommended controlled ejection altitude. The MA rolled out of the left 280° turn on a heading of approximately 195°.

Descending through 2,600 ft MSL (1,500 ft AGL), at 126 KIAS, and 1 minute and 50 seconds into the emergency, the MIP pulsed the PCL past midrange and back to the OFF position in an incorrectly executed **sixth airstart** attempt. No changes in engine performance occurred as well as no indication the starter switch was activated. The MSP notified the MIP of the need to eject. The MIP acknowledged and stated his intention of another airstart. The MSP confirmed this would be the last attempt, which the MIP affirmed.

The MIP attempted the **seventh airstart** by applying the correct BOLDFACE procedures as the MA descended through 2,400 ft MSL (1,300 ft AGL). N1 stagnated at 23-24% for 16 seconds at which point the MIP terminated the airstart. Airspeed during the seventh airstart attempt varied from 124 to 130 KIAS.

The MIP notified the MSP to prepare for ejection, as the MIP attempted the **eighth and final airstart** descending through approximately 1,800 ft MSL (700 ft AGL).

The MIP activated the starter switch and placed the PCL to IDLE where it remained through ground impact. Upon confirmation the MSP was ready for ejection, and as the MA reached 1,680 ft MSL (580 ft AGL), the MIP gave the command to eject and pulled the ejection handle. This initiated the ejection sequence for the MC, with the MA at approximately 115 KIAS, on a 1800 heading, approximately wings level, and in a slight climb.

The AIB report explains the Egress and Aircrew Flight Equipment.

All aircrew flight equipment functioned properly. The ejection took place within the ejection envelope, however, it was initiated 1,420 ft below the minimum recommended controlled ejection altitude of 2,000 ft AGL.

The post-ejection trajectories of the MSP and MIP resulted in their parachutes opening in extremely close proximity. From approximately wings level and 115 knots, the MIP initiated ejection and both seats ejected with the proper sequencing. However, once the MSP (front cockpit) exited the aircraft, the seat rotated slightly forward, then flipped backward 180 degrees so the MSP's head was pointing down and his feet were pointing up at man/seat separation. At the opening shock of the parachutes, the MIP looked up to check his canopy and discovered the MSP's boots and legs were touching the MIP's parachute canopy.

They maneuvered away from each other and executed their parachute landing fall.

The Mishap Student Pilot (MSP) suffered a significant back injury as well as minor injuries and the Mishap Instructor Pilot (MIP) suffered minor injuries.

Human factors analysis

The AIB concluded that the cause of this mishap was pilot error. The mishap instructor pilot (MIP) generated an emergency by inadvertently shutting down a functioning engine, executed procedural errors on airstarts, and missed a forced landing opportunity.

The Department of Defense Human Factors Analysis and Classifications Systems is comprised of a list of potential human factors that can be contributory or causal to a mishap. The following human factors were identified and described below for this mishap.

1. Inadvertent Operation

Inadvertent operation is a factor when an individual's movements inadvertently activate or deactivate equipment, controls or switches when there is no intent to operate the control or device. This action may be noticed or unnoticed by the individual.

According to the report, departing the area on the second rejoin, the MIP inadvertently operated the engine cut-off gate handle during flight and pulled the PCL past the cut-off gate to the OFF position. This initial inadvertent switch actuation was noticed by the individual, and began the IFE that eventually led to the MC ejection, and loss of the aircraft.

2. Checklist Error and Procedural Error

Checklist Error is a factor when the individual, either through an act of commission or omission makes a checklist error or fails to run an appropriate checklist and this failure results in an unsafe situation. Procedural error is a factor when a procedure is accomplished in the wrong sequence or using the wrong technique or when the wrong control or switch is used. This also captures errors in navigation, calculation or operation of automated systems.

According to the report, the MIP made multiple Checklist and Procedural Errors during the course of the mishap. The MIP failed to execute the Immediate Airstart (PMU Norm) BOLDFACE checklist correctly by not actuating the starter switch on the second airstart attempt which resulted in a "no start."

Procedurally, during an airstart attempt the PCL may be advanced out of IDLE upon reaching 67% N1. On the third airstart, the MIP incorrectly advanced the PCL out of IDLE passing 37% N1. This action resulted in excessive fuel flow to the engine and an excessive heat condition which produced irrevocable damage within the engine.

3. Necessary Action – Rushed.

Necessary action - Rushed is a factor when the individual takes the necessary action as dictated by the situation but performs these actions too quickly and the rush in taking action leads to an unsafe situation.

According to the report, the MIP advanced the PCL out of IDLE during the third airstart before N1 reached idle RPM (approximately 67% N1) in a rushed attempt to generate usable thrust. This action resulted in excessive fuel flow to the engine and an excessive heat condition which produced irrevocable damage within the engine.

4. Acts- Error due to Misperception.

Error due to Misperception is a factor when an individual acts or fails to act based on an illusion; misperception or disorientation state and this act or failure to act creates an unsafe situation.

According to the report, on the first airstart attempt, the MIP inadvertently moved the PCL to the OFF position and then immediately moved the PCL above midrange. The engine recovered, but the MIP perceived the engine was decelerating and moved the PCL to the OFF position. This action resulted in shutting down a functioning engine.

5. Decision-Making During Operation

Decision-Making During Operation is a factor when the individual through faulty logic selects the wrong course of action in a time-constrained environment.

According to the report, the MIP failed to identify the nearest suitable airfield and instead chose an unreachable airfield. The MC had two suitable airfields within gliding distance, for which they failed to get on profile. He instead made a delayed attempt to reach an airfield further away.

6. Preconditions - Task Delegation.

Task Delegation is a factor when the crew or team members failed to actively manage the distribution of mission tasks to prevent the overloading of any crewmember.

According to the report, the MIP delegated to the MSP the task of obtaining the bearing to Wizard and at one point maintaining aircraft control. However, the following tasks were not delegated due to channelized attention: referencing appropriate checklists, locating the nearest suitable airfield, and communicating within the flight or controlling agency.

7. Channelized Attention.

Channelized Attention is a factor when the individual is focusing all conscious attention on a limited number of environmental cues to the exclusion of others of a subjectively equal or higher or more immediate priority, leading to an unsafe situation and may be described as a tight focus of attention that leads to the exclusion of comprehensive situational information.

According to the report, after inadvertent inflight engine shutdown, the MIP became channelized on restarting the engine. The focused attention on restarting the engine resulted in the MC not identifying the nearest suitable airfield nor placing the MA on profile for an airfield in a timely manner. The delayed decision resulted in a controlled ejection.

8 F-15E Spatial Disorientation

Figure 26: F-15E (Source: US AIB report).

The United States Air Force Aircraft Accident Investigation Board (AIB) describes in their report that:

On Wednesday, 28 March 2012 at approximately 2003 local time, the Mishap Aircraft (MA), an F-15E, Tail Number 90-0235, impacted the ground approximately 18 nautical miles west, southwest of the deployed operating location of the 391st Expeditionary Fighter Squadron in Southwest Asia. The Mishap Weapon Systems Officer (MWSO) initiated ejection for the Mishap Crew (MC) and ejected safely with only minor injuries. The Mishap Pilot (MP) was fatally injured when his ejection sequence was interrupted by contact with a 377-foot tower that was part of a large radio tower array. The MA was destroyed after contacting the radio tower and subsequently the ground.

The MC was participating in a large force exercise as the flight lead of a two-ship of F-15Es in a strike package of approximately 27 aircraft. At the conclusion of the tactical portion of the mission, the MC removed their night vision goggles (NVGs) and proceeded back to the base.

Below 10,000 feet above mean sea level (MSL), blowing dust and sand obscured the horizon (with or without NVGs).

At approximately 3,100 feet MSL, five degrees nose low and in a wings-level attitude, the MP incorrectly interpreted the visual scene in front of him and began a series of abrupt maneuvers that ultimately resulted in him rolling the MA into an inverted attitude 1,800 feet above ground level and 25 degrees nose low. Due to the lack of any significant topographical features, the expected lack of cultural lighting, the reduced visibility and the lack of a discernable horizon, the MP became disoriented by the cultural lighting in the vicinity of the mishap site and incorrectly perceived that the MA was inverted. This misperception caused the MP to roll the MA into a truly inverted attitude, at which time the MWSO became convinced the MP had become disoriented and took control of the MA. After attempting to recover the MA, the MWSO initiated ejection for the MC.

The evidence suggests that the MP did not have the electronic attitude director indicator (EADI), the primary source of aircraft attitude, up on any of his cockpit displays at the time of the mishap. The MP was likely using his head-up display and the visual environment as the source of his attitude.

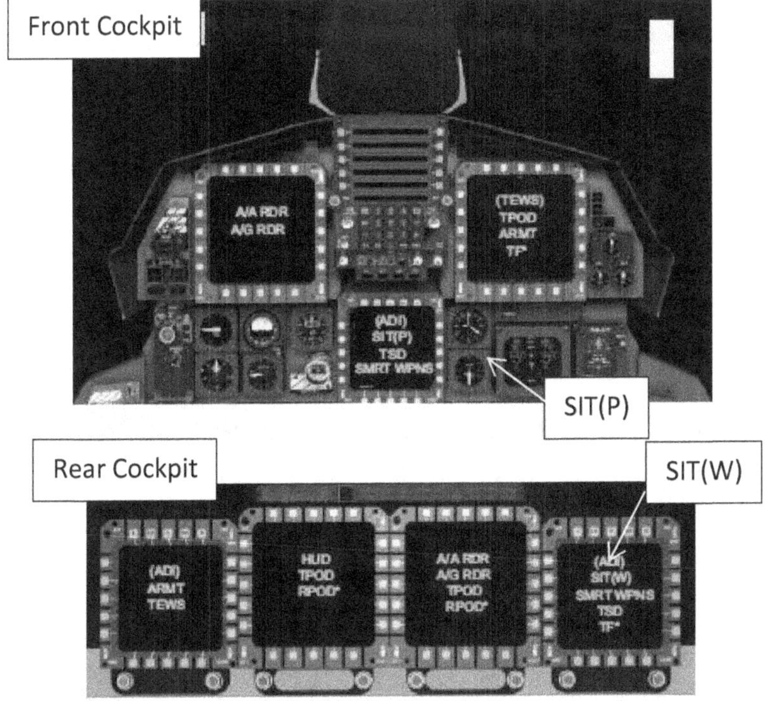

Figure 27: F-15E Cockpit Display Setup (Source: US AIB report).

Subsequently, visual stimuli from light sources on the ground caused the MP to misinterpret his attitude and because this illusion was so strong, he initially did not make any attempt to call up the EADI or confirm his attitude with his standby instruments. Instead, he maneuvered the MA in accordance with his mistaken visual interpretation of his attitude and flew the MA into an inverted position. By not having the EADI in his crosscheck, the MP lacked a vital instrument that could have helped him avoid or overcome his disorientation. In addition, the combination of environmental and procedural aspects of the approach to the base created an environment where the MP was very susceptible to a visually induced illusion and offered a very small window of opportunity with which to correct his misperception.

Accident cause

The Accident Investigation Board (AIB) President found by clear and convincing evidence that the cause of the mishap was the MP becoming spatially disoriented due to a visual illusion during his nighttime recovery to his deployed operating location. Further, the AIB President found by a preponderance of the evidence that the following factors substantially contributed to the mishap:

(1) the lack of an effective instrument crosscheck by the MP and

(2) a combination of the environmental and procedural factors present on the approach to the base.

Accident summary

According to the AIB report, this is the Summary of Accident:

The MC took off at 2003 local time and flew southeast into the operating area (OA) as directed by the standard departure procedure. They proceeded to their holding area as briefed and rejoined with the MW. Despite taking off late, the MC arrived in holding 22 minutes prior to their push time.

Note: Push time is when the MF must leave holding enroute to their target area in order to achieve their assigned "time on target."

As the AIB report says, while on climb during the departure, the MC made several comments expressing concern with the weather, specifically regarding the poor visibility. However, the weather call was made as "full-up clear of clouds," meaning that there was no weather that would affect the mission, and that all mission aircraft must maintain their own visual meteorological conditions (VMC) cloud clearances in accordance with AFI 11-214 night training rules.

After entering holding in the block 20,000 feet mean sea level (MSL) to 24,000 feet MSL, the MC verbalized putting on their NVGs and did not comment on the weather again. Several crews who flew during the Large Force Exercise (LFE) reported the weather was clear above about 10,000 feet MSL with a discernable horizon. Several crews also noted seeing stars above 10,000 feet MSL while on NVGs.

At push time, the MC did not know the exact location of the aircraft they planned to follow into the target area. After a short period, the MC positively identified the flight they were supposed to be following on the Situation Display (SIT) and pushed behind them on time. It appeared the MP used the SIT a majority of the time for deconfliction, only relying on radar and visual cues as a back-up. The MF dropped their training weapons successfully and egressed the target area uneventfully.

The report noted the MF did not have any air-to-air engagements during the mission. During target egress, the MP identified a potential deconfliction issue with other package aircraft and used the SIT along with NVGs to establish deconfliction. This deviation from the plan worried the MF and elevated their concern about the potential for breakdowns in the deconfliction plan.

The AIB investigator says in his report once clear of these aircraft, the MF reestablished itself in holding and remained there to burn fuel and to await their assigned recovery time. While in holding, the MC had a brief discussion about how to fly the recovery and then contacted the Air Traffic Control (ATC) agency for approach instructions.

The MP called for the MF to take off their NVGs and the MC did so. The MW left their NVGs until they were established in the descent due to concerns about deconfliction on the recovery. Then the MF began their recovery back to the deployed location.

ATC initially directed the MF to maintain an arc 20 NM from the TACAN, a navigation aid used to fly the instrument approach. The 20 NM arc is nonstandard for the recovery because the published approach is via the 17 NM arc. As the MP turned to maintain the 20 NM arc, the MWSO questioned this action. The MP told him that ATC had instructed this change to the recovery procedure.

At that same time, ATC cleared the MF to 5,000 feet MSL. As the MP leveled the MA at 5,000 feet MSL, ATC directed them onto the 17 NM arc and cleared them to 4,000 feet MSL.

The MP made two turns of approximately 45 degrees of bank to establish the MA on the 17 NM arc while descending to 4,000 feet MSL.

The MP accurately maintained his relationship with regard to the TACAN station on both the 20 and 17 NM arcs. The MP likely had an HSI displayed on his right Multi-Purpose Display (MPD) because it would be difficult to maintain position on an arc without having an HSI displayed and pilots typically run the HSI on the right MPD.

The MP had just established the MA on the 17 NM arc at 4,000 feet MSL when ATC cleared him to 3,000 feet MSL. He responded to ATC with a correct read-back of the instructions and began a steady five degree nose low descent in a wings-level attitude.

At approximately 3,400 feet MSL, the ATC controller queried the MP if he was "radar contact" with the aircraft in front of him on the arc passing the 270 degree radial. The MP replied affirmatively to ATC that he had radar contact, and the controller cleared him to descend to 2,000 feet MSL behind that aircraft.

In reality, the MP did not use the radar to gain situational awareness on the aircraft's location. Instead, he took control of and used the Pilot's Situation Display (SIT(P)) for this purpose.

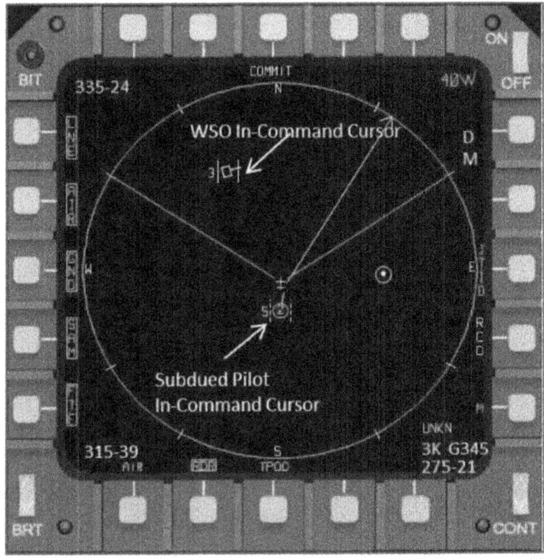

Figure 28: WSO Situational Display (SIT (W)) (Source: US AIB report).

Based on this information and because the MA was in a descent, the aircraft in front of him would have appeared slightly above him and ten degrees left of the MA's midline.

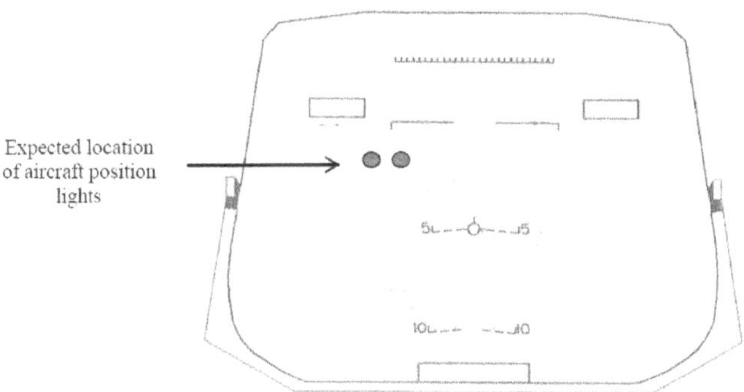

Figure 29: A representation of what the MP expected (Source: US AIB report).

The MP was in control of and actively moving his cursor on the SIT. All evidence suggests the MP was using the SIT(P) on the MPCD rather than viewing an EADI.

As the MA passed through 3,100 feet MSL, the MP pulsed the stick backwards and forwards. This caused a quick pitch up and then a pitch down of the MA. The MP simultaneously pushed the throttles forward from less than full power to full afterburner for two seconds.

The MP then aggressively pushed the stick forward, inducing -2.6 gravitational force (g) on the MA.

Next, the MP expressed verbal concern about what was going on around him, pulled the throttles back to less than full power and rolled the MA left, dwelling about one second in approximately 70 degrees of left bank and 20 degrees nose low.

The MWSO was not sure which way the jet rolled and did not tell the MP to recover because he worried that any input on his part might have made the situation worse.

The MP expressed further concern as he continued to roll another 110 degrees left to a fully inverted position approximately 1,800 feet AGL and 25 degrees nose low.

At that point, the MWSO believed that the MP did not know which way was up.

The MWSO grabbed the controls and rolled the MA left towards a near wings-level position. The ground collision warning system went off at that time, giving the MC an arrow on all of the displays, including the HUD, indicating the fastest way to pull to the horizon. The MWSO then pulled 11 g while rolling left to wings-level.

The final frame of HUD footage on the Digital Video Recording System (DVRS) displayed the MA had a positive vector away from the ground and a radar altimeter reading of 88 feet above ground level (AGL). As the MWSO rolled the MA to nearly level flight, he initiated ejection for the MC.

The MA airspeed read 352 knots in the last frame of the HUD video.

Had a radio tower not been in the flight path, the MA would have recovered prior to impacting the ground.

The time from the first abrupt maneuver and verbal concern by the MP to the time of ejection was approximately 11 seconds.

Impact

The AIB report describes the Impact as follows:

The MA impacted the terrain about 18 NM west, southwest of the deployed location in Southwest Asia. The MA was in the same configuration at impact as it was prior to take-off. The MA struck a 377-foot tall radio tower and crashed approximately 0.5 NM northeast of the tower. Based on the damage to the MA, it appears the right wing of the MA struck the radio tower. The impacted radio tower was part of a large tower array just north of a major east-west running well-trafficked highway.

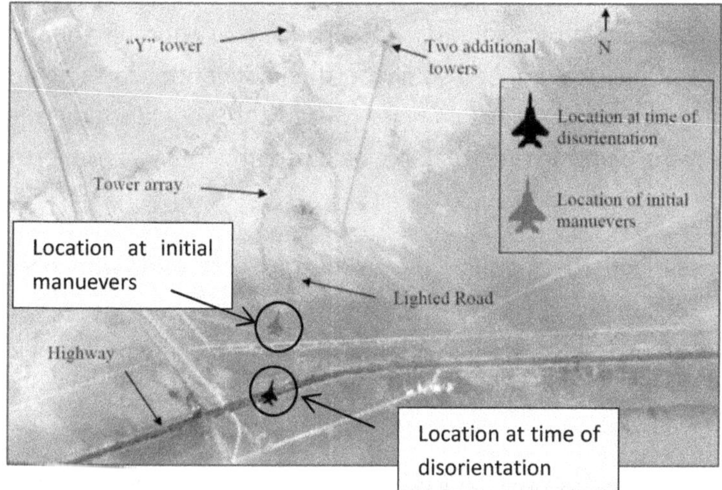

Figure 30: An aerial view of the mishap location (Source: US AIB report).

Human factors analysis

AFI 91-204, Safety Investigations and Reports, Attachment 5, contains the Department of Defense Human Factors Analysis and Classification System which lists potential human factors that can play a role in aircraft mishaps. The following human factors were relevant to this mishap:

1. Spatial Disorientation (Type 2) Recognized

Spatial Disorientation is a failure to correctly sense a position, motion or attitude of the aircraft or of oneself within the fixed coordinate system provided by the surface of the earth and the gravitational vertical. Spatial Disorientation (Type 2) is a factor when recognized perceptual confusion is induced through one or more of the following senses: visual; vestibular; auditory; tactile; proprioception or kinesthetic. Proper control inputs are still possible.

According to the report, the MP became spatially disoriented (Type 2) due to a visual illusion. As the MC was flying the approach back to base, the MP may have focused on lights that appeared from a nearby radio tower array and highway. In an environment devoid of traditional visual cues, most notably the lack of a true horizon, the MP may have relied solely on the lights and incorrectly inverted the MA. It is unknown which specific image caused the MP's disorientation, but the MP's maneuvers demonstrate that he believed the MA was inverted and five degrees nose low.

Witnesses described the night of the mishap as very dark with no discernable horizon.

Additionally, the MP was briefed that the recovery arc would be dark with no cultural lighting.

There were no discussions pertaining to highway lights or radio towers.

The mishap occurred at an isolated radio tower array 18 NM west, southwest of the base.

This array forms a horseshoe shape and consists of 31 primary towers. These towers are of varying heights with the tallest being 377 feet in height. Each radio tower contains one or two closely spaced steady red lights at the top of the tower and two to four steady red lights at the midpoint.

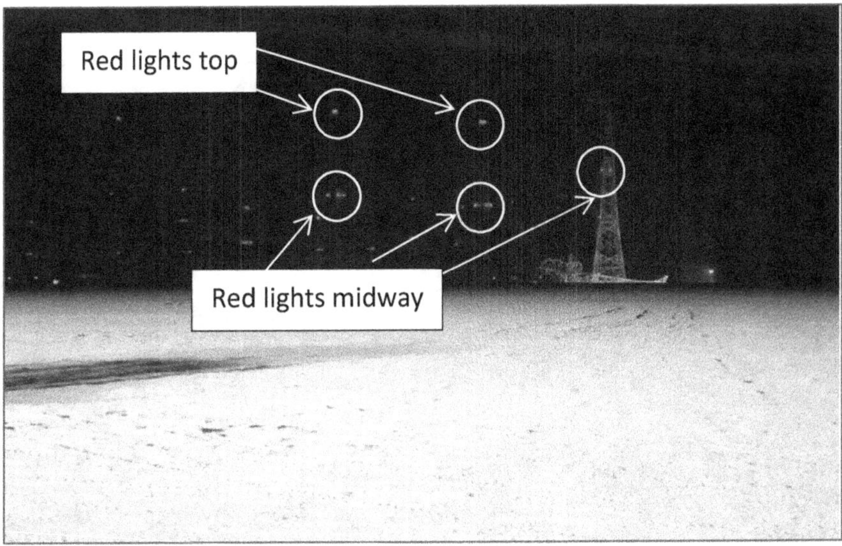

Figure 31: An image of tower lights at night with one to two red lights on top and two to four red lights midway up the tower (Source: US AIB report).

There is one distinct "Y" shaped tower 1,403.31 meters to the north of the main tower array. Directly east of this tower are two additional towers with buildings at their base. There are several buildings in the center of the tower array, which all have white security lights. A lighted road leads out of the horseshoe south towards a major east-west running well-trafficked highway.

There is a heavily trafficked, lighted highway south of the radio tower array. There are palm trees planted at a set interval along the side of the highway, which causes a flickering image at night due to the headlights of passing vehicles. In addition, many of the trucks commuting along this road have flashing yellow lights on the top of their freight.

Figure 32: A view of the palm trees planted along the road. The radio tower array can be seen in the background (Source: US AIB report).

As the MA descended through 3,400 feet MSL, the lighting from the radio towers and highway traffic would have come into the MP's view.

At that moment, the MP was looking down to manipulate the SIT and therefore, was unaware of the approaching lights. When the MP looked up, the lights from the main tower array would have already been under the MA's nose and only the "Y" shaped tower would have been in his focal view. The MP's verbal concerns indicate he looked up from his SIT and became disoriented by the cultural lighting.

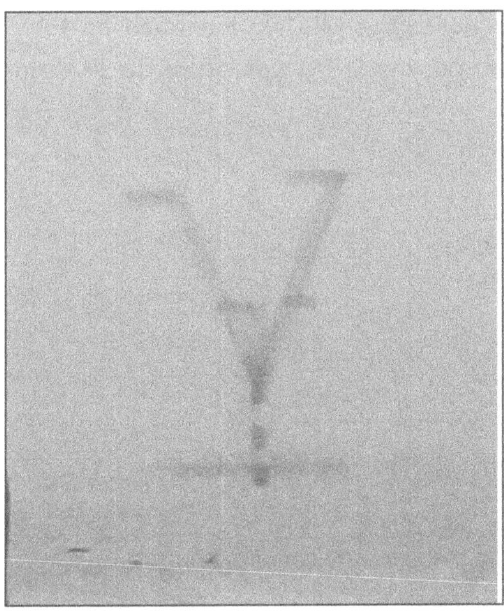

Figure 33: "Y" tower located north of the tower array (Source: US AIB report).

Due to the location of the MA, the highway lights would have been recognized by the MP's peripheral vision.

Peripheral vision has a strong influence on an individual's orientation in relation to the environment. In other words, it plays a big part in determining which way is "up." Prior to this event at a higher altitude, the MP would have seen stars above him in his peripheral vision, thereby verifying the feeling that stars were "up."

The flickering lights of the highway could have been interpreted by the MP as twinkling stars. If the MP interpreted the flickering lights below him as stars, it would have been spatially disorienting since it conflicted with what he expected.

A visual illusion is difficult to combat since visual cues are the primary source of a pilot's orientation. A dark night with no discernable horizon would prevent the MP from correctly orienting himself to any outside reference. Below are possible circumstances which may have disoriented the MP.

First, the radio tower lights that came into the MP's focal view may have been perceived as the position lights of another aircraft. The MA was behind an aircraft on the recovery arc, which the MP had identified on the SIT(P). The expected location of the aircraft per the SIT(P) was left of the MA's midline just below the horizon.

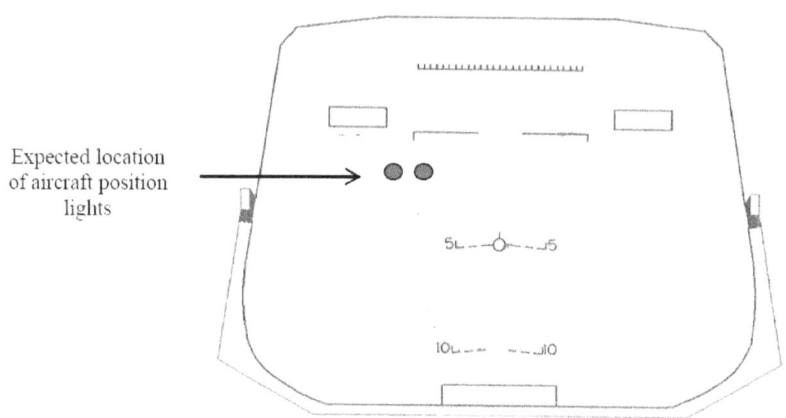

Figure 34: A representation of what the MP expected (Source: US AIB report).

If the MP misinterpreted the two lights on top of the "Y" tower as that aircraft, then that image would have conflicted with what he expected because it appeared right of the MA's midline and 10 degrees low.

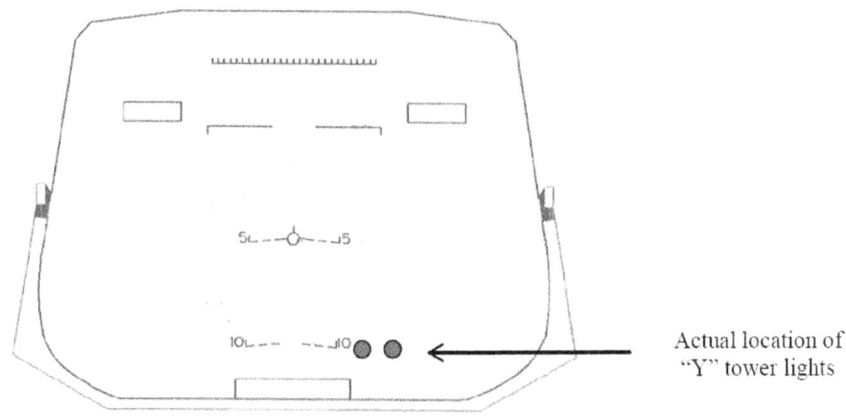

Figure 35: Actual representation of MA HUD (Source: US AIB report).

As a result, the MP incorrectly perceived the MA as inverted.

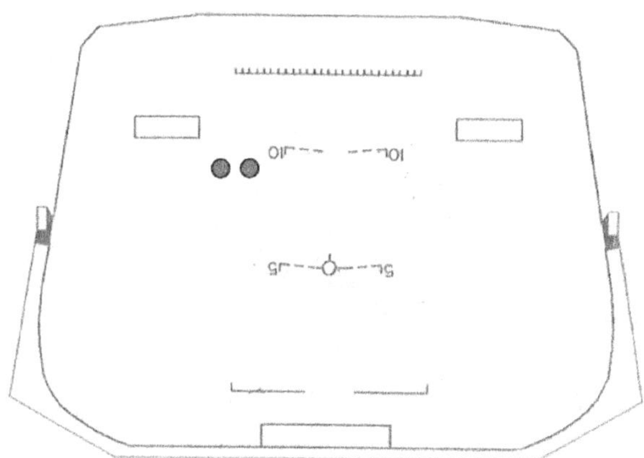

Figure 36: A representation of the HUD if the MA was truly inverted (Source: US AIB report).

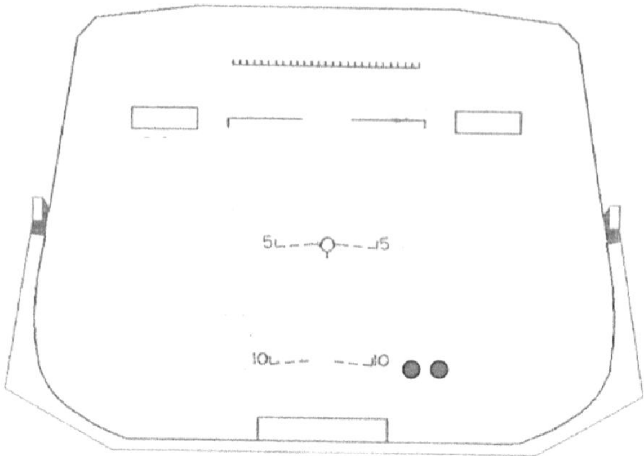

Figure 37: A representation of what the MP may have mistakenly perceived due to a visual illusion (inverted and five degrees nose low) (Source: US AIB report).

Secondly, the MP may have perceived the tower lights located on left side of the array as a false horizon.

The flickering lights of the highway would have entered the MP's peripheral vision at the same time the lights of the "Y" tower would have entered his focal vision. When the MP pushed the nose of the MA over in an attempt to orient himself to the "Y" tower's lights, the left line of tower lights would have also come into his focal view. The MP may have attempted to correct to this false horizon by placing the line of lights in the center of his vision and rolling left to situate the lights in a more traditional horizontal orientation.

A third possibility takes into consideration that the MP may have utilized his FLIR due to the environmental conditions. This may have allowed the MP to correctly identify the light in front of him as a tower. However, he still may have incorrectly believed he was inverted.

This would be due to the aforementioned highway lighting in his periphery and the atypical orientation of this isolated "Y" tower. This radio tower in the MP's focal view would have been an unfamiliar shape, wide at the top and narrow at the bottom. A typical radio tower would be the opposite shape, with a wide base and a narrow top. Instead of realizing he was viewing an unusual "Y" shaped tower, the

MP may have thought he was viewing a "typical" tower that appeared like a "Y" because he was inverted.

 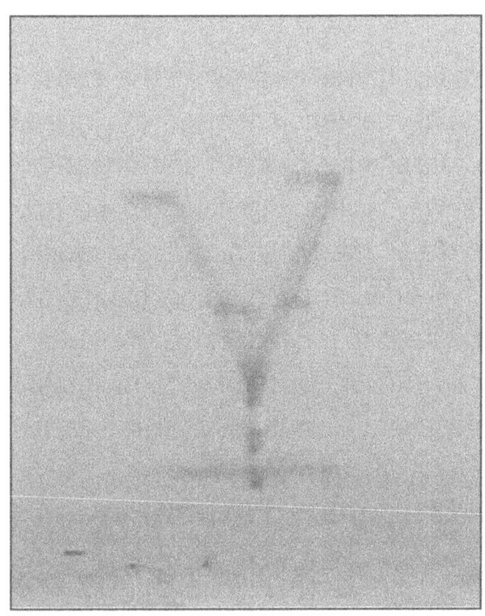

Figure 38: The left image shows a "typical" tower, wide at the bottom and narrow at the top. The right image shows the "Y" tower located north of the tower array (Source: US AIB report).

Vestibular disorientation was ruled out as a factor due to the lack of significant movements by the MA along any of its three axes. In the time period leading up to the mishap, the MP was performing a benign descent with no angular rotation or significant bank. That lack of motion also removes the likelihood of tactile, proprioception or kinesthetic disorientation. An auditory illusion is also unlikely, as the MP had good communication with the MWSO and ATC at all times. No other sounds were identified on the DVRS recording.

2. Vision Restricted by Meteorological Conditions

Vision Restricted by Meteorological Conditions is a factor when weather, haze or darkness restricted the vision of the individual to a point where normal duties were affected.

According to the report, due to the weather conditions and the fact that the MP was not wearing his NVGs at the time of the mishap, the MP's vision was restricted by meteorological conditions.

Visual references provide the most important sensory information to maintain spatial orientation during flight. These visual references provide information about distance, speed, depth and orientation. As the MA approached the towers and highway, lights once blocked by poor visibility and distance suddenly became visible to the MP. These lights would have been his only point of reference for visual orientation. It is possible the MP based his false orientation solely on these lights due to the lack of reliable visual cues (e.g., horizon, city lights). It would have been difficult for the MP to maintain his attitude in this environment without an instrument crosscheck using the EADI or standby ADI.

3. Channelized Attention

Channelized Attention is a factor when the individual is focusing all conscious attention on a limited number of environmental cues to the exclusion of others of a subjectively equal or higher or more immediate priority, leading to an unsafe situation. It may be described as a tight focus of attention that leads to the exclusion of comprehensive situation information.

According to the report, the MP was manipulating the SIT(P) prior to mishap. Because he may have been concerned with deconfliction in a heavy traffic area and the location of the aircraft in front of him, the MP focused his attention on the SIT(P) to maintain his situational awareness. This channelized attention resulted in an inadequate crosscheck of the other instruments/displays that are designed to assist the pilot with maintaining proper aircraft orientation.

4. Breakdown in Visual Scan

Breakdown in Visual Scan is a factor when the individual fails to effectively execute learned/practiced internal or external visual scan patterns leading to an unsafe situation.

According to the report, in accordance with Air Force Manual (AFMAN) 11-217, Vol 1, a proper crosscheck includes a visual scan of the outside environment, as well as using the HUD and an ADI to provide a pilot with the aircraft's correct attitude. As described above, the SIT provides a bird's eye view of the surrounding area but lacks information on aircraft attitude. The MP channelized his attention to the SIT(P), causing a breakdown in his visual scan.

The evidence suggests the MP looked up from the SIT(P) as he was flying over the highway near the radio tower array . The lights would have been unexpected and appear to have immediately disoriented the MP. The MP may have been better equipped to combat this illusion or avoid it completely if he had continuously utilized an effective crosscheck. Maintaining a visual scan outside the cockpit would have allowed the radio towers to slowly develop into the MP's line of sight instead of the immediate image that may have caused his sudden disorientation. In addition, the evidence suggests that the EADI was not part of the MP's display panel at the time of the mishap. The EADI would have displayed the MA's true upright orientation. By not having the EADI in his visual scan, the MP lacked a vital instrument that could have helped him avoid/overcome his disorientation.

5. Expectancy

Expectancy is a factor when the individual expects to perceive a certain reality and those expectations are strong enough to create a false perception of the expectation.

According to the report, the MP may have experienced the following three individual factors of Expectancy: The environment of the area was repeatedly briefed to the MP as "very dark". The MP did not expect to see cultural lighting until he was approaching the runway at the deployed location. The appearance of red tower lights and flickering highway lights were unexpected and may have been interpreted by the MP as lights above an indiscernible horizon.

Based on what he was seeing on the SIT(P), the MP expected the aircraft in front of him to be to his left. A tower light misinterpreted as an aircraft would have appeared to be on the MP's right. This perceived inverted image of the expected scene, along with the peripheral lighting of the highway below, could have caused the MP to become disoriented.

The MP's disorientation caused him to believe that he was inverted and five degrees nose low. The MP attempted to level the MA to his perceived horizon by pushing forward on the MA controls. The MP expected this maneuver to push the nose of the MA toward the horizon. In reality, the MA acted in accordance with the forward stick input and pitched further away from the horizon. This increased nose low attitude contradicted the MP's expectation of what the MA should have done. The MP likely was then attempting to identify why the MA did not follow his command, which would have caused further disorientation.

6. Error due to Misperception

Error due to Misperception is a factor when an individual acts or fails to act based on an illusion; misperception or disorientation state and this act or failure to act creates an unsafe situation.

According to the report, the MP performed recovery maneuvers to correct his perceived orientation. He pitched the MA down 20 degrees nose low and rolled left 70 degrees. The MP maintained this position for approximately one second and then continued to roll left to a fully inverted position.

The recovery maneuvers were incorrect, as the MP inverted the MA at approximately 1,800 feet AGL and 25 degrees nose low, creating an unsafe situation for the MC. Stick force analysis revealed all movements were controlled by the MC.

7. Air Traffic Control Resources

Air Traffic Control Resources is a factor when inadequate monitoring of airspace, enroute navigational aids or language barriers in air traffic controllers causes an unsafe situation.

According to the report, the MP was instructed by ATC to descend to 2,000 feet MSL earlier than expected or briefed. That caused a decrease in the vertical distance between the MA and the radio tower, which resulted in a corresponding increase in the visibility of the radio towers' lights and the highway lighting. The MA being five degrees nose low also introduced the lights into the MP's focal vision.

As was their common practice, ATC made frequent requests to the aircraft participating in the LFE to descend to 2,000 feet MSL earlier than depicted on the approach plate and was not consistent with what was briefed. By isolating aircraft at 2,000 feet MSL early, ATC was able to spend more time and attention on controlling the remaining aircraft entering the arc.

However, this practice of placing an aircraft at lower altitudes for longer periods of time and earlier than planned or expected, decreased the margin for error.

9 MC-12W Afghanistan Stall

Figure 39: MC-12W (Source: U.S. AIB report).

The United States Air Force Aircraft Accident Investigation Board (AIB) describes in their report that:

On 27 April 2013, at approximately 1243 local time (L) in Afghanistan, an MC-12W, tail number 09-0676 impacted terrain 110 nautical miles northeast of Kandahar Airfield (KAF) while on a combat intelligence, surveillance, and reconnaissance (ISR) mission. The four crewmembers on board were the Mishap Mission Commander (MMC), Mishap Pilot (MP), Mishap Sensor Operator (MSO), and Mishap Tactical Systems Operator (MTSO). The four airmen were killed instantly on impact and the Mishap Aircraft (MA), was destroyed. The crew and MA were deployed to the 361st Expeditionary Reconnaissance Squadron, 451st Air Expeditionary Wing, KAF, Afghanistan.

According to the AIB report, the four aircrew were highly respected airmen and combat veterans with 4,845 combat flying hours and 836 combat sorties between them.

The MMC, who had 1,749 flying hours, was assigned to Scott Air Force Base (AFB), Illinois as an aircraft commander in the KC-135, and was on temporary duty with the MC-12W program.

The MP, who had 2,434 flying hours, was newly assigned to Beale AFB, California as a new MC-12W mission commander and had extensive combat experience in the EC-130H from his previous assignment.

The MSO, who had 3,147 flying hours, was assigned to Tinker AFB, Oklahoma as an instructor air surveillance technician in the E-3, and was on temporary duty with the MC-12W program.

The MTSO, who had 1,494 flying hours, was assigned to Beale AFB, California and had extensive combat experience in the MC-12W and other tactical Intelligence Surveillance Reconnaissance (ISR) aircraft.

The MA, callsign Independence 08, departed KAF at 1157L. The MA encountered deteriorating weather in the orbit and was climbing from 20,000 to 23,000 feet mean sea level (MSL) at to fly above the weather when the mishap occurred. In addition, the crew had found an enemy combatant and was in the process of adjusting their orbit to enhance mission success.

Accident cause

The board president found, by clear and convincing evidence, the cause of the mishap was a stall due to insufficient airspeed, while in a climbing left turn, which developed into a left spin followed quickly by a left spiral, from which the crew was unable to recover.

Additionally, the board president found, by a preponderance of evidence, each of the following three factors substantially contributed to the mishap:

(1) orbit weather that impeded visibility and masked the horizon;

(2) pilot inexperience in the MC-12W; and

(3) known MC-12W program risks associated with sustaining required combat capability in theater. The MC-12W program accepted increased risk with mitigation measures and enabled the capture or killing of over 700 high value enemy combatants, while improving over-watch surveillance for coalition ground forces.

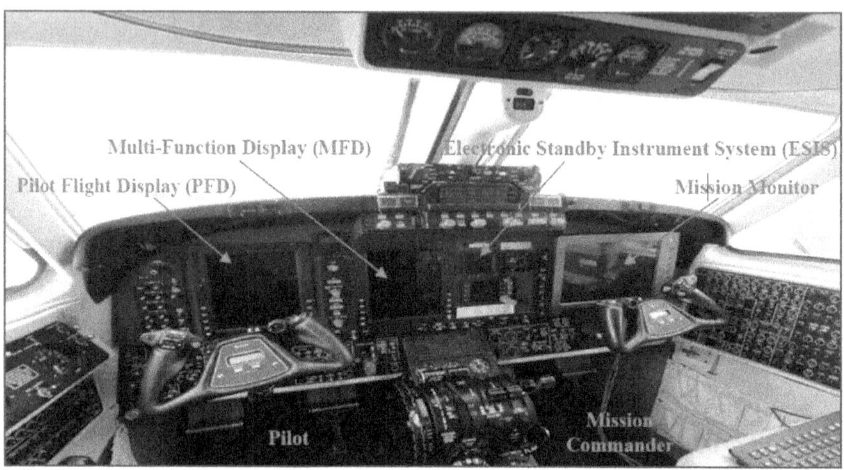

Figure 40: MC-12W Cockpit (Source: U.S. AIB report).

Accident summary

The AIB details the accident as follows:

After takeoff at 1157L, the MA encountered isolated towering cumulus buildups en route to their operating area. They stowed and unstowed the sensor ball on two occasions during their climb and en route to their orbit, indicating visible moisture above the freezing level. The MSO reported on-station in Internet Relay Chat (mIRC).

Note: mIRC was the MA's primary method of communication with Air Traffic Control (ATC) and Supported Unit.

Upon entering the operating area, they encountered a cloud deck partially covering their orbit area and a large, rapidly building towering cumulous (TCU) cloud in the center of their orbit area from 17,000 ft to 24,000 ft mean sea level ((MSL), all altitudes are in MSL unless otherwise indicated).

The report said that while in their first orbit, the MA was in the clouds approximately one-half of the time, and the conversation on board indicated they were flying in light to moderate turbulence. The sensor field of view (FOV) showed ground visible below the Towering Cumulous (TCU) with no intermediate cloud layers.

The MSO made the following weather comment in mIRC, "…looking at scattered and broken 16-170 [cloud base at 16,000 to 17,000 ft], plus this giant thing we're flying around going up to about FL240 [24,000 ft]". The TCU continued to grow and drift into the MA's orbit, prompting a request to climb from 20,000 ft to 23,000 ft. This translates to climbing from 13,800 to 16,800 ft above ground level (AGL), or height above terrain. The request and approval were transmitted over mIRC. mIRC communications were tasked to the MMC while the MP was at the controls. The MA was in a left hand orbit, preparing to shift the orbit, when the MP initiated the climb with the autopilot on. They were in IMC, meaning that they were in weather conditions that required reliance on aircraft instruments for attitude reference.

The MP initiated the climb in auto-pilot, utilizing either the constant pitch or constant vertical speed (VS) mode rather than the Flight Level Change (FLC or "filtch") mode. In each of these three possible modes, the pilot manually sets the throttles. The FLC mode will hold a constant airspeed and climb at a rate commensurate with the additional power increase. Since the other two modes will not self-adjust commensurate with power input, power application must be more closely monitored when using the constant pitch or VS mode. It has been estimated that about half the pilots use a similar technique and execute flight level changes, or changes in altitude, with the auto-pilot in VS mode.

While or just after initiating the climb, the MP continued working an orbit adjustment to better service tracking an active target, and approximately ten seconds after the climb was initiated, the climb rate increased. Fifteen seconds afterward the MP noticed he had allowed the MA airspeed to decrease during the climb, stating, "A little slow, correcting." Seven seconds later, the MMC said,

"Alright, firewall," meaning to advance the throttles as far forward as they would go, and one second later, the auto-pilot was disengaged.

The report explains that, the propellers on the MC-12W do not counter-rotate, and advancing the power in the MC-12W produces left-handed torque and P-factor, creating a left yaw and making the aircraft to want to turn left; the MA was already in a left-hand turn and left bank. Two seconds after calling to "firewall" the throttles, and one second after auto-pilot disengagement, video feed was lost and the bank angle warning tone sounded, indicating the MA left bank had rapidly increased to greater than 50 degrees. The MMC again called for full power, and four seconds later, the MMC directed "eyes inside," telling the MP to refer to his instruments for attitude and airspeed information; contemporaneously, the stall warning sounded. The stall warning horn stopped after five seconds, and a second later, background noise indicates items began flying around within the cockpit and the bank angle warning stopped.

The bank angle warning can stop even when an aircraft is in excess of 50 degrees of bank when the pilot flight display (PFD) reverts to "No Computed Data" mode due to excessive roll, pitch, or yaw changes. In "No Computed Data" mode, the PFD would remove all data except for red chevrons that would cue the pilot to "pull up" in the direction of the chevrons to recover the aircraft from an unusual attitude. Right after background noise indicated items began flying around within the cockpit and the bank angle warning stopped, the MP stated, "Whoa, pull up".

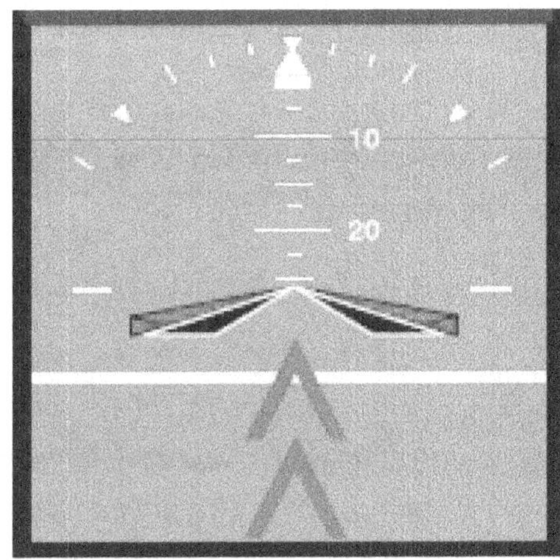

Figure 41: Declutter Display (Source: U.S. AIB report).

The MMC then advised the MP to look at his airspeed and the MMC took the aircraft, calling for a reduction in power. Four seconds after the MMC took the aircraft, the aircraft overspeed warning sounded, followed by the landing gear horn sounding. The landing gear horn indicates the throttles were reduced toward idle, and it did not sound until 15 seconds after initial stall warning sounded. The CVR stopped at this point. The MA reached a maximum recorded height of 20,900 ft. and lost approximately 15,000 ft before impacting the ground

A description of the last 94 seconds of flight, integrated with words and sounds from the cockpit voice recorder follows:

12:40:48 MMC: Alright, go ahead and push up the power. I asked for 230 [23,000 ft] for now just to keep us out of this for a little while anyway. So, go ahead and climb to 230. And as soon as you're ready.

12:40:58 MP: Oh we're already approved? Okay cool. The MP begins a shallow climb and airspeed begins to decrease.

12:41:00 MMC: Yup. As soon as you're ready you can go direct to that new start point and -

12:41:04 MP: Yea, once we make this turn here, I'll get that set in there. It's ready to be inserted.

12:41:08 MMC: Oh, cool. I'll let you do your business then.

1241:10 MA pitch increases, climb rate increases and airspeed decreases. From approximately 10 seconds from climb initiation until loss of feed, the climb rate increases and the airspeed decreases at a rapid rate.

12:41:12 MP: Cool. So once we make this turn I'll keep the roll going and then uh-.

12:41:15 MMC: Roger, roger.

12:41:25 MP: A little slow, correcting. MP acknowledges the airspeed decayed while in the climb. If power is added, while at a high angle of attack, the engines' torque/p-factor causes a left-rolling tendency for the aircraft, which the autopilot would compensate for by repositioning the yoke and control surfaces to a "right bank" position. This characteristic of MC-12W departure from controlled flight is similar to a previously-recorded incident.

12:41:32 MMC: Alright, firewall. "Firewall" is jargon for maximum power, or pushing the throttles to the full forward position.

12:41:33 Aural tone indicates MP has disengaged the auto-pilot. If the yoke is displaced to the right by the autopilot as discussed above, neutralizing the yoke upon auto-pilot disengagement would put the aircraft into further left bank almost immediately.

1241:34 Video feed lost due to MA unusual attitude. At loss of feed, calibrated airspeed was approximately 116 nautical miles per hour, or "knots". Coordinates of last known position plot are less than a mile from impact site.

12:41:34 Contemporaneously, the "bank angle" warning is activated, indicating the aircraft has exceeded 50 degrees bank.

12:41:34 MMC: Max power, max power. If the throttles were not at full power already, adding more power would increase left yaw.

12:41:38 MMC: Alright, eyes inside, eyes inside. An "eyes inside" call would advise the MP to reference the cockpit instruments for aircraft attitude and performance information instead of looking outside for visual cues. The aircraft was "in the weather," or in Instrument Meteorological Conditions, at the time.

12:41:38 Stall warning comes on; bank angle warning continues.

12:41:41 Mode C (altitude-encoded transponder return) indicates MA reaches a maximum recorded altitude of 20,900 ft. "Mode C" is a channel that emits altitude information.

12:41:42 MP: Max power. MP confirms he has advanced throttles to maximum power.

12:41:43 Stall warning horn stops.

12:41:44 Background noise indicates items flying around within the aircraft. This would occur if the aircraft violently entered a spin. A spin could result from uncoordinated flight to correct excessive left bank, while in a stall, combined with the left-yawing tendency of two engines at maximum torque.

12:41:44 Bank Angle warning stops. If a pilot flight display (PFD) reverted to "No Computed Data" mode due to excessive roll, pitch, or yaw change (in excess of 125 degrees per second), the audible bank angle warning would stop, and the PFD would be blank except for red chevrons cueing the pilot to "pull up" in the direction of the chevrons.

12:41:45 MP: Whoa, pull up. Adding up elevator, in other words, "pulling up," or back on the yoke, would be counter to proper spin or spiral recovery procedures.

12:41:48 MMC: Eyes inside. Look at your airspeed.

12:41:49 Bank angle warning comes on and stays on until loss of audio.

12:41:54 MMC: Eyes inside, eyes inside, my aircraft, power back.

12:41:56 MA Mode C indicates MA at 18,000 ft; descent rate of 11,600 fpm (this equates to 116 nautical miles per hour (knots) vertical velocity).

12:41:57 MP: Your aircraft.

12:41:58 Overspeed warning tone is activated. Overspeed warning comes on when the aircraft exceeds approximately 245 knots.

12:42:00 "Gear warning" horn sounds, indicating throttles pulled towards idle. Time from stall warning ceasing to overspeed warning is approx 15 seconds. Such rapid acceleration is indicative of an extreme nose-down attitude.

12:42:02 Last CVR data.

12:42:03 Mode C indicates MA at 14,700 ft; descent rate of 28,285 fpm (i.e. 283 knots vertical velocity).

12:42:23 Last ATC Radar return indicates MA ground speed of 316 knots.

The MA lost approximately 15,000 ft before impacting the ground.

Impact

The AIB report describes the Impact as follows:

The MA impacted valley terrain at approximately 1243L on 27 April 2013 approximately 110 NM northeast of KAF. The MA impacted with the fuselage slightly nose-low, in a left bank, with minimal forward momentum. The MA was destroyed upon impact and burned during the post-crash fire. With the exception of the right wingtip and winglet, which was located 500 meters (1,640 ft) from the impact site, all other aircraft wreckage was within a 50-meter (164 ft) radius. A Local National (LN) witness reported seeing the MA descending in a left turn, and reported seeing either a puff or trail of black smoke prior to impact.

Human factors analysis

A taxonomy was developed to identify hazards and risks, called the DoD Human Factors Analysis and Classification System (DoD-HFACS). This guide is designed for use as a comprehensive tool for human error investigation, data identification, analysis and classification. It is designed for use by all members of an investigation board to accurately capture and recreate the complex layers of human factors. The human factors relevant to this mishap are discussed below.

Since the mishap aircrew perished, no firsthand accounts of the immediate events leading up to the mishap are available. Human factors are extrapolated from CVR data, witness testimony, radar logs, and reconstruction of the accident through sensor feeds. It should also be noted that while each factor is independently relevant, many of the factors are interrelated, and they are not mutually exclusive.

1. Program and Policy Risk Assessment.

Program and Policy Risk Assessment is a factor "when the potential risks of a large program, operation, acquisition or process are not adequately assessed and this inadequacy leads to an unsafe situation".

According to the report, in this case, the potential risks were assessed, but program and policy risks are still relevant to the mishap. Since its inception in 2008, the MC-12W program consistently trains nearly 300 pilots per year, flies 75% of all ISR missions, and shoulders 25% of total combat flying missions in the Air Forces Central Command (AFCENT) Area of Operation AOR. Nearly 20,000 sorties and over 100,000 combat flying hours have been accomplished in the last five years with a success rate of 99.96%. It is the single most requested asset in the AOR, has been instrumental in the capture or elimination of over 700 high value targets, and has saved countless coalition lives through over-watch and improvised explosive device (IED) detection.

Program success came with the assumption of certain risks including rapidly implemented training programs and the delay of program normalization. Normalization refers to aligning a program with accepted Air Force common practices. This lack of normalization is evidenced by a "flow-through" manning process with its associated challenges, crew position waivers, and a non-standard aircraft certification/testing process for the mission-required MC-12W modifications. "Flow-through" manning is a process wherein a crew member is removed from their major weapons system (MWS), trained and deployed in the MC-12W, and then returned to their MWS. These program risks are most visible from a human factors perspective in organizational training gaps and limited pilot experience.

2. Organizational Training Issues.

According to the DoD HFACS, organizational training issues are a factor, "when one-time or initial training programs, upgrade programs, transition programs or other training that is conducted outside the local unit is inadequate or unavailable and this creates an unsafe situation".

According to the report, MC-12W training is divided into two parts: Initial Qualification Training (IQT) and Mission Qualification Training (MQT). IQT teaches crews how to fly a civilian King Air 350, and MQT teaches crews to employ the MC-12W in combat.

IQT consists of six simulator rides, is provided at three sites by contract instructors, and is the same training civilians receive to be qualified in the King Air 350.

MQT consists of 15 sorties, is provided by military units at Beale AFB, and focuses on mission-related tasks. The first two MQT sorties transition the pilot from IQT and focus strictly on basic airmanship, or flying skills. IQT and MQT are relevant to this mishap because both training and aircraft experience affect basic airmanship skills including recognition of and recovery from unsafe aircraft attitudes.

IQT is conducted in a King Air 350 simulator and is not MC-12W specific. The King Air 350 was designed for executive transport, and this mission shapes IQT.

The MC-12W is physically different, its mission is different, and it is more mentally demanding and challenging than the King Air 350. For example, the MC-12W has additional parts and systems, and different aerodynamic characteristics. It is fitted with extra fuel tanks and an array of antennae and other external equipment, weighs more, and has more drag than the King Air 350.

This point is very important, the MC-12W did not undergo normal developmental or operational testing to account for these differences.

According to the report, Orbit stall training was limited. This is significant as a typical mission sortie includes substantially more time in orbit than in any other phase of flight, and the orbit is flown relatively close to stall speed. Four previous MC-12W orbit stalls that resulted in significant, near catastrophic altitude loss highlight this limited training. These four near misses occurred in adverse weather and also show why training and experience in weather is important. Training in the often unpredictable weather experienced in Afghanistan cannot be replicated at Beale AFB, where it is largely clear all summer and has mild winter weather.

Before the mishap flight, the MP had not flown in Instrument Meteorological Conditions (IMC) in 67 days.

After IQT, pilots transition to MQT. MQT is focused primarily on mission employment rather than on basic airmanship or "stick and rudder" training. Additionally, unlike more normalized airframes, there was no combat mission ready top-off program to bridge the gap between MQT and crews deploying to combat.

The Pilot Flight Display in the MC-12W has "Declutter" and "No Computed Data" modes. During unusual aircraft attitude scenarios, these modes automatically replace the normal instrument display with a simplified recovery mode, which displays only essential data. Pilots may be unfamiliar with the "Declutter" or "No Computed Data" modes since neither IQT nor MQT emphasize them, nor can they be safely replicated in the aircraft. Unfamiliarity with the "Declutter" or "No Computed Data" modes could lead to confusion and delayed or improper stall/spin recovery.

3. Limited Recent Experience.

According to the DoD HFACS, limited recent experience is a factor, "when the supervisor selects an individual whose experience for a specific maneuver, event or scenario is not sufficiently current to permit safe mission execution".

According to the report, in this mishap, although all crewmembers were current, limited recent experience is still relevant.

The MP had 2,434 hours in an EC-130H, but had only 21 primary hours and 41.7 total hours in the MC-12W/King Air 350 and had not flown the MC-12W for 45 days before the mishap. Most mission commanders are deployed with approximately 40 hours of MC-12W flight time, only about half of which is primary flight time. The MP's last flight prior to the mishap sortie was in an unmodified King Air 350, and occurred 26 days prior to the mishap. On the mishap sortie, the

MP was flying in the left seat. His most recent flight in the left seat of the MC-12W was 64 days prior, and the mishap sortie was his first flight in combat.

The MMC had a total of 1,749 hours, primarily in a KC-135. He had 242 combat hours in the MC-12W; however, he was not instructor qualified and the mishap sortie was his first ride as a "certifier". The MSO and MTSO were both current and qualified, and both were highly experienced in the MC-12W.

According to the report, both pilots were on their first MC-12W deployment and were inexperienced in their roles on the mishap sortie. Their limited recent experience was compounded by the fact that they had not flown together in the past.

4. Vision Restricted by Meteorological Conditions.

According to the DoD HFACS vision restricted by meteorological conditions is a factor, "when weather, haze, or darkness restricts the vision of the individual to a point where normal duties are affected".

According to the report, Sensor camera data, coalition surface personnel, and mIRC data indicate the crew's vision was restricted by clouds near the time of departure from controlled flight and they likely did not have a visually discernible horizon. Cloud tops reached 24,000 feet during the time of the mishap.

Weather is relevant because lack of external visual cues is almost universally causal to known instances of spatial disorientation. Spatial disorientation, which is a failure to correctly sense a position, motion, or attitude of the aircraft or one's self in reference to the ground, can lead to unrecognized dangerous aircraft attitudes. In this case, the mishap crew's visual cues were limited during their climb and initial departure from controlled flight, and their initial recovery actions would have occurred in an environment lacking a visually discernible horizon.

5. Breakdown in Visual Scan

Breakdown in Visual Scan is a factor "when the individual fails to effectively execute learned/practiced internal or external visual scan patterns leading to an unsafe situation".

According to the report, Breakdown in Visual Scan is relevant because increased attention on weather, the evolving mission, and other associated tasks may have resulted in a breakdown of the normal visual scan pattern. The cockpit voice recorder (CVR) indicates there were mission and weather-related task changes as the MP initiated his climb. The MA airspeed decreased from 150 knots to 116 knots during the final seconds of controlled flight. The MP's visual scan failed to timely identify the decreasing airspeed.

6. Procedural Error

Procedural Error is a factor "when a procedure is accomplished in the wrong sequence or using the wrong technique or when the wrong control or switch is used".

According to the report, Procedural Error is relevant because though the MP exercised a "max power" procedure in conjunction with the slow airspeed and subsequent stall warning, there is no evidence of an immediate pitch correction to reduce the angle of attack and avoid a stall. Due to left-turning tendencies of propeller-driven aircraft, power application without reducing the angle of attack could lead to additional yaw in the same direction as the established turn. Both stall and yaw are necessary preconditions for a spin. In addition, after departure from controlled flight, the MP delayed 15 seconds in executing a "power idle" procedure. Finally, the MP called "Whoa, pull up," and may have prematurely pulled up as a "No Computed Data" screen on the PFD would have prompted. Pulling up too early will exacerbate either a spin or a spiral.

10 HH60G Ground Impact

Figure 42: HH-60G (Source: U.S. AIB report).

The United States Air Force Aircraft Accident Investigation Board (AIB) describes in their report that:

On 5 August 2013 at approximately 1610 hours local time (L), the mishap aircraft (MA), an HH-60G, tail number 91-26354, assigned to the 33rd Rescue Squadron, 18th Wing, Kadena Air Base (AB), Japan, while flying in formation on a pre-deployment spin-up training mission, impacted terrain approximately 14 nautical miles northeast of Kadena AB in the Central Training Area (CTA).

Mishap Pilot (MP), Mishap Copilot (MCP) and Mishap Aerial Gunner (MAG) exited the MA shortly after impact sustaining minor to major injuries. Mishap Flight Engineer (MFE) was fatally injured. MA was significantly damaged upon impact and subsequently destroyed by ensuing fire.

MA was in a formation flight to the CTA as the wingman of the Mishap Flight Lead Aircraft (MFLA). Once in the area, MFLA, followed by MA, infiltrated their pararescuemen into a landing zone near a simulated downed helicopter with a survivor.

Following the infiltration, MFLA and MA, now with MA in the formation lead position and MFLA as the trailing aircraft/wingman, proceeded to fly in a northwest-southeast oriented figure eight-like racetrack pattern at 150 feet above ground level.

On the last turn prior to the mishap, MA, with MCP on the flight controls, turned to the right (east), and in a direction opposite previous turns in order to correct their pattern, which had drifted to the west. MFLA was at MA's five o'clock position at the beginning of the turn, in an effort to maintain desired gun pattern ground track. There was no indication of discussion or that anyone on the Mishap Crew was aware as to the location of MFLA in relation to MA other than in being in trail.

After approximately 90 degrees of turn, MP was surprised to see MFLA off his right side and perceived an immediate conflict with potential for mid-air collision. However, MFLA crew did not have the same perception. Based upon this perception, MP immediately took control of MA, and proceeded to increase bank and initiated a descent to avoid MFLA.

Accident cause

The Accident Investigation Board (AIB) President found by clear and convincing evidence that the cause of the mishap was MP, based upon his perception of a potential for a mid-air collision with the formation wingman, maneuvered MA at low altitude in a manner that resulted in excessive altitude loss and MP's inability to stop the helicopter's descent prior to ground impact.

Furthermore, the AIB President found by a preponderance of evidence that each of the following factors substantially contributed to the mishap:

(1) MCP turned in a direction opposite previous racetrack turns and into the flight path of the trailing aircraft; and

(2) MP was not aware of trailing aircraft's specific position prior to turning, which resulted in MP's surprise upon seeing the trailing aircraft and MP's belief that immediate maneuvering was required to avoid collision.

Accident summary

MF actual takeoff time was 1535L. MF flew for approximately 15 minutes to the Initial Point (IP), approximately 14 NMs northeast of Kadena AB. The scenario for the training mission was located at Landing Zone (LZ) Peacock in the CTA.

MFLP's game plan, upon arrival at the IP, was to fly a racetrack pattern between the SDH and any potential threat. Upon arriving at the terminal area and before dropping off the CRO and PJs near the Simulated Downed Helicopter (SDH) survivor, MF entered into a northwest-southeast oriented gun-pattern racetrack initially planned for 300 feet above ground level (AGL) with MFLA in the formation lead position.

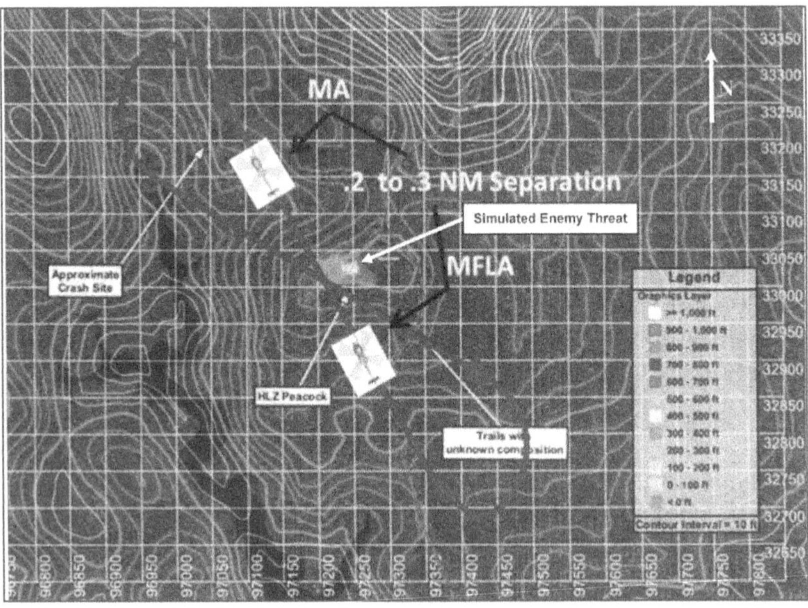

Figure 43: Desired Turn Reversal Racetrack (Source: U.S. AIB report).

MF infiltrated the Pararescueman (PJs) as planned and without incident. MFLA landed in the Landing Zone (LZ) first and dropped off the Combat Rescue Officer (CRO) and two PJs.

MFLA subsequently lifted off and proceeded to fly back into the established racetrack pattern, then cleared MA to land. MA landed, dropped off two PJs, then lifted off and rejoined the racetrack pattern. However, due to the timing of the re-entry into the gun pattern upon takeoff, MA ended up in the formation lead position, although MP is not flight lead certified.

This type of formation, where a non-flight lead certified aircraft commander is in the lead, periodically occurs during formation gun procedures in an effort to maximize guns on target.

MCP was on the flight controls of MA on all racetracks after departing MF gun pattern following infiltration was at a speed of 80 knots, 150 feet AGL with a separation of.2 to .3 NMs between aircraft.

All turns on the northwest end of the racetrack were to the left, or west, at maximum rate-turn bank angles, while turns on the southeast end of the track were reversed and to the right, at the same bank angles. The desired straight-and-level portion of the racetrack was between the SDH survivor and simulated enemy forces and on a heading as directed by MFLP on each subsequent turn. Shortly after MF was re-established in the overhead gun pattern, the PJ ground teams were engaged by simulated enemy forces attacking. Subsequently, the enemy forces were simulated killed by MF.

MF continued to fly racetrack patterns, in between the last known enemy threat area and the friendly ground forces. In order to maximize target effect and keep MF between friendly ground forces and the last known enemy threat, MFLP continued to reverse the turns at each end of the racetrack.

MF conducted approximately four to six gun patterns in this manner. While executing these patterns, the MA, allowed its ground track to shift to the west, thus placing the friendly ground forces between the MA and the last known threat area. As noted by MFLP, MA had a weapons engagement confliction or area where they were unable to fire weapons because of the location of the survivor. Therefore, on the last southeast leg of the racetrack, MFLP directed the LZ except for the last half of the mishap turn.

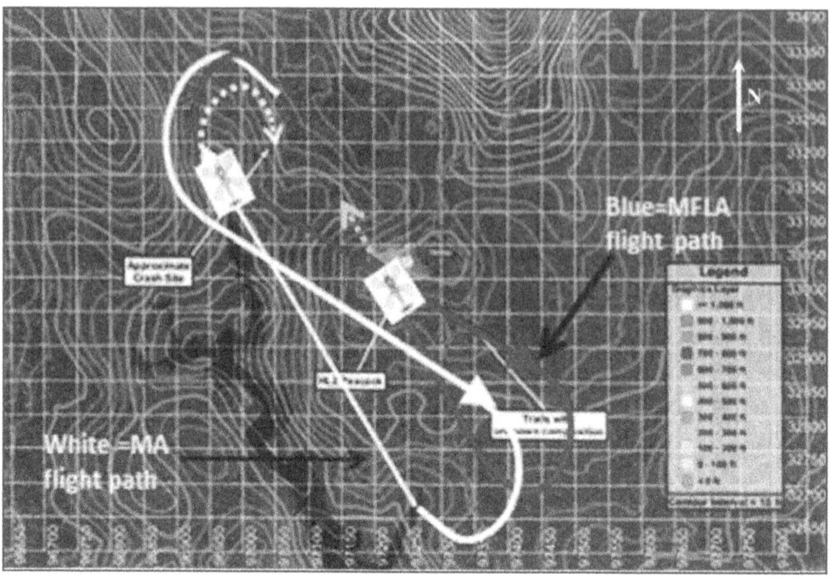

Figure 44: Mishap Aircraft and Mishap Flight Lead Aircraft Separate Ground Track (Source: U.S. AIB report).

MA to correct their pattern by shifting back to the east, to once again place MA between friendly forces and the last known threat area. The pattern shift was acknowledged by the MC.

At the same time, MFLA continued to follow the ground track between survivor and anticipated threat, thus placing it east of MA. After the MF turned right to a northeast heading, MFLP noted that MA was still west of desired ground track and MFLP again directed a pattern correction to the east, which again the MC acknowledged. During all racetracks, the MFLA, flying in the trailing formation position, maintained the desired ground track, which was between the SDH survivor and simulated threat and to the east of the MA ground track on the last racetrack. In order for MFLA to maintain the desired ground track, they had to fly at the seven o'clock position of MA when flying southeast and at the five o'clock position when flying northwest, while maintaining .2 to .3 NMs separation. Flying within the 5 o'clock to 7 o'clock position is where MP and MCP stated they would have expected the trailing aircraft to be.

As MA entered the northwest end of the racetrack pattern, and based on previous patterns, MFLP and MFLCP anticipated MA would perform a left-hand turn as in previous turns. However, MCP chose to execute a right turn in order to shift the pattern to the east, as previously directed by MFLP. This right turn was neither communicated to MFLA nor does MC remember any internal discussions about turning right to fix the pattern. Per testimony, MP remembered all turns at this end of the track to be to the right, while MCP, MFLP and MFLCP recalled all previous turns being to the left. Likewise, Mishap Flight Lead Crew (MFLC) did not communicate with MC, as a result of MCP turning in a direction opposite than was expected by MFLP and MFLCP.

However, neither the MFLP nor the MFLCP stated they felt this was a problem because they were deconflicted by distance and believed the MFLA was correcting their pattern spacing to the east by turning to the east, although opposite the direction of previous turns. MFLA continued straight for approximately five seconds to keep the guns on the right side of the helicopter pointed at the simulated threat for as long as possible then initiated a short turn to the left in order to avoid a conflict and a set up for a subsequent right turn to follow MA. MFLP stated that just prior to starting the left avoidance turn, the MA had completed approximately 90 degrees of its right turn.

It is at this point, approximately 90 degrees through the maximum performance (turning as fast as possible with the smallest radius possible for a specified airspeed) right turn, MP saw MFLA through the green house window (the window in the ceiling), which was not where MP expected to see MFLA. MP perceived that MFLA was closing on the MA and there was danger of a midair collision.

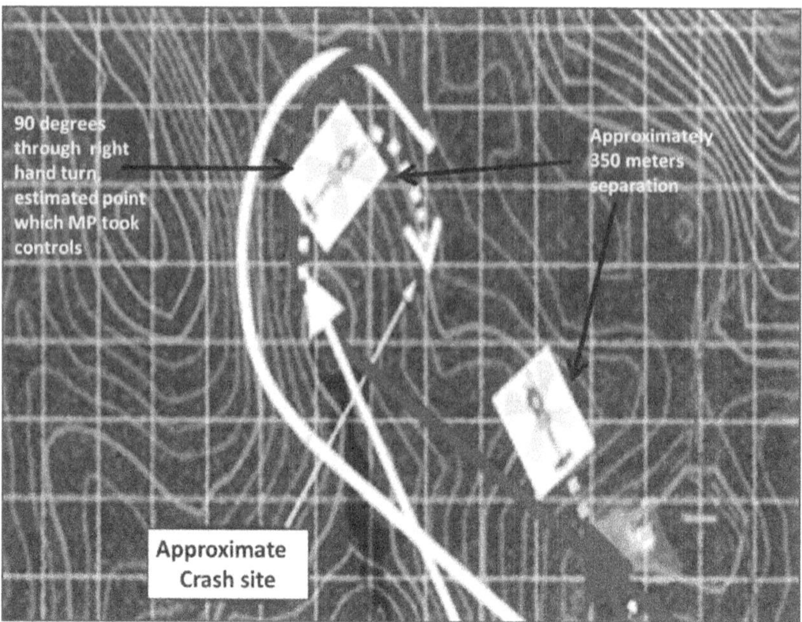

Figure 45: Mishap Pilot's Perceived Conflict Approximate Location (Source: U.S. AIB report).

However, MFLP, MFLCP, and MFLFE indicated otherwise. While MFLP acknowledged that had he done nothing with MFLA there would have been a conflict, which is normal for this type of pattern, MFLP negated this conflict by turning to the left, with subsequent intent to follow MA in the right turn.

Further MFLP, MFLCP and MFLFE reported no sense of urgency and stated that MA and MFLA remained .2 to .3 NM distance apart. In addition, the MP stated the MFLA was approximately 1,000 feet at the time he first saw the MFLA.

As a result of his perception, MP took the flight controls from MCP and increased the angle of bank from the 40-50° to an unspecified steeper angle. MP also decreased the collective (the collective changes pitch of the main rotor blades causing an increase or decrease in lift) by approximately 3-4 inches. MP's intent was to avoid MFLA's flight path by tightening MA' s turn in order to break phase and plane (turn through MFLA's flight path in a descending turn) and reversing the turn to continue around until MA would eventually rejoin behind MFLA in the gun pattern. While every aircraft ultimately has a responsibility for collision avoidance, in HH60G gun patterns, the formation lead aircraft is responsible for ground track while the wingman is primarily responsible for spacing and collision avoidance. Although MP intended to descend during this maneuver, upon rolling out, MA was lower than MP anticipated. Realizing MA was about to hit the trees, MP pulled in as much collective as he could but described MA as "mushing through" or "didn't have enough power" in his efforts to stop the descent. At some point during the maneuver, MP and MCP heard a warning horn from the MA, an indication of either low rotor revolutions per minute (RPM) (below 95%) or compressor gas turbine RPM below 55% (engine failure). Due to their attention being drawn outside, neither MP nor MCP could confirm the source of the warning horn.

Once MP realized he was unable to recover MA and that descent into the trees was imminent, he decelerated as much as possible in order to enter the trees vertically and with minimal forward airspeed.

Impact

MA impacted the ground into upward sloping terrain at 1610L, approximately 14 NMs northeast of Kadena AB. At the time of the impact, MA attitude was assessed to be approximately wings level, nose high, at an unknown rate of descent, and having minimal forward airspeed. MA impacted hard enough to partially stroke MP and MCP's seats (intentional seat design to collapse for aircrew crash survivability). MA rolled onto its right side after impact. The only change from the original configuration at the time of impact was the weight reduction due to offload of MPJ1 and MPJ2, and fuel burned during flight, estimating fuel remaining to be 4000 pounds.

Human factors analysis

AFI 91-204, Safety Investigations and Reports, 24 September 2008, Attachment 5, contains the Department of Defense Human Factors Analysis and Classification System which lists potential human factors that can play a role in aircraft mishaps.

1. Cross-Monitoring Performance

AFI 91-204, page 130 defines cross-monitoring performance as a factor when crew or team members failed to monitor, assist or back-up each other's actions and decisions.

According to the report, MC failed to recognize that the final right-hand turn (which was opposite previous directions at this end of the racetrack) would be in the direction of the MFLA, which was at their 5 o'clock position. MC received a shift pattern east call, to which MCP initiated a right turn to the east, although neither MP nor MCP recall any internal communication as to the choice of turning right being different than previous turns. MP did not recall that this turn direction was different than previous turns. Likewise, surviving members of MC did not recall whether or not there was any internal communication as to clearing MA's flight path relevant to MFLA.

2. Misperception of Operational Conditions

AFI 91-204, page 129 defines misperception of operational conditions as a factor when an individual misperceives or misjudges altitude, separation, speed, closure rate, road/sea conditions, aircraft/vehicle location within the performance envelope or other operational conditions and this leads to an unsafe condition.

According to the report, MP perceived a situation unfolding that if uncorrected would lead MF into a situation that would prevent either aircraft from having enough energy to maneuver as required, although evidence suggests otherwise. Due to MA displacement from the desired ground track, MFLP chose to fly the desired ground track putting them at MA's 5 o'clock position, where MP and MCP stated they would have expected MFLA to be. MFLAG detected MA's right hand turn, which was in the direction of MFLA's flight path, and alerted MFLP to the condition that if left uncorrected would lead to a conflict. Since this type of potential conflict is common in this formation pattern, MFLP assessed there was adequate space to continue flying ahead for approximately five seconds to complete the gun pattern before turning to avoid a conflict. At the end of the five seconds and just prior to MFLP initiating the turn to the left is when MP sees MFLA at approximately 1,000 feet away. MFLP and MFLCP' experienced no significant sense of urgency as the situation progressed; nor did they feel the need to communicate their intentions with MA. MP felt MA and MFLA where going to hit each other although MFLP and MFLCP, who were continually watching MA throughout the right turn, perceived the separation was appropriate.

3. Overcontrol / Undercontrol

AFI 91-204, page 116 defines overcontrol / undercontrol as a factor when an individual responds inappropriately to conditions by either overcontrolling or undercontrolling the aircraft / vehicle / system. The error may be a result of preconditions or a temporary failure of coordination.

According to the report, MP recalled in detail the actions that he took to maintain adequate separation from MFLA. MP testified that after MCP initiated a right hand turn, MP perceived a possible conflict between MA's and MFLA's flight paths. Upon detection of the impending conflict, MP took control of MA, and made flight control inputs to further increase the rate of turn while simultaneously descending to gain separation. However, MP's controlling of MA resulted in a loss of altitude greater than allowable due to terrain.

There is evidence to suggest these human factors were factors in the mishap.

11 U-28A Spatial disorientation

Figure 46: U-28A (Source: U.S. AIB report).

The United States Air Force Aircraft Accident Investigation Board (AIB) describes in their report that:

On 18 February 2012, at approximately 1918 local time (L), a United States Air Force U-28A aircraft, tail number 07-0736, crashed five nautical miles (NM) southwest of Ambouli International Airport, Djibouti. This aircraft was assigned to the 34th Special Operations Squadron, 1st Special Operations Wing, Hurlburt Field, FL, and deployed to the 34th Expeditionary Special Operations Squadron, Camp Lemonnier, Djibouti. The aircraft was destroyed and all four aircrew members died instantly upon impact.

The mishap aircraft (MA) departed Ambouli International Airport, Djibouti at 1357L, to accomplish a combat mission in support of a Combined Joint Task Force.

The MA proceeded to the area of responsibility (AOR), completed its mission in the AOR and returned back to Djiboutian airspace at 1852L arriving overhead the airfield at 1910L to begin a systems check.

The MA proceeded south of the airfield at 10,000 feet (ft) Mean Sea Level (MSL) for 10 NM then turned to the North towards the airfield, accomplished a systems check and requested entry into the pattern at Ambouli International Airport.

This request was denied due to other traffic, and the MA was directed to proceed to the west and descend by Air Traffic Control (ATC). The MA began a left descending turn to the west and was directed by ATC to report final. The mishap crew (MC) reported they were passing through 4,000 ft MSL and would report when established on final approach. The MA, continuing to descend, initiated a right turn then reversed the turn entering a left turn while continually and smoothly increasing bank angle until reaching 55 degrees prior to impact. Additionally, the MA continued to steadily increase the descent rate until reaching 11,752 ft per minute prior to impact. The MC received aural "Sink Rate" and "Pull Up" alerts with no apparent corrective action taken. The MA impacted the ground at approximately 1918L, 5 NM southwest of Ambouli International Airport, Djibouti.

Figure 47: Descent profile provided by Enhanced Ground Proximity Warning System, looking west (Source: U.S. AIB report).

The MC never lost control of the aircraft; there are no indications of mechanical malfunction; and there are no indications the crew took any actions to control or arrest the descent rate and nose down attitude.

Accident cause

The evidence demonstrates that the MC did not recognize the position of the aircraft and, as a result, failed to take appropriate corrective actions. The only plausible reason for the MC not recognizing the situation or reacting to aural alerts is the cognitive disconnect associated with spatial disorientation. The Board President found that the clear and convincing evidence indicated the cause of the mishap was unrecognized spatial disorientation.

Additionally, the Board President found by a preponderance of the evidence that failing to crosscheck and ignoring the "Sink Rate" caution substantially contributed to the mishap.

Accident summary

The MA departed the airfield, climbed to altitude, and proceeded into the AOR uneventfully. The MC completed the assigned mission uneventfully and returned to Djiboutian airspace at 1852L. The MA arrived over the airfield at 10,000 ft MSL and was given permission by the Ambouli control tower to proceed to the South of the field for systems checks. The control tower told the MC to remain at 10,000 feet MSL due to traffic leaving the airfield. The MA proceeded south of the airfield at 10,000 feet MSL and turned back to a North heading to initiate the systems check. After the completion of the systems check, the MC requested a descent for the right base, a right turn to final for runway 09, but the Ambouli control tower instead cleared the MC to descend west of the airfield due to traffic. The MC acknowledged and said that they would report for a left base, a left turn to final.

According to testimony, the normal procedure for descending from 10,000 ft MSL to enter into the visual pattern at Ambouli at night and on Night Vision Goggles (NVGs) is to slow down below 177 knots indicated air speed (KIAS), lower the gear, then descend ensuring to not exceed 236 KIAS at 15 to 20 degrees nose low attitude.

According to the radar tracks from the approach control radar at Ambouli, the MA was using this normal procedure to descend to the west. According to testimony; the MP would normally perform this maneuver on NVGs. The radar track shows a left descending turn with an initial descent rate of 6,000 fpm which slows to 2,400 fpm until an altitude of 6,300 ft MSL where the descent rate begins to climb to 8,400 fpm until leveling off at 4,400 ft MSL. The MA is level at 4,400 ft MSL for approximately 5 seconds until the MA begins another descent starting at 8,400 fpm. At 1917L, the MA is told by the control tower to report final for runway 09, and the MC responds with "Ratchet 33 passing 4,000 feet in the descent west of the field, we'll report final."

At 2,972 ft MSL, the onboard EGPWS shows a descent of 2,443 fpm and a 24.5 degree right turn with 195 knots ground speed. The EGPWS shows data every second and shows the MA in a relatively constant descent, a decreasing right turn, and decreasing ground speed for ten seconds. The MA enters into a steadily increasing left bank eventually reaching 55 degrees, while increasing the descent rate from 2,985 fpm to 11,752 fpm, and decreasing the ground speed from182 knots to 165 knots.

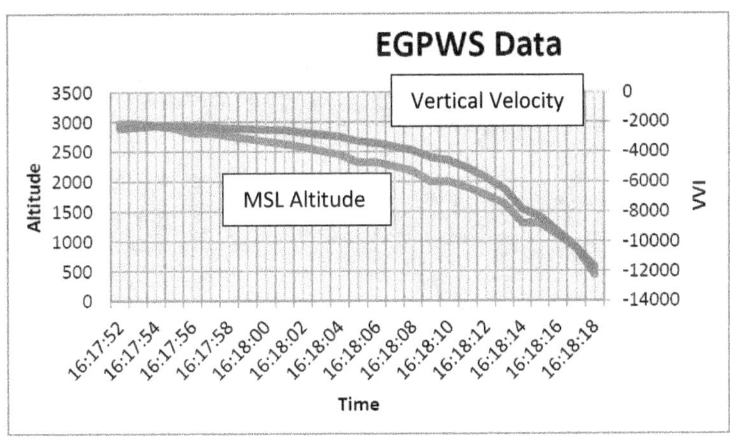

Figure 48: Enhanced Ground Proximity Warning System Data showing Altitude and Decent Rate in feet per minute (Source: U.S. AIB report).

Approximately seven seconds prior to impact, the EGPWS emitted an aural warning to the MC of "Sink Rate, Sink Rate," advising the MC that there was an excessive descent rate occurring.

This warning occurred at 1,800 ft MSL, approximately 1,600 ft above ground level (AGL), with an approximate descent rate of 5,400 fpm. Another warning was issued by the EGPWS approximately four seconds prior to impact that instructed the MC to "Pull up, Pull up." This warning occurred at 1,302 ft MSL, approximately 1,102 ft AGL, with a 8,000 fpm descent rate and 174 knots ground speed. The last EGPWS data for the MA prior to impact shows the MA was in a 55 degree left bank, 11,752 fpm descent rate, and at 165 knots ground speed. The times on the EGPWS are running clock time. To have accurate times, the radar track data, EGPWS data, and radio transmissions were compared to correlate the times to a synchronized time.

Figure 49: Aerial view of crash site from CH-53, looking west northwest (Source: U.S. AIB report).

Impact

The MA impacted the ground five miles southwest of Ambouli International Airport in an uninhabited and remote location strewn with boulders up to a two to three of feet in diameter, at North 11° 31.61' East 043° 04.41', 265 ft MSL. After initial impact, most of the MA cleared the ridgeline before breaking apart.

Human factors analysis

The board considered the following human factors and found them to be relevant:

1. Spatial Disorientation (Type 1) Unrecognized

Spatial Disorientation is a failure to correctly sense a position, motion or attitude of the aircraft or of oneself within the fixed coordinate system provided by the surface of the earth and the gravitational vertical. Spatial Disorientation (Type 1) Unrecognized is a factor when a person's cognitive awareness of one or more of the following varies from reality: attitude; position; velocity; direction of movement or acceleration. Proper control inputs are not made because the need is unknown.

According to the report, there is no evidence that there was a mechanical failure with the MA. There is no evidence for a sudden medical incapacitation prior to impact with any of the MC. The flight profile flown by the MC is consistent with spatial disorientation. There is no indication that the MC applied any flight control inputs showing that they were aware of the correct position of the MA, which is indicative of unrecognized spatial disorientation.

Unrecognized Spatial Disorientation would explain the failure of the MC to take corrective action in response to the position of the MA.

2. Illusion – Visual

Illusion – Visual is a factor when visual stimuli result in an erroneous perception of orientation, motion or acceleration, leading to degraded performance. The MA was sent to the west of the airfield because of traffic in the pattern.

According to the report this area has minimal cultural lighting and a "black hole" was described out to the west and south of the airfield. At the time of the mishap there was no lunar illumination. With the use of NVGs the field of view is limited and depth perception is reduced. This reduction in visual clues could have caused the MC to have a false perception of their altitude, attitude and descent rate.

This could have caused the MC to become spatially disoriented.

3. Illusion – Vestibular

Illusion – Vestibular is a factor when stimuli acting on the semicircular ducts or otolith organs of the vestibular apparatus cause the individual to have an erroneous perception of orientation, motion or acceleration leading to degraded performance. The G-excess illusion occurs when a pilot enters a greater than 1 G (1 times the force of gravity) turn with the aircraft, looks back into the turn and experiences the sensation that the aircraft is leveling out from the roll and having a pitch up attitude. Given this input the pilot will often apply more bank and nose-down pitch in order to maintain the desired bank angle and pitch. (Newman, David G, An overview of spatial disorientation as a factor in aviation accidents and incidents, Flight Medicine Systems Pty Ltd, Dec 2007) The unintended consequence is that the aircraft experiences significant overbank and descent.

According to the report, in a situation where the aircraft is already at a low altitude, this could cause a controlled flight into terrain. The G-excess illusion causes pilots to increase bank angle and pitch forward as they perceive the aircraft to be leveling out and pitching up, which matches the mishap flight profile. This could have caused the MC to become spatially disoriented.

4. Caution/Warning – Ignored

Caution/Warning – Ignored is a factor when a caution or warning is perceived and understood by the individual but is ignored by the individual leading to an unsafe situation.

According to the report, when replicating the flight parameters in the simulator, the MA could be controlled and pulled out of the descent if the MC had applied the correct flight control inputs when auditory alerts were given by the EGPWS. There is no evidence to indicate that the MC applied any corrective inputs to the flight controls when the EGPWS issued the auditory alerts of "Sink Rate" and "Pull Up." This factor was felt to contribute to the mishap.

5. Channelized Attention

Channelized Attention is a factor when the individual is focusing all conscious attention on a limited number of environmental cues to the exclusion of other of a subjectively equal or higher or more immediate priority, leading to an unsafe situation. It is a tight focus of attention that leads to the exclusion of comprehensive situational awareness.

According to the report, when looking at the data retrieved from the EGPWS, the MC showed no signs of pulling up in response to the "Sink Rate" and "Pull Up" auditory alerts. This could happen if they were focusing all of their attention on some other factor and these alerts were not consciously addressed. The evidence raises the possibility of this being involved.

6. Fatigue – Physiological/Mental

Fatigue – Physiologic/Mental is a factor when the individual's diminished physical or mental capability is due to an inadequate recovery, as the result of restricted or shortened sleep or physical or mental activity during prolonged wakefulness. Fatigue may additionally be described as acute, cumulative or chronic.

According to the report, the MP had recently had a change in his duty schedule where he advanced his duty day almost 12 hours. He was given 2 days off from the flying schedule to adjust to this new schedule. The day prior to the mishap, the MP was issued four zolpidem (Ambien) tablets. Ambien is a medication that is approved for use in aviators as an adjunct to the aircrew fatigue management program.

The MCP and MOP1 had just arrived at the deployed location 2 days prior to the mishap and had shifted 9 hours ahead during that timeframe. These changes in the circadian rhythm of these three members of the MC could have led to them suffering from acute fatigue. While this was not likely incapacitating, it is possible that fatigue could have delayed a necessary response in a situation where a time-critical decision had to be made.

12 AC-130J Flight Test

Figure 50: AC-130 (Source: U.S. AIB report).

The United States Air Force Aircraft Accident Investigation Board (AIB) describes in their report that:

On 21 April 2015, at approximately 12:18:40 hours local time (L), AC-130J, tail number 09-5710, assigned to the 413th Flight Test Squadron, 96th Test Wing, Eglin Air Force Base (AFB), Florida, departed controlled flight over water approximately 41 nautical miles (NM) south of Eglin AFB and then was recovered and landed safely. There were no significant injuries to the crew or anyone else. Post-flight engineering analysis revealed that the mishap aircraft (MA) exceeded the Design Limit Load (DLL), thus rendering it unsafe for further flight.

The mishap occurred on a medium risk flying qualities test sortie out to the edges of the flight envelope. The mishap pilot (MP) was attempting to execute a Steady Heading Sideslip (SHSS) to the RUDDER Special Alert of the Advisory Caution and Warning System (ACAWS). This is normally a prohibited maneuver, but the

Director of Operations at Air Force Materiel Command (AFMC/A3) signed a waiver approving the test team to fly to this limit. The MA exceeded 14.5 Angle of Sideslip (AoS), triggering the RUDDER Special Alert and continued increasing AoS until it departed controlled flight, eventually tumbling to an inverted position.

Shortly thereafter, the MA recovered from the departure and the mishap copilot (MCP) took the controls to recover from the near vertical dive. In the process of the departure and recovery, the aircraft lost approximately 5,000 feet of altitude, experienced 3.19 times the normal force acceleration (Gs), and over sped the flaps by over 100 knots. The over G exceeded the aircraft's DLL, thereby nullifying the airworthiness of the MA, rendering it a total loss.

The Accident Investigation Board (AIB) President found, by a preponderance of the evidence, the cause of this mishap was the MP's excessive rudder input during the test point followed by inadequate rudder input to initiate a timely recovery from high AoS due to Overcontrolled/Undercontrolled Aircraft and Wrong Choice of Action During an Operation.

Additionally, the AIB President found, by a preponderance of the evidence, the following factors substantially contributed to the mishap: Instrumentation and Warning System Issues, Spatial Disorientation, Confusion, and the fact the test team was Provided Inadequate Procedural Guidance or Publications.

Accident summary

The MA took off at 10:46:34L and conducted a series of flying qualities test points at approximately 15,000 feet MSL in the Gulf of Mexico just South of Eglin AFB, FL. During earlier SHSS test points in the flight, the crew had discussions about the recovery technique. In one instance, the MP mentored the mishap copilot (MCP) with the advice "don't dance on the rudders during recovery".

At 12:10L, the crew began performing SHSS with flaps at 100%, gear down and a speed of 140 Knots Calibrated Airspeed (KCAS). Per the test safety build-up, SHSSs to the right were conducted first. The MP was able to reach but not stabilize at the rudder alert, even though he was applying as much as 278 lbs of rudder pedal force. He made the statement that his feet were all the way on the floor. The test point to the right was terminated and then the test proceeded to the left.

The MP stabilized at the SIDESLIP Special Alert (the first alert) for nearly 10 seconds, applying approximately 125 lbs of rudder pedal force. The mishap test conductor (MTC) began to clear the MP to proceed to the second Special Alert, the MP was already increasing rudder pedal force; within two seconds of increasing force, he reached 180 lbs. Less than one second later, the RUDDER Special Alert annunciated immediately after the MTC finished the words "continue nose left, second alert" at approximately 14.5 AoS, with a force of 204 lbs. The rudder pedal force peaked at 229 lbs one and a half seconds later, already greater than 17 AoS. At approximately four seconds after the RUDDER Special Alert annunciated, the MP modulated rudder pedal force back down to 160 lbs, but the AoS was already greater than 21 (test termination criteria) and getting worse. At this point, the MP began to completely release all rudder pedal force immediately prior to the MTC calling, "Recover". The rudder was in an overbalance state or "locked" since there was no pilot rudder force applied, yet the rudder was still deflected.

The MCP made several directive call outs to assist including "Nose down," "Power out," and "Let go, Let go". The MA eventually inverted and recorded over 56 of sideslip although the instrumentation may be considered unreliable at those extreme conditions. The MA violently dropped its nose, rolled and inverted. The MP never applied corrective rudder. Since only the left seat rudder pedals were instrumented, it is impossible to tell when or if the MCP began applying any corrective forces, but the rudder pedal position did not approach neutral or an "unlocked" state until 12:18:55L. Just one second prior, the rudders were deflected to 55% of rudder pedal position. The MP became distracted during the sequence of events when his checklist or some object from the cockpit hit him in the head and momentarily distracted him from recognizing the aircraft was recoverable.

AOS_Boom	6.0 DEGREES
AOS_Bus	39.8 DEGREES
Baro_Correct_Alt	14430 FT

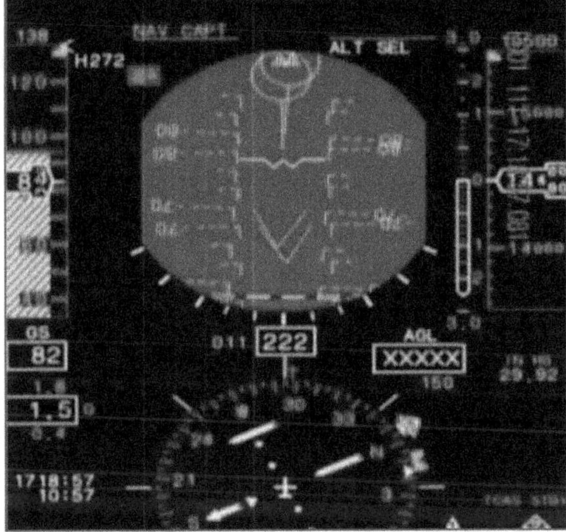

Figure 51: Attitude of the MA and cockpit presentation after the MA went inverted during the departure (Source: U.S. AIB report).

The picture above is from animation produced by LM, created from flight data that shows the attitude of the MA and cockpit presentation after the MA went inverted during the departure.

At some undetermined point, the MCP began flying the aircraft to recover it from the dive. He pulled the aircraft out of the dive, retracted the flaps, and recovered with under 10,000 ft of altitude. The MA was over G'd, reaching 3.194 Gs during the recovery, and the flaps were over sped by more than 100 knots.

Immediately following the recovery, the crew responded to an alarm for smoke in the cargo compartment and the crew began donning oxygen masks. The mishap loadmaster (ML) realized it was not smoke, but rather powder from a fire extinguisher which had been thrown around during the violent aircraft movement.

The crew requested the safety chase aircraft to perform a damage assessment, a visual inspection in flight. The MP then performed a controllability check. The crew elected not to change the flaps or gear any further since those structures had been over-sped. The crew declared an in-flight emergency (IFE). The MP performed a flaps up landing uneventfully. The crew was met by emergency response and the IFE was terminated.

Human factors analysis

Air Force Guidance Memorandum 2015-01, 14 April 2015, to AFI 91-204, Safety Investigations and Reports, with corrective actions applied on 10 April 2014, contains the Department of Defense Human Factors Analysis and Classification System (DoD HFACS) 7.0. DoD HFACS 7.0 lists potential human factors (including organizational influences, supervision, preconditions, and specific acts) that may play a role in aircraft mishaps. The following human factors were relevant to this mishap:

1. Overcontrolled/Undercontrolled Aircraft/Vehicle/System

Overcontrolled/Undercontrolled Aircraft/Vehicle/System is a factor when an individual responds inappropriately to conditions by either over- or undercontrolling the aircraft/vehicle/system. The error may be a result of preconditions or a temporary failure of coordination.

Evidence supports that the MP overcontrolled the rudder during test point while transitioning from the SIDESLIP Special Alert to the RUDDER Special Alert to the left.

The MP stabilized at the SIDESLIP Special Alert for nearly 10 seconds, applying approximately 125 lbs of rudder pedal force. As the MTC began to clear the MP to proceed to the second Special Alert, the MP was already increasing rudder pedal force; within two seconds of increasing force, he reached 180 lbs. Less than one second later, the RUDDER Special Alert annunciated immediately after the MTC finished the words "continue nose left, second alert" at approximately 14.5 AoS (per design for the test point conditions), with a force of 204 lbs. The rudder pedal force peaked at 229 lbs one and a half seconds later, and already greater than 17 AoS. At approximately four seconds after the RUDDER Special Alert annunciated, the MP modulated rudder pedal force back down to 160 lbs but the AoS was already greater than 21 and getting worse. The MP eventually reduced all pressure against the left rudder, but the aircraft had already departed from controlled flight.

According to previous flight test data provided by the OEM to the Air Force in July 2013, the rudder force required to achieve 14.5 AoS for 100 percent flaps is approximately 150 lbs. The 150 lbs required was less than 180 lbs of force reached within two seconds of being cleared to continue to the second alert and much less than the 229 peak force used. Therefore, the aircraft was overcontrolled for the test point conditions.

Overcontrolling can happen for a variety of reasons. One of the possible reasons is the difficulty of the task. Several test pilots commented on how difficult the task is due to the variation in sensitivity on the rudder pedals required for each test point condition compounded by the waffling flight characteristics of the Dutch Roll.

Test Pilot 1 (TP1) stated the following:

"So, you are doing a fine motor skill task with your quadriceps, right? And so, it's about like trying to drive a finish nail with a sledgehammer, okay? Um, it's not an easy task to do that and you have to move in very small discrete increments. And the task is different at higher speeds than it is at slower speeds. At higher speeds you've got a lot of force your pressing on the rudder, at the slower speeds, -- you know, and so you are kind of metering force. At the slower speeds you are metering position because your -- because your forces get a lot lighter and so you don't want to -- you don't want to just honk on like you were doing up at those faster speeds. So, as you build down in speed, you're, I don't want to say you're changing your technique, but you are probably changing how you, at least when I do it, how I -- how I am monitoring what I am doing, and I'm using the flight test display is feedback on the position when we're doing it...So, um, I mean, there is probably 100 different ways of how to officially work through these tests point, you know, whether you do it all left leg, all right leg, whatever. The reason why we were swapping between the two is, honestly, is fatigue.

Because, although left seat instrumented so the left seat guys are the ones doing all the test points when it comes to this. Um, and so as you, um, as you work through it, just by the nature of the way we are doing it, you know -- luckily when you get to the slowest speeds it's the lightest forces, because you're tired by then, but you also got to watch what you're doing because you're tired by then. Um, make sure that you're not over controlling the rudder, so a lot depended upon the pilot to monitor his fatigue level and there were a couple of flights where I would turn around look at the flight testing units and say were done today. You know, three hours of me doing this and my legs are shot. And so, but its, um, but yeah, there's just no other way to do it, I mean, we were slowly and incrementally stepping out trying to nibble at the edge of this thing without, without, you know, running over the top -- running over a cliff somewhere. And so, there was no other good way to do it, um, other than build down speed and build up in rudder force. I mean, it was the only way that made sense as far as from a safety standpoint, but obviously there is a, there is a lot of pilot technique and an pilot ability stuff that comes in there, because, you know, the difference between, you know, the first point the next point may be, you know, three quarters of an inch of rudder travel, you know. You know, when you're going from first alert to the second alert, that is two degrees of side slip and so it may literally be an inch or less of rudder travel to get you to that point...So, you get out and trying to nail a test point and trying to nail a position there in the nose is kind of wanting to hunt on you a little bit, and so it just -- some days it was easier than others to get that thing to stop where you wanted it to."

Evidence also supports that the MP undercontrolled the rudder during the recovery.

In accordance with 1C-130(A)J-1, page 2E-8, HIGH SIDESLIP RECOVERY PROCEDURES:

"If either RUDDER Special Alert occurs, immediately apply the indicated rudder to center the sideslip display on the HUD. . . If rudder overbalance is encountered (one pedal pushes against the pilot's foot as the rudder floats towards the stop), the rudder pedal must be pushed back immediately towards center. Rudder pedal force to accomplish this can vary from 50 lbs at slow speeds to over 200 lbs at 180 knots".

Similarly the test team recognized this possibility when applying for the waiver. The test team wrote:

"If the pilot continues to push the pedals, the rudder pedal force continues to decrease until the rudder floats toward full deflection by itself. This is called rudder overbalance. If this condition occurs, the other pedal must be pushed to bring the rudder back toward center (opposite rudder pedal, 50 – 200+ lbf required). If this is not accomplished quickly, the airplane reaches extreme sideslip and may roll to a high angle of bank. Up to 5,000 feet of altitude loss could occur during the recovery".

According to the data, the MP released left rudder pedal force but never applied right rudder pedal force as required by the procedure. Immediately after the MA was recovered, the MP told the MCP, "Well I was trying to not overcontrol". Therefore, the aircraft was undercontrolled for the recovery from departure from controlled flight.

Several test pilots cited their reluctance to be aggressive with the rudders and felt reducing rudder pedal force was preferred to being too aggressive with applying rudder inputs). During a previous test point on the mishap flight, the MP stated, "For the most part we don't dance on the rudders at all during the recoveries". He later commented, "I think in the back of -- any pilot of an aircraft of a rudder or fin, it's always in the back of our minds that large abrupt motions on the rudder can cause an overstress condition and, you know, could have structural damage". However this reluctance to use the rudder seems more tied to spatial disorientation than anything else since the MP answered, "I think if I had known what I know now, and I knew that what we were in was a sideslip departure or a spin motion, I wouldn't have hesitated to apply the correct procedure".

2. Wrong Choice of Action During an Operation

Wrong Choice of Action During an Operation is a factor when the individual, through faulty logic or erroneous expectations, selects the wrong course of action.

The test cards, THAW, and waiver directed, "Recover IAW PTO (extreme AoA procedures)" for a departure from controlled flight. The first steps of the extreme AoA procedures include "1. Lower the nose, apply appropriate rudder (step on the ball or 'dog house,' as indicated by the special alert and reduce asymmetric power. (Set all power levers to FLT IDLE if the nose is very low.) 2. Once the turn rate stops, neutralize the rudder and recover from the dive...". The MP never stepped on the right rudder as previously discussed. Also, the MP never reduced the throttles completely even though he was instructed by the MCP. Furthermore, during the event, the MCP directed the MP, "Nose down, nose down" to lower the nose and the MP responded "pushing, pushing, pushing". The MP pushed the nose down and rolled right, but the aircraft continued to yaw even more to the left.

According to the MP, he was disoriented during the departure from controlled flight and all that made sense was airspeed; he thought it was the one thing he could control so he pushed forward on the control column. This action, along with his right roll inputs exacerbated the left yaw condition due to a flight dynamics phenomenon known as "coupling". The MP admitted that he knew that the rudder was locked, he would have applied correct rudder, "if I knew exactly we were in an overbalanced condition and the fin was stalled or was beginning to stall, I don't think I would have hesitated to put the correct action in".

There are various reasons why the wrong choice of action was applied. One reason may be confusion. Confusion will be further discussed in an upcoming section. Another possibility includes an inaccurate expectation or disposition by the test team to think departures from controlled flight would occur during a stall. When Test Pilot 2 (TP2) was asked if it would have made sense to use the high AoS recovery procedure for SHSS test points instead of the extreme AoA procedure, the witness responded, "We had one data point that basically said it worked" referring to the fact that he thought during the February 2014 AC-130J, T/N 09-5710, Class A, 21 April 2015 23 departure the aircraft was recovered by breaking the stall. However, according to the non-safety privileged analysis of the first departure, the aircraft self-recovered due to coupling dynamics that reduced sideslip. If the pilots expected the aircraft to depart during a stall rather than a sideslip excursion, this could have predisposed them to take actions to recover from a stall rather than an overbalance. The waiver that allowed the test team to proceed to the RUDDER Special Alert contained the fact that opposite rudder pedal force must be used to overcome a rudder overbalance and could require between 50 and 200 lbs or force. The guidance goes on to say, "If this is not accomplished quickly, the airplane reaches extreme sideslip and may roll to a high angle of bank. Up to 5,000 feet of altitude loss could occur during the recovery," which is basically what happened.

3. Instrumentation and Warning System Issues

Instrumentation and Warning System Issues is a factor when instrument factors such as design, reliability, lighting, location, symbology, size, display systems, auditory or tactile situational awareness or warning systems create an unsafe situation.

The current design of the aircraft's sideslip warning system visual cues provides only limited real-time positional information beyond the SIDESLIP Special Alert (2o) and freezes at the RUDDER Special Alert. The sideslip warning system visual cues consist of a sideslip indicator and sideslip limit fence symbols in the HUD. The space between these symbols represents the difference between the airplane sideslip angle and the sideslip limit. When the sideslip indicator touches the "fence," the SIDESLIP Special Alert is activated; if sideslip continues to increase until the sideslip indicator extends halfway through the "fence," the RUDDER Special Alert is activated. After RUDDER Special Alert is activated, the sideslip indicator does not move beyond half way through the fence, regardless of a continual increase in sideslip.

The PTO 1C-130(A)J-1 does not make it clear that the sideslip indicator freezes once it bisects the fence and according to TP1, this fact was not understood by the test team.

TP1 stated:

"Um, a little hard to define where that second alert is other than just eyeballing it. What I didn't realize, until after we started a lot more in-depth discussion on this, and I guess I should have, as many as these test points as I've done, is once it gets to the second alert it does not move any further. So it stops, so, you have no indication past -- if you've gone past that point and if so how far. With the OEM's assumption being is that once you've hit that point you don't need to be going any further than that so I'm not going to tell you how much further you can go. So, so if I were to change that, I would change that mechanization somehow to, to show if I've gone past that how far past that I have gone".

Similarly, the MTC observed, "...there is an audio alert that you get, but there is hysteresis in the audio alert. So, if you were to touch the fence and come away from the fence, the audio alert will continue to sound...So, if the audio is sounding, that means we're -- could be getting close to the test point...or at the test point or past the test point".

Therefore, the test crews had no indication if they were stabilized beyond the RUDDER Special Alert. The MP stated, "I think the biggest and obvious one [human factor] was I didn't have a good way to tell what the motion of the aircraft was, that the sideslip had continued to increase. I had no cultural references. And the one piece, the doghouse, stopped moving, and I wasn't able to use it to help me determine what the aircraft was doing".

4. Spatial Disorientation

Spatial Disorientation is a factor when an individual fails to correctly sense a position, motion, or attitude of the aircraft/vehicle/vessel or of oneself. Spatial Disorientation may be unrecognized and/or result in partial or total incapacitation. The MP describes his challenge correctly to sense motion, confusion about what was happening and how he tried to respond below:

"As I moved from initial alert to the second alert, I recognized the rate that I was not intending to occur, and I decreased the pressure I was putting on the pedal. Near the same time the flight test engineer recognized my force being removed from the pedal and called "recover." I further reduced my pressure on the pedal as far as I could, and the resulting motion of the aircraft as I did that instantaneously and debilitating disoriented me. I couldn't quite recognize why the aircraft was continuing to do what it was doing. Out of all the things that I could see, in my field of view, the only thing that I could recognize as status of the aircraft was the airspeed. I saw the airspeed bleeding down at a rate that was not inconsistent with I saw since that's the only thing I could verify at the time. I attempted to decrease the pitch of the aircraft by pushing forward on the yoke to arrest the decrease in airspeed. The elevator did not move with the authority that I was hoping it would have, and the airspeed continued to decrease... I recall not fully having my SA about me. When the FT called recover, I was -- I don't know the appropriate word, but I was disoriented in a way that I don't remember ever feeling before in an aircraft. It was almost like the aircraft was doing something that I couldn't figure out why it was doing it. And while hindsight may appear like it was something that I caused when I removed the force on the rudder, I couldn't ascertain what the aircraft was actually doing. And so the only thing I could actually latch onto was the airspeed decreasing, and I believe a left rolling tendency. That's the only thing that I could definitely say the aircraft was doing, and so I tried to correct those two conditions by putting in right roll and pushing forward on the yoke to eliminate the decrease in airspeed...We were far south in the water ranges; so I had no cultural references to ascertain motion of the aircraft; so I was fully dependent on the HUD and the instrumentation inside the aircraft".

During his interview, the MCP stated, "At one point, I remember looking at the water and I just remember the water—it was very difficult to make a reference of which way was what because of the water. We still had the HUD, but the water was—there was no ground reference". This is consistent with the first AC-130J departure event in 2014 according to a witness who stated that the crew thought they were spinning to the right when in fact they were spinning to the left. The MP and MCP described conditions that are most conducive to spatial disorientation including lack of visual references, loss of situational awareness, and distraction.

5. Confusion

Confusion is a factor when the individual is unable to maintain a cohesive and orderly awareness of events and required actions, and instead experiences a state characterized by bewilderment, lack of clear thinking or (sometimes) perceptual disorientation.

The MP described some of his confusion during the MA's departure from controlled flight, saying to the MCP after recovery, "I was unsure, bringing the power back if the reverse gyroscopic effects would undo something". He later stated, "I was trying to analyze everything . . . I was just, I was trying to contemplate everything. There were just too many things". During the MP's interview, he stated, "I couldn't quite recognize why the aircraft was continuing to do what it was doing. Out of all the things that I could see, in my field of view, the only thing that I could recognize as status of the aircraft was the airspeed. I saw the airspeed bleeding down at a rate that was not inconsistent with I saw since that's the only thing I could verify at the time".

6. Provided Inadequate Procedural Guidance or Publications

Provided Inadequate Procedural Guidance or Publications is a factor when written direction, checklists, graphic depictions, tables, charts or other published guidance is inadequate, misleading, or inappropriate.

Test card 14 contained a table and chart that identified expected activation of the SIDESLIP Special Alert and the RUDDER Special Alert. These predictions would have the test crew not expect the RUDDER Special Alert for high power settings (greater than 10,000lb total horsepower) to activate prior to 16 AoS. In fact, the RUDDER Special Alert activates at 14 AoS for high power settings. The Board retrieved a document believed to be the source for test card 14 which identified a Lockheed Martin employee as the author. The data contained within the table and chart conflict with a subsequent version of expected alert activation Lockheed Martin provided after the mishap. The expected alert activations identified in the chart provided by Lockheed Martin after the mishap are 1.5 lower than the alert activations identified in test card 14 for both sideslip and rudder activation.

Despite these errors, they likely did not contribute substantially to how the MP flew the aircraft.

He stated, "It was more up to me to use the cues and the HUD to determine what rudder position would be required for me to get those alerts". What they did affect was the boundaries placed on the IADS display and therefore what a safety monitor may be looking at.

7. Distraction

Distraction is a factor when the individual has an interruption of attention and/or inappropriate redirection of attention by an environmental cue or mental process.

The MP stated he was distracted after the MA's departure from controlled flight just prior to the dive recovery by an unsecured item, possibly a checklist, hitting him in the head as the MA inverted.

13 C-17A Afghanistan Overrun

Figure 52: C-I7A Globemaster III (Source: U.S. AIB report).

The United States Air Force Aircraft Accident Investigation Board (AIB) describes in their report that:

On 23 January 2012, at approximately 0749 Zulu (12 19 Local), a C-I7A Globemaster III aircraft, tail number 07-7189, assigned to the 437th Airlift Wing, Joint Base Charleston, South Carolina, landed on runway 34R at Forward Operating Base (FOB) Shank, Afghanistan. The mishap aircraft (MA) was unable to stop, departed the prepared runway surface, struck an embankment, and came to rest approximately 700 feet from the end of the runway. The MA sustained damage to the landing gear, cargo floor, undercarriage, antennas, and main structural components. There were no passengers, fatalities, significant injuries, or damage to civilian or other military property.

The 816th Expeditionary Airlift Squadron, in support of Operation ENDURING FREEDOM, operated the MA from Al Udeid Air Base, Qatar. The mishap crew consisted of the Mishap Pilot (MP), Mishap Copilot (MCP), Mishap First Pilot,

Mishap Loadmaster 1 , and Mishap Loadmaster 2. Additionally, a Mishap Flying Crew Chief was assigned as mission essential personnel.

Accident cause

The accident investigation board (AIB) president found, by clear and convincing evidence, that the cause of the mishap was the MP and MCP failed to identify that the landing distance required to safely stop the aircraft exceeded the runway length.

Additionally, the AIB president found by the preponderance of evidence, that failure to assess runway conditions for fixed wing operations at FOB Shank substantially contributed to the mishap.

Accident summary

At approximately 0034Z, the MA departed Al Udeid AB. Qatar, and at 0145Z completed an uneventful sortie to Kuwait City International Airport, Kuwait. At Kuwait City International, the MC uploaded 111.498 lbs of cargo, 43.921 lbs of fuel and received the mission paperwork for the mishap sortie. The total gross weight of the MA when it departed Kuwait City International was 565.526 lbs. The MC considered the MA to be "heavy,' but within limits (maximum permitted takeoff gross weight of a C-17A is 585.000 lbs).

The FOB Shank day shin sweeper crew. ITT Exelis contract employees, reported for duty and at 0045Z began snow removal operations on runway 34R. Upon arrival at runway 34R the sweeper crew noted that it was snowing and several inches of snow covered the runway. The sweeper crew completed removing the bulk of the snow off runway 34R. However approximately one-half of an inch of snow and ice remained on the runway. At 0300Z the SWEEPER applied deicing fluid to runway 34R. At 0400Z the SWEEPER finished applying deicing fluid to runway 34R.

While waiting for the deicing fluid to work the SWEEPER began snow removal operations on other parts of the airfield. At approximately 0400Z, the SWEEPER SUPERVISOR told the FOB Shank Mishap Air Traffic Controller I (MATC I) that the runway would be clear at 0500Z . The SWEEPER SUPERVISOR intended to communicate to Tower that at 0500Z runway 34R would be clear of men and equipment, not that the runway would be clear of ice and snow. However, MATCI understood SWEEPER SUPERVISOR's communication to mean that runway 34R was "clear and deiced".

The MA departed Kuwait City International for FOB Shank. The takeoff and cruise phase of flight into Afghanistan were uneventful. For the sortie to FOB Shank the MP was in the left pilot's seat, the MCP was in the right pilot's seat. The MFP was seated in the Right Additional Crewmember (RACM) seat and the ML2 was seated in the Left Additional Crewmember (LACM) seat. The ML1 was seated downstairs at the forward loadmaster station and the MFCC was seated in the crew rest area.

The MP conducted the Combat Entry brief, discussed the upcoming landing at FOB Shank, and noted they had a maximum brakes on speed (Vbo). Vbo is the highest speed at which maximum braking effort should be initiated. The C- 17A Flight Manual cautions pilots to not apply wheel brakes above Vbo, as damage to the brakes and tires could result if this restriction is not observed.

Approximately 15 minutes later, the MC discussed the NOTAM that closed the first 1.500 ft of runway 34R and the need to use the full length of the runway.

A CASA-212 (C-212) short takeoff and landing aircraft, landed on runway 34R at FOB Shank and reported to the FOB Shank Air Traffic Control Tower (Tower) a braking action of "fair". Braking action of "fair" is a runway condition report indicating reduced braking action level, with a corresponding increase in aircraft landing distance.

The MC discussed the landing at FOB Shank and identified a "Vbo split" of 2.000 ft. "Vbo split" indicates that the aircraft touchdown speed is higher than Vbo. Using the Vbo procedures increases aircraft landing distance due to the delay in brake application. The resulting landing distance is called "Vbo landing distance".

The MC ran the Combat Entry checklist and called the Combat Entry brief complete.

According to the report, the MC ran the Descent checklist and discussed the approach for FOB Shank. The MC identified a "20 knot (kt) split between touchdown and Vbo." stated the Vbo landing distance as "just 6.000" ft. and discussed delaying braking until the MA was under Vbo (128 kts).

The MC established radio contact with the Tower and requested the current weather conditions.

The MATCl responded with the most current observation:

"Sir. as of 0655 Zulu. visibility is unrestricted, sky conditions are clear, temperature's minus zero six [Celsius], dew point minus one one [Celsius], altimeter's three zero two six, aerostat is down sir, and as of 0635, braking action for runway three four right was a fair from C-212, how copy?"

The MCP responded:

"Moose 89 copies all, can I get current winds and runway in use?"

MATC1 replied:

"Roger sir, winds estimated two five zero at three, runway in use three four right".

The MCP stated to Tower,:

"I'd like to confirm that the full length of the runway will be useable. We're going to need full length to land".

MATC1 responded:

"that's a negative sir, full length landing will be at pilot's own discretion due to personnel and equipment east of the tower, and that area is not visible from the tower, sir...you can make a go around if you need to or overfly but landing will be at pilot's own discretion"

During MATC1's response there was a simultaneous radio transmission from Kabul center to the MC on a different frequency.

Approximately one minute later, MATC1 asked the MC:

"Moose 89, did you copy full length will be at pilot's own discretion?".

The MP responded. "affirmative" and again stated. "yeah. we'll need full length. Did you say you can coordinate for the personnel to be out of the way though?".

MATC1 responded. "Moose 89 standby, we'll contact airfield management".

The MC then began a descent from flight level 27.000 ft down to 17.500 ft.

MATC1 contacted MC and responded, "I talked to the ATC Chief and they're basically saying the same thing sir, they said you can do a low approach or a touch and go if you need to sir, they would not move the equipment, they are unable to and full length will be at pilot's own discretion".

The MP asks the MCP, ".....what's your thoughts (sic) on this runway thing he's talking about: we have to land 1200 feet down?".

The MCP responded, "They've been there the whole time, they are not on the runway, think well... as we're on the approach, if we see anything that looks fishy, we'll go around".

The MP responded, "Yeah...we can't land super long".

The MC entered a Visual Flight Rules (VFR) downwind pattern from the north and ran the Approach checklist. As part of the Approach checklist, both the MP and MCP stated, "TOLD checked". The MP's crew brief was "right base for three four, full flap, full stop, complete". The VFR pattern was stable, in accordance with criteria from C- 17 Operations Procedures.

The MCP visually acquired the airfield environment and stated. "I'm not making out the runway yet though. I think I'm seeing it but it actually just looks pretty, like snow covered, but I think it's just white".

The MC turned to the final approach course and ran the Before Landing check list. At this time, the Tower called and stated. "Moose 89. check wheels down, landing full length runway 34R will be at pilot's own discretion, landing area is not visible from the tower, wind estimated two seven zero at three, report clear of the active".

The MCP responded, "Moose 89 is gear down, cleared to land, and understand all".

The MA was established on the final approach course and the MIP stated, "I got the runway in sight."

The MCI' responded. "I've got the runway in sight as well, so it looks like the landing zone is...." MI' interrupted. "black and little pieces of white".

The MI' then stated. "Cleared to land. Expect poor... fair he said

The MCIP then stated. " I'm gonna go ahead and give us a twelve on that". At this time, the MCP attempted, but failed to enter RCR of 12 into the mission computer.

According to the report, RCR of 12 correlates to the reported braking action of "fair". RCR is the measure of the coefficient of friction between the aircraft tires and the runway surface. RCR values less than 23 indicate that aircraft stopping performance is degraded. The MA was stable on final approach in accordance with criteria from C-17 Operations Procedures.

The MA touched down on speed approximately 1000 ft - 1.200 ft past the approach end of runway 34R .

The MCP then stated;

 "Good ground spoilers... four blue...brakes".

This indicated the ground spoilers and all four thrust reversers deployed and the MA was below Vbo. The MIP applied MA brakes and noted less than expected deceleration. The MCP noted the minimal deceleration and also applied his aircraft brakes. Post mishap analysis found no defects with the anti-skid system or aircraft brakes.

Impact

Approximately 20 seconds after the MA touched down on runway 34R, the MA departed the runway, struck an embankment, and came to rest approximately 700 ft past the end of the runway. The nose landing gear (NLG) was destroyed on impact with the embankment and the front of the MA came to rest on its belly.

The rear of the MA remained supported by both the left and right main landing gear (MLG) assemblies. When the MA departed runway 34R, the brake pedals were fully depressed, slats were extended, the flaps were fully extended, and all four thrust reversers (TRs) deployed.

The MA sustained damage to the landing gear, cargo floor, undercarriage, antennas and main structural components. Additionally, a pallet in the aerial delivery system (ADS) broke free during the impact. The pallet slid forward, struck the forward bulkhead.

Human factors analysis

A DoD taxonomy was developed to identify hazards and risks called DoD Human Factors Analysis and Classification System (DoD-HFACS), referenced in Attachment 5 of AFI 9 1-204. Safety Investigations and Reports. 24 September 2008. All human factors enumerated in Attachment 5 to AFI 91-204, including channelized attention, task saturation, complacency, and distraction, were carefully analyzed for possible contribution to the mishap sequence. The relevant human factors are discussed below.

1. Procedural Error

Procedural Error is a factor when a procedure is accomplished in the wrong sequence or using the wrong technique or when the wrong control or switch is used. This also captures errors in navigation, calculation or operation of automated systems (AFI 9 1 -204, attach 5).

According to the report, although the MP and MCP both correctly correlated the reported braking action of "fair" to an RCR value of 12, four procedural errors prevented them from identifying the correct landing distance. After Tower relayed a reported braking action of "fair" to the MC, the following procedural errors occurred:

a) The MP and MCP called "TOLD-Checked" on the approach checklist without recognizing the mission computer did not contain the RCR value of 12, and therefore without noting the Vbo landing distance was greater than the runway length. IAW TO IC -17A- I, paragraph 2-126, the aircrew is required to check the TOLD to be used for the approach and landing.

b) The MP failed to brief the Vbo landing distance as part of the crew brief on the approach checklist. IAW TO IC-17A- I, paragraph 2-126, the pilot flying conducts a comprehensive briefing to prepare the crew for the approach.

c) After the approach checklist was completed, the MCP attempted, but failed, to update the TOLD in the mission computer with an RCR value of 12. TO IC17A-I, paragraph 2-126, warns pilots to adjust their TOLD in the primary aircraft computer for reported wet/slushy conditions on the runway.

d) The MP failed to verbalize landing distance during the VFR pattern. IAW AFTTP 3-3.C-17, paragraph A3.3.1. 12.1, during a VFR pattern the pilot flying always states the value of the mission computer Vbo landing distance or ground roll.

Note: Landing distance is the total distance from a 50 foot height above the runway to the point where the aircraft can be completely stopped and ground roll is the total runway distance from touchdown to a point where the aircraft can be completely stopped. Vbo landing distance and ground roll are based on delaying brake application until maximum brakes on application speed (Vbo) to prevent damage to aircraft brakes and tires.

The AIB reconstructed the MA TOLD with a mission computer in the C-17A simulator. Using variables identical to those in the MA mission computer at the time of the mishap, including aircraft gross weight, temperature, winds, pressure altitude, runway available, and RCR, the AIB confirmed the Vbo landing distance of 6,047 ft.

Leaving all other variables unchanged, the AIB changed the RCR to 12.

The mission computer then no longer displayed a value for landing distance or Vbo landing distance, an indication that the landing distances exceeded the available runway. The mission computer in the aircraft operates identically. When the AIB manually changed the runway is available in the mission computer in order to generate landing distances, the values were 7,930 ft for landing distance and 8,642 ft for Vbo landing distance. Both of these values exceed the runway length at FOB

Shank. The main runway on FOB Shank, runway 34 right (R)/16 Left (L), is 7,425t (ft) long, including 300 ft overruns at both ends of the runway.

Note: The mission computer displays a calculated landing distance only if this distance is less than runway available, or a ground roll distance if it is less than runway available and runway available is less than landing distance.

In the AIB reconstruction, when the RCR value was changed to 12, the mission computer calculated a ground roll of 6,587 ft and a Vbo ground roll of 7,288 ft. Both ground roll and Vbo ground roll distance s were less than the length of runway 34R.

However, use of the ground roll distance when a Vbo is indicated in the mission computer requires procedures cautioned against in the C-17 Flight Manual. Use of Vbo ground roll distance in this case would allow for a touchdown zone of only 137 ft.

2. Miscommunication

Miscommunication is a factor when correctly communicated information is misunderstood, misinterpreted, or disregarded.

According to the report, snow removal and deicing operations on runway 34R were in progress, not completed, at the time of the mishap. At approximately 0400Z, the SWEEPER SUPERVISOR told the FOB Shank Mishap Air Traffic Controller I (MATC I) that the runway would be clear at 0500Z. The SWEEPER SUPERVISOR intended to communicate to Tower that at 0500Z runway 34R would be clear of men and equipment not that the runway would be clear of ice and snow. However, MATC I understood SWEEPER SUPERVISOR's communication to mean that runway 34R was "clear and deiced ".

Due to this miscommunication, Tower thought runway 34R was clear of ice and snow when the MA arrived. An inspection conducted immediately following the accident revealed a combination of water, slush, ice and snow covered runway 34R.

3. Task/Mission-In-Progress Re-Planning

Task/mission-in-progress re-planning is a factor when crew or team members fail to adequately reassess changes in their dynamic environment during mission execution and change their mission plan accordingly to ensure adequate management of risk.

According to the report, MP and MCP failed to evaluate the risk of landing on runway 34R once they received the reported braking action of fair and correlated this braking action to an RCR of 12.

4. Supervision-Policy

Supervision-Policy is a factor when policy or guidance or lack of a policy or guidance leads to an unsafe situation.

According to the report, TF Corsair did not have local policies or guidance requiring daily airfield inspections at the time of the mishap. Further, TF Corsair did not have a standard process to verify that snow and ice removal operations were completed and runway 34R was safe to use for fixed wing operations.

5. Airfield Resources

Airfield Resources are a factor when runways, taxiways, ramps, terminal, ATC resources or navaids, lighting systems, SOF/RSU resources or the environment surrounding the airfield are inadequate or unsafe.

According to the report, TF Corsair did not have equipment capable of determining an RCR reading at the time of the mishap. In addition Tower personnel could not see the entire fixed-wing runway due to the location of the ATC tower at FOB Shank. Tower personnel relied upon communication from sweeper personnel to assess the runway conditions.

14 F-22 Oxygen system emergency

Figure 53: F-22A (Source: U.S. AIB report).

The United States Air Force Aircraft Accident Investigation Board (AIB) describes in their report that:

On 16 November 2010, at approximately 19:43 hours local time (L), an F-22A, tail number 06-4125, assigned to the 525th Fighter Squadron, 3rd Wing, Joint Base Elmendorf-Richardson (JBER), Alaska, impacted the ground during controlled flight approximately 120 nautical miles (NM) northeast of JBER. The mishap pilot (MP) did not attempt ejection and was fatally injured upon impact. The mishap aircraft (MA) was destroyed.

The mishap occurred on a 3-ship night opposed surface attack tactics (SAT) training mission. Opposed SAT missions typically consist of F-22As fighting their way into a target area protected by enemy forces and dropping Joint Direct Attack Munitions (JDAM) on specified targets. During the return-to-base portion of the mission while the MP was attempting to rejoin with his flight lead, the MA experienced an engine bleed air leak malfunction.

The airflow to MP's oxygen mask stopped. The MP entered a 240-degree roll through inverted flight, and the nose down (ND) pitch attitude increased. The MP initiated a dive recovery. Three seconds later, the MA impacted the ground in a left bank at approximately 48 degrees ND at a speed greater than 1.1 Mach (M).

Accident cause

The Board President found, by clear and convincing evidence, the cause of the mishap was the MP's failure to recognize and initiate a timely dive recovery due to channelized attention, breakdown of visual scan, and unrecognized spatial disorientation.

Additionally, the Board President found, by a preponderance of the evidence, organizational training issues, personal equipment interference, controls and switches, and inadvertent operation were factors that substantially contributed to the mishap.

Accident summary

Jake flight took off at 18:05L; Rocky flight departed 10 minutes later. Departure and entrance into the Dice MOA was uneventful, and the weather in the airspace was clear with high moon illumination. Jake flight arrived at the designated airspace first. As Rocky flight entered the airspace, Jake flight completed their first mission and proceeded to the KC-135 air refueling tanker as briefed. After refueling, Jake flight returned to the airspace, executed their second SAT mission opposed, because Mig flight had additional fuel available, and returned to JBER.

Rocky flight's first opposed SAT mission against Mig flight was uneventful. Rocky 02 reached a previously briefed fuel quantity prior to the MFL and MP, and proceeded to the tanker as a single aircraft, and refueled. The MFL and MP followed Rocky 02 to the tanker to refuel. While on the tanker, Rocky 02 was troubleshooting minor, non-safety-of-flight related avionics issues. The MFL directed Rocky 02 to return to Dice MOA to continue troubleshooting. Once the issues were resolved, the MFL directed Rocky 02 to fly an unopposed SAT mission as a single aircraft and RTB.

After receiving fuel, the MFL and MP executed a second unopposed SAT mission, in accordance with the brief. Upon completion of tactical maneuvering, the flight proceeded towards the airspace exit point to RTB.

The last recorded data from the MFL IFDL showed the MA 13 NM in front of the MFL bearing 131 degrees, heading 183 degrees, 1.6 M at 38,400 ft MSL.

The MFL directed the MP to rejoin to a 2 NM trail formation. The MP acknowledged the MFL's directive to rejoin and made no further communications. The MP began a climbing right-hand turn to rejoin. The MA climbed to a maximum altitude of 51,720 ft MSL, crossed the MFL's projected flight path and then began a descent to the north.

The MA was at 50,870 ft MSL, 315 knots calibrated airspeed (KCAS), 1.23 M, with an attitude of 1-degree nose up, 69 degrees right wing down (RWD), heading 323 degrees, 1.5-Gs, and with a vertical velocity indication (VVI) of -1,700 ft per minute (fpm). At this time, the fire protection system (FPS) detected a bleed air leak in the center bleed air ducting from both engines. In response to the FPS, the Integrated Vehicle Subsystem Controller (IVSC) asserted the C BLEED HOT caution ICAW while it requested the Environment Control System (ECS) to isolate the center bleed system. "CAUT" was displayed in the head-up display (HUD) advising the MP of the caution ICAW.

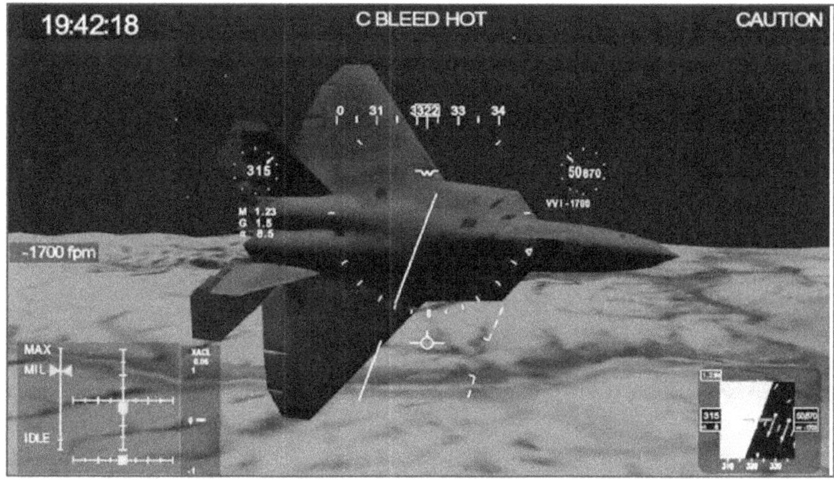

Figure 54: MA parameters at assertion of C BLEED HOT caution ICAW (Source: U.S. AIB report).

According to TO 1F-22A-1, a caution ICAW message warns a pilot of an "aircraft operation that could result in damage to aircraft. Corrective procedures may be required, but not immediately." When the C BLEED HOT caution ICAW asserted, the following functions were automatically shutdown to protect against a bleed air induced aircraft fire:

1) ECS
2) Air Cycle System (ACS) forced air cooling
3) On-board oxygen generating system (OBOGS)
4) On-board inert gas generating system (OBIGGS)
5) Cabin pressure

Despite the loss of these functions, the flight control system and both engines were operating normally and responding to pilot inputs.

The C BLEED HOT caution ICAW cleared after the IVSC commanded the bleed air ducts to the closed position and stopped the flow of bleed air to the ECS. The OBOGS FAIL caution ICAW asserted when the OBOGS output pressure dropped below 10 pounds per square inch (psi). The CSMU data showed partial pressure to the MP's oxygen mask stopped shortly after.

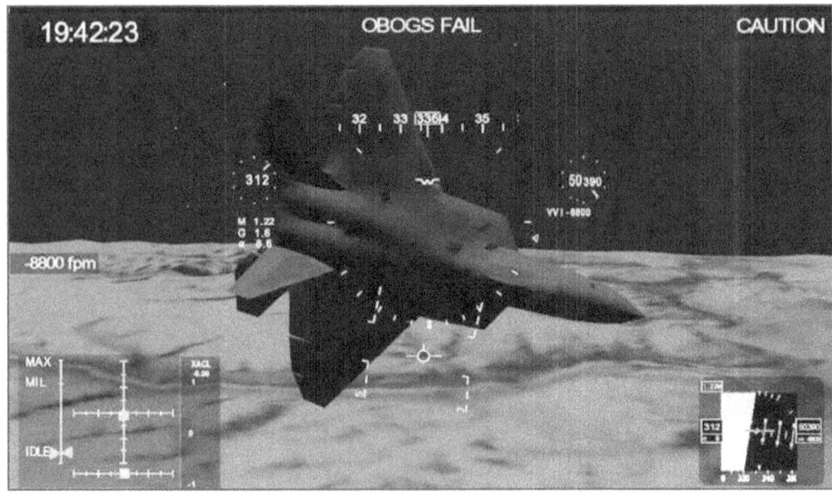

Figure 55: MA parameters at assertion of OBOGS FAIL caution ICAW (Source: U.S. AIB report).

From the assertion of the OBOGS FAIL caution ICAW, the MP retarded the throttles to IDLE power and continued a controlled, descending right-hand turn. The MA was at 41,460 ft MSL, 390 KCAS, 1.29 M, 30 degrees ND, 44 degrees RWD, 1.7-Gs, and with a VVI of -33,700 fpm.

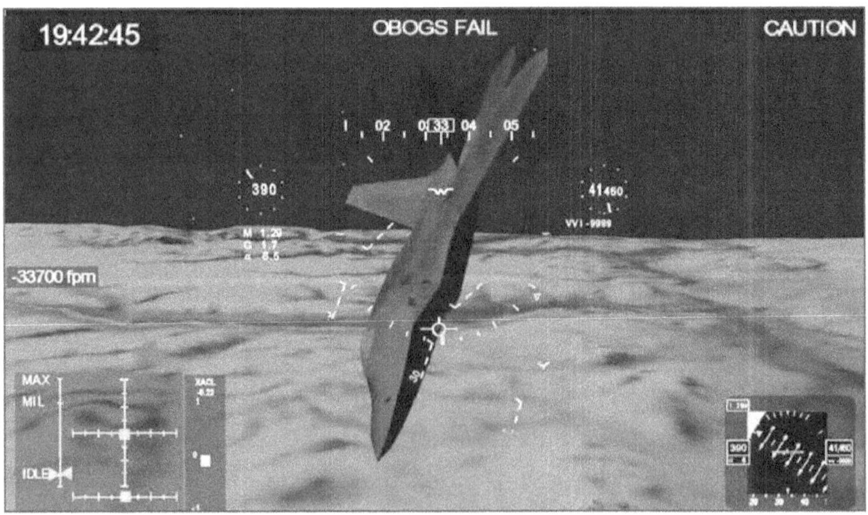

Figure 56: MP deliberately flew to a controlled attitude of 30 degrees ND and 44 degrees RWD (Source: U.S. AIB report).

For eight seconds, the MP made no inputs to the stick, pedals, or throttles, and the MA maintained a relatively stable bank angle and attitude. The MA was at 37,110 ft MSL, 470 KCAS, 1.35M, 30 degrees ND, 46 degrees RWD, 0.8-G, with a VVI of -37,700 fpm. -- MA parameters after 8 seconds of zero MP inputs to stick, pedals, or throttles.

The MP input a combination of right forward stick and right pedal which initiated a 240-degree descending right roll at greater than 45 degrees per second.

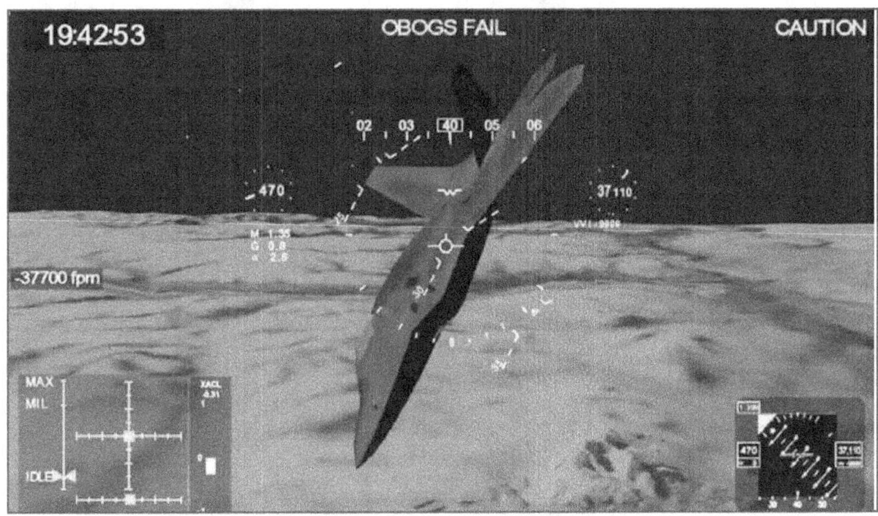

Figure 57: MA parameters after 8 seconds of zero MP inputs to stick, pedals, or throttles (Source: U.S. AIB report).

The MA had rolled through inverted flight, experienced less than 1-G of gravitational force, reversed turn direction from RWD to left wing down (LWD), increased ND attitude, and significantly increased the descent rate. The parameters at this time were 24,070 ft MSL, 627 KCAS, 1.39 M, 44 degrees ND, 81 degrees LWD, 0.8-G, with a VVI of -57,800 fpm.

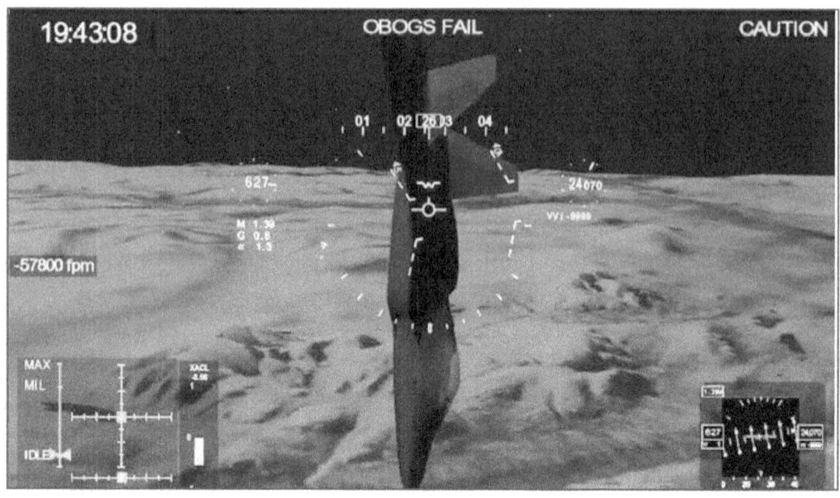

Figure 58: MA parameters after the 240-degree roll (Source: U.S. AIB report).

There were no stick inputs and only very minor pedal inputs for the next 15 seconds. During this time, the descent rate of the MA increased to greater than 1,000 feet per second (fps), and as the MA passed approximately 19,000 ft MSL, a CABIN PRESSURE caution ICAW asserted based on cockpit pressurization exceeding its normal schedule.

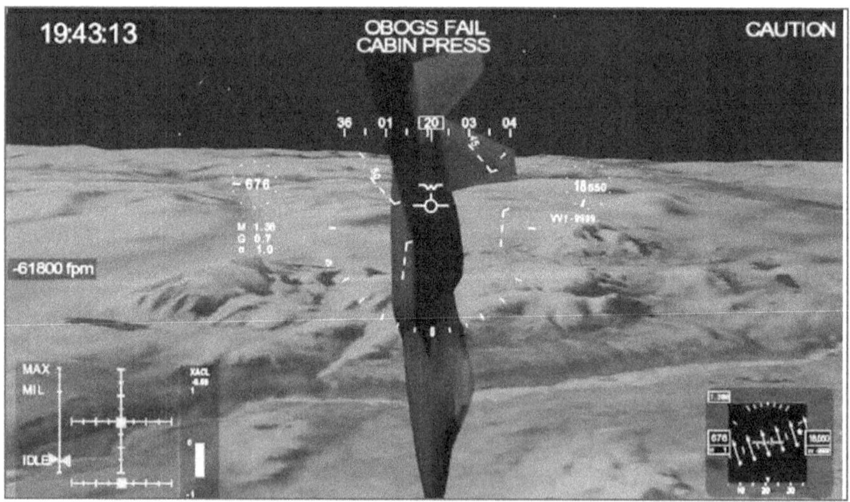

Figure 59: MA parameters at assertion of CABIN PRESS caution ICAW (Source: U.S. AIB report).

Passing 12,400 ft MSL, an AIR COOLING caution ICAW asserted. This AIR COOLING caution ICAW asserted 60 seconds after the C BLEED HOT caution ICAW asserted, which meant the MA was not receiving an adequate cooling air source to its avionics.

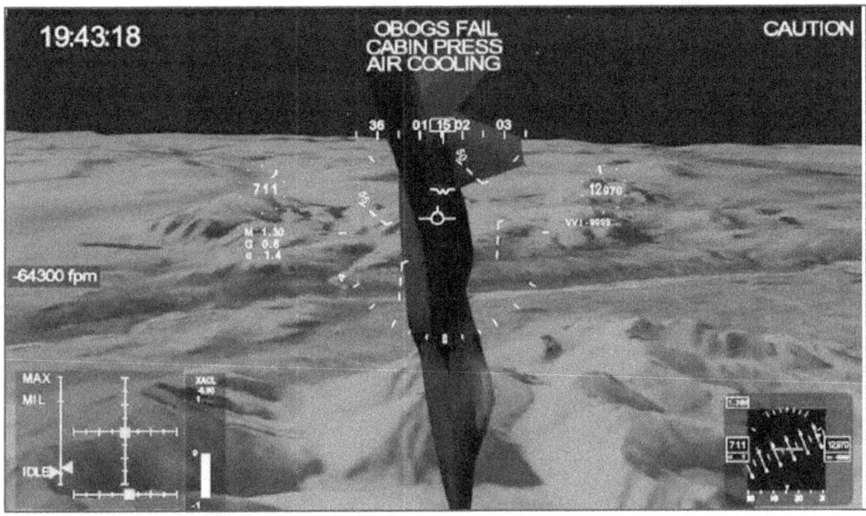

Figure 60: MA parameters at assertion of AIR COOLING caution ICAW (Source: U.S. AIB report).

The MP performed a dive recovery at 5,470 ft MSL by pulling aft on the stick, producing a 7.4-G pull up maneuver. By this time, the MA had transitioned below the minimum safe recovery altitude. The MA impacted the ground three seconds later, inflicting fatal injuries to the MP and destroying the MA.

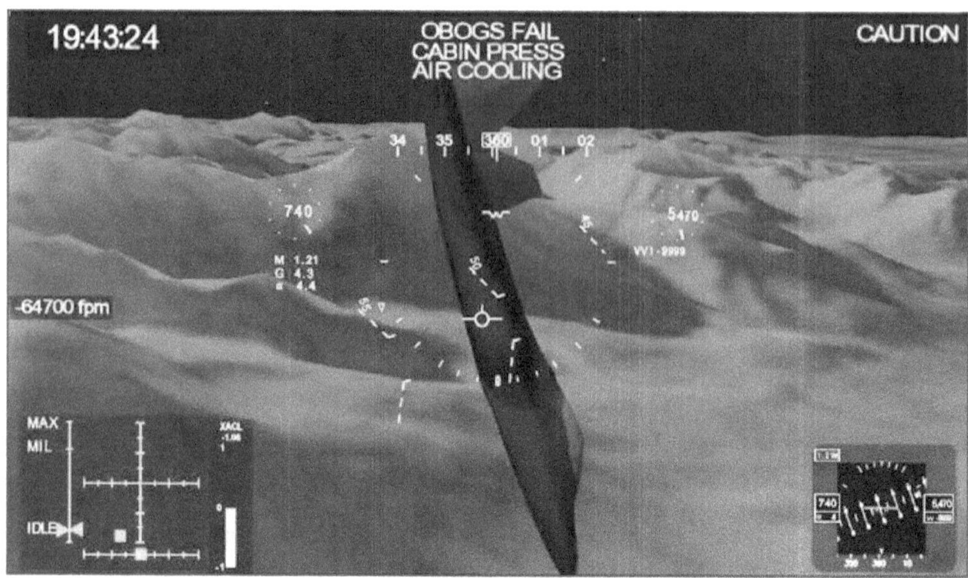

Figure 61: MP initiates full aft stick pull to start dive recovery at 5,470 ft MSL (Source: U.S. AIB report).

Impact

The MA impacted the ground at 735 KCAS, 1.17 M, 48 degrees ND, 48 degrees LWD, 7.4-Gs, with a VVI of -57,900 fpm. The impact site is approximately 120 NM north of JBER, AK, in the Talkeetna Mountain range. The site is approximately 3,100 ft MSL near the edge of a south-west to north-east running valley. The impact crater is located at the valley floor where it begins to slope upwards towards the southeast. The valley floor is approximately one-half mile wide at this point and has a stream running through it approximately 60 yards west of the impact point.

The debris field consisted of small aircraft and engine pieces extending approximately one-quarter mile from the crater. The upslope wall of the crater and aircraft impact angle appear to have focused the debris pattern in a 60-80 degree wide arc from west to north.

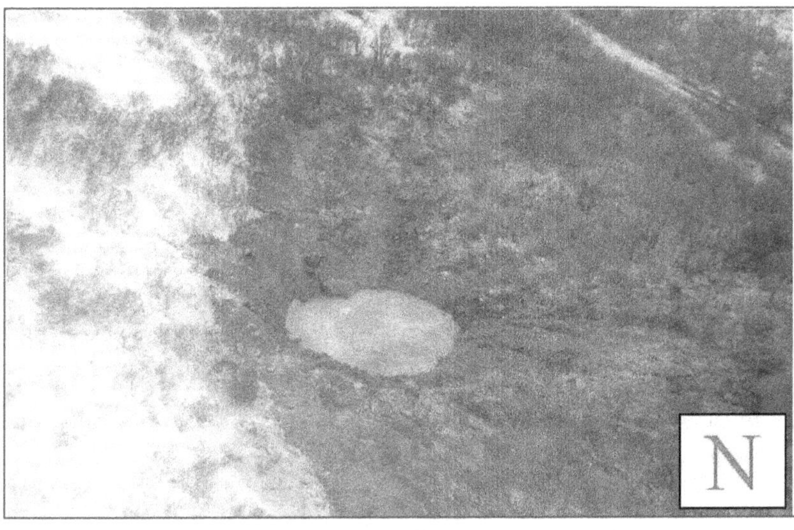

Figure 62: Impact Crater (Source: U.S. AIB report).

Human factors analysis

AFI 91-204, Safety Investigations and Reports, 24 September 2008, Attachment 5, contains the Department of Defense Human Factors Analysis and Classification System, which lists potential human factors that can play a role in aircraft mishaps. The following human factors were relevant to the mishap:

1. Organizational Training Issues/Programs

Organizational Training Issues/Programs are a factor when one-time or initial training programs, upgrade programs, transition programs or other training that is conducted outside the local unit is inadequate, unavailable, etc. creating an unsafe situation. Failure of an individual to absorb the training material in an adequate training program does not indicate a training program problem.

According to the report, United States Air Force aircrew are highly trained to handle multiple and/or severe aircraft emergencies. The MP had recently reviewed the C BLEED HOT caution ICAW emergency procedures during monthly Supervised Emergency Procedure Training (SEPT) on 2 November 2010. However, emergency procedure simulator/ground training does not expose the pilot to all in-flight, real-world stressors and cockpit conditions, such as those experienced in this situation (for example, CAT III cold weather gear, NVG usage, G-forces, cockpit pressurization, motion or restricted breathing). Additionally, the F-22A simulator presented a C BLEED HOT malfunction and associated ICAWs concurrently, which is different than the ICAW presentation timing in an actual aircraft.

Nonetheless, TO 1F-22A-1 guidance and procedures, SEPT and simulator training all encourage immediate EOS activation during oxygen system related emergency procedures (for example, "Emergency Oxygen – Activate" is the first step in the C BLEED HOT caution ICAW checklist procedure.). As such, pilots are predisposed to activate the EOS when experiencing physiological symptoms, based on training and block position.

TO1F-22A-1 checklist procedures. Therefore, there is evidence to suggest that Organizational Training Issues/Programs were a factor in the mishap.

2. Personal Equipment Interference

Personal Equipment Interference is a factor when the individual's personal equipment interferes with normal duties or safety.

According to the report, the AIB conducted multiple ground simulations of the mishap sequence. The simulations were conducted with the pilot advisor in an actual F-22A cockpit. The pilot advisor is of similar build and size as the MP, and wore the same types of CAT III cold weather gear, life support equipment and NVGs as the MP wore during the MS. All harnesses, safety restraints and life support equipment were connected and secure.

The pilot advisor performed multiple repetitions of reaching for, visually locating, activating, and dropping the EOS activation ring. The EOS activation ring is seated on the left aft edge of the ejection seat.

With the canopy up during the ground simulation, the pilot advisor was able to successfully pull the EOS activation ring. The pilot advisor also simulated what could have occurred if the MP had difficulty pulling and subsequently dropped the EOS activation ring between the seat and the console. The pilot advisor had significant difficulty retrieving the dropped EOS activation ring while wearing cold weather gloves. The pilot advisor also could not visually locate the EOS activation ring without twisting his torso due to the bulky flight gear and EOS activation ring's design, size and location. When the pilot advisor lowered the canopy and performed the same actions with NVGs donned, the AIB members noted that the NVGs impacted the canopy when the pilot advisor moved his head to visually locate the EOS activation ring.

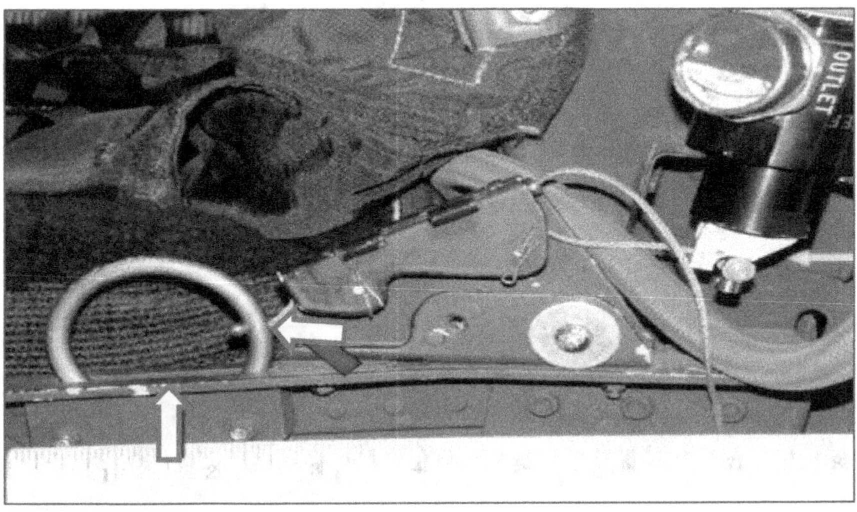

Figure 63: Notice the position of the EOS activation ring within the seat (arrows) based on wedge block position (Source: U.S. AIB report).

Ground simulations demonstrated reduced mobility in the cockpit due to the bulkiness of CAT III gear. Additionally, the NVGs hit the canopy, interfering with the pilot advisor's ability to look from side to side and down at the consoles. Therefore, there is evidence to suggest that Personal Equipment Interference was a factor in the mishap.

3. Controls and Switches

Controls and Switches is a factor when the location, shape, size, design, reliability, lighting, or other aspect of a control or switch is inadequate and this leads to an unsafe situation.

According to the report, the AIB examined the process of manually activating the EOS. The TO 1F-22A-1 states: "To manually activate the EOS, pull the green ring up and out of the retaining slot (approximately 33 pound pull), then pull directly forward minimizing inboard/outboard and upward motion. The pull force required to activate the EOS may be in excess of 40 lbs. The green ring will travel approximately two inches and will not release from the seat side. There is no obvious detent to indicate that the EOS has been activated."

During ground simulation, the pilot advisor successfully manually activated the EOS. The pilot advisor also unseated the EOS activation ring and dropped it between the seat and console prior to EOS activation. This was done to simulate a failed initial pull, which may have occurred. Retrieval of the ring from between the seat and console would be difficult based on the seat position, night environment, CAT III cold weather gear, and NVGs.

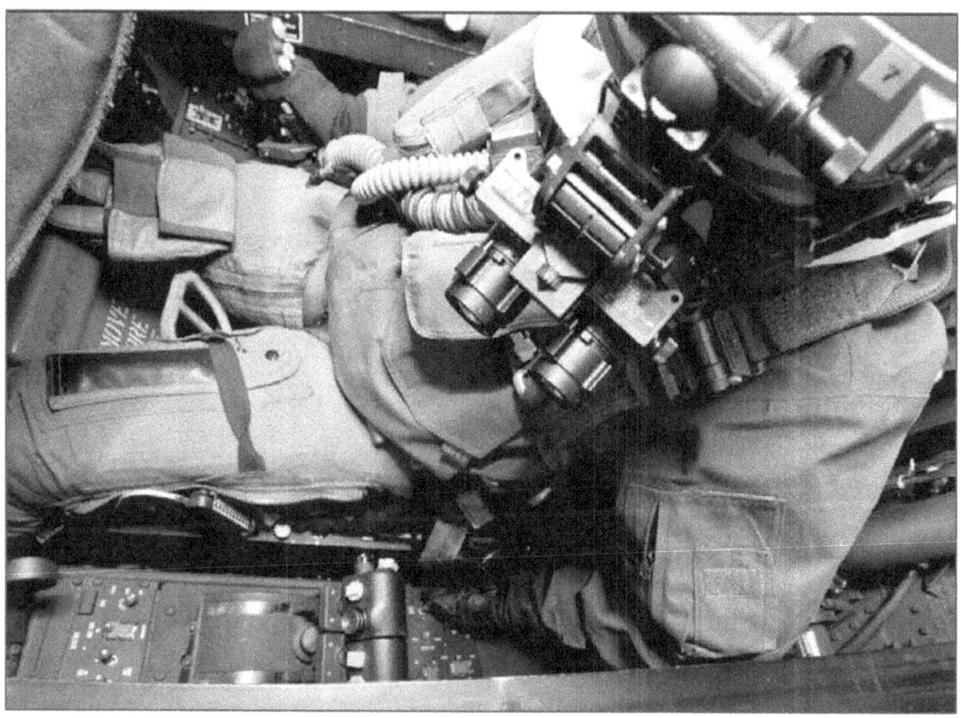

Figure 64: Pilot advisor pulling EOS activation ring. NVGs interfering with EOS activation ring visualization (Source: U.S. AIB report).

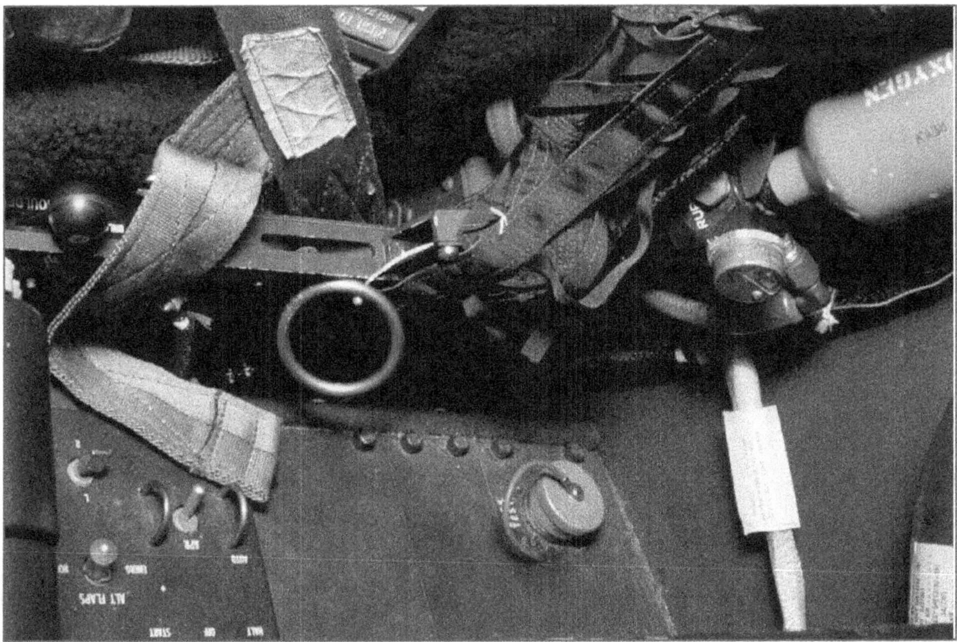

Figure 65: Manual EOS activation ring fallen below lip of seat (Source: U.S. AIB report).

According to the report, therefore, there is evidence to suggest that the design, size and location of the EOS activation ring were factors in the mishap.

4. Inadvertent Operation

Inadvertent Operation is a factor when individual's movements inadvertently activate or deactivate equipment, controls, or switches when there is no intent to operate the control or device. This action may be noticed or unnoticed by the individual.

According to the report, the MP input a combination of right forward stick and right pedal, which initiated a 240-degree descending right roll at greater than 45 degrees per second. At the completion of these stick and pedal inputs, the MA had rolled through inverted flight, experienced less than 1-G of gravitational force, and went from a RWD to LWD attitude, and the descent rate of the aircraft significantly increased.

The AIB determined these control inputs to be inadvertent because they had no clear goal or objective, resulted in an unusual attitude, and do not reflect expected or intentional inputs consistent with basic aircraft control. During ground simulations, the AIB observed that the pilot advisor made similar inadvertent control stick and pedal movements while twisting his torso to visually locate the EOS activation ring.

According to the report, therefore, there is evidence to suggest that inadvertent operation was a factor in the mishap.

5. Channelized Attention

Channelized attention is a factor when the individual is focusing all conscious attention on a limited number of environmental cues to the exclusion of others of a subjectively equal or higher or more immediate priority, leading to an unsafe situation. This factor may be described as a tight focus of attention that leads to the exclusion of comprehensive situational information.

According to the report, the following evidence indicates the MP initially exhibited channelized attention while attempting to restore oxygen flow IAW his training and checklist procedures. The first step in the C BLEED HOT caution ICAW checklist is:

"Emergency oxygen – Activate,"

a procedure recently reviewed by the MP during the monthly SEPT on 2 November 2010.

Additionally, the OBOGS FAIL caution ICAW checklist warns pilots to activate the EOS if they experience any physiological symptoms. As such, pilots are predisposed to activate the EOS when experiencing physiological symptoms, based on training and TO 1F-22A-1 checklist procedures.

Airflow to MP's oxygen mask stopped, which would have caused a restricted breathing condition. The MP most likely experienced a sense similar to suffocation. This restricted breathing condition would not have been incapacitating, but would have been a physiological symptom prompting him to immediately activate the

EOS, based on his training and TO 1F-22A-1 checklist procedures. However, post-mishap forensic evidence indicated that the EOS was most likely not activated.

Additionally, the MP input a combination of right forward stick and right pedal, which initiated a 240-degree descending right roll at greater than 45 degrees per second. The MA had rolled through inverted flight, experienced less than 1-G of gravitational force, went from a RWD to LWD attitude, and the descent rate of the aircraft significantly increased. The roll rate and change in gravitational force were above the minimally detectable threshold and should have been recognized by the MP. These flight control inputs do not reflect expected or intentional inputs consistent with basic aircraft control.

According to the report, there is evidence to suggest that the MP initially channelized his attention on restoring oxygen flow while attempting to manually activate the EOS. When the airflow stopped to the MP's oxygen mask, the MP tightly focused his attention inside the cockpit. This may have precluded the MP from perceiving the detectable attitude changes and corresponding unusual attitude.

6. Breakdown in Visual Scan

Breakdown in visual scan is a factor when the individual fails to effectively execute learned/practiced internal or external visual scan patterns. The breakdown can lead to an unsafe situation.

According to the report, the evidence suggests that intentional flight control inputs stopped and did not resume for approximately 39 seconds. However, during this period, the MP input a combination of right forward stick and right pedal, which initiated a 240-degree descending right roll at greater than 45 degrees per second. The MA had rolled through inverted flight, experienced less than 1-G of gravitational force, went from a RWD to LWD attitude, and the descent rate of the aircraft significantly increased. In a single-seat aircraft, the pilot is solely responsible for maintaining aircraft control while managing other cockpit tasks. A continuous cross-check of in-flight parameters via cockpit instruments or outside references is essential. Had the MP focused on the flight instruments or looked outside (based on high moon illumination and a discernible horizon), the MP would have recognized the change in aircraft orientation and made corrective flight control inputs. Since the MP did not take corrective action until below the minimum dive recovery altitude, there is evidence to suggest that breakdown in visual scan was a factor in the mishap.

7. Spatial Disorientation (Type 1) Unrecognized

Spatial Disorientation is a failure to correctly sense a position, motion, or attitude of the aircraft or of oneself within the fixed coordinate system provided by the surface of the earth and the gravitational vertical. Spatial Disorientation (Type 1) Unrecognized is a factor when a person's cognitive awareness of one or more of the following varies from reality: attitude, position, velocity, direction of motion or acceleration. Proper control inputs are not made because the need is unknown.

According to the report, IAW the OBOGS FAIL checklist, the MP was in a deliberate and controlled descent to a lower altitude after the assertion of the OBOGS FAIL caution ICAW. However, the MP input stick and pedal movements for approximately 15 seconds, causing a 240-degree descending right roll. At the completion of these stick and pedal inputs, the MA had rolled through inverted flight, experienced less than 1-G of gravitational force, transitioned from a RWD to LWD attitude, and significantly increased the descent rate. This increased descent rate shortened the amount of time available to recover the aircraft. The MP did not take corrective actions until approximately three seconds prior to impact. By the time the MP recognized the unusual attitude and applied dive recovery flight control inputs, the MA had transitioned below the minimum safe recovery altitude.

The AIB determined the MP lost cognitive awareness of the MA's location and orientation relative to the ground, and he did not make proper control inputs because the need was unknown, until it was too late.

According to the report, therefore, there is evidence to suggest that unrecognized spatial disorientation was a factor in the mishap.

Although non-contributory to the mishap, the following human factors warrant discussion: Hypoxia, Effects of G Forces (G-LOC, etc.), and Sudden Incapacitation/Unconsciousness.

8. Hypoxia

Hypoxia is a factor when the individual has insufficient oxygen supply to the body sufficient to cause an impairment of function.

According to the report, the AIB examined the possibility that the MP suffered from any form of hypoxia during the MS. There are four forms of hypoxia; anemic, histotoxic, hypoxic and stagnant:

Anemic hypoxia is a reduction in the oxygen carrying capacity of the blood. Causes include carbon monoxide poisoning, hemorrhage, reduced hemoglobin concentration, and increased red cell destruction/decreased red cell production. In aerospace medicine, the most feasible concern is carbon monoxide poisoning. The data recovered from the MA showed there was no evidence of carbon monoxide contamination in the MP's air supply. There was insufficient tissue for a toxicological assessment for carbon monoxide in the MP. Finally, review of the MP's medical record did not identify any evidence to support other possible causes. Therefore, because the MP was able to pull over 7-Gs prior to impact, there is no evidence to suggest that anemic hypoxia was a factor in the mishap.

Histotoxic hypoxia is the inability of cells to take up or utilize oxygen from the bloodstream, despite physiologically normal delivery of oxygen to such cells and tissues. Histotoxic hypoxia results from tissue poisoning, caused by oxygen toxicity and/or cyanide. Oxygen toxicity is caused by breathing 100% oxygen for 24 hours or more, or breathing 100% oxygen at increased ambient pressure, neither of which was present during the MS. There was no apparent mechanism for exposing the MP to cyanide during the MS. Therefore, there is no evidence to suggest that histotoxic hypoxia was a factor in the mishap.

Hypoxic hypoxia occurs when the oxygen tension in the arterial blood becomes insufficient for normal function. The MP was operating at high altitude for a majority of the MS, based on the F-22A cabin pressurization schedule, the cockpit altitude would not have exceeded 23,000 ft. Additionally, based on the F-22A oxygen concentration schedule, the MP would have been breathing 90% to 94% oxygen. This would have caused his body to have a high oxygen saturation level prior to the MA malfunction. The recovered CSMU data showed no EOS fault codes prior to 19:42:23L, when the OBOGS FAIL caution ICAW asserted. Therefore, the evidence suggests that prior to the OBOGS FAIL caution ICAW, the OBOGS system was functioning as designed, and the MP would not have been incapacitated due to hypoxic hypoxia.

The MP was at high altitude requiring supplemental oxygen when the bleed air malfunction occurred and would have had the oxygen mask secured to ensure proper oxygen concentration flow IAW his training and AFI 11-202, Vol. 3, Paragraph 6.4, Table 6.2. At 19:42:37L, airflow to MP's oxygen mask stopped, which would have caused a restricted breathing condition. The MP most likely experienced a sense similar to suffocation. This restricted breathing condition would not have been incapacitating, but would have been a physiological symptom prompting him to immediately activate the EOS, based on his training and TO 1F-22A-1 checklist procedures. Activation of the EOS would have restored oxygen flow to the MP's oxygen mask. However, as previously discussed, the EOS was most likely not activated. Therefore, the AIB had to determine whether the MP suffered a hypoxic event during the mishap sequence after the airflow to the MP's oxygen mask stopped. The AIB considered two scenarios: (1) the MP lowered or partially lowered his mask to take a breath; or (2) the MP kept his mask secure and held his breath for the duration of the mishap sequence.

(1) If the MP lowered or partially lowered his mask by releasing one mask bayonet or simply pulling the mask away from his face, he would have been breathing cockpit air. Based on the cabin pressurization schedule and CSMU data, the cockpit altitude never exceeded 23,000 ft during the mishap sequence of events. According to research, the MP would have more than three to five minutes of time of useful consciousness (TUC) at that cockpit altitude. Additionally, the cockpit altitude continued to decrease throughout the mishap sequence of events as the MA descended to lower altitude, allowing a longer TUC. Therefore, the evidence suggests that the MP would not have been incapacitated due to hypoxic hypoxia in this scenario.

(2) The AIB also examined the scenario where the MP kept his mask secure and did not take a breath for the duration of the mishap. Given the oxygen concentration schedule and the high affinity of oxygen to hemoglobin (oxygen-carrying molecule in the blood), the MP's body would have been highly saturated with oxygen. This would have substantially increased the

MP's breath holding time and reduced his respiratory drive. A reduced respiratory drive would enable the MP to endure a breathing restriction/suffocation by increasing his TUC. Based on the conditions, analysis showed that the MP, at a minimum, had approximately 68 seconds of breath holding time following the airflow shutoff to the MP's oxygen mask. Although the mishap sequence of events from the assertion of the C BLEED HOT caution ICAW to impact was 69 seconds, the time from airflow shut-off to impact was only 50 seconds. Therefore, the evidence suggests that the MP would not have been incapacitated due to hypoxic hypoxia in this scenario.

Stagnant hypoxia is the reduction in blood flow to the body's tissues. Causes of stagnant hypoxia include exposure to cold temperatures and sustained exposure to high accelerations (for example, pilots performing high-G turns). Evidence collected from the crash site indicated the MP was appropriately wearing the required cold weather gear during the MS, and therefore CSMU data from the last few minutes of flight indicated the MA was not in a high-G environment until the 7.4-G recovery pull three seconds prior to impact. There is no evidence to suggest that stagnant hypoxia was a factor in the mishap.

9. Effects of G Forces (G-LOC, etc.)

Effects of G Forces (G-LOC, etc) is a factor when the individual experiences G-induced loss of consciousness (GLOC), greyout, blackout or other neurocirculatory affects of sustained acceleration forces.

According to the report, the AIB considered the possibility that the MP suffered the effects of G Forces during the mishap sequence to include almost loss of consciousness (A-LOC). A-LOC "consists of a transient incapacitation without complete loss of consciousness that often occurs during and after relatively short-duration, rapid-onset gravitational forces."

The MP was a highly trained and experienced pilot familiar with, and physiologically conditioned to, the effects of high-G maneuvering. The AIB reviewed the MP's centrifuge training tape that demonstrated the MP had an adequate anti-G strain technique and a resting G tolerance of 4.8-Gs.

Based on recovered data, prior to the aircraft malfunction, the MA was flying a low-G forces profile while attempting to rejoin with the MFL. During the mishap sequence of events, the MA did not exceed 2.5-Gs prior to the 7.4-G attempted dive recovery three seconds prior to impact. Therefore, there is no evidence to suggest that G Forces were a factor in the mishap.

10. Sudden Incapacitation/Unconsciousness

Sudden Incapacitation/Unconsciousness is a factor when the individual has an abrupt loss of functional capacity / conscious awareness. (NOT GLOC)

According to the report, the AIB considered the possibility that the MP suffered sudden incapacitation/unconsciousness. The most reasonable causes of sudden incapacitation include: cardiovascular events (i.e. heart attack), neurologic events (i.e. seizure), and increased age (i.e. above 50 years old). The MP's age at the time of the mishap was well below the threshold for the age associated sudden incapacitation. Additionally, the AIB medical advisor documented that the MP was medically qualified for flight duty and had no information in his medical record that would indicate that the MP would have been susceptible to either cardiac or neurologic events leading to disqualification from flight duties.

Further, the AIB referred to a medical review published in 1991 by McCormick and Lyons titled Medical causes of in-flight incapacitation: USAF experience 1978-1987.

In this publication, the analysis included an examination of 23 in-flight incidents of incapacitation due to significant underlying medical conditions, such as the aforementioned causes of sudden incapacitation. The researchers calculated a frequency of incapacitating events to be 0.19 events per 1,000,000 flying hours. Given the MP's total flying hours was 959.7 hours, this resulted in a 0.018% probability that the MP suffered from incapacitation during the final moments of the MS.

The evidence suggests the MP was conscious and actively flying the MA throughout the MS. At the assertion of the OBOGS FAIL caution ICAW until 19:42:45L, the MP retarded the throttles to IDLE power and deliberately continued a controlled, descending right hand turn to descend to a lower altitude IAW the checklist. While there are 39 seconds when the MP appears to not be deliberately controlling the MA, the MP executed a 7.4-G dive recovery maneuver three seconds prior to impact demonstrating the MP was conscious and positively controlling the MA at the time of impact. There is no evidence that the MP suffered an unconscious event during the 39 seconds, regained consciousness, and then attempted to recover the MA.

According to the report, therefore, there is no evidence to suggest that sudden incapacitation/unconsciousness was a factor in the mishap.

15 F-16 Fog in the Cockpit

Figure 66: F-16C (Source: U.S. AIB report).

The United States Air Force Aircraft Accident Investigation Board (AIB) describes in their report that:

On 28 July 2011, at approximately 1120 hours local time (L), an F-16C, tail number 87-0296, assigned to the 100th Fighter Squadron, 187th Fighter Wing, Dannelly Field, Alabama departed the prepared runway surface of Wittman Regional Airport (KOSH) causing damage to the mishap aircraft (MA). The mishap pilot (MP) egressed the aircraft unharmed; there was only minor damage to Wittman Regional Airport.

The MP was number two of a two-ship formation on a continuation training (CT) mission to the AirVenture 2011 air show at KOSH. After an uneventful flight from Alabama to KOSH, the flight entered the airport landing pattern. During the MP's landing roll, the MA's environmental control system (ECS) caused extreme fogging that completely obscured the MP's visual cues and severely affected the correct execution of his normal landing procedures. The MP correctly applied the defog procedure without effect, resulting in the MA running off the end of the airport's 8002 ft runway.

The weather at the field was 1400 broken, 6 miles visibility, and calm winds. The weather forced the mishap flight (MF) to fly a lower than normal overhead pattern resulting in a flat final turn. The MA landed above computed touchdown speed with the speedbrakes closed. The MP attempted to aerobrake, but could not gauge the angle of attack (AOA) because of ECS fog. The MA never achieved the desired aerodynamic braking resulting in the jet exiting the prepared surface coming to rest approximately 300 ft into the grass infield. The MP egressed and emergency vehicles responded.

Accident cause

The board president found by clear and convincing evidence that the cause of the mishap was extreme fogging in the MA cockpit, caused by the MA ECS that completely obscured the MP's vision.

The board president found by a preponderance of the evidence that substantially contributing factors were an inadequate aerobrake, a fast touchdown speed, and closed speedbrakes.

Aerodynamic braking provides the most effective braking in the F-16 during landing. The ECS fog denied the MP the ability to establish a proper aerobrake increasing his landing distance. The fast touchdown speed increased the landing distance, but would have been negated by a proper aerobrake.

Speedbrakes would add some minor aerodynamic drag during the landing roll, but would not have prevented the MA's runway departure. The speedbrakes' primary purpose is to increase drag which at landing airspeeds provides for a higher power setting allowing for faster engine spool up in the event of go around. If not for the lack of visual and instrument references, the MP could have executed a proper aerobrake, come to a complete stop on the runway, and still had approximately 1000 ft of runway remaining.

Accident summary

The MP took off from Montgomery/Dannelly Field (KMGM) approximately 0950L and proceeded to rejoin with the MFL into line-a-breast tactical formation while climbing to 28,000 ft. The departure and enroute portions of the sortie were uneventful.

During the descent, the MFL reformed the formation to 1-2 mile data link trail while descending into instrument meteorological conditions (IMC). Milwaukee Approach Control descended the flight via radar vectors to the runway 36L ILS final approach course.

During the final descent, the flight flew into visual meteorological conditions (VMC) and obtained visual contact with the KOSH airfield. On initial contact with the control tower, the field was reported VFR (Visual Flight Rules) with ceiling 1,400 ft broken. The MFL requested and was cleared by KOSH tower direct to the overhead pattern for a low approach and subsequent closed overhead traffic patterns. The MP followed the MFL in trail to initial runway 36L.

On the downwind leg, a scattered layer of clouds drove a lower than expected pattern altitude which lead to overshooting final turns by both MFL and MP. The flight executed low approaches and a closed overhead pattern onto downwind for a second low approach. The second downwind leg was flown wider, but still resulted in slightly overshooting final turns.

Based on the weather the MFL informed the tower that the next landing would be a full-stop, and the MFL landed uneventfully and cleared the runway at taxiway A-1.

Crash Survivable Flight Data Recorder (CSFDR) and photographic evidence shows the fuel weight of 2,850 lbs and a total MA weight of 24,500 lbs at landing.

CFPS computed approach and landing speeds for the MA were 151 and 140 knots respectively.

The MP lowered the landing gear and commenced the final turn. The final turn was slightly overshooting and slow, requiring the MP to increase power and adjust his flight path. Speedbrakes were not used during the landing rollout. This is not IAW normal procedures. The AIB was unable to ascertain if they were never opened or if they were closed during the final turn while the MP adjusted airspeed.

The MP landed touching down just past the 1,000 ft runway marker which was confirmed by witness testimony and photographic analysis. The AIB estimates the touchdown was approximately 1000-1300 down runway 36L and at approximately 165-175 knots with the speedbrakes closed.

Cockpit ECS fog started developing in the MA as it approached the flare. As the throttle was retarded to idle, fog began to envelope the entire cockpit. As the MP began to set a pitch attitude for the aerobrake passing through 10-11 degrees, he lost sight of the HUD gun-cross and was unable to use the Nose Wheel Steering (NWS) indicator and AOA indexers for a visual reference. CSFDR data indicates that the aerobrake varied between 5 and 11-degrees AOA during the rollout. The MP started losing forward visibility first. Using the view out the side of the canopy, the MP focused on keeping the aircraft tracking down the runway. The MP reached for the DEFOG lever and shoved it full forward. He held it in that position for one or two seconds with no effect and then recycled, with yet again no change in ECS fog or airflow. The MP then experienced brief vertigo, almost a tumbling sensation, and considered ejection but was concerned for spectators and aircraft along the runways.

The MP did not consider initiating a go-around because of the disorientation and no assurance that the ECS fog would dissipate, rendering the MP blind while navigating through the congested traffic pattern.

The MP momentarily read 140 knots on the MA airspeed indicator during the rollout and thought he had enough runway, but could not see any runway remaining markers. The MP then applied main landing gear wheel brakes and the nose came down from the aerobrake. The MP felt the brake anti-skid system cycle and continued to brake as hard as he could. The MP never saw the end of the runway approaching, but felt that he had enough remaining runway to stop. Runway 36L has no overrun or arresting gear. As the MA departed the runway surface, the MP felt a bump and rumbling, and then the nose dug in. The ECS fog cleared as the engine ingested dirt and sod. After the MA came to a stop, the MP raised the canopy and egressed over the left canopy rail jogging northwest away from the MA.

Figure 67: MFL IMMEDIATELY POST LANDING (NO FOG IN COCKPIT) (Source: U.S. AIB report).

Figure 68: MP IMMEDIATELY POST LANDING (FOGGED COCKPIT) (Source: U.S. AIB report).

Impact

Aircraft S/N 87-0296 departed KOSH runway 36L at approximately 1120L on 28 July 2011, at approximately 80 knots and 25 ft left of runway centerline. As it entered the soft soil, the nose wheel turned and broke off. The nose contacted the ground, breaking off both the nose and avionics bay, just forward of the cockpit bulkhead. The engine intake ingested dirt and sod as the aircraft came to a stop. Photographs show that the nose wheel failed at approximately 150 ft off the end of the runway,

Human factors analysis

The board evaluated human factors relevant to the mishap using the analysis and classification system model established by the Department of Defense (DoD) Human Factors Analysis and Classification System (HFACS) guide, implemented by Air Force Pamphlet (AFPAM) 91-204, USAF Safety Investigations and Reports, dated 24 September 2008. A human factor is any environmental, technological, physiological, psychological, psychosocial, or psycho-behavioral factor a human being experiences that contributes to or influences his performance during a task. The DoD has created a framework to analyze and classify human factors and human error in mishap investigations.

The relevant factors to this mishap are discussed below.

1. Vision Restricted by Icing/Windows Fogged/Etc.

Vision Restricted by Icing/Windows Fogged/Etc is a factor when it is determined by the investigator that icing or fogging of the windshield/windscreen or canopy restricted the vision of the individual to a point where normal duties were affected.

According to the report, the fog caused the MP to lose "total visual," which he found "disorienting" and similar to having a "white plastic bag" placed over his head. The extreme fogging of the cockpit disoriented the MP, causing him to experience "vertigo" or "feel like there's some movement happening when nothing really is happening" but in reality the movement is not as drastic as perceived. In this regard, the fogging of the cockpit restricted the vision of the MP to a point where proper control of the aircraft was diminished or made extremely difficult. If not for the thick fog, the MP could have landed the aircraft safely.

Furthermore, the fog in the cockpit caused the MP to lose both inside and outside reference points. The MP stated that he "was able to just get a quick focus on the 140 and then nothing". Furthermore, the fog causing him to lose his reference point for the desired angle of attack in order to perform a proper aerobrake. He stated that "I just obviously wasn't high enough". The fog caused the MP to lose track of his closure rate and ground speed, which ultimately led to an unsafe situation.

2. Procedural Error.

Procedural error is a factor when a procedure is accomplished in the wrong sequence or using the wrong technique or when the wrong control or switch is used. This also captures errors in navigation, calculation or operation of automated systems.

According to the report, Procedural error was determined to be a contributory factor to this mishap as the MP did not deploy the speedbrakes prior to touchdown. This unintended error contributed to a faster touchdown speed and a longer touchdown distance.

The MP correctly managed the defogging procedure and this was not a factor. He reported engaging the defog lever at least twice but without effect. He initiated this procedure in a timely manner.

3. Distraction.

Distraction is a factor when the individual has an interruption of attention and/or inappropriate redirection of attention by an environmental cue or mental process that degrades performance.

According to the MP's testimony, he may not have deployed the speedbrakes because the multiple tasks required to follow his lead to the runway distracted him. The MP did not recall why he did not use the speedbrakes, but opined that he may have been "preoccupied with the pattern or preoccupied with the traffic" or with "other stuff going on in the cockpit".

However, the MP was not distracted by the copious fog that obscured his vision. The MP's attention was not redirected; rather the fog in the cockpit caused the MP to become even more focused on the landing roll out, actually bringing the MP to a heightened sense of attention. In his interview, the MP states he was extremely concerned about the crowds to the left of the runway along with the other planes. Concerned that the "airplane was veering slightly to the left" and could threaten the safety of civilians and other aircraft, he focused on maintaining control and ruled out ejecting as an option in order to guide the plane safely.

Clearly, his attention was centered on completing a safe landing.

4. Temporal Distortion.

Temporal distortion is a factor when the individual experiences a compression or expansion of time relative to reality leading to an unsafe situation.

According to the report, the MP, denied any visual reference through the fog, experienced a perceptual quickening of time, describing it as a "very short time" in which everything "happened very quickly". He goes on to state that he realized, from a temporal standpoint, when he looked down and saw his speed was at "140" that, based on his extensive experience, his aero-brake was "nowhere near" what he needed. This subjective experience of time compression relative to reality may have led to an unsafe situation in that the MP was unaware of ground speed (distance x time) and the fast approaching end of the runway. Although brakes were applied, the MP could not see the end of the runway and therefore did not receive a feedback response to determine if his braking was achieving the desired goal, namely to slow down the aircraft in a timely manner.

16 F-16 Loss of Consciousness

Figure 69: F-16C (Source: U.S. AIB report).

The United States Air Force Aircraft Accident Investigation Board (AIB) describes in their report that:

On 28 June 2011, at 1716 local time, an F-16C aircraft, tail number (TIN) 85-1413, impacted the ground approximately 95 miles north of Nellis Air Force Base (AFB), while participating in a training mission. The mishap pilot (MP) was killed. The MP was assigned to the 53rd Wing out of Eglin AFB, but was based at Nellis AFB with the 422d Test & Evaluation Squadron (TES).

The mishap aircraft (MA) belonged to the 57th Wing at Nellis AFB. The MP was flying a basic fighter maneuver (BFM) training mission with a mishap wingman (MW) in a second F-16C. The MW is assigned to the United States Air Force Warfare Center, but flies missions with the 422 TES. The MA was completely destroyed upon impact. The MA crashed in an unpopulated Bureau of Land Management wilderness area causing incidental damage to a small area of vegetation but no damage to property.

The primary purpose of this mission was to provide a final proficiency training sortie for the MP prior to his start at USAF Weapons Instructor Course (WIC), which was to begin the following week. The MP was focused on WIC preparation and needed one more sortie to complete the attendance prerequisites.

The mishap occurred during F-16 simulated air-to-air combat engagements between the MP and MW. The training engagements subjected the pilots to high levels of sustained gravitational forces (G forces, or Gs) of up to 9 Gs, often at high G onset rates (greater than 6 Gs per second).

Twenty-six minutes into the mission, during a planned high-speed turning maneuver likely involving 8 or more Gs, the MA stopped maneuvering and began a steep descending flight path consistent with an aircraft no longer being controlled by the pilot. The MA impacted the ground.

There was no evidence of an attempt by the MP to eject or to maneuver the MA prior to impact.

Accident cause

The AIB President found clear and convincing evidence to conclude the cause of the mishap was a G-Induced Loss of Consciousness (G-LOC) experienced by the MP during the high G maneuver.

The AIB President found by a preponderance of the evidence that the MP did not adequately perform an anti-G straining maneuver (AGSM) which led to the G-LOC. A preponderance of evidence indicates the MP had excessive motivation to succeed during his fourth engagement and had slight fatigue, which resulted in the MP not adequately performing an AGSM. Furthermore, the MA was in a clean configuration (minimal external stores) that would have enabled a higher G onset rate than what the MP was used to flying.

The AIB President found no evidence the MP's physical or mental condition, or Operations' supervision and training contributed to the accident. Additionally, a thorough review of maintenance procedures revealed no problems or adverse trends which could have contributed to the accident.

Accident summary

The MF taxied to runway 21 (the active runway). The MF took off from Nellis AFB and departed on a "Dream 2" departure. "Dream 2" is a standard departure procedure that aircraft follow en route to the Caliente Military Operating Area (MOA), the airspace assigned to the MF that day. The MF was established in the Caliente MOA and performed a G warm up. This maneuver is a 90 degree turn involving 4 to 5 Gs, and is used to ensure that the G-suit, pressure breathing equipment, and the inflatable bladder in the Combat Edge Helmet are working properly.

Immediately following the G warm up, the MF completed a G awareness maneuver. This is a 180 degree turn that involves flying the aircraft to body or aircraft G limits (the 422 TES standard is 6 to 7 Gs). While the G warm up is used to test the operation of Anti-G equipment, the G awareness maneuver gives the pilot the chance to practice the Anti-G Straining Maneuver (AGSM). The AGSM is a muscle-tightening and breathing procedure employed by pilots during high G maneuvers to ensure sufficient blood flow to the brain to maintain consciousness. Following the G warm up and the G awareness exercises, neither member of the MF reported any Anti-G system or body related G force problems.

The mission for the day involved four engagements:

The first engagement of the day was a 9,000 feet (9K) offensive BFM set for the MF and began at 1704L.

This fight was started at 18,000 feet Mean Sea Level (MSL), with the MP's aircraft 9,000 feet (9K) behind the MW's aircraft. After the fight, the MP debriefed the fight over the radio. He talked about being stuck in "lag" without enough airspeed to continue an effective attack on the MW. Lag pursuit occurs when the nose of the offensive aircraft points behind the defensive aircraft.

The fourth engagement was the mishap engagement. This set was also a high aspect BFM set and started at approximately 18,000 feet MSL. After the aircraft passed each other, the MW lost sight (momentary loss of sight in this type of engagement is not abnormal) of the MA. After scanning the sky where he expected to see the MA (aft and slightly low), the MW felt that something had gone wrong and began looking low and high.

Approximately 25 seconds after the two aircraft merged, the MW saw a bright flash below him, which was the MA impacting the ground. In an attempt to determine whether the impact was the MA or some other training in the Test Range, the MW made multiple "status" calls. The term "status" is a request for information on the location of the other aircraft. The MW received no response from the MP.

Simulator Analysis of Mishap Engagement

Because the MA's flight data recorders were destroyed in the accident, the AIB lacked detailed objective data on the MA's flight parameters during its final seconds of flight. However, the AIB was able to estimate these parameters based upon information from the MW's Digital Video Recorder (DVR) and the MP's previously briefed high aspect BFM game plan.

The AIB sought to improve the fidelity of this estimate by re-enacting the final sequence of events via flight simulation. The AIB conducted the following re-enactment using an F-16 simulator at Nellis AFB.

The AIB pilot member simulated the MP, flying a profile based upon the briefed high aspect BFM game plan, resulting in a G-Induced Loss of Consciousness (G-LOC) profile (G-LOC is defined below in Section 11, Human Factors). In this profile, the AIB pilot member passed the merge point, selected afterburner and entered a slightly descending 7 to 8 G turn for 5 seconds, then over rotated 60 degrees nose low, increasing to 9 Gs (the MP's briefed game plan).

The AIB pilot member then selected military power (based on post impact engine analysis) and released the control stick as if he had lost consciousness. Each time, after control stick release, the simulated MA accelerated in a nose-low attitude and impacted the ground. The following approximate parameters resulted from the simulation:

- Speed: 650+ knots
- Pitch Attitude: 85 degrees nose low

- Time of Impact: 17:16:20L

In this scenario, the simulated MA's starting parameters were very close to the actual MA's airspeed, altitude, attitude, location, and time reported in the accident.

Human factors analysis

The AIB found no evidence of maintenance or egress crew complacency, overconfidence, low motivation, distraction, disruption, supervisory pressure, channelized attention, uncharacteristic mistakes or other degradation that may have led to the accident.

The AIB found no indications of latent failures, but did identify active failures. The AIB found the Operations supervision to be effective, proficient and professional and not causal to this mishap.

1. Effects of G Forces (G-LOC, etc)

"The Effects of G Forces" are defined by HFACS as factors wherein the individual experiences G-LOC, greyout, blackout or other neuro-circulatory affects of sustained acceleration forces. The brain is extremely sensitive to oxygen deprivation. Oxygen is delivered to the brain through normal blood flow. If the brain is deprived of oxygen for 4-6 seconds it is unable to continue normal function. If the rate of G onset is not too rapid, the body will experience warning signs of decreased blood flow to the eyes. Individuals will experience "tunnel vision," a dimming of their central vision (greyout), or a complete loss of vision (blackout). If the rate of onset of Gs is high, G-LOC can occur before any other symptoms are noticed, including visual manifestations.

According to the report, the MP's fourth engagement in his sortie was a high aspect BFM set. He was planning to execute a lift vector low to intercept the MW. This maneuver would cause the MA to point at the ground during the high G pull. It would also place a large amount of G force on the MP's body, approximately 8 or 9 Gs. The MA was in a clean configuration (minimal external stores), thereby decreasing its drag and causing the rate of G onset to be incredibly fast during this maneuver. If the MA's rate of G onset was 6 Gs per second or higher, it could have caused the MP to G-LOC within 4 seconds, without any visual warning signs to precede it.

G-LOC incapacitation has been divided into two time periods: absolute incapacitation (unconsciousness) and relative incapacitation (confusion/disorientation). The average absolute incapacitation lasts for approximately 12 seconds (range of2-38 seconds). The average relative incapacitation that follows is approximately 15 seconds (range of 2-97 seconds). A pilot would be unable to control his aircraft during either of these phases. The average total incapacitation time, therefore, is approximately 28 seconds (range of 9-110 seconds).

Recent studies performed at Wright-Patterson AFB shows that these times may be even longer. This study showed that cognitive performance degrades on average 3.2 seconds prior to rapid acceleration induced G-LOC and does not return to normal until 55.6 seconds later. This would leave the pilot incapacitated for nearly 1 minute without aircraft control. Evidence recovered from the MA revealed that the MP was leaning forward in his seat consistent with being unconscious, his right shoulder further forward than his left.

Part of the control mechanism for the ejection seat was recovered and showed that no attempt was made to eject. Two eye witnesses reported seeing no attempts being made to recover the MA from its dive, again indicating that the MP was unconscious at the time of the mishap.

2. Inadequate Anti-G Straining Maneuver

"Inadequate AGSM" is defined by OOOHFACS as a factor wherein the individual's AGSM is improper, inadequate, poorly timed or non-existent, leading to adverse neurocirculatory effects.

According to the report, the AGSM is a two part muscle contraction and breathing procedure employed by pilots and aircrew during high G maneuvers that increases blood flow to the eyes and brain to assist in maintaining sight and consciousness in high stress environments. The muscle contraction consists of maximal straining of the legs, thighs, buttocks and abdomen. The breathing element consists of a maximal inspiration of air prior to the onset of Gs. Repetitive sharp, quick air exchanges are made every 3 seconds. This maneuver is maintained until after the G forces on the body have returned to normal (1 G). The MP was an experienced and seasoned pilot who had many engagements in a high G environment, although, as stated in the discussion on G-LOC, if the rate of G onset is high, G-LOC can occur rapidly without any visual warning signs. During the MP's final engagement he performed a maneuver that would place his body under high Gs and would have resulted in a high G onset rate. A pilot not anticipating such a high G onset may succumb to G-LOC.

3. Excessive Motivation to Succeed

"Motivation to Succeed - Excessive" is defined by OOOHFACS as a factor when the individual is preoccupied with success to the exclusion of other mission factors, leading to an unsafe situation. This was the MP's last sortie and the last high aspect BFM engagement that he would perform prior to starting WIC.

According to the report, it is likely that he was highly motivated to perfect this engagement.

The MP had attempted to perform a lift vector low maneuver during his third engagement of the sortie. During that engagement the MP lost sight of the MW. The MP was not satisfied with his performance and ended the engagement early. After a brief discussion with the MW, the MP decided to attempt that same scenario again. The MP was focused on success and may have positioned his body and/or head in such a way as to keep the MW in sight.

This may have placed him in a less optimal position to effectively counteract the G forces he was about to endure.

4. Emotional State

"Emotional State" is defined by OOOHFACS as a factor when the individual is under the influence of a strong positive or negative emotion and that emotion interferes with duties.

According to the report, the MP received the news of the death of his grandfather the day prior to the mishap. He had been scheduled to fly on 27 June 2011, but removed himself from the schedule due to the emotional impact that news had on him. Witnesses reported that the MP was so preoccupied by the news of his grandfather that he did not exit the freeway at the proper exit on his way to work that day. By the day of the mishap, the MP appeared to be in better spirits and was coping well with the death of his grandfather. By all witness accounts he was back to his normal countenance/mindset and appeared focused. He told his division commander that he was ready to fly. During his sortie, he showed clarity of thought and excellent clear, concise and directive communications to the MW. He had no lapses of thought and made no incorrect radio calls. After reviewing all witness testimonies and the MW's HUD tape, the AIB assessed the MP's emotional state to have been a minor factor, at most, for cause ofthe accident. By all accounts he appeared ready to fly.

5. Physical Fatigue

"Physical Fatigue" (over-exertion) is defined as a factor when the individual's diminished physical capability is due to overuse (time/relative load) and it degrades task performance. It includes the effects of prolonged physical activity, or the effects of brief but relatively extreme physical activity, either of which taxes a person's physical endurance or strength beyond the individual's normal limits.

According to the report, on 28 June 2011 the temperature at the time of the preflight inspection was 106 degrees F, resulting in FITS danger. The AIB assessed physical fatigue as a minor factor at most to this mishap. Witness testimonies all indicate the MP was rested and ready to fly. It is possible that after his third training engagement, the MP was slightly fatigued. Most F-16 G-LOCs occur on the third or later engagement due to fatigue.

There is no evidence of MP inattention, confusion, complacency, over-aggressiveness, overconfidence, distraction, hypoxia, special disorientation, motivational exhaustion, disruption, task oversaturation, external pressure, channelized attention, medication or alcohol misuse, preexisting physical illness, uncharacteristic mistake or other degradation as causes of the accident.

The AIB evaluated all available evidence, such as witness testimonies, radio transmissions and the MW's HUD tape. The evidence of the engagement - a high G and high rate G onset maneuver, the MP's body position at time of impact as revealed by shoulder harness markings, his lack of communication, eye witness testimony of the impact, and evidence supporting no ejection effort - suggests that the MP suffered rapid onset G-LOC and did not regain consciousness prior to the impact of the MA.

17   B-747 Struck its tail at Landing

Figure 70: E-4B (Source: U.S. AIB report).

The United States Air Force Aircraft Accident Investigation Board (AIB) describes in their report that:

On 12 May 2010, at approximately 2310 local time, an E-4B aircraft, tail number (T/N) 73-1676, struck its tail approximately 1,300 feet past the threshold of runway 30 at Offutt Air Force Base (AFB), Nebraska (NE), after completing a National Airborne Operations Center (NAOC) Alert weather avoidance mission. No injuries or lost work were incurred by the Mishap Crew (MC).

The AIB explains that the mishap aircraft (MA) is based at Offutt AFB, NE, and assigned to the 1st Airborne Command and Control Squadron of the 55th Operations Group, 55th Wing, to provide the President and Secretary of Defense with a survivable command center for directing United States forces during all conditions of peace and war, and for supporting the federal government during military, national, and natural emergencies. The MA was damaged on the underbody of the tail section upon impact, and the mishap caused no damage to the runway.

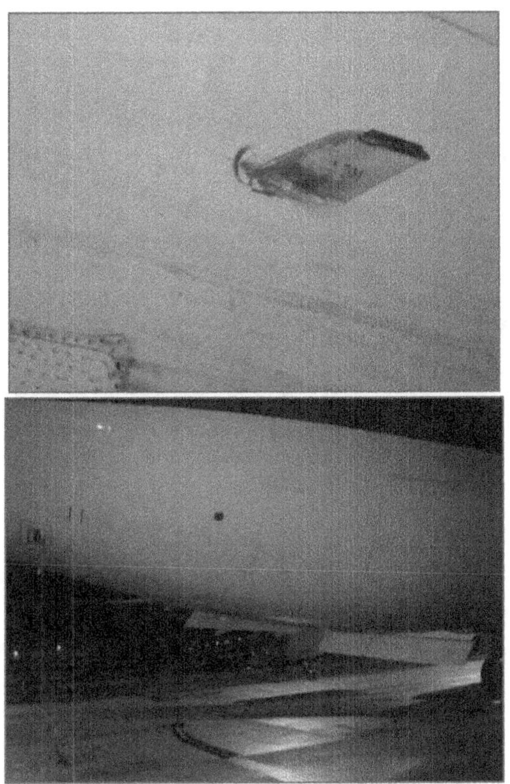

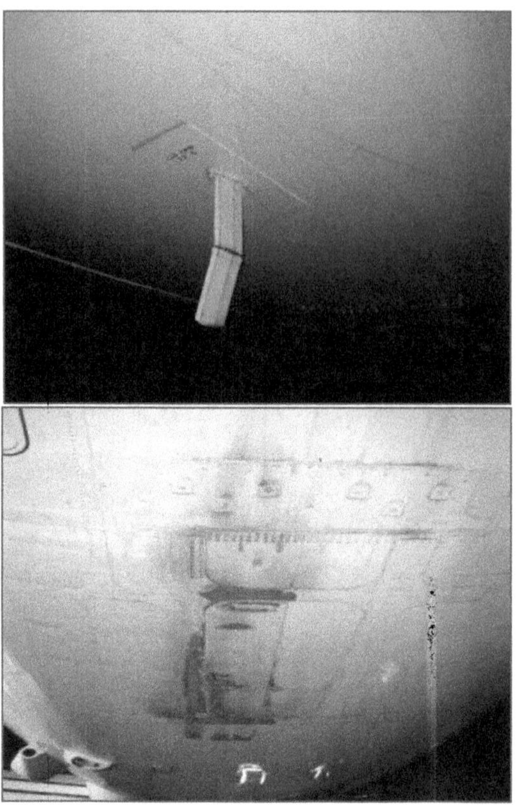

Figure 71: Damage to the aircraft was photographed immediately following the mishap after the aircraft taxied to parking (Source: U.S. AIB report).

The report describes that two hours and 32 minutes after takeoff, Mishap Pilot 1 (MP1) flew an uneventful, stable on speed precision approach to short final. Digital flight data recorder (DFDR) information and testimony reveal that on short final, MP1 flew a slightly low glide path with a higher than normal descent rate. MP1 applied a large pitch-up control movement to the yoke at approximately 30 feet above touchdown, culminating in a firm touchdown at a 9-degree pitch angle and a subsequent bounce. During the bounce, MP1 applied back pressure to the yoke, increasing the aircraft pitch angle to 11 degrees as the aircraft settled back to the runway about 800 feet past the first touchdown point, resulting in the tail of the aircraft impacting the runway 2-3 feet right of the centerline, approximately 1,300 feet past the threshold. MP1 and the MC brought the MA to a stop on the runway, ensured the MA was safe for taxiing, and exited the runway uneventfully.

Accident cause

The Aircraft Investigation Board (AIB) president found by clear and convincing evidence the cause of the mishap was pilot error by MP1 and Mishap Pilot 2 (MP2). During the bounce, MP1 increased the pitch angle of the MA to more than twice the pitch angle specified by the flight manual for landing, resulting in the tail striking the runway nearly simultaneously to the landing gear. As the Aircraft Commander for the sortie, MP2 did not ensure the safe and effective conduct of the flight, giving no input to MP1 during the landing, bounce, and second touchdown.

Additionally, the AIB president found as contributing factors that the E-4B flight manual and training programs did not state, discuss, or address any risk of tail strikes during landings or bounce recovery and that the manufacturer did not provide the Air Force information concerning risks of tail strikes for 747 aircraft during landing or bounce recovery.

Accident summary

The MA departed Offutt AFB at 2038L. There was no schedule for this mission, as National Airborne Operations Center (NAOC) operational missions flown for weather avoidance are executed on an as needed basis.

The report describes:

Following an uneventful take off, the MA climbed to a cruise altitude of 31,000 feet and headed towards the Gopher VORTAC (GEP), a navigational aid near Minneapolis, MN. From there the MA proceeded to the Aberdeen VOR/DME (ABR), a navigational aid in SD, then to the Sioux Falls VORTAC (FSD), another navigational aid in SD, then towards the Fort Dodge VOR/DME (FOD), a navigational in IA. At this point, the MC deviated from the flight plan, after determining a need to remain aloft longer in order to allow time for any remaining severe weather in the Offutt AFB area to clear. The MC requested to proceed to the area of North Platte VOR/DME (LBF), in NE. From there the MC approached Offutt AFB from the west and commenced an en route descent, briefing an

Instrument Landing System (ILS) approach to Runway (RW) 30 at Offutt AFB. The MC then flew a Standard Terminal Arrival (STAR), terminating the STAR with vectors from Omaha Approach to the RW 30 ILS.

During the en route descent and vectors to the RW 30 ILS, the MC configured the MA for the approach in accordance with the applicable checklists from T.O 1E-4B(II)-1. Once established on the final approach segment of the ILS to RW 30, the MC continued to configure the MA for a full stop landing in accordance with T.O 1E-4B(II)-1, selecting landing gear down and wing flaps 30 percent for the full stop landing.

During the en route descent and final approach, the Mishap Pilot 1 (MP1) was flying the aircraft from the right, or copilot seat. Mishap Pilot 2 (MP2), the pilot not flying, was the Aircraft Commander, and sat in the left seat monitoring the approach. The Mishap Flight Engineer (MFE) was at his assigned station, as was the Mishap Navigator (MN).

MP1, as the pilot flying, was utilizing one of the three autopilots installed on the E-4B to fly the en route descent and most of the final approach portion of the RW 30 ILS. MP1 kept the autopilot engaged on the ILS through approximately 800 feet above ground level (AGL), when he disconnected it shortly after passing through a thin cloud deck on final approach to the runway.

MP1 manually flew the aircraft from that point through the rest of the approach.

Weather was good below the cloud deck, with a visibility of at least 7 nautical miles (NM) as observed by the MC and reported by Offutt AFB Weather. MP1 testified to seeing the Precision Approach Path Indicator (PAPI) as three red lights and one white light initially, then two white and two red after correcting. Two red and two white lights indicate an aircraft is on the proper glide slope for landing. MP1 was not able to precisely recall the last time he saw two red and two white PAPI lights.

At approximately the Decision Height (DH) of 1,172 feet above Mean Sea Level (MSL), or 200 feet AGL on the ILS RW 30, MP2 testified he saw three red, and one white light on the PAPI during short final, indicating the aircraft was slightly below glide slope.

While on short approach, MP1 and MFE both heard a faster than normal —50, 40, 30, 20, 10 feet remaining until touchdown countdown from the automated system as the MA was crossing the runway threshold, indicating the descent rate was slightly faster than normal.

When MP1 realized that he was actually slightly low and descending slightly faster than normal, MP1 made a faster and larger than normal pitch up input to the steering column, or yoke (pulled back on the yoke). The result was that the aircraft touched down in a firm landing, with a 9- degree pitch attitude. The touchdown point was short—500 feet past the threshold (approximately 500 feet short of the PAPI point of intercept and the thousand foot —Captain's Bars runway marking in the recommended touchdown zone). Upon landing, the aircraft bounced.

As the MA's wheels initially touched down on the runway, the aircraft's spoilers automatically deployed as they were designed to do when the speed brake lever is placed in the armed position. The armed position was in accordance with the Before-Landing Checklist in T.O 1E-4B(II)-1. The ground function of the spoilers raises all six panels on the upper surface of each wing to help the aircraft slow down by reducing lift, thus causing the aircraft wheel brakes to be more effective. In flight, the spoilers add drag to slow the aircraft, and also tend to raise the pitch of the aircraft slightly.

Immediately after the initial touchdown, the MA became airborne again, with no members of the MC immediately aware they were airborne. Upon the first touchdown, MP1 had initially relaxed aft control column pressure (released backpressure on the yoke).

However, when he realized the MA was again airborne, MP1 pulled back on the yoke again in an attempt to smooth the subsequent landing. While airborne from the bounce, pitch on the MA came up to approximately 11 degrees, due in part to MP1's aft control column input. As the MA then settled back towards the runway, portions of the lower aft fuselage made contact with the runway surface, causing a —tail strike.

The Aircraft Commander for the sortie, MP2, gave no verbal or physical input to MP1 or the MA during the landing, bounce, and second touchdown.

The report continued:

As the MA landed, the tower watch supervisor noted a bright flash and sparks from the MA and notified the aircrew. Following the full stop landing, the MA taxied clear of RW 30, and was instructed by the Offutt control tower to hold position. The tower controller initiated the Offutt Crash Net, effectively declaring an emergency. Offutt fire/crash rescue personnel performed a visual inspection of the aircraft and discovered damage on the aft fuselage, enabling them to conclude that the bright flash and sparks seen by the tower controller and Supervisor of Flying (SOF) were from tail contact with the runway and not from any other malfunction. Following this inspection, the MC taxied the MA to parking under its own power

Human factors analysis

The board and two additional human factors experts (a trained Air Force (AF) physiologist, and an AF doctor trained in aerospace psychology) considered all of the environmental and individual human factors elements contained in AFI 91-204 attachment 5, Department of Defense (DoD) Human Factors Analysis and Classification System (HFACS), and paragraph 8.7.8.11 of AFI 51-503.

The AIB evaluated every action the MC took during the mishap sequence using all available evidence, such as witness testimony, radio transmissions, and Digital Flight Data Recorder (DFDR) information. The following information was reviewed: MP1, MP2, MFE, and MN witness interview transcripts DFDR Information.

Nighttime viewing of runway, its associated horizon, and touchdown points Re-creation of flight simulation (animation) Electronic Medical Records of MP1 and MP2 14-day and 72-hour histories of all MP1, MP2, MFE, and MN.

Nine human factors from the DoD HFACS model AFI 91-204, attachment 5) are relevant to this mishap: (1) Misperception of Operational Conditions; (2) Breakdown in Visual Scan; (3) Overcontrol/Undercontrol; (4) Procedural Error; (5) Inattention; (6) Procedural Guidance/Publications; (7) Local Training Issues/Programs; (8) Supervision – Policy; (9) Cross-Monitoring Performance.

The RW 30 profile and its varying up gradient and its possible effect on the pilots is also discussed in this section.

1. Misperception of Operational Conditions.

Misperception of Operational Conditions is a factor when an individual misperceives or misjudges altitude, separation, speed, closure rate, road/sea conditions, aircraft/vehicle location within the performance envelope or other operational conditions and this leads to an unsafe situation.

According to the report, it is relevant in this mishap because evidence suggests MP1 misjudged his altitude, glide path, and descent rate within the performance envelope of the MA on short final.

2. Breakdown in Visual Scan.

Breakdown in Visual Scan is a factor when the individual fails to effectively execute learned /practiced internal or external visual scan patterns leading to unsafe situation.

According to the report, it is relevant in this mishap because evidence suggests MP1 did not notice, or noticed late, he was slightly low during a night landing performed using visual references.

3. Overcontrol/Undercontrol.

Overcontrol/Undercontrol is a factor when an individual responds inappropriately to conditions by either overcontroling or undercontroling the aircraft/vehicle/system. The error may be a result of preconditions or a temporary failure of coordination.

According to the report, Overcontrol/Undercontrol is relevant because of MP1's reaction once he recognized the increased descent rate on short final. His reaction was basically correct but was an —over control input to the yoke, resulting in an aircraft designed to touch down at 5 degrees of pitch touching down at 9 degrees of pitch. The —over control of the control column prior to the initial touchdown was assessed can be described as an —uncharacteristic mistake (per paragraph 8.7.8.11 of AFI 51-503) by MP1 because he is not characterized by mistakes in his training or evaluation records and the E-4B has not sustained a tail strike in its employment history in the AF since 1980.

4. Procedural Error.

Procedural Error is a factor when a procedure is accomplished in the wrong sequence or using the wrong technique or when the wrong control or switch is used. This also captures errors in navigation, calculation or operation of automated systems.

According to the report, Procedural Error is relevant because MP1 moved the control column aft during the bounce, increasing the pitch angle even further above the 5 degrees specified in the flight manual to 11 degrees. MP1's recovery technique from the initial bounce resulted in too much pitch.

5. Inattention.

Inattention is a factor when the individual has a state of reduced conscious attention due to a sense of security, self-confidence, boredom or a perceived absence of threat from the environment which degrades crew performance. (This may often be a result of highly repetitive tasks. Lack of a state of alertness or readiness to process immediately available information).

According to the report, Inattention is relevant because inattention during an approach can lead to similar circumstances of being below glide slope while having an elevated descent rate.

6. Procedural Guidance/Publications.

Procedural Guidance/Publications is a factor when written direction, checklists, graphic depictions, tables, charts or other published guidance is inadequate, misleading or inappropriate and this creates an unsafe situation.

According to the report, In this case, Procedural Guidance/Publications is relevant because the flight manual neither quantifies the degrees of pitch that will result in a tail strike nor contains a note, caution, or warning about the risk of tail strike during landing In addition, there are no Air Force (AF), Air Combat Command

(ACC), or unit level tail strike prevention programs or tail strike threat awareness programs.

7. Local Training Issues/Programs.

Local Training Issues/Programs are a factor when one-time or recurrent training programs, upgrade programs, transition programs or any other local training is inadequate or unavailable (etc) and this creates an unsafe situation.

According to the report, in this case, Local Training Issues/Programs is relevant because there is no training in place to help prevent or avoid tail strikes or how to properly handle the E-4B in a bounce recovery, despite the fact that the manufacturer and commercial operators know this to be a risk to safe 747 —classic operations.

8. Supervision – Policy.

Supervision – Policy is a factor when policy or guidance or lack of a policy or guidance leads to an unsafe situation. In this case, Supervision – Policy is relevant because there was no policy or guidance related to tail strikes in an aircraft susceptible to tail strikes.

According to the report, in this instance, however, as far as the AIB was able to tell, the information related to tail strikes was not passed from the manufacturer to the Air Force, and supervision was unaware of the elevated potential for such occurrences. Accordingly, though relevant for discussion, the AIB did not find error or fault in Air Force supervision or policy.

9. Cross-Monitoring Performance.

Cross-monitoring performance is a factor when crew or team members failed to monitor, assist or back-up each other's actions and decisions.

According to the report, Cross-Monitoring Performance is relevant because MP2 did not provide input to the pilot flying to help him recognize the low glide path, slow the descent rate, or prevent the over control and the increase of the pitch attitude during the bounce to 220% of the 5 degrees specified for landing in the flight manual.

The report added the following information related to Human Factor investigation:

Careful analysis of DFDR information, witness testimony, and expert witness evaluation reveals MP1 made what can be classified as an uncharacteristic mistake by MP1.

DFDR data indicates that at approximately 18 seconds prior to the first touchdown, MP1 corrected what was a minor glide path deviation on the low side. MP1 made this correction by adding a slight bit of power, and reducing the rate of descent using aft control column movement.

MP1 testified that after this correction, he was on glide slope, observing two red and two white on the PAPI. Based on MP1 testimony, this is the last time in the mishap sequence where he referenced the PAPIs. At some undetermined time, MP1 had a momentary loss of Situational Awareness (SA) and this momentary loss ceased when he heard the radar altimeter calling off the 50, 40, 30, 20, and 10 foot calls more rapidly than normal.

The AIB consulted a trained physiologist and a doctor trained in aerospace psychology factors in an effort to determine what factors might have been influencing the MC.

Writing a joint report, they determined that MP1 displayed evidence of being tired, but did not characterize the MC as fatigued. In other words, there was the potential for minor performance deviations based on the fact that MP1 had been awake for almost 18 hours, and was past the point at which he would be sleeping on a non-duty night. Their report notes that a momentary loss of SA, such as that theorized to have occurred with MP1, is likely to have arisen because of MP1 being tired. In addition, the expert testimony suggests that a common human reaction to a momentary loss of SA and the realization that an action is needed, is to make the correct action to a larger degree than normal or required, resulting in —over control of the control column with a greater than normal pitch up movement.

The report continued:

Analysis of the physiologist and psychologists report, in conjunction with the DFDR information and witness testimony suggests that MP1 suffered a momentary loss of SA at some point after making a pitch/glide slope correction at approximately 18 seconds prior to the first touchdown. After making a pitch correction back to the proper glide slope, the MA then assumed a pitch/descent rate that was slightly greater than nominal, resulting in a three red and one white on the PAPI, as noted by MP2.

The increased descent rate resulted in an aim point and touchdown short of the 1,000-2,000 feet down the runway target used by E-4B aircrews. MP1 did not notice the deviations. However, MP2, seeing three red and one white on the PAPI, noticed the deviations but did not believe they were enough of a concern to verbalize them to MP1. MP1 testified that he was slightly surprised when radar altimeter call outs, starting with the 50 foot call, came in at a rate perceived to be faster than normal.

The AIB also explored human factors affecting both MP1 and MP2 for reasons why neither MP1 nor MP2 were able to discern, via visual reference from looking out the pilot windows, the excessive pitch attitude of the MA prior to the tail strike and second touchdown.

One relevant factor is the runway profile at Offutt AFB. The Offutt AFB runway is not level, with a published .7% up gradient for the entire length of RW30.

From USAF Flight Information Publications, and as used to calculate aircraft performance, the gradient is considered constant over the length of the runway. However, the actual gradient for RW30 is not constant.

The first approximately 2,200 feet of RW30 is relatively flat, followed by an upslope approximately 4,000 feet long, where approximately 50 feet of vertical change is seen, and then the rate of gradient change decreases, but still moves up to gain another approximately 25 feet of vertical change over the remaining 3,700 of the runway length. Over the final 7,700 feet of runway, the 75 foot rise equates to about a 1.0 gradient upslope (equivalent to a .6 degree upslope). The net effect is that the horizon the pilots used at the end of RW 30 to establish a reference for landing was higher than the level part of the runway they landed on in the landing zone (first 3,000 feet).

The AIB carefully considered how this upslope condition would affect a crew landing an E-4B at night, at the end of a 16-hour duty day, experiencing an unexpected bounce, and without training or guidance to prevent over-rotation.

Pilots are taught to evaluate aircraft height above the ground, and pitch, via visible references during the landing phase. In the case of RW 30 at Offutt, the true horizon (or the end of a level runway used by pilots to determine height above a runway while landing) lies behind the hill presented by the increasing gradient of RW 30. This can affect a crew's ability to visually perceive height above runway and pitch. The memo at and consultation with a prominent Air Force runway visual illusions expert suggests that this gradient can affect a pilot's ability to determine aircraft pitch solely by visual means, but the exact amount of this effect, in mathematical terms, cannot be determined.

18 F-16C Midair collision

Figure 72: F-16Cs (Source: U.S. AIB report).

The United States Air Force Aircraft Accident Investigation Board (AIB) describes in their report that:

On 20 October 2014, at 1421 hours (time local), two F-16Cs, tail numbers (T/N) 89-2019 and 89-2034, assigned to the 125th Fighter Squadron, 138th Fighter Wing, Tulsa Air National Guard Base (ANGB), collided during a training mission near Moline, Kansas. Mishap pilot 1 (MP1), was an instructor pilot with over 2,400 hours of flight time in the F-16. Mishap pilot 2 (MP2) was a student pilot with 106 flying hours in the F-16. MP1 ejected and experienced minor injuries; MP2 was unharmed. Mishap aircraft 1 (MA1), T/N 89-2019 was destroyed. Five feet of the right wing tip was severed from mishap aircraft 2 (MA2), T/N 89-2034.

The mishap flight (MF) departed Tulsa ANGB at 1403 for an air combat maneuvers (ACM) training mission. The MF included three F-16s; MP1 and MP2 planned to operate as a coordinated two ship, while mishap pilot 3 (MP3) would play the role of simulated adversary.

The MF flew 83 nautical miles (NM) northwest to the Eureka Military Operating Area (MOA), to perform a series of ACM engagements, wherein MP1 and MP2 would patrol the Eureka MOA and MP3 would approach from an unknown direction to simulate an attack, to which MP1 and MP2 must respond. MP1 and MP2 would fill the role of either an engaged fighter (EF) whose primary responsibility is to kill the adversary, or supporting fighter (SF) whose primary responsibilities are to maintain visual and ensure flight path de-confliction with the EF.

The first engagement finished without incident.

For the second engagement, MP3 approached from the north, separated by 20 NM. By default, MP1 was the EF and MP2 was the SF. MP1 and MP2 were headed north with MP1 left of MP2. MP3 targeted MP2, and MP1 then directed MP2 to bracket right, but did not initiate an exchange of EF and SF roles.

MP2 saw MP1 for the last time before impact, 16 seconds later. MP2 stated he had merged with MP3. MP2 then took a hard left turn in an attempt to get behind MP3. MP1 saw MP2 turn but misperceived it as a right turn, away from him, and accordingly focused on simulating a kill on MP3. MP2 made a request to exchange roles; MP1 then saw MA2's belly on a rapid collision course. MP1 and MP2 collided. The impact resulted in sheering MA1's right wing flaperon and horizontal tail, causing MP1 to lose control. MP1 successfully ejected from MA1 and landed near Moline, Kansas. MP2 landed MA2 safely at Tulsa ANGB.

Accident cause

The Accident Investigation Board (AIB) president found, by clear and convincing evidence, the cause of the mishap was MP2's failure to fulfill his primary responsibilities of maintaining visual and flight path de-confliction with MP1.

Additionally, the AIB president found, by a preponderance of evidence, three factors substantially contributed to the mishap:

1) MP2's failure to call "blind" when he could not see MP1,

2) MP1's misperception of MP2's turn at the merge, and

3) MP1's failure to initiate a role exchange when MP2 was most defensive.

Accident summary

Start, taxi, and arming the aircraft were all uneventful. The flight took off at 1403 from Tulsa ANGB, OK in a 2+1 formation with 1 NM between the mishap element (ME) and MP3 to Eureka MOA. There was nothing of note with Air Traffic Control (ATC) or weather during the departure to the MOA. After entering the airspace, the MF performed a G-Awareness exercise, which is a turning exercise to determine a pilot's tolerance of gravitational force, prior to beginning air to air engagements. As mentioned previously, they planned a "Tap the Cap" scenario with one continuous fight. The ME was holding in the center of the airspace with the adversary free to engage at any point throughout the flight after the "FIGHTS ON" call.

The second engagement began, when MP1 picked up radar histories and directed MP2 to target that group. The adversary was 15-20 NM off their nose, which was shorter than planned. MP2 called targeted. MP1 then directed MP2 to bracket right to the east. The mishap element (ME) maneuvered in an offensive manner in order to identify, and if hostile, attack the adversary. MP2 called that he was targeted by the adversary and defended to the northeast. At this point, MP2 was the most defensive fighter. MP1 could have given MP2 the EF role by calling "2 PRESS" at any point from now until MP2 merged (as in opposite traffic on a two lane highway) with MP3; however, he did not initiate a role exchange. MP1 acknowledged that he should have initiated a role exchange to give the engaged fighter responsibilities to MP2 since he was clearly the most defensive fighter in accordance with AFTTP 3-3, but did not initiate this role swap.

MP2 did not defend effectively enough to defeat MP3's radar, so MP3 continued to attack MP2 as per the briefing.MP1 called "1's TALLY ONE" to indicate that he is in sight of the adversary, but unable to make a declaration of hostile intent. MP1 turned into the adversary to be in a position to take a shot if MP2 identifies the adversary as hostile. MP2 called "TWO's IN 14 THOUSAND" at an altitude of 14,600 feet, three seconds after his "TALLY" call. During an interview with MP2, he stated this call was made to inform MP1 that MP2 was maneuvering into the fight; however, MP2 subsequently acknowledged this was an incorrect and mistimed call.

The correct term would have been "greasing in". At this point, MP2 looked at MP1 for the last time, and assumed de-confliction for the remainder of the engagement without maintaining the visual on the EF, MP1. MP2 called "2'S MERGED HOSTILE VIPER,". MP2 turned across MP3's tail in an effort to fight his best Basic Fighter Maneuvers (BFM); however, he did not have sight on MP1 and was still the SF. At this point, MP1 saw that the adversary turned away from him to the east and towards his wingman in a vertical type maneuver. MP1 misperceived that MP2 had also turned away from him to the east. Viewing an F-16, 1.5-2 NM away, rotating either toward or away from you, and similar in color, top and bottom can be misperceived as attested by MP1.

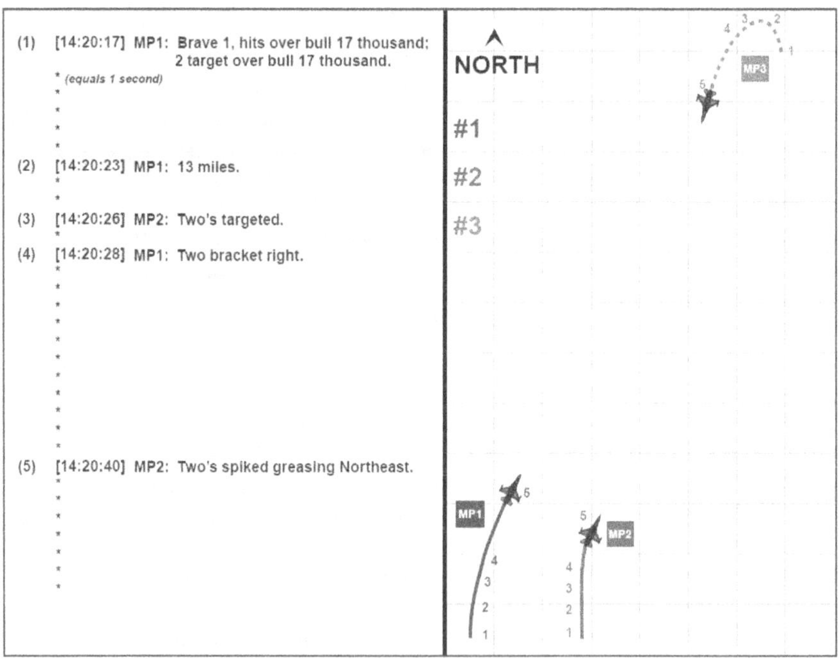

Figure 73: Mishap Engagement Illustration First Half (Source: U.S. AIB report).

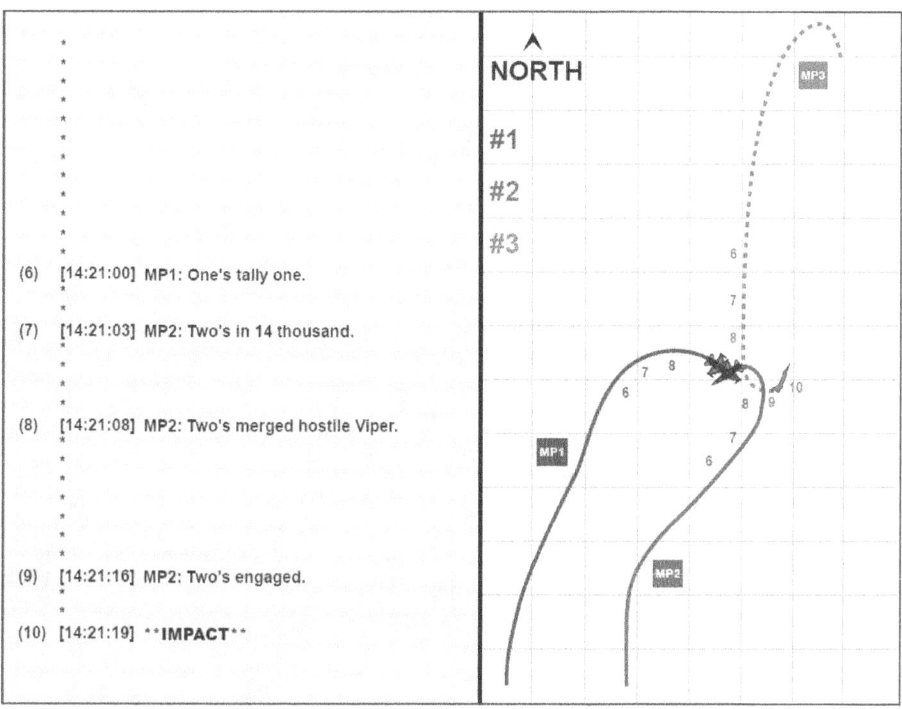

Figure 74: Mishap Engagement Illustration Second Half (Source: U.S. AIB report).

Due to MP1's misperception of turn direction as the EF, MP1 continued to point at and radar locked MP3 without continuing to crosscheck MP2's position. He assessed his range and clear avenue of fire and employed his first weapon at the adversary. He then assessed range and clear avenue of fire again, and took a second shot before looking for MP2. A total of eight seconds passed during this process, MP2 called "2's ENGAGED," which was three seconds prior to impact. At this point, the aircraft were between 2,000-2,500 feet apart with over 800 knots of closure. MP1 realized that MP2 made a left hand turn when he saw the belly of MP2's aircraft.

MP1 described their orientation as co-altitude, with zero line-of-sight, at a range of 1,000 feet from MP2, and closing on a collision course. MP1 attempted to react and maneuver out of the way by bunting the aircraft or pushing it down. However, he was unsuccessful and the two aircraft collided.

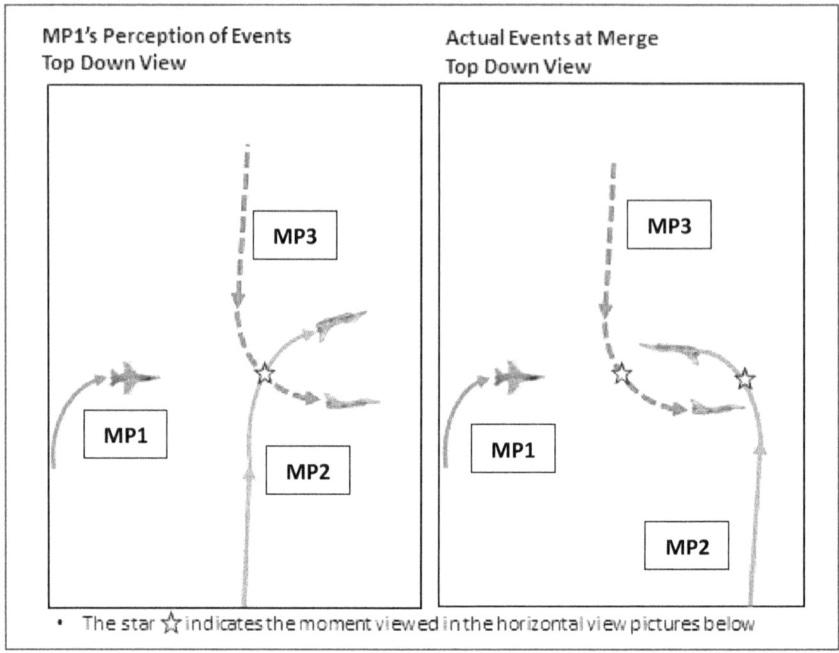

Figure 75: Merge View from MP1 (Source: U.S. AIB report).

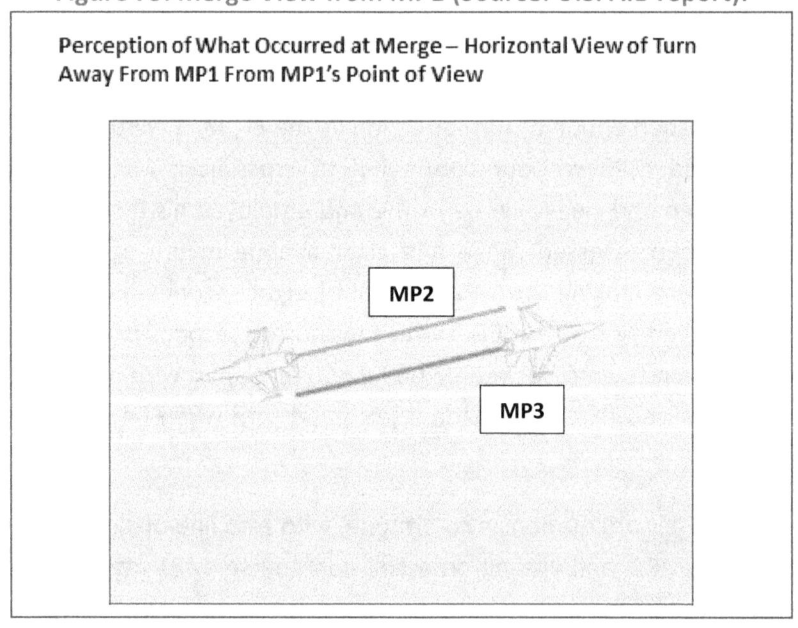

Figure 76: Horizontal View of MP1 (Source: U.S. AIB report).

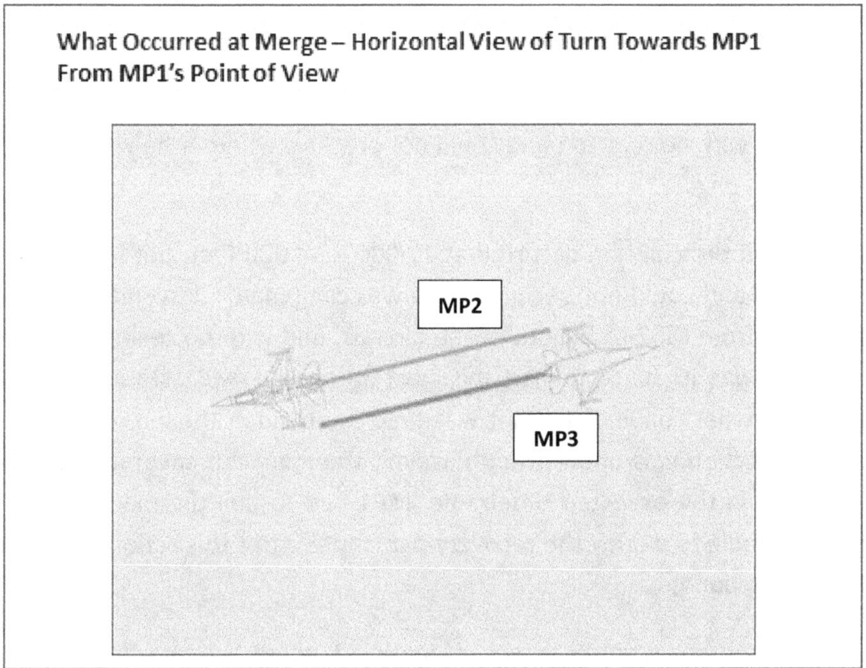

Figure 77: Horizontal View of MP1 #2 (Source: U.S. AIB report).

MP2 did not call "blind" during the engagement and focused exclusively on MP3 following his "2'S IN 14 THOUSAND" call. MP2 never saw MP1 prior to the collision and described the impact as passing through jet wash. After impact, MP3 initiated a "knock-it-off" call several times to end the fight. While recovering his aircraft, MP2 saw MP1's aircraft trailing white smoke and appeared as though it was skidding across the ground with a high angle of attack. MP2 realizing MA1 had departed controlled flight, called "BAILOUT, BAILOUT, BAILOUT" in an effort to convince or direct MP1 to eject from the aircraft.

MP2's right wingtip missile and five feet of his right wing sliced through MP1's right wing root, destroyed the flaperon, severed the fuel manifold and shattered the entire right horizontal tail. MP1's aircraft was uncontrollable. He described the scene in the cockpit as violent and was unsure if the aircraft was out of control. His vision, memory, and senses were foggy after impact. MP1 was unsure whether the fog was due to smoke in the cockpit or his reaction to the violent event. MP1 received warnings from most of his systems. He could barely see the bright warning lights on the glare shield and his vision outside the cockpit was only of light or dark fog in relation to being pointed at the sky or at the ground. MP1 described the fall of the aircraft as a leaf falling from a tree. MP1 attempted to add control inputs with no reaction and could not perceive whether he was getting any thrust from his engine.

MP1 estimated the collision occurred at 12,000 – 14,000 feet, but he was unsure of his altitude and could not decipher if he was climbing or descending. He heard the radio call from MP2 to bailout of the aircraft, and with no real understanding of where he was in space, pulled the ejection handle. MP1 stated that MP2's bailout call is what convinced him it was time to abandon the aircraft. The initial part of the ejection was uneventful; however, the man-seat separation sequence did not occur in the expected timeframe. MP1 had to pull the manual man-seat separation handle to deploy the recovery parachute. After this action, MP1 landed safely on the ground.

MP2's right wing was severed outside of Station 7, about five feet from the end of the wing. He joined with another F-16C, call sign Loco 3, another aircraft that was not part of the MF. They performed a controllability check over an unpopulated area before making the decision to return to Tulsa ANGB. It was determined during the controllability check that MA2 was controllable at approach and landing speeds, even though part of the right flaperon was missing

MP1 and MP2 collided approximately 15 NM from the north border of the Eureka MOA. At impact, MP1's aircraft was heading between 128 to 139 degrees True, 5 to 60 degrees right wing down and between 1 to 12 degrees nose up, 395 knots calibrated air speed (KCAS), or approximately 472 knots true airspeed (KTAS).

MP2's aircraft was heading approximately 222 degrees True, 78 degrees left wing down and 10 degrees nose down, 292 KCAS, or 369 KTAS. The right wing of MP2's aircraft outboard of station 7, impacted the right side of MP1's aircraft from the wing root to the horizontal tail on an axis of approximately 83 to 94 degrees right of the nose. The aft portion of the AIM-120 on station 9 of MP2's aircraft between the missile wings and fins hit the right wing root of MP1's aircraft. The Captive Training Missile (CATM)-9X on station 8 of MP2's aircraft remained intact except for the missile seeker. There were two marks on the right side of the engine duct of MP1's aircraft that appeared to be from an aft fin from the CATM-9X on station 8 of MP2's aircraft. The rest of the damage to MP1's aircraft, including the right horizontal tail, appears to be a result of the collision with the right wing of MP2's aircraft outboard of station 8.

MP2's station 8 missile rail and CATM-9X were relatively intact. They had separated from each other and were found close together, approximately 215 degrees True at 0.6 NM from the mid-air collision point. MP2's AIM-120 and station 9 missile rail were broken into numerous pieces and found in various areas of the main debris field.

Figure 78: MA1's and MA2's Mishap Sortie Configuration (Source: U.S. AIB report).

Station 1: LAU-129 missile launcher and CATM-120

Station 2: 16S301 pylon LAU-129 missile launcher and AMD pod

Station 3: Weapons pylon and MAU-12

Station 4: Empty

Station 5: Centerline pylon and MAU-12

Station 6: Empty

Station 7: Weapons pylon and MAU-12

Station 8: 16S301 pylon LAU-129 missile launcher and CATM-9M

Station 9: LAU-129 missile launcher and CATM-120

There was a gray paint smear on the right side of MP2's vertical tail that was probably from pieces of its wing and/or flaperon that separated on collision.

Human factors analysis

AFI 91-204, Safety Investigations and Reports, 24 September 2008, Attachment 5, contains the Department of Defense (DoD) Human Factors Analysis and Classification System which lists potential human factors that can play a role in aircraft mishaps.

1. Task Misprioritization

Task Misprioritization is a factor when the individual does not organize, based on accepted prioritization techniques, the tasks needed to manage the immediate situation. The following events represent misprioritization errors made during the engagement.

According to the report, MP2 was the SF during the entire mishap engagement. The SF's highest priorities are maintaining visual and flight path de-confliction. MP2 was not de-conflicting from MP1. From shortly before the merge until collision, MP2 focused exclusively on MP3 and did not maintain visual on MP1. MP2 mistakenly assumed that he was de-conflicted from MP1.

MP2 made his "ENGAGED" call too late. MP2 realized that he was targeted by MP3 and was more defensive than MP1 at the merge, which is the latest point he should have called "ENGAGED". MP2 called "ENGAGED" 8 seconds after the merge. This is a key mistake for if he would have obtained the engaged fighter role he would have been relieved of his primary responsibilities of flight path de-confliction and maintaining the visual and able to give his full attention to fighting his best BFM.

Conversely, MP1 realized that MP2 was more defensive and testified that he should have exercised his option to call "2 PRESS" and initiate the change to make MP2 the engaged fighter. MP1's failure to initiate this role exchange also represents a task misprioritization because the most defensive fighter should have priority over the flight lead to be the EF.

2. Cognitive Task Oversaturation

Cognitive Task Oversaturation is a factor when the quantity of information an individual must process exceeds their cognitive or mental resources in the amount of time available to process the information.

According to the report, MP2 showed signs of task oversaturation during the engagement. During the second engagement, he was behind normal pacing due to a reduced range of separation from the adversary. In a short period of time, MP2 was required to: 1) Turn to bracket the adversary, 2) defend against an attack from MP3, 3) maintain visual of MP1, 4) acquire TALLY of MP3 with the aid of HMCS, 5) set up for the merge, 6) make radio calls, 7) perform Anti-G Straining Maneuver, 8) keep sight of MP3 during hard turn, 9) fight his best 1 v 1 BFM, and 10) kill MP3. Based on MP2's relative inexperience, he may have been overwhelmed by having to make a number of nearly simultaneous decisions.

3. Channelized Attention

Channelized attention is a factor when the individual is focusing all conscious attention on a limited number of environmental cues to the exclusion of others of a subjectively equal or higher or more immediate priority, leading to an unsafe situation (Tab BB-34). Channelized attention may be described as a tight focus of attention that leads to the exclusion of comprehensive situational information.

According to the report, the following event represents a channelized attention error made during the engagement. From a point shortly before the merge until impact, MP2 channelized his attention on killing MP3. He fully understood there had been no role exchange and he was still the SF. MP2 failed to maintain visual and flight path de-confliction with MP1 due to his exclusive focus on MP3.

4. Communicating Critical Information

Communicating critical information is a factor when known critical information was not provided to appropriate individuals in an accurate or timely manner.

According to the report, the following errors in Communicating Critical Information occurred during the engagement:

MP2 made an "engaged" call that MP1 did not hear. Additionally, this call was not made in a timely manner, and as a result, MP1 did not have time to respond even if he did hear it.

MP2 never called "blind" when he lost visual of MP1. MP2 had visual on MP1 until shortly before he merged with MP3. MP2 never had visual on MP1 again until after the collision and never made a "blind" call that would be typically expected within approximately two seconds of losing visual on the engaged fighter.

5. Misperception of Operational Conditions

Misperception of Operational Conditions is a factor when an individual misperceives or misjudges altitude, separation, speed, closure rate, road/sea conditions, aircraft/vehicle location within the performance envelope or other operational conditions and this leads to an unsafe situation.

According to the report, MP1 continued as the EF when MP2 merged with MP3 and continued to pursue MP3 during

MP2's left turn. MP1 believed that MP2 turned right at the merge.

MP2 turning right at the merge would have de-conflicted MP1 and MP2's flight path to allow MP1 to engage MP3. The misperceived turn resulted in MP2 belly-up, blind, and quickly on a collision course without MP1s awareness.

19 F-16CJ Pilot inadvertently engine shutdown

Figure 79: F-16CJ (Source: U.S. AIB report).

The United States Air Force Aircraft Accident Investigation Board (AIB) describes in their report that:

On 2 June 2016 at 13:00 local time an F-16CJ was destroyed by ground impact after the Mishap Pilot (MP) ejected south of Peterson Air Force Base (AFB), CO. The MP sustained a minor injury and no other personnel were injured. The Mishap Aircraft (MA) Tail Number 92-3890 and the MP are assigned to the 57th Wing, United States Air Force Air Demonstration Squadron (USAFADS), Nellis AFB, NV. The MA, was destroyed.

The mishap occurred as part of a six F-16 aircraft, USAFADS flyby and airshow combination for a United States Air Force Academy graduation ceremony,

Colorado Springs, CO. The mission was uneventful until the MA entered the Peterson AFB traffic pattern in preparation for landing.

When the MA was positioned on downwind (parallel to, and opposing the active landing runway), the highly experienced MP inadvertently placed the throttle to cutoff position (engine shutdown). This normally requires both (a) an actuation of the throttle cutoff release trigger switch (throttle trigger), which then permits (b) full throttle grip rotation outboard -- enabling the throttle to be retarded aft (pulled backwards), past the cutoff stop. Below the minimum altitude/airspeed required for either an engine restart or flame-out landing, the MP was forced to eject over a grass field in El Paso County, CO.

The throttle trigger must be physically actuated (depressed, squeezed, pulled) to overcome the spring-force in its un-actuated position. Analysis by Air Force Research Laboratory/Materials Integrity Branch identified intermittent sticking/binding of the MA throttle trigger, causing the throttle trigger to remain in the retracted/stuck position after actuation. The throttle trigger bushing was examined and determined to be damaged and worn due to throttle trigger clevis pin misalignment, along with metallic-particle debris contamination -- both increasing the chance of throttle trigger sticking/binding. In addition, lubricant to the throttle trigger assembly was identified (inconsistent with maintenance technical orders), which exacerbated the debris contamination condition.

Accident cause

The Accident Investigation Board President found by a preponderance of the evidence the cause of this mishap was a throttle trigger actuation and subsequent malfunction (throttle trigger stuck in retracted position) followed by the MP's inadvertent full-rotation of the throttle grip while retarding the throttle aft to cutoff position. Substantially contributing factors include maintenance Technical Orders that lack sufficient detail to consistently identify either a throttle trigger clevis pin misalignment or a sticking/binding throttle trigger.

Accident summary

The MF was delayed on the ground approximately 20 to 25 minutes after engine start due to longer than- expected graduation proceedings. Since the MF was still on the ground, the amount of fuel consumed was negligible.

Flyby timing was coordinated with Pilot 7, who was the safety observer and located near on a hill near the stadium. After the flyby, the airshow proceeded without incident. The terrain around the show site was described as "difficult" with sloping terrain.

The MF flew IAW with USAFADS standard procedure for a visual flight rules landing pattern with all six aircraft in close formation flying over the runway of intended landing at a low altitude before individually and sequentially turning 180 degrees and climbing to parallel the runway on the downwind leg and prepare the aircraft for landing.

The MP was the last to ascend and turn onto the downwind leg (parallel to and opposing the landing runway, where the pilot typically configures the aircraft for landing) with 1,000 to 1,100 pounds of fuel remaining, 3,000 feet behind Pilot 5. Thunderbird procedure on downwind includes turning off the display smoke when abeam the approach end of the runway.

The Data Acquisition System (DAS) recorded the initial throttle movement to the cutoff position. The throttle had been previously positioned at the idle position (lowest selectable power setting above engine cutoff) for approximately 15 seconds prior to the initial movement to cutoff position.

The MP stated, "I remember pulling my hand back to get to slow down" and then after that movement "I remember feeling something that didn't feel right".

However, the MP did not recall if he had actuated the throttle trigger or rotated the throttle grip. To place the throttle to the cutoff position, the pilot must normally squeeze the throttle trigger to allow the throttle grip to fully rotate outboard before it can be pulled aft over the idle cutoff stop.

The MP stated that the throttle trigger is "obviously a switch that is very important and is one that we, again, from day one are trained to avoid via hand placement and being deliberate".

 The MA was established at 222 knots, 2,045 feet AGL, abeam the approach end of Runway 35R when the throttle was first placed to the cutoff position.

Placing the throttle to cutoff cuts ignition and fuel flow, causing the engine to shutdown.

At the initial placement of the throttle to the cutoff position (1st Cutoff), the MA was at too low an energy state (a combination of airspeed and altitude) for engine restart prior to ground impact.

If an aircraft is at an altitude between 4,000 and 10,000 feet AGL (MP was at approximately 2000 AGL), there is probably time for one airstart prior to minimum recommended ejection altitude. Additionally, at this first movement of the throttle to cutoff, the MA was already at too low an energy state to glide to the runway. Due to RPM decreasing below idle, the MP exercised efforts to restart the engine. IAW airstart procedures, he intentionally placed the throttle to cutoff (2nd Cutoff).

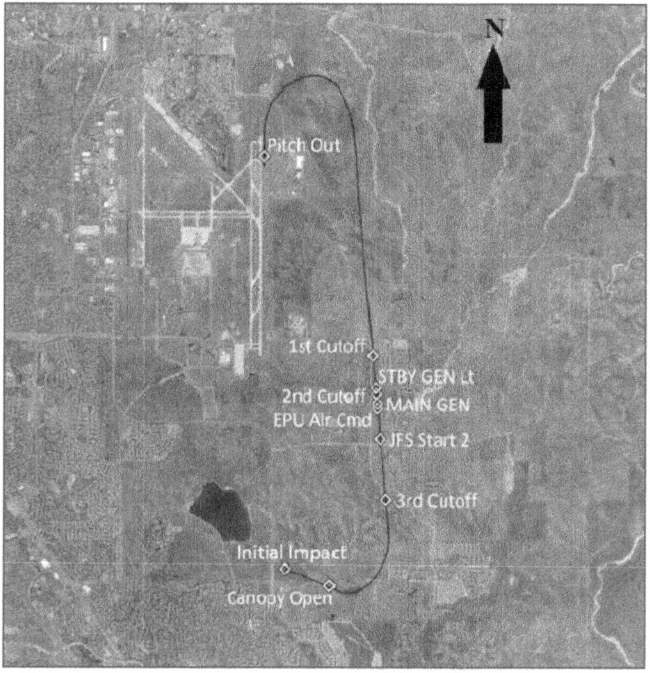

Figure 80: MAGround Track (Source: U.S. AIB report).

To restart a failed engine (Pratt & Whitney 229) in flight, the throttle must be placed to cutoff position, then placed midrange, followed by actuation of the Jet Fuel Starter (JFS).

While executing those Critical Action Procedures (CAPs), the MP recalled "there was no hang ups on the hump [idle cutoff stop] or anything like that" in reference to moving the throttle to the cutoff position the first time, and "I don't remember if there was anything weird about the lever [throttle trigger]" in reference to trigger switch actuation, though admitting that the throttle trigger was not the focus of his attention at the time.

The MP made a radio call over the interflight frequency stating he had a problem.

Figure 81: MA post impact (Source: U.S. AIB report).

Pilot 5 had started the final turn and visually acquired the MA, assessing that the MA appeared slower and lower than usual.

The Emergency Power Unit (EPU) had automatically activated and spun up to the operating range, providing the MA with the electrical power and hydraulic pressure needed to operate its flight controls.

The MP activated the JFS by placing the JFS switch to the START 2 position, providing additional airflow to increase RPM and assist in the airstart.

The MP made a radio call on Peterson AFB Tower's radio frequency describing that the engine had cycled off and on, and that he was steering it away from houses and "getting out". Pilot 1 then immediately directed Pilot 4 to go-around, which meant Pilot 4 would discontinue his landing approach.

The MP moved the throttle slightly above idle. The MP recalled perceiving the "hump" that indicates movement from cutoff position to idle when he moved the throttle forward. Checking the engine Revolutions Per Minute (RPM) gauge, the MP saw the "RPM gauge decreasing as if it's failing," and additionally perceived reduced engine noise.

The MP states multiple times that he was initially confused about whether or not he had truly pulled the throttle to the cutoff position. The throttle in the MA was placed in and out of cutoff a third time (3rd cutoff), as the MP perceived the airstart was not progressing as he'd hoped.

The MP began a turn to the right, anticipating that if the engine restarted, he might "get just enough thrust to make it to the runway".

The MP continued his turn to avoid houses. The MP ejected at an altitude of 270 feet AGL and airspeed of 149 knots.

The MP deliberately chose to delay ejection below the minimum recommended ejection altitude specified in the Dash 1.

The MP stated that, at first, he hoped to get the engine restarted quickly even though his airspeed and altitude were below the minimum required for an airstart. Once the MP realized a quick restart would not occur, he stayed with the MA to maneuver it to an open field. Both Pilot 4 and Pilot 5 observed the MP ejection, and Pilot 5 made a radio call over the interflight frequency that he observed the MP was under a good (successful) parachute. Pilot 4 established the airborne on scene command for the pending search and rescue effort.

Impact

The MA impacted the ground at 13:00 in an open grassy field, off-base. The MA impacted at relatively wings level, slightly nose high, and came to rest 1,240 feet from initial impact on a slight uphill slope. The MP's parachute was found 1,450 feet southeast from the initial impact point. The impact area was two miles south of Runway 35R at Peterson AFB, and just to the north of a residential area.

Figure 82: MA Crash Site Looking Northwest (Source: U.S. AIB report).

Figure 83: MA Crash (Source: U.S. AIB report).

Human factors analysis

AFI 91-204, Safety Investigations and Reports, 12 February 2014, Attachment 6, contains the Department of Defense (DoD) Human Factors Analysis and Classification System (HFACS) which lists potential human factors that can play a role in aircraft mishaps.

The human factors listed below are those that were determined to be relevant to the determination of cause or substantially contributing factors to the mishap.

1. Inadvertent Operation

A factor when an individual's movements inadvertently activate or deactivate equipment, controls or switches when there is no intent to operate the control or device. This action may be noticed or unnoticed by the individual.

According to the report, there was inadvertent operation when the MP applied outboard rotation to the throttle grip with aft-pressure while the throttle was in the idle position, moving the throttle to the cutoff position.

In order to move the throttle aft to cutoff position, first the throttle cutoff trigger must be actuated permitting full outboard rotation applied to the throttle grip. There are no known reported incidences of the F-16 throttle being placed to cutoff position without full throttle grip rotation outboard.

2. Procedural Guidance/Publications

Procedural Guidance/Publications is a factor when written direction, checklists, graphic depictions, tables, charts or other published guidance is inadequate, misleading, or inappropriate and this creates an unsafe situation.

According to the report, TOs lack sufficient detail to consistently identify either a throttle trigger clevis pin misalignment or a sticking/binding throttle trigger.

20 C17 Stall during Airshow

Figure 84: C-17A (Source: U.S. AIB report).

The United States Air Force Aircraft Accident Investigation Board (AIB) describes in their report that:

On 28 July 2010, at approximately 1822 hours local time (L), a C-17A, Tail Number 00-0173, executed a takeoff from Runway 06 to practice maneuvers for the upcoming 31 Jul 10 Arctic Thunder Airshow at Joint Base Elmendorf-Richardson (JBER). After the initial climbout and left turn, the mishap pilot executed an aggressive right turn. As the aircraft banked, the stall warning system activated to alert the crew of an impending stall. Instead of implementing stall recovery procedures, the pilot continued the turn as planned, and the aircraft entered a stall from which recovery was not possible. Although the pilot eventually attempted to recover the aircraft, he employed incorrect procedures, and there was not sufficient altitude to regain controlled flight.

The aircraft impacted wooded terrain northwest of the airfield, damaged a portion of the Alaskan Railroad, and was destroyed.

The mishap aircraft was assigned to the 3rd Wing based at Joint Base Elmendorf-Richardson, Alaska. The mishap crew was an integrated crew with members from both the 249th and 517th Airlift Squadrons. The mishap crew consisted of the mishap pilot, the mishap copilot, the mishap safety observer and the mishap loadmaster. All four aircrew members died instantly. There were no civilian casualties.

Accident cause

The board president found clear and convincing evidence that the cause of the mishap was pilot error. The mishap pilot violated regulatory provisions and multiple flight manual procedures, placing the aircraft outside established flight parameters at an attitude and altitude where recovery was not possible. Furthermore, the mishap copilot and mishap safety observer did not realize the developing dangerous situation and failed to make appropriate inputs. In addition to multiple procedural errors, the board president found sufficient evidence that the crew on the flight deck ignored cautions and warnings and failed to respond to various challenge and reply items.

The board also found channelized attention, overconfidence, expectancy, misplaced motivation, procedural guidance, and program oversight substantially contributed to the mishap.

Accident summary

Mission

The mishap sortie (MS) was a practice flight for the JBER Arctic Thunder Airshow, scheduled for the weekend of 31 July 2010. It was planned and briefed as an aerial demonstration proficiency and currency flight, involving one C-17A aircraft, aerial demonstration flights typically consists of a single aircraft, which conducts a series of practice demonstration maneuvers, defined by Air Force Instruction (AFI) 11-246, Vol. 6, as "profiles".

For this particular flight, the mishap crew (MC) planned to fly a known as the 12-minute profile.

The relevant components of Profile 3 as related to this mishap were: maximum performance climb to 1,500 feet AGL, 80/260-degree reversal turn, and the 500-foot AGL highspeed pass.

The maximum performance climb requires the pilot to pitch the aircraft nose upward to achieve minimum climbout speed, defined as Vmco.

Note: Vmco is the speed required to clear an obstacle if the C-17 only has three of the four engines operating. This speed demonstrates the climb-capability of the aircraft.

After climbout, the aircraft utilizes an 80/260-degree reversal turn to transition the aircraft from the original outbound direction in order to align with the runway and perform a high-speed pass. The demonstration pilot will perform the reversal turn in three segments.

First, an 80-degree turn away from the initial heading establishes an outbound leg.

Second, the aircraft flies to a safe distance from the runway.

Third, a 260-degree reversal turn towards the runway.

The 500-foot AGL high-speed pass is accomplished by descending from 1,500 feet to 500 feet AGL during the 80/260-degree reversal turn. Upon reaching 500 feet, the aircraft accelerates to 250 kts, flying past the spectators at "show center" (the center of the viewing area; represented by the star in the diagram.

C-17 Aircrew Positions

The MP was the aircraft commander, and the pilot flying (PF) during the flight. He was in the left front seat during the MS. The MCP, also known as the pilot monitoring (PM), was in the right front seat. The MSO was in the right additional crew member (RACM) seat, and had a view of most of the flight deck displays and switches. The MLM was seated in the right-rear area of the cargo compartment.

Weather Observation Flight

Thirty minutes prior to the mishap sortie, the MC flew the MA in the local area to observe the weather. The purpose of this flight was to determine if the weather was acceptable for their demonstration practice. During the nine-minute flight, the MC evaluated winds and observed flight conditions around the airfield. The MA flew normally and the weather was within limits.

Aerial Demonstration Practice Flight (Mishap Sortie)

After the weather observation flight, the MC landed and waited approximately 30 minutes to begin their aerial demonstration practice. Once they received clearance, the MP aligned the aircraft on the runway and released brakes.

During the takeoff sequence, the MP "rotated" (raised the nose of the aircraft) and attained a maximum pitch angle of 40 degrees nose-high. The target climbout airspeed was 133 kts. The highest airspeed attained during the climbout was 107 kts.

As the aircraft passed 800 feet AGL, the MP initiated the first segment of the 80/260-degree reversal turn.

He turned the aircraft left at 57 degrees of bank to a heading of 340 degrees and leveled-off at 852 feet AGL. After completing the turn, the MCP initiated flap retraction when the airspeed reached 151 kts. The minimum flap retraction speed (Vmfr) was 150 kts. The MP continued outbound for seven seconds as the flaps completed retraction.

The MP turned right at an initial bank angle of 53 degrees to begin the third segment of the 80/260-degree reversal turn.

The MCP initiated slat retraction when the airspeed reached 188 kts. The minimum slat retraction speed (Vmsr) was 193 kts. Five seconds into the right turn, the stall warning system activated. At this time, the MA's configuration was full right rudder, the control stick aft, and slats retracting. The airspeed was 199 kts, 6 kts below stall airspeed.

When the stall warning occurred, the MCP responded "acknowledged crew . . .temperature, altitude lookin' good."

The MP continued the turn using full right rudder, which increased the MA's bank angle to 62 degrees. The maximum allowable bank angle for the C-17 is 60 degrees. The MP also continued to apply control stick pressure, which increased the force of gravity on the aircraft to a factor of 2.4.

Approximately 62 seconds into the mishap sortie, the MA stalled. By this time, the deep stall protection system (the Angle of Attack Limiter System (ALS)) was active, but was overcome by the MP's rapid and aggressive maneuvers.

Within seconds, the MA's bank angle increased to a maximum of 82 degrees. The aircraft began to descend and ultimately reached a descent rate of 9,000 feet per minute, as airspeed decayed to 184 kts.

One-and-a-half seconds into the stall, several events occurred simultaneously: the MCP said "not so tight, brother"; the MSO said "watch your bank" three times; and the MP moved the control stick full left, applied left rudder, but maintained constant control stick pressure.

Five seconds prior to impact, the slats fully retracted. Approximately two seconds prior to impact, the MP was able to initiate a left roll of the aircraft, however, the roll rate was minimal due to the stall. The stall protection system remained active until impact.

Impact

The MA impacted wooded terrain northwest of the airfield at 63.6 degrees of right bank, 16.9 degrees nose-low at 184 kts on 28 July 2010 at 1822L. The MA exploded, burned for approximately 36 hours and was destroyed.

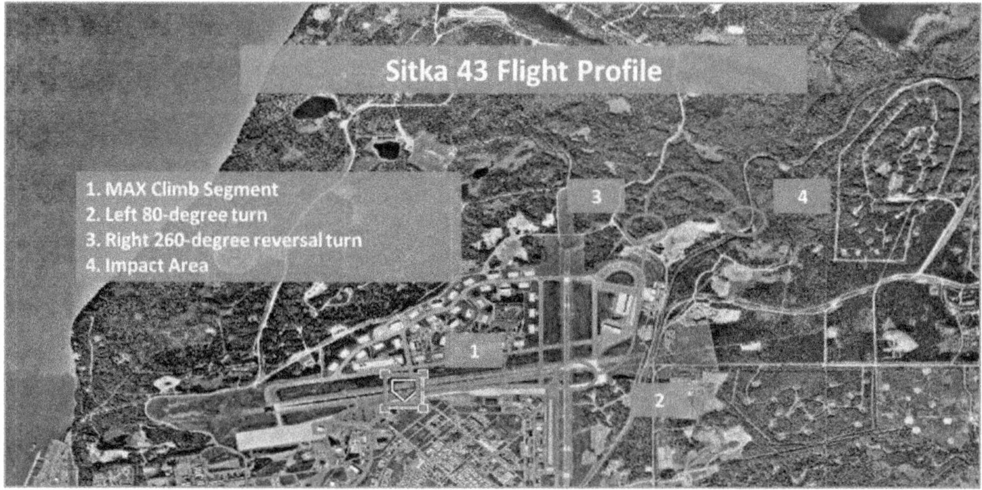

Figure 85: C-17A Flight Profile (Source: 1U.S. AIB report).

Human factors analysis

Human Factors contributing to this mishap were evaluated using the Department of Defense (DoD) Human Factors Analysis and Classification System (DoD-HFACS).

The Board reviewed a substantial amount of evidence during its proceedings to include, but not limited to, cockpit voice recorder transcripts, flight data recorder information, video recordings, and witness interviews. Numerous human factors were relevant to the mishap, and the MC's actions during the mishap sortie were highly uncharacteristic of their experience level and reputation.

1. Procedural Error.

Procedural Error is a factor when a procedure is accomplished in the wrong sequence or using the wrong technique or when the wrong control or switch is used. This also captures errors in navigation, calculation or operation of automated systems.

According to the report, the MP committed two procedural errors during the mishap sortie. He replaced aerial demonstration procedures with his own techniques; and failed to implement proper stall recovery procedures.

(A) Incorrect Combination of Aerial Demonstration Techniques (Energy Management).

The basic concept of energy management (i.e., maintaining sufficient speed and altitude for a specific aircraft configuration in order to sustain controlled flight) is paramount.

Without proper energy management, an aircraft can enter a low energy state and depart controlled flight.

The MP committed pilot error by executing the demonstration profile using the following techniques:

- Attempted 60-degree bank turns, instead of the prescribed 45 degrees.
- A climbout to approximately 850 feet AGL instead of the AFI-directed altitude of 1,500 feet AGL.
- A climbout pitch angle of 40 degrees, instead of climbing out at a minimum climbout speed.
- Maintained full right rudder and control stick pressure to facilitate the 80/260 reversal turn.

These actions resulted in a low energy state that was insufficient to sustain controlled flight. Depending on conditions, these techniques, in and of themselves, may not be unsafe. However, when combined, they will diminish flight safety margins. The stated purpose of the C-17 Aerial Demonstration program is to demonstrate aircraft capabilities, not to achieve maximum performance of the aircraft ("Max Perform").

When flown IAW AFI 11-246, the profile results in an energy state sufficient to sustain safe flight. The MP's execution of Profile 3 "max performed" the aircraft at the threshold of a stall. Flying at the threshold of a stall is the very definition of a low energy state.

The MP planned an aggressive and unsafe profile based on 60-degree bank turns in an effort to keep the aircraft as close to the show center as possible.

This plan forced him to minimize his timing on his outbound segments, and left him no alternative but to use 60 degrees of bank, fly through stall warnings, maintain control stick pressure, and use full rudder, in order not to cross the extended show centerline.

During the mishap sortie, the MP used 40 degrees of pitch angle on initial takeoff without considering the minimum climbout speed (Vmco). He leveled-off at approximately 850 feet AGL, 26 kts below Vmco. This low altitude and airspeed led to an initially low energy state.

Although the MA accelerated during the first and second segments of the 80/260-degree reversal turn, the MA's overall energy state remained low. The configuration change, coupled with 60 degrees of bank, full right rudder and control stick pressure, further decreased the energy state, which led to the departure from controlled flight.

(B) MP Failed To Employ Proper Stall Recovery Procedure.

The C-17 stall recovery procedure is:

1) apply forward stick pressure;
2) apply maximum available thrust; and
3) return to or maintain a level flight attitude. Large rudder inputs should be avoided.

Despite numerous stall warnings during the mishap sortie, the MP continued to aggressively execute the 260-degree reversal turn. The MP failed to employ proper stall recovery procedures. Even when the MA stalled, the MP maintained control stick pressure, which did not sufficiently reduce the angle of attack to recover controlled flight. As a result, the MA remained in a stall until impact.

2. Overaggressive

Overaggressive is a factor when an individual or crew is excessive in the manner in which they conduct a mission.

According to the report, the MC planned, briefed, and flew the mishap sortie Air Show Demonstration Profile with bank angles, altitudes, timing, and use of rudder beyond the procedures in AFI 11-246.

Once certified as a demonstration pilot, the MP manipulated the standard profile to enhance the airshow performance. He planned and regularly flew 60 degrees of bank for the 80/260-degree maneuver with full rudder to minimize the turn radius and displacement from crowd.

During his upgrade training, an instructor counseled him for being "aggressive" to keep the turns "tighter to the runway". The MP "was also very intent on crisp turns, roll in, roll out efficiently . . . providing a good show to the spectators".

In previous performances, the MP continued to execute his 260-degree reversal turn despite lengthy stall warnings.

On the day of the mishap sortie, the MP's techniques diminished flight safety margins, and caused the aircraft to stall. Specifically, he planned for an initial climbout altitude range of 1,000 to 1,500 feet AGL at 35 to 40-degree nose high attitude, while disregarding minimum climbout speed. During climbout, the MP achieved a 40-degree nose-high attitude, and flew 26 kts below a safe climbout speed. An average nose-high attitude for the initial climbout is 25-35 degrees. Executing maneuvers below the minimum climbout speed is a safety-of-flight issue, and is not advised.

Additionally, the MP disregarded the stall warning when it activated during the 260-degree reversal turn. It remained active until impact; a total of 12 seconds.

The MP's overaggressive actions also caused the mishap.

3. Caution/Warning – Ignored and Challenge and Reply.

Caution/Warning – Ignored is a factor when a caution or warning is perceived and understood by the individual but is ignored by the individual leading to an unsafe situation.

According to the report, Challenge and reply is a factor when communications did not include supportive feedback or acknowledgement to ensure that personnel correctly understood announcements or directives.

As the lead C-17 aerial demonstration pilot for JBER, the MP routinely instructed and planned to ignore stall warnings during aerial demonstrations. Five seconds into 260-degree reversal turn, the stall warning system activated. In response, the MCP said "Acknowledged Crew . . . Temperature, altitude lookin' good." Although the warnings continued, the MP neither replied nor adjusted his control inputs, and continued the turn. The MP made no attempt to implement stall recovery procedures, and neither MCP nor MSO directed recovery until the MA stalled.

The MP also routinely instructed demonstration co-pilots to retract flaps and slats "on speed" automatically, without a challenge or reply. During this mishap sortie, the MCP automatically retracted flaps and slats, as trained. This resulted in the MCP retracting the slats five kts below Vmsr. There is no indication that the MP or MSO understood the configuration of the MA.

Automatically configuring the aircraft does not provide supportive feedback or acknowledgement to ensure situational awareness.

4. Channelized Attention

Channelized Attention is a factor when the individual is focusing all conscious attention on a limited number of environmental cues to the exclusion of others of a subjectively equal or higher or more immediate priority, leading to an unsafe situation. May be described as a tight focus of attention that leads to the exclusion of comprehensive situational information.

According to the report, the MP displayed two instances of channelized attention. First, the MP continued to aggressively turn the MA in a low energy state, while ignoring the stall warning system. The MP intended to fly crisp, tight, aggressive maneuvers, in an attempt to keep the aircraft close to show center.

Second, when the stall occurred, the MP moved the control stick full left. However, the MP maintained control stick pressure and applied left rudder. Maintaining these control inputs did not sufficiently reduce the angle of attack to recover controlled flight. As a result, the MA remained in a stall until impact.

5. Overconfidence

Overconfidence is a factor when the individual overvalues or overestimates personal capability, the capability of others or the capability of aircraft/vehicles or equipment and this creates an unsafe situation.

According to the report, during simulator training, the MP taught stall warnings were an "anomaly." The warnings were considered inaccurate and transitory due to aggressive aerial demonstration maneuvers. The MP "was not concerned" about stalling in the profile. The MP also believed these warnings would cease at completion of the turns and not adversely affect the aircraft.

He flew numerous aerial demonstrations in the aircraft with the stall warnings active and without incident. The MP's overconfidence in both his abilities and the C-17 capabilities led to the stall.

6. Misplaced Motivation

Misplaced Motivation is a factor when an individual or unit replaces the primary goal of a mission with a personal goal.

According to the report, the MP wanted to "put on a good airshow," keeping his turns crisp, tight, and aggressive. The MP planned a compressed profile based on timing and 60-degree bank turns. The MP utilized unsafe techniques in an effort to keep the aircraft as close to the airfield as possible, impress the crowd, and improve the airshow.

As previously stated, the purpose of the C-17 Aerial Demonstration program is to demonstrate aircraft capabilities, not to max perform the aircraft. The MP's enthusiasm "to put on a good show" for the spectators benefit led him to plan an aggressive and unsafe profile.

7. Expectancy

Expectancy is a factor when the individual expects to perceive a certain reality and those expectations are strong enough to create a false perception of the expectation.

According to the report, the MC consistently planned, practiced and flew the profile, with the stall warnings activated during the 260-degree maneuver. Additionally, the MP taught aerial demonstration pilots that the stall warning was an anomaly or otherwise transient. He believed these warnings would cease at some point during the maneuver and not adversely affect the aircraft.

When the MC experienced the same warnings during the mishap sortie, they responded as trained. The MC falsely perceived the aircraft would not stall.

8. Procedural Guidance/Publications

Procedural Guidance/Publications is a factor when written direction, checklists, graphic depictions, tables, charts or other published guidance is inadequate, misleading or inappropriate and this creates an unsafe situation.

According to the report, Air Force Policy Directive (AFPD) 11-2, Aircraft Rules and Procedures, para. 1 states:

"The Air Force establishes rules and procedures that meet global interoperability requirements for the full range of aircraft operations. Adherence to prescribed rules and procedures is mandatory for all personnel involved in aircraft AFI 11-246, Vol. 6, Chp. 3, describes the Air Show Demonstration profiles for the C-17 aircraft."

The AFI states in the General Instructions:

"Aircrews from all MAJCOMS will adhere to the flying procedures in Profiles 1 through 4. Profiles 1, 2 and 3 are demonstrations of Aircraft High Performance Maneuvering."

In or around April 2008, the MP underwent aerial demonstration upgrade training and was recommended as a safety observer. The MP's initial instructor taught crews "to start lowering the nose at 1000 feet while continuing to climb to 1500 feet AGL" on the initial take-off. Additionally, he taught to make the initial 80-degree turn at a speed 15 kts above flap retract speed. He taught that the use of rudder was a technique, but "always taught that there was no requirement for use of the rudder on this airplane." The instructor stressed AFI 11-246, Vol. 6. Chp. 3 is "procedure," not technique.

In or around December 2008, the MP completed upgrade training as a demonstration pilot. During this training, his upgrade instructor emphasized adherence to AFI 11-246. He also taught MP to "level off at 1500 feet" on the initial climbout; the use of a longer outbound segment allows for greater airspeed and displacement from the runway; the use of bank angles and rudder to avoid overshooting the "extended runway centerline" for safety reasons. Once certified as a demonstration pilot, the MP manipulated the standard profile to enhance the airshow performances. Specifically, he planned for an initial climbout altitude range of 1,000 to 1,500 feet AGL at 35 to 40 degree nose high attitude, while disregarding minimum climbout speed. He also planned and regularly flew 60 degrees of bank for the 80/260-degree maneuver with full rudder to minimize the turn radius and displacement from crowd.

Although the first paragraph on page 3 in AFI 11-246, Vol. 6, Chp. 3 states, "The procedures in these profiles are general guidelines", it also directs that "Aircrews will not deviate from the mission plan except for safety considerations."

The MP's aerial demonstration technique violated the intent of the AFI. They are inappropriate and created an unsafe situation.

9. Program Oversight/Program Management

Program Oversight/Program Management is a factor when programs are implemented without sufficient support, oversight or planning and this leads to an unsafe situation.

According to the report, the MP had a reputation in both squadrons of being an extremely precise and knowledgeable aviator. His extensive experience as a simulator instructor and his 3,251 total C-17 hours garnered him the utmost respect from squadron leadership and his peers.

They also held his instructor abilities in the highest of esteem. Because he was an accomplished aviator, leadership allowed him to operate independently with little or no oversight. Prior to the mishap, 3 OG Commander took a vested interest in the C-17 aerial demonstration program for the upcoming airshow. He was scheduled to fly onboard the MA in order to evaluate the performance of the MC. However, due to a last minute F-22A fighter aircraft emergency, he could not attend the scheduled flight. 176 OG Commander also intended to observe demonstration flights, but was TDY during the times they practiced. From the time of the MP's certification as a demonstration pilot to this mishap, his supervisors assumed he was within regulatory compliance, and did not inquire or review the MP's techniques or performances. Without checks and balances, the MP's aerial demonstration techniques evolved into an unsafe program.

21 F-35A uncontained engine fire during engine start

Figure 86: F-35A (Source: U.S. AIB report).

The United States Air Force Aircraft Accident Investigation Board (AIB) describes in their report that:

On 23 September 2016, at approximately 0852 hours local time, the Mishap Aircraft (MA), an F-35A, tail number 12-5052, assigned to the 61st Fighter Squadron, 56th Fighter Wing, Luke Air Force Base (AFB), AZ, but temporarily stationed at Mountain Home AFB, ID, experienced an uncontained engine fire during engine start. The MA aborted the start and the Mishap Pilot (MP) safely egressed the still burning aircraft. Maintenance crew members responded and extinguished the fire. The aft (rear) two thirds of the MA sustained significant fire damage.

Accident cause

The AIB concluded:

That the cause of the mishap was the tailwind present during engine start. The tailwind forced hot air into the inlet of the Integrated Power Pack, which led to a series of events resulting in insufficient torque applied to the MA engine during start, and thus the engine rotation speed slowed. At the same time, fuel continued to be supplied to the engine at an increasing rate which enabled an uncontained engine fire. The fire came out the engine exhaust and was carried along the outer surfaces of the MA by the tailwind, causing significant damage. The fire was extinguished approximately twenty seconds after the initial visual indications of a fire.

Accident summary

The AIB explain that the MP initiated an aircraft engine start on the parking ramp by placing the engine switch on the MA to RUN.

Twenty four seconds later, hot gas was ingested into the Integrated Power Pack (IPP) inlet causing a corresponding increase in the IPP Exhaust Gas Temperature (EGT). An IPP FAIL Integrated Caution, Advisory, Warning (ICAW) occurred 19 seconds later as the IPP performed an auto shutdown due to an EGT over-temp. The IPP FAIL ICAW was followed four seconds later by a FIRE GEAR ICAW, which indicated fire detection sensors located in the main landing gear wheel wells detected fire.

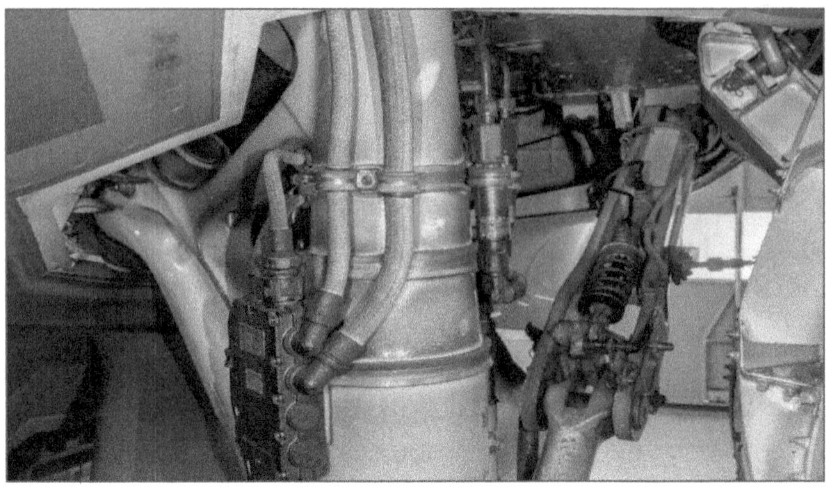

Figure 87: Right Side Landing Gear (Source: U.S. AIB report).

During these events, several aircraft maintenance members witnessed flames come out of the engine exhaust, and then surround the aircraft moving toward the front of the MA. The Mishap Crew Chief informed the MP of the fire. The MP accomplished most of the EGRESS procedures and safely evacuated the scene while maintenance crew members used a fire bottle (large fire extinguisher) to extinguish the fire. The fire burned for approximately 20 seconds. The fire damaged the aft two thirds of the MA's middle fuselage area before it was extinguished.

The report describes the Integrated Power Pack (IPP) as:

The IPP is a mechanical system with a conventional auxiliary power unit and an emergency power unit combined. The IPP operates in two primary modes: burn mode (when the IPP is powering itself using its own combustion motor) and bleed mode (when the IPP is powered via bleed air from a running aircraft engine). During burn mode, air is drawn into the IPP motor through the IPP inlet and, after combustion, the air is pushed out through the IPP exhaust duct.

The IPP is a major component for a normal F-35A aircraft ground engine start. The IPP is started and runs in burn mode for a few minutes before the pilot initiates aircraft engine start by moving the engine switch in the cockpit to RUN. The IPP then provides electrical power to the Integrated Converter/Controllers (ICCs), which in turn provide and regulate electrical power to the Engine Starter/Generator (ES/G). The ES/G converts the electrical power into mechanical power which is transferred to a shaft that rotates the aircraft engine during engine start.

Once the aircraft engine reaches a self-sustaining rotation speed, the start sequence through the ES/G, ICCs, and the IPP is complete and the IPP transfers to bleed mode.

To understand the accident the AIB explain in detail the Power and Thermal Management System (PTMS), it monitors the entire start sequence. The PTMS monitors IPP inlet temperature because if the temperature rises, indicating hot-gas ingestion, the IPP motor becomes less efficient and turns at a slower speed. The PTMS recognizes this and takes action to return the IPP to full speed. The actions taken include reducing the electrical output to the Integrated Converter Controllers (ICCs) (this reduces the load on the IPP) and increasing fuel flow to the IPP motor. These actions, known as hot-gas ingestion logic, continue until either the condition is cleared or an unsafe system operation is reached, which would then cause the PTMS to shut down the IPP. One indication of unsafe system operation is the IPP EGT becoming too high.

The MA IPP started and performed normally up through the beginning of aircraft engine start on the day of the incident. However, the IPP inlet temperature rose 24 seconds after the initiation of aircraft engine start. The only sources of hot gas in the vicinity were the IPP exhaust and the engine exhaust from the MA.

The report noted:

The F-35 engine, like all combustion engines, has a fire in it while running. Under normal circumstances, the fire is contained in the combustion section of the engine. During this mishap, however, the fire became uncontained due to the increased amount of fuel added while the engine rotation speed was slowing. Once the uncontained fire started coming out the aircraft exhaust, the tailwind carried it rapidly along the exterior surfaces of the jet.

The report added:

A direct tailwind of 30 knots or greater was present during engine start.

Figure 88: POSITION OF MA WITH RELATIVE WIND (Source: U.S. AIB report).

The report continued:

Operations were conducted and systems were operated within the designated limits. There was a NOTE in the pilot checklist stating issues could occur when starting the aircraft engine when a tailwind was present. However, there was no mention of a tailwind limit.

Human factors analysis

The Board evaluated human factors relevant to the mishap using the analysis and classification system model established by the Department of Defense Human Factors Analysis and Classification System guide, implemented by AFI 91-204, Safety Investigations Reports.

The investigators found that there were the following relevant Human Factors that may have contributed to the mishap:

1. Procedural Guidance/Publications

Procedural Guidance/Publications is a factor when written direction, checklists, graphic depictions, tables, charts or other published guidance is inadequate, misleading or inappropriate and this creates an unsafe situation.

The pilot checklist in use at the time of the accident contained a NOTE on the ENG START ABNORM page, indicating engine start with a tailwind may cause IPP FAIL, requiring movement of the engine switch to the OFF position. This NOTE was not included as part of the Normal Procedure Chapter in ENG START checklist.

Neither publications nor guidance and training were adequate for the circumstances surrounding this incident. IPP and engine start issues with a tailwind were known prior to the incident.

However, the publications were written and communicated in such a way that the F-35A pilot community had only vague awareness of the issue. This vague awareness led to inadequate training for engine starts with a tailwind. Training also resulted in complacency and an over-reliance on aircraft automation. Thus, the MP was not trained adequately and was not as ready for the abnormal engine start and resulting fire as he could have been. Preponderance of evidence shows if there had been an expectation of engine startup problems with a tailwind, the MP may have relied less on aircraft automation, and may have identified an abnormal engine start earlier.

2. Organizational Training Issues/Programs

Organizational Training Issues/Programs are a factor when one-time or initial training programs, upgrade programs, transition programs or other training that is conducted outside the local unit is inadequate or unavailable (etc) and this creates an unsafe situation. (Note: the failure of an individual to absorb the training material in an adequate training program does not indicate a training program problem.

Since this limitation was not included in the manuals, during the training definition, it was not included in the course syllabus, so pilots did not receive adequate training at this point.

Pilots were not trained on tailwind engine start procedures and were not aware of any specific concerns related to tailwinds. Additionally, they did not have knowledge of specific limits or engine parameters to monitor during engine start, other than simply identifying that the aircraft displays were green/yellow/red.

3. Automation, Perceptions of Equipment, Overconfidence, Complacency, Inattention.

Automation is a factor when the design, function, reliability, use guidance, symbology, logic or other aspect of automated systems creates an unsafe situation.

Perceptions of Equipment is a factor when over or under confidence in an aircraft, vehicle, device, system or any other equipment creates an unsafe situation.

Overconfidence is a factor when the individual overvalues or overestimates personal capability, the capability of others or the capability of aircraft/vehicles or equipment and this creates an unsafe situation.

Complacency is a factor when the individual's state of reduced conscious attention due to an attitude of overconfidence, undermotivation or the sense that others "have the situation under control" leads to an unsafe situation.

Inattention is a factor when the individual has a state of reduced conscious attention due to a sense of security, self-confidence, boredom or a perceived absence of threat from the environment which degrades crew performance. (This may often be a result of highly repetitive tasks. Lack of a state of alertness or readiness to process immediately available information.)

The F-35A engine start process is heavily automated, which drove a perception among pilots the aircraft handled virtually all of the starting procedures and so long as the dials were "green" there were no problems.

This is one of the dangers of automatisms that leave the pilot out of the loop. The human being is not very good when it comes to monitoring automatic systems, especially when the systems are very reliable. This leads to complacency and relaxation.

4. Checklist Error, Distraction, Thermal Stress – Heat

Checklist Error is a factor when the individual, either through an act of commission or omission makes a checklist error or fails to run an appropriate checklist and this failure results in an unsafe situation.

Distraction is a factor when the individual has an interruption of attention and/or inappropriate redirection of attention by an environmental cue or mental process that degrades performance.

Thermal Stress – Heat is a factor when the individual is exposed to heat resulting in compromised function.

The AIB report discusses in depth these matters Checklist Error, Distraction, Thermal Stress – Heat such a Human Factors, we will look closely at their examination:

Upon recognition of the aircraft fire, MP initiated egress procedures per the F-35A pilot checklist. The MP stated he lifted the cover for the engine switch with the intent to turn it off, but could not recall whether he had actually moved the switch to the OFF position.

The aircraft Flight Data Recorder memory indicated the engine switch was never moved to the OFF position. Further, examination of the switch immediately following the incident found it in the RUN position. Based on this objective evidence, the MP failed to move the engine switch to OFF, as directed by the checklist.

The MP was under duress and distracted immediately upon recognition of the fire.

The burn injuries sustained to his head, neck, face, and ears are further supportive of the urgency surrounding his circumstances and the necessity to prioritize egress from the aircraft above all else.

The fire's ferocity and close proximity impaired the MP's ability to follow the checklist. The MP did not move the engine switch to OFF in accordance with the EGRESS checklist while he was egressing the MA. Within the first few seconds of the fire, the flames had reached the main landing gear and the Crew Chief was telling the pilot there was a fire. The fire burned for at least 20 seconds around the outside of the aircraft. The report highlight that if the engine switch had been moved to OFF at the first indication of fire, fuel would have been shut off to the engine nearly immediately and the fire would not have burned as long.

But as the report tells us, the pilot at the time was under duress and did not have enough situational awareness of being able to analyze what was happening to turn off the engine at the first fire signal. When the fire spread it was already too late to do so and he had to decide whether to immediately egress or turn the switch to OFF.

The burn injuries sustained to his head, neck, face, and ears are further supportive of the urgency surrounding his circumstances and the necessity to prioritize egress from the aircraft above all else.

Editorial note: This article was adapted from a report prepared by the U.S. Air Force Accident Investigation Board regarding mishap of an F-35A, tail number 12-5052. This report includes diagrams and illustrations and was obtained from US Air Force official web side.

22 UH-1N Impact Terrain

Figure 89: UH-1N (Source: U.S. AIB report).

The United States Air Force Aircraft Accident Investigation Board (AIB) describes in their report that:

On 27 April 2011, at approximately 1115 local time, a UH-1N, T/N 69-6603, crashed at a remote landing zone near Kirtland Air Force Base (AFB), New Mexico (NM).

The mishap crew (MC) was performing hoist operations when the rescue device, in this case a forest penetrator, snagged on a stationary F-111 capsule. The mishap aircraft (MA) entered a descending right turn and impacted terrain. After the MA came to a rest, the MC egressed the MA unharmed. The MA is assigned to the 512th Rescue Squadron, 58th Special Operations Wing, Kirtland AFB, NM. The MC was conducting an initial instructor flight engineer checkride involving hoist operations. The MC consisted of two pilots (MP1 and MP2) and two flight engineers (MF1 and MF2).

During one of the hoist operations, the hoist cable was lowered to the ground with the forest penetrator attached. MF1 initiated a hoist malfunction to test MF2's ability to troubleshoot. During the operation, the MA's hover drifted forward and left. When MF2 cleared the malfunction the hoist cable retracted unexpectedly. When the cable retracted, the forest penetrator raised off the ground and swung forward, snagging a stationary F-111 capsule's window. The MA banked right and MP2 instinctively applied maximum power in an attempt to recover the MA. The MA entered a sharp descending right turn while tethered to the F-111 capsule. When the forest penetrator ripped free, the MPs leveled out the MA before impacting terrain. The MA's main rotor struck the ground twice and the MA came to rest on its left side.

The MC egressed with no major injuries. A fire ignited shortly after impact completely destroying the MA.

Accident cause

The Accident Investigation Board (AIB) President found by clear and convincing evidence that the cause of the mishap was a combination of four actions by the mishap crew (MC), including three by the mishap flight engineers (MF1 and MF2) and one by the mishap pilot (MP2). These actions included:

(1) MF2's troubleshooting sequence,
(2) MF1's checkride supervision,
(3) MF2's channelized attention, and
(4) MP2's control inputs.

In addition, the AIB President found by a preponderance of the evidence that the use of an old F-111 capsule as a training target during hoist operations and miscommunication between the crew substantially contributed to the incident.

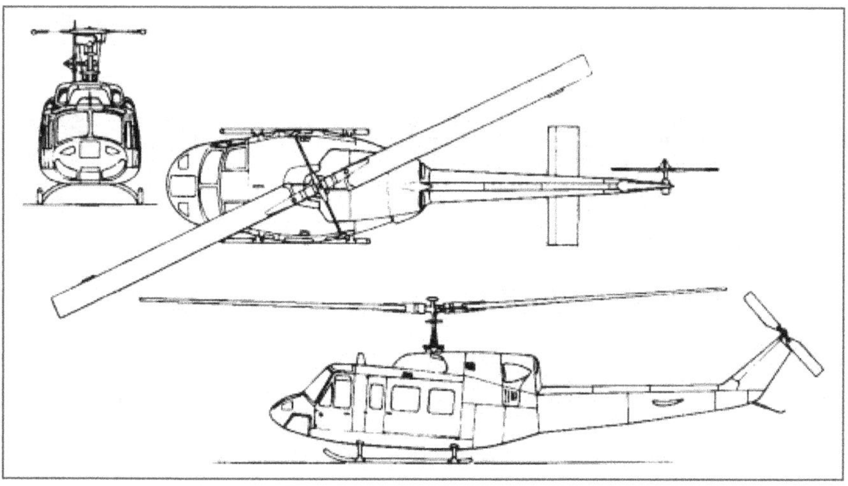

Figure 90: UH-1N (Source: U.S. AIB report).

Accident summary

The AAIB then explain in the report that the MC and FC started the mission as a formation. Startup, taxi, and takeoff occurred without incident. The formation took off 12 minutes early at 0948L. The formation departed via the South Departure and proceeded to Site 37. While enroute to Site 37, the formation descended below 300 feet above ground level (AGL) to conduct tactical low-level operations, including two practice evasive maneuvers. The formation did three approaches at Site 37 with one go-around called by MF2. Upon completion of training objectives for the formation portion of the sortie, MC and FC disbanded the formation per the mission plan.

After, the MC flew to Site 15 to conduct remote operations. Site 15 is located in a bowl-shaped depression along a series of ridgelines at an elevation of 5382 feet mean sea level (MSL). The surveyed landing area is surrounded by rising terrain on the northeast and southwest sides. Due to terrain, the best approach and escape headings are 110 or 290 degrees. The landing area is 263 feet long and 160 feet wide. An F-111 capsule was located on a downward slope approximately 145 feet northwest of and 12 feet lower in elevation than the landing area. The F-111 capsule is an entire cockpit pod from an F-111 usually resulting from an ejection.

The capsule on Site 15 weighed 2,060 pounds and was missing multiple window coverings.

Figure 91: F-111 Capsule with Snag Point and Forest Penetrator (Source: U.S. AIB report).

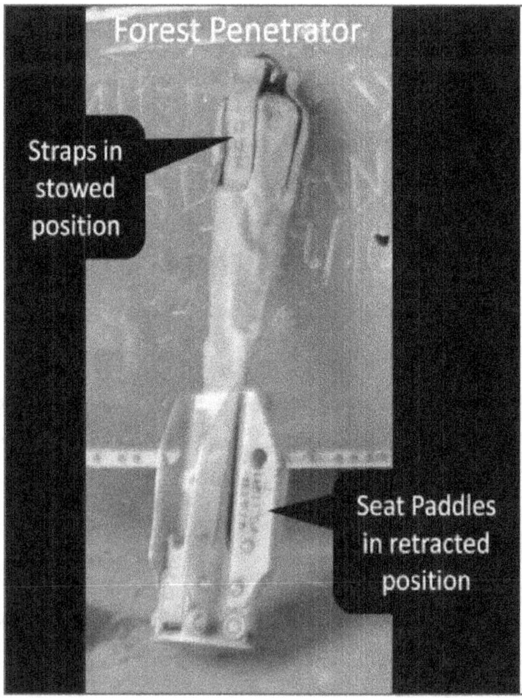

Figure 92: Forest Penetrator with Retracted Seat Paddles (Source: U.S. AIB report).

The report said: the MC arrived at Site 15 at approximately 1055L. MP2 accomplished a site evaluation and landed in the surveyed landing area. While on the ground, the MC took a five minute restroom break.

After that, the MP1 took off, orbited, and came back around for a 50 foot Alternate Insertion/Extraction (AIE) near the F-111 capsule. For the first AIE, MF1 assumed the role of the student and took control of hoist operations in order for MF2 to act as an instructor. The approach was performed into the wind with a northwest heading. MF1 directed the aircraft to hover 10 to 20 feet south of the F-111 capsule. During the hover, MF1 purposefully made minor mistakes to simulate being a student, and MF2 corrected those mistakes as the instructor candidate. The MC concluded the first AIE without incident.

Next, MF1 expressed that he wanted to see MF2 operate the hoist, so the MFs switched positions. MP2 assumed control of the MA and performed the next approach. MP2 performed an approach to the same spot as the first AIE and settled into a stable hover. MP2 held the hover between 44 and 48 feet, utilizing approximately 80 percent power. MF2 demonstrated operating the hoist, providing instruction to MF1 as he would to a student. MF2 lowered the cable and set the forest penetrator on the ground at the intended target, approximately 10 to 15 feet south of the F-111 capsule. Until this moment everything had gone as planned, it is then when the problems begin.

Source: U.S. AIB report. Hoist Up Limit Switch and Hook

As part of the instruction the MF1 induced a failure with the object that the student in this case the MF2 performed the troubleshooting following the appropriate procedures.

As MF2 was lowering the cable, MF1 leaned over MF2 and induced a simulated hoist malfunction by holding the up limit switch to the full up position. The up limit switch is designed to stop cable retraction once the cable fully retracts. Holding the up limit switch up prevented the hoist from retracting the cable but allowed it to extend. In accordance with procedure, MF2 attempted to retract the hoist cable by using his pendant. MF2 noticed that the hoist was not retracting. MF2 began trouble-shooting the hoist malfunction in accordance with the 512th Standard Operating Procedures.

MF2 announced to the MC that the cable was not coming up and asked the MPs if the hoist power was on. The MPs confirmed that it was on. MF2 then asked the MPs if they could double check their circuit breakers, and it was confirmed that the circuit breakers were in. MF2 again checked his pendant. MF2 then misdiagnosed the simulated malfunction as a pendant failure. He then asked MP2 to raise the hoist cable by using the pilot hoist control switch on the pilot's cyclic. MP2 responded in the affirmative that he was using the pilot's hoist control switch to attempt to retract the cable. MF2 announced that "nothing was happening."

Figure 93: Pilot Controls (Source: U.S. AIB report).

Upon seeing that MF2 had not yet correctly identified the simulated malfunction, MF1 interjected and queried MF2 on the cause. MF2 then looked at the hoist, noticed that MF1 was holding the up limit switch, and promptly identified and corrected the simulated malfunction by swiping MF1's hand from the switch.

This is the key moment of the accident, the MP2 was still activating the pilot hoist control switch because the MF2 did not tell him that he should stop activating it. The MF2 should have instructed the MP2 to release the switch according to the approved procedure. MF2 did not confirm that MP2 had released the pilot's hoist control switch before clearing the simulated malfunction. This sequence resulted in an unanticipated full rate cable retraction.

Since the up limit switch was no longer activated, the cable immediately began retracting at full rate in the low speed setting (125 feet per minute). MF2 did not immediately notice the retraction. MF1 sat down in the transmission seat in the middle of the cabin to observe MF2.

MF2's Troubleshooting Sequence is as follow:

The error in the execution of the procedure was as follows. The MF2 initially thought that the failure was due to the non-functioning of the pendant and therefore performed the first two steps of the corresponding procedure, see table below. When the pilot was pressing the hoist control switch he discovered that the problem was due to the Up-limit switch and instead of finishing the "Pendant Failure" procedure he had initiated and indicate to MP2 to stop acting on the hoist control switch, he changed directly to the procedure "Up limit switch failure" in his first step of "Ensure that the Up limit switch actuator is not stuck in the up position" without having previously made sure that the pilot stopped acting his hoist control switch.

The normal trouble shooting sequence for up-limit switch failure has the pilot try his hoist control switch two steps after the FE has already ensured the up limit switch actuator is not in the up position. MF2 executed the first steps of the pendant failure troubleshooting sequence followed by the first step for up limit switch failure. MF2 did not confirm that MP2 had released the pilot's hoist control switch before clearing the simulated malfunction. This sequence resulted in an unanticipated full rate cable retraction.

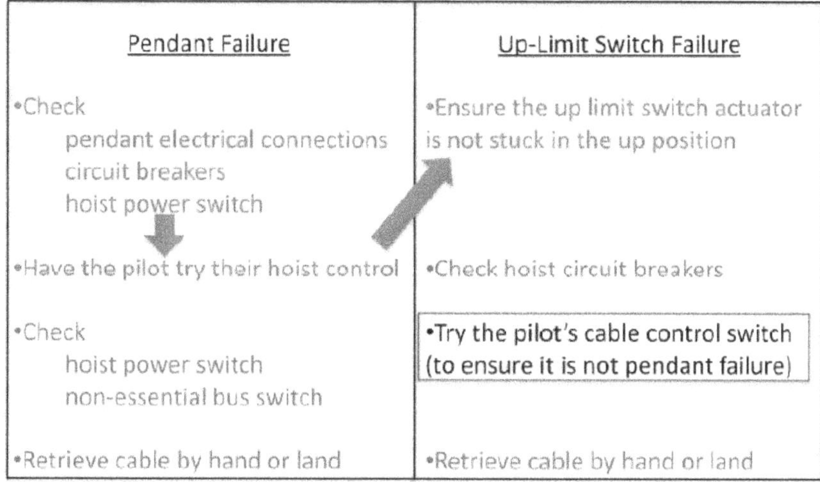

Figure 94: Hoist Troubleshooting Steps (Source: U.S. AIB report).

According to the AIB report, next came the second event of authentic bad luck, the penetrator snag in the front left F-111 capsule window and the cable became taut.

While MF2 was focused on the malfunction inside the cabin, the MA had an undetected drift forward and left, positioning the MA 5 to 10 feet west of the capsule. Upon clearing the simulated malfunction, MF2 looked back outside and noticed that the forest penetrator was already off the ground and swinging. Within approximately 2 seconds, MF2 saw the penetrator snag in the front left F-111 capsule window. He noticed the cable becoming taut and immediately called "stop up, stop up." Neither MP1 nor MP2 heard this call.

MF2 channelized his attention on the simulated hoist malfunction, which drew his attention away from the MA's hover position. Ordinarily, MF2 would correct the hover before cable retraction. When the cable unexpectedly retracted, the MA was not over the forest penetrator.

The forest penetrator subsequently swung like a pendulum and lodged into the F-111 capsule. MF2 made a "stop up, stop up" can after the forest penetrator hit and lodged into the F-111 capsule. This call was not successfully communicated to the MPs. Successful communication of this critical information might have reversed the pilot's actions on the collective and mitigated the ensuing rapid descent.

Due to the snag, the MA experienced a violent jerk, creating a right roll and right yaw. Based on the unexpected aircraft movement and abnormal control feel, MP2 instinctively pulled up on the collective, which would normally move the MA away from the ground. MP2 glanced inside and noticed the torque showing 100 percent or maximum power available. Simultaneously, MP1 placed his hand to the right of the cyclic to ensure that control inputs were not causing the right bank. MP1 noticed that the right bank was not being caused by the cyclic and decided to mirror the controls because of the MA's erratic behavior.

The AIB report says the MA started a descending right turn which prompted MF1 to call for cable cut. MF2 reached for the cable cut switch on the back side of the hoist. With the hoist swung out for operations, the cable cut switch faced the inside of the cabin. MF1 initially saw both MPs on the flight controls, and attempted to reach the cable cut switch on the center console, but was unable to due to his restraining device. MP1 also reached for the center console to activate the cable cut switch. MP2 remained on the controls attempting to recover the MA.

The MA turned to a northeastern heading, positioning itself into a direct crosswind from the northwest. At that point, the forest penetrator ripped free from the F-111 capsule. The MA departed from its radial path and slid left and forward towards the rising terrain. Just prior to impact, MP1 returned to mirroring the flight controls. Both MP1 and MP2 realized that they could not recover the MA and applied aft cyclic to level the skids with the rising terrain. Approximately 3 to 5 seconds passed between the cable snagging and the MA impacting the terrain. The cable was sheared by the hoist cable cut mechanism close to impact.

Impact

The AIB report explains the Impact:

The MA impacted rising terrain with an approximate 15 degree nose up attitude and a forward left drift. Effort was made to impact with the skids as level as possible in order to increase the chance of occupant survivability. Upon initial impact, the main rotor blades came in contact with the higher terrain to the northeast. This caused the nose of the aircraft to spin right and the fuselage to roll left. The MA came to rest on its left side. Even though MF1 and MF2 were wearing restraining devices, the impact and left roll tossed both of them onto the left side of the cabin MP1 and MP2 remained restrained in their seats throughout the impact.

Figure 95: Approximate Mishap Terrain Vertical Reference (Source: U.S. AIB report).

Human factors analysis

The report continued with HUMAN FACTORS ANALYSIS:

The Department of Defense Human Factors Analysis and Classification System (DoD-HFACS) is a systematic and comprehensive tool that is comprised of a list of potential human factors that can be contributory or causal to a mishap.

A total of seven human factors were identified and described below for this mishap:

1. Authorized Unnecessary Hazard

Authorized Unnecessary Hazard is a factor when supervision authorizes a mission or mission element that is unnecessarily hazardous without sufficient cause or need. This includes intentionally scheduling personnel for missions or operations that they are not qualified to perform.

The F-111 capsule had been on Site 15 for over a decade. At one point aluminum sheeting covered all the openings, but several panel coverings were missing at the time of the mishap. Without these panels, the capsule was an entanglement hazard. Previous site surveys noted the F-111 capsule's presence. Multiple members in the 512 RQS verified that the capsule was a frequently-used reference point for AIE operations. MF1 selected an aim point for the hoist approximately 10 to 15 feet from the capsule.

2. Channelized Attention

Channelized Attention is a factor when the individual is focusing all conscious attention on a limited number of environmental cues to the exclusion of others of a subjectively equal or higher or more immediate priority, leading to an unsafe situation. This may be described as a tight focus of attention that leads to the exclusion of comprehensive situational information.

The FE is responsible for clearing the aircraft of obstacles on the side and rear, directing the pilots' inputs for aircraft position and altitude, and monitoring the hoist during its operation. MF2 channelized his attention on troubleshooting the hoist malfunction. MF1 was focused on his student's actions. Due to MF1 and MF2's channelized attentions, neither initially noticed the aircraft drifting or the hoist cable retracting and lifting the penetrator.

3. Cross-Monitoring Performance

Cross-Monitoring Performance is a factor when crew or team members failed to monitor, assist or back-up each other's actions and decisions.

All instructors and evaluators are tasked to immediately correct breaches of flight safety. MF1 stated he was able to monitor students' abilities and the situation by observing their body language, head movements, and verbalizations. After MF2 cleared the hoist malfunction, MF1 sat and observed MF2 raise the hoist cable. Since MF1 was sitting and no longer standing over MF2, he was unable to visually monitor the forest penetrator. This placed him in a position where he could not quickly recognize and correct the impending unsafe situation.

4. Miscommunication

Miscommunication is a factor when correctly communicated information is misunderstood, misinterpreted or disregarded.

Both FEs state a "stop up" call was clearly communicated by MF2. MP1 and MP2 did not hear a stop up call. This discrepancy displays a communication issue. MF2 may have made the statement and it may have been unintentionally disregarded by the pilots.

5. Inadvertent Operation

Inadvertent Operation is a factor when individual's movements inadvertently activate or deactivate equipment, controls or switches when there is no intent to operate the control or device. This action may be noticed or unnoticed by the individual.

MF1 controlled the up-limit switch on the hoist and simulated a malfunction. MF2 eventually identified the simulated malfunction and swiped MF1's hand away from the switch, releasing the hold on the cable retraction. MF1 and MF2 failed to ensure that MP2 was not activating the pilot's hoist control switch when the up limit switch was released. As a result, the hoist cable retracted inadvertently.

MF2 made a "stop up, stop up" can after the forest penetrator hit and lodged into the F-111 capsule. This call was not successfully communicated to the MPs. Successful communication of this critical information might have reversed the pilot's actions on the collective and mitigated the ensuing rapid descent.

6. Mission Briefing

Mission Briefing is a factor when information and instructions provided to individuals, crews, or teams were insufficient, or participants failed to discuss contingencies and strategies to cope with contingencies.

The AIE portion of the brief was conducted without MF1 present, and he was not back-briefed. This part of the brief covered AIE contingencies, including transfer of cable cut authority. MF1 had attended multiple AIE briefs in the past and even though he was fully aware of how to cope with those contingencies, his attendance at that brief was expected and required.

7. Inadequate Rest

Inadequate Rest is a factor when the opportunity for rest was provided but the individual failed to take the opportunity to rest.

All crewmembers were afforded sufficient time for crew rest. MF2 was on a night schedule two days prior to the MS. Per squadron policy, he was given one day prior to the day MS to shift his sleep cycle. MF2 did not change his sleep schedule on his day off and only slept for 5 hours the night prior to the MS.

8. Training Aid

The F-111 capsule was utilized routinely as an aide for both search training and alternate insertion and extraction (AIE) events. The capsule's deterioration increased the likelihood that a rescue device could entangle with the capsule. I bough increasing the realism of the training, the routine use of the capsule as an AIE reference and training target unnecessarily increased risk.

23 F16 Out of Control

Figure 96: F-16C (Source: U.S. AIB report).

The United States Air Force Aircraft Accident Investigation Board (AIB) describes in their report that:

On 27 December 2012, at approximately 1533 local time (L), the mishap aircraft (MA), an F-16C Fighting Falcon, tail number (T/N) 87-0315 assigned to the 144th Fighter Wing, Fresno Air National Guard Base (ANGB), California (CA) went out of control during a training mission and impacted the ground 84 nautical miles east of Fresno, CA. The mishap pilot (MP) ejected safely with minor injuries. The MA was destroyed upon impact with total loss. The aircraft impacted the ground in a desolate area. There was no damage to private property and there were no civilian casualties.

The mishap flight (MF) departed Fresno ANGB as a formation of two F-16Cs. The MF mission included air to air training opposing a separate two-ship of F16Cs. The

MF then split up to accomplish one-against-one air combat training, or Basic Fighter Maneuvers (BFM). On the third and mishap BFM engagement, the MP maneuvered the MA into a nose high and low airspeed state.

The MP's actions to recover from this nose high, low airspeed state were inappropriate and not in accordance with published guidance, resulting in the MA departing controlled flight. The MP incorrectly applied out of control emergency procedure actions and was unable to recover the MA from the out of control situation. The MP safely ejected below recommended ejection altitude.

Accident cause

The board president (BP) found, by clear and convincing evidence, the cause of the mishap was failure of the MP to properly recover the MA from a high pitch, low airspeed state resulting in an inverted deep stall.

In addition, the MP failed to properly apply Out-of-Control Recovery Critical Action Procedures, resulting in an inability to recover the MA before ejection was initiated.

Furthermore, the BP found three human factors causal to the mishap: Complacency evident throughout the entire flight, Pressing beyond reasonable limits, and Procedural Error in the last few minutes of flight. Finally, by a preponderance of the evidence, the BP found six other human factors substantially contributed to the mishap: Violation-Lack of Discipline in three separate areas, Seating and Restraints, Illusion-Vestibular, Spatial Disorientation (Type 1) Unrecognized, Channelized Attention, and Error Due to Misperception.

Accident summary

Preflight

The aircraft was configured with two external wing fuel tanks, two missiles on the outboard ends of each wing, three missile launcher rails on each wing, an empty pylon on the centerline fuselage, and a safe gun. The MF started on time IAW the brief and completed all normal ground procedures without incident.

The MF taxied on time in accordance with the lineup card. Prior to takeoff, the MP noticed a degraded navigation system. The MF took off from Fresno Yosemite International Airport (IAP) and departed on an R2508A stereo route to the R2508 military operating area (MOA). On departure, the MP performed an in-flight alignment (IFA) of the navigation system due to MA position error in excess of 100 miles.

The MF entered R2508 on a subsection of R2508 clearance that included the Owens, Saline, and Panamint areas below flight level 290 (29,000 ft.). Neither the MP nor the MW accomplished the planned and required G-Awareness Exercise.

Note: The G-Ex is a maneuver involving two tactical turns of increasing Gs to check both pilot and aircraft tolerance for follow on high G maneuvers.

The tactical portion of the mission involved three TI engagements with Dogs 41 as Red Air followed by two High Aspect Basic Fighter Maneuver (HABFM) and one 9000 ft. perch Basic Fighter Maneuver (BFM) engagement. The MF executed all three TI engagements with Razor 31 flight as planned.

The second engagement on the MS was also a nonstandard, in-flight directed HABFM set with a 6,000 ft. altitude differential. This set started with a 2.3 NM separation and Dogs 41 as the low fighter. During this set, the MP experienced the low speed warning tone during two vertical maneuvers. The low speed warning tone sounds to aid the pilot in recognizing that critical high pitch, low airspeed flight conditions have been reached. The first low speed warning tone lasted approximately eight seconds and the second approximately 12 seconds. During the engagement, the MP reset an air data converter (ADC) caution light while continuing to maneuver, ending the set approximately 30 seconds later.

The ADC light notifies the pilot of a possible flight control malfunction.

The final BFM engagement, which led to the mishap, was set a 9,000 ft. perch BFM with Dogs 42 in a 1.5 NM trail at 18,000 ft. mean sea level (MSL) with the MP as the defensive fighter.

The MP executed a right-hand defensive break turn of 7.5 Gs ten degrees nose low, bleeding airspeed to approximately 210 knots indicated airspeed (KIAS). The MP executed a vertical nose down maximum aft stick maneuver resulting in a high aspect merge with the MW. The MP continued maximum aft stick pull into the vertical from 13,840 ft. and 241 KIAS. The MP held maximum aft stick input constant with the aircraft established on the angle-of-attack (AOA) limiter as airspeed decreased and pitch attitude increased.

According to AFMAN 11-217, Volume 3, Flying Operations Supplemental Flight Information, paragraph 3.4.8, the AOA is the difference between pitch and flight path angle. The low speed warning tone sounded at approximately 165 knots with the MA nose nearly in the pure vertical position. The MP then commanded a maximum left roll stick input while continuing the maximum aft stick pull. The MP maintained aft and left stick maximum inputs until the aircraft was no longer in controlled flight as communicated by the MP calling "ballistic" over the radio.

The MA sliced into an inverted attitude as forward momentum slowed, and entered a negative AOA departure. A departure is defined as a loss of aircraft control characterized by significant, large amplitude, and uncommanded motions. The automatic flight control system (FLCS) features of the F-16 normally prevent departures but may be defeated if maneuvering limits are not observed. The F-16 depends on its horizontal tails to limit AOA and typically reaches its controllability limit at approximately ±40 degrees AOA. Exceedance of the AOA value is used for departure recognition. This type of departure is characterized as a pitch departure, because the inability to control AOA leads to an out-of-control situation. Pitch departures are typically slow speed where the MA is in a nose high pitch attitude. Airspeed is bled off until the ballistic path of the airplane drives AOA to increase quicker than the tail can control due to limited control authority. If the departed aircraft does not self-recover, a deep stall may develop.

The MA did not self-recover and established in an inverted deep stall with an approximate descent rate of 12,000 ft. per minute. The MP attempted to execute an Out-of-Control Recovery using Critical Action Procedures (CAPS) by letting go of the flight controls and moving the throttle to idle IAW the CAPS. During inverted deep stalls in analog F-16s, such as the MA, the yaw rate limiter is not active, meaning the pilot must provide anti-spin inputs to the rudder. The MP did not use rudder control inputs in an attempt to control yaw. The MP proceeded to attempt pitch rocking with the manual pitch override (MPO) switch engaged as required for deep stall recovery IAW the CAPS. The MPO switch allows the pilot to manually override the FLCS limiter allowing maximum deflection of the horizontal tail.

After multiple failed recovery attempts and two check altitude radio calls from the MW, the MP initiated a successful ejection at approximately 6200 ft. (3000 ft. above ground level (AGL)) with no significant injuries.

The MP contacted the MW on UHF Guard frequency (243.0) via his survival radio stating he was okay and was proceeding to walk towards the highway with an F-18 Hornet overhead.

Historical Comparison

Analysis from 416th Flight Test Squadron (FLTS) flight testing provided comparison for departures resulting from the maneuvers performed with similar aircraft configurations to the MA. Out-of-Control Recovery characteristics for maneuvers performed with the wing tank loadings resulted in recovery from all departures within two pitch rocking cycles.

Historically, during test programs, the 90th percentile altitude lost during recovery is 6100 ft., while the 98th percentile altitude lost during recovery is 8500 ft. Post-maneuver analysis determined insufficient rudder pedal force was applied to counter the yaw rates, and that pitch rocking was not performed in phase with pitch cycles, both of which combined to delay the recovery.

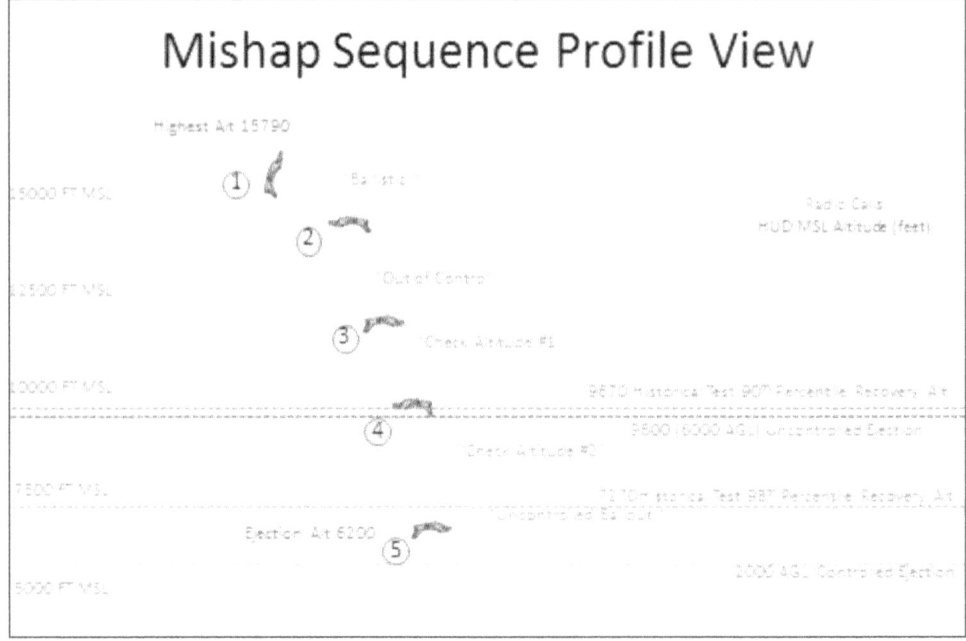

Figure 97: Figure overlays the historical 90th and 98th percentile recoveries with the mishap sequence and parameters (Source: AIB).

Human factors analysis

The AIB evaluated human factors relevant to the mishap using the analysis and classification system model established by the Department of Defense (DoD) Human Factors Analysis and Classification System (HFACS) guide, implemented by AFI 91-204, USAF Safety Investigations and Reports, dated 24 September 2008.

1. Complacency

Complacency is a factor when the individual's state of reduced conscious attention due to an attitude of overconfidence, undermotivation or the sense that others "have the situation under control" leads to an unsafe situation.

According to the report, there is evidence that a high level of complacency existed for both the MP and the MW throughout the MS planning, briefing and execution.

MP testimony stated little mission planning time was available, required, or dedicated to the MS.

While a combined motherhood and coordination brief occurred, the separate MF brief was lacking in detail and did not cover critical BFM-specific training rules or include any BFM tactical discussion. Additionally, there appeared to be little to no discussion with regard to BFM setups, desired learning objectives, designated training aids/limitations, low speed warning tones, and basic operating limitations with regard to configuration. This is evident during the three BFM engagements when the MP was forced to audible directions to the MW multiple times regarding position, altitude, and setups. The MP referenced the simple nature of the mission and the frequency of similar missions as justification for the minimal planning, and while all required items were completed, this highlighted complacency in mission preparation.

The Head-Up Display (HUD) tape revealed multiple examples of complacency. After taxi, the MP elected to take off six minutes early with a known corrupt navigation system. The MP attempted to correct the bad system without referencing the EGI failure checklist. While performing the second HABFM set, the MP reset the FLCS in response to an ADC malfunction. However, the MP again failed to reference the associated checklist and failed to TERMINATE/KIO IAW AFI 11-2F-16, Volume 3, paragraph 7.1.6. The MW also reset a FLCS light between BFM sets without checklist reference, querying the MP on procedures. The MP testified that he would normally reference the checklist or expect the wingman to reference the checklist in both instances. The MP failed to complete the planned and required G-Ex IAW AFI 11-214, Air Operations Rules and Procedures, paragraph 3.2 and AFI 11-2F-16, Volume 3, paragraph 3.11.1. Furthermore, the MW failed to provide in-flight cross monitoring to ensure that this required exercise took place.

The MS consisted of three BFM sets. The two HABFM sets started from inconsistent and nonstandard parameters. There were several variances in starting parameters apparent on the HUD video with regard to the BFM setups (approximately 50 knots in airspeeds, 7,000 ft. in altitude, and 2 NM in separation).

Additionally, the MP attempted three separate over the top maneuvers during the second and third BFM sets with setup airspeeds of 278, 260, and 241 knots. During these maneuvers, the MP activated and remained within the low speed warning tone for approximately eight to 12 seconds, demonstrating little urgency to correct the low speed condition IAW AFI 11-2F-16, Volume 3, paragraph 3.9.5 and IAW T.O. 1F-16C-1, Flight Manual USAF Series F-16C/D Blocks 25, 30, and 32 Aircraft or ceasing to fight IAW AFI 11-214, paragraphs 3.4.1.1, 3.4.1.2, and 3.4.3.1.3.

A combination of these factors indicated an air of complacency, which resulted in direct violation of multiple guidelines and training rules.

2. Pressing

Pressing is a factor when the individual knowingly commits to a course of action that presses them and/or their equipment beyond reasonable limits.

According to the report, F-16 T.O.s and AFIs define low speed limitations, rules, and pilot actions. AFI 11-214, paragraphs 3.4.1.1, 3.4.1.2, and 3.4.3.1.3 state that KIO/TERMINATE is required when safety of flight is a factor, Desired Learning Objectives (DLOs) are unattainable, or training rules or other limits are met. T.O. 1F-F16-1, section six, states the low airspeed warning tone sounds to aid in recognizing that critical high pitch, low airspeed flight conditions have been reached. AFI 11-2F-16, Volume 3, paragraphs 3.9.4 and 3.9.5 state that minimum airspeed is activation of the low speed warning tone; upon activation, the pilot will take action to correct the low speed condition, and will not assault two or more limiters at low airspeed.

According to T.O. 1F-F16-1, maximum maneuvering in a low speed state, especially maximum roll coupled with maximum aft stick, significantly predisposes the aircraft to departure.

All pilot testimony, including the MP, agreed that upon activation of the low speed warning tone, the pilot should take immediate action to alleviate the condition, indicating a clear understanding of the above limitations and rules.

All pilot testimony, including the MP, described continuous activation of the low speed warning tone beyond two to three seconds as excessive and would warrant some degree of debrief or counseling . Additionally, the MP demonstrated a clear understanding of the limitation precluding assault of two or more limiters. In consideration of setup airspeeds for over the top maneuvers in a two-tank configuration, the local culture seemed to agree that it would vary depending on the individual pilot. Nonetheless, there did appear to be a consensus that 300 to 350 knots was the required minimum airspeed in order to safely accomplish the maneuver in a two-tank configuration.

The MP testified to an established personal minimum setup speed of 250 knots. While the MP conceded that he "swore it [airspeed] was 245…" at the setup of the final maneuver, he would have remained below his personally established minimum of 250 knots and well below the culturally accepted minimum of 300-350 knots for a two-tank configuration.

The MP attempted three over the top (vertical loop) maneuvers during the second and third BFM sets. During the initial maneuver of the second BFM set, as exhibited in the unclassified HUD tape, the MP completed a 278 knot setup with continuous activation of the low speed warning tone for approximately eight seconds without a TERMINATE/KIO. During the second maneuver of the second set, the MP completed a 260 knot setup with continuous activation of the low speed warning tone for approximately 12 seconds without a TERMINATE/KIO. During the final setup that led to departure, the MP reached a maximum airspeed of 241 knots and continuously activated the low speed warning tone for approximately 10 seconds without a TERMINATE/KIO. This low speed state coupled with inappropriate/aggressive recovery maneuvers, as discussed below, predisposed the MA to an uncontrolled departure.

These instances of progressively borderline starting airspeeds for over the top maneuvers, excessive time spent within the low speed warning tone with little urgency to terminate or recover, and aggressive maneuvering in a low speed state indicated a tendency of pressing beyond reasonable limits. This tendency ultimately placed the MA in a position where departure was imminent.

3. Procedural Error

Procedural Error is a factor when a procedure is accomplished in the wrong sequence or using the wrong technique or when the wrong control or switch is used. This also captures errors in navigation, calculation or operation of automated systems.

According to the report, Procedural errors occurred during two critical phases of the MS, the low speed warning tone recovery and the Out-of-Control Recovery. T.O. 1F-F16C-1, section six, states to avoid a departure, specific control techniques are required. A pilot should first release aft stick pressure to reduce AOA and then smoothly roll inverted to the nearest horizon. After completing the roll, the pilot should smoothly apply aft stick pressure as required to keep the nose tracking towards the horizon. All pilot testimony, to include the MP, agreed that upon activating the low speed warning tone, the pilot should take immediate action to alleviate the condition, IAW the techniques described in the T.O. guidance. The MP testified that upon hearing the low airspeed warning tone, he proceeded to recover the MA. The CSFDR data showed maximum aft stick continued upon activation of the low speed warning tone while adding maximum left roll. This unsuccessful recovery technique was not IAW T.O. 1F-F16C-1. The MA subsequently departed controlled flight.

Out-of-Control Recoveries are detailed in section three of T.O. 1F-F16C-1. Successful recoveries require CAPS per AFI 11-2F-16, Volume 3. The AFI directs pilots to immediately accomplish the procedures in the published sequence without reference to the checklist. These include (1) controls release (2) throttle idle (3) rudder opposite yaw direction (4) MPO switch override and hold with (5) forward and aft cycling of the stick in phase with nose oscillation. T.O. guidance further states any deviations or delay could reduce effectiveness of the recovery and therefore delay recovery.

The MP correctly accomplished steps one, two and four as required. The third step was omitted due to contributing factors discussed below. Proper pitch rocking, step five, is accomplished by allowing the nose to lead stick motion and maintaining full stick inputs until the maximum pitch attitudes are reached. Data analysis reflects the MP pitch inputs were not held to maximum values or for sufficient duration. Additionally, these MP pitch inputs were not performed in phase with pitch cycles. These inputs are clearly illustrated in the Comparison of Recovery Inputs Figure of the 416 FLTS mishap analysis. The MP control inputs (solid blue lines) are overlaid upon the proper control technique (black dashed lines). According to the 416 FLTS analysis, "Comparison of the MP technique and proper technique show that aerodynamic recovery was unlikely to occur since the insufficient duration and magnitude of commands did not result in sufficient trailing edge down deflection of the horizontal tail at any point".

4. Violation - Lack of Discipline

Violation - Lack of Discipline is a factor when an individual, crew or team intentionally violates procedures or policies without cause or need. These violations are unusual or isolated to specific individuals rather than larger groups. There is no evidence of these violations being condoned by leadership.

According to the report, as described within the human factors of Complacency, Pressing and Procedural Error, there were several violations of AFIs, Training Rules, and T.O.s within the MS. The AIB found evidence the MP intentionally violated these regulations without cause or need. There is no indication the MP was unaware or unfamiliar with any rules or regulations. There is also no evidence to suggest a lack of experience given the MP had more than 2000 flying hours and was a highly experienced four-ship flight lead.

The MP knowingly and intentionally took off with an inaccurate navigation system with a positional error in excess of 100 NM. This was in direct violation of AFI 11-2F-16, Volume 3, paragraph 7.1.1: "Do not accept an aircraft for flight with a malfunction which is addressed in the emergency/abnormal procedures section of the flight manual until appropriate corrective actions have been accomplished." Additionally, 144 FW In-Flight Guide, page 2-13, lists the Inertial Navigation System (INS) on the Mission Essential Subsystem List. This was without cause or need, especially considering that the MP took off six minutes ahead of schedule which would have afforded time to correct the problem.

The MP knowingly and intentionally reset a Flight Control System Malfunction and continued to engage the opposing fighter. This was in direct violation of AFI 11-2F-

16, Volume 3, paragraph 7.1.6: "For actual/perceived flight control malfunctions, pilots will terminate maneuvering and take appropriate action." This was without cause or need given the engagement could have been terminated at any point for any reason without significant consequence.

While attempting over the top maneuvers on three separate occasions, the MP entered the low speed warning tone for a duration of 8-12 seconds without a TERMINATE/KIO and continued aggressive maneuvering in multiple axes of flight.

This was in direct violation of AFI 11-2F-16, Volume 3, paragraph 3.9.5: "The minimum airspeed for all maneuvering is based upon activation of the low speed warning tone. When the low speed warning tone sounds, the pilot will take action to correct the low speed condition."

Intent was demonstrated by the MP during the MS by the number of times entering the low speed warning tone, the excessive duration of continuous activation of the warning tone with little urgency to recover, and progressively borderline setup parameters. According to MP testimony, these setup parameters are what he intentionally uses on a routine basis. It is implausible that a pilot would not encounter or expect to encounter the low speed warning tone in a two-tank configuration using these parameters; particularly, if a pilot employs more aggressive setup parameters for a maneuver immediately following one in which the tone was encountered using less aggressive parameters. These actions indicated the MP's intent to repeatedly place the MA in a low speed state with little urgency to recover or TERMINATE/KIO. This was done without cause or need given the engagement could have been terminated at any point for any reason without significant consequence.

The above violations indicate a lack of discipline by the MP.

5. Seating and Restraints

Seating and Restraints is a factor when the design of the seat or restraint system, the ejection system, seat comfort or poor impact-protection qualities of the seat create an unsafe situation.

According to the report, the MP recalled appropriate and adequate application of the lap belt prior to takeoff.

Specifically, he stated that it is his routine to "...keep the seat kit loose, so I can turn and look over my shoulder in the jet but I tighten the lap belt up as tight as I can get it". Nonetheless, during the inverted departure the MP recalled falling away from the seat at least "1-2 inches" resulting in axial/inferior transfer of body mass to the canopy.

This transfer left the MP with his helmet pinned against the canopy causing forward flexion of his neck, pulled his feet off the rudders, caused difficulty finding and deflecting the MPO switch in a timely manner, and caused difficulty maintaining positive control of the stick.

The MP specifically recalls that the abutment of his helmet to the glass of the canopy restricted his field of vision and limited his ability to effectively visualize terrain. He recalled being disoriented in this position, but not incapacitated. Even so, the MP stated that he never perceived the yaw rate. At this point, he was focused solely on the nose of the MA in an effort to track vertical movement of the nose and cycle appropriate pitch rock maneuvers. He did not perceive horizontal movement of terrain.

The inadequate restraint also hindered his ability to implement the MPO in a timely manner. The MP stated in his testimony that "...I kind of had to feel for it and I was using my right hand to hold onto the towel rack and kind of trying to push myself into the seat and brace myself a little bit with the right hand". This assertion is further supported by CSFDR data that showed a 31-second delay from aircraft departure to MPO switch deflection. Given his altitude at departure (15,770 ft. according to HUD tape) and the typical altitude required for recovery according to Lockheed Martin Flight Engineers, any delay in time would have been invaluable for MA recovery prior to ejection altitude.

Finally, the MP's displaced position within the cockpit affected his ability to make appropriate stick inputs. MP stated difficulty maintaining positive control of the stick since he required use of his stick hand/arm to improve his position within the cockpit using the right body positioning handle or "towel rack". Lockheed Martin mishap analysis of the CSFDR data revealed stick inputs of a duration and magnitude inadequate to provide an effective pitch rock maneuver, particularly in the forward/push cycle. Specifically, the data showed that several forward/push cycles did not move beyond neutral. This is clearly illustrated in the Comparison of Recovery Inputs Figure of the 416 FLTS Mishap Analysis where the MP control inputs (solid blue lines) are overlaid upon the proper control technique (black dashed lines). Since the FLCS automatically applies trailing-edge-up commands (or aft stick pull), it is critical for the pilot to apply full forward (push) stick force to facilitate successful recovery. A positional displacement towards the canopy and a resultant maximum extension of the MP's right arm could have precluded his ability to push the stick beyond neutral to an effective magnitude. Therefore, this positional displacement contributed to the procedural anomaly of ineffective pitch rocking, precluding effective recovery.

The aforementioned factors resulting from inadequate restraint, in combination or alone, contributed to a significant delay in effective MA recovery from a negative AOA departure prior to ejection altitude.

6. Illusion – Vestibular

Illusion – Vestibular is a factor when stimuli acting on the semicircular ducts or otolith organs of the vestibular apparatus cause the individual to have an erroneous perception of orientation, motion or acceleration leading to degraded performance.

7. Spatial Disorientation (Type 1)

Unrecognized Spatial Disorientation is a failure to correctly sense a position, motion or attitude of the aircraft or of oneself within the fixed coordinate system provided by the surface of the earth and the gravitational vertical. Spatial Disorientation (Type 1) Unrecognized is a factor when a person's cognitive awareness of one or more of the following varies from reality: attitude, position, velocity, direction of motion or acceleration. Proper control inputs are not made because the need is unknown.

8. Channelized Attention

Channelized Attention is a factor when the individual is focusing all conscious attention on a limited number of environmental cues to the exclusion of others of a subjectively equal or higher or more immediate priority, leading to an unsafe situation. This may be described as a tight focus of attention that leads to the exclusion of comprehensive situational information.

9. Error Due to Misperception

Error due to Misperception is a factor when an individual acts or fails to act based on an illusion, misperception or disorientation state, and this act or failure to act creates an unsafe situation.

According to the report, the MP stated he did not perceive yaw at any time during the departure. Following the onset of the negative AOA (inverted) departure, the MP recalled his field of vision being restricted due to a positional displacement into the canopy where his helmet had contacted the canopy. While the MP denied incapacitation, he did recall some degree of disorientation during the deep stall. The MP recalled focusing his attention on the pitot tube on the nose of the MA as he attempted to cycle the pitch rocking maneuver in phase with vertical oscillation. He did not recall the terrain or horizon moving in the horizontal plane. The MP never assessed the turn and slip indicator for direction and magnitude of yaw (Tab V-1.29). Secondary to fixed attention on the vertical oscillation on the nose and limited field of vision due to his displaced position within the cockpit, the MP was unable to employ visual indicators of yaw. Particularly in a daylight scenario, visual cues serve as the most reliable indicators for perceptual orientation.

Consequently, the MP was forced to rely solely on vestibular cues that erroneously suggested a state of neutral yaw. Data reproduced by the CSFDR revealed a consistent yaw rate between 10 to 30 degrees per second, which was evident on the HUD tape as horizontal terrain movement and rate of change of the heading angle.

Appropriate CAPS for recovery from an inverted deep stall IAW AFI 11-2F-16, Volume 3, as compared to the MP's actions were previously reviewed in detail.

While the MP did eventually deflect the MPO switch and made an attempt at the pitch rock maneuver, CSFDR data revealed no rudder inputs were made to neutralize yaw. Given the MP did not perceive yaw for the reasons discussed above, he made no attempt to input rudder. T.O. 1F-16C-1 states attempts at pitch rocking before the yaw rotation stops or is minimized reduces the effectiveness of pitch rocking and delays successful aerodynamic recovery. According to the Lockheed Martin and Edwards AFB flight engineer departure analysis for similar F-16 configurations, the MA should have recovered within two pitch rocking cycles assuming yaw rate control and proper pitch inputs. In this instance, several cycles of the pitch rocking maneuver alone proved ineffective in recovering the MA prior to ejection altitude.

The MP's erroneous and unrecognized perception of neutral yaw coupled with channelized attention on the nose to the exclusion of reliable indicators of yaw rate led to the subsequent procedural failure to control yaw with rudder input.

24 T-38C severe damage during landing

Figure 98: T-38C (Source: U.S. AIB report).

The United States Air Force Aircraft Accident Investigation Board (AIB) describes in their report that:

On 11 February 2011, at 2017 Central Standard Time, the Mishap Aircraft (MA), a T-38C, serial number 65-0337, sustained damage during an attempted landing on Runway 22 at Ellington Field, Houston, Texas. The MA and Mishap Pilot (MP) were assigned to the 14th Flying Training Wing, Columbus Air Force Base (AFB), Mississippi. The MP suffered minor injuries. The MA sustained damage to the landing gear, engines, right wing, and tail section.

Accident cause

The Accident Investigation Board (AIB) President found by clear and convincing evidence this accident was caused by the following:

(1) Geographic Misorientation of the MP in relation to the landing runway, which led to a series of perception and performance errors that ultimately resulted in the runway impact;

(2) the authorization and execution of a mission profile having an unnecessarily high level of risk relative to the real benefits.

Operational Risk Management (ORM) was inadequate on three fronts: inadequate risk analysis of the overall cross-country weekend plan as well as the MP's individual plan, an inadequate risk assessment matrix, and a culture of risk tolerance in the squadron.

Inappropriate supervisory policy, combined with inadequate ORM, led to the MP flying a high-risk mission profile

 The AIB President also found by a preponderance of the evidence that the MP's fatigue substantially contributed to the mishap.

Accident summary

The MP was flying his fourth sortie of the day as a night solo continuation training sortie into Ellington Field on a squadron cross-country mission.

Figure 99: T-38C Talon (Source: U.S. AIB report).

The MP requested a visual approach to runway 17 Right. He did not sufficiently monitor his position and became geographically misoriented. As a result, when he was three miles from the airfield, the MP misidentified runway 22 as runway 17 Right.

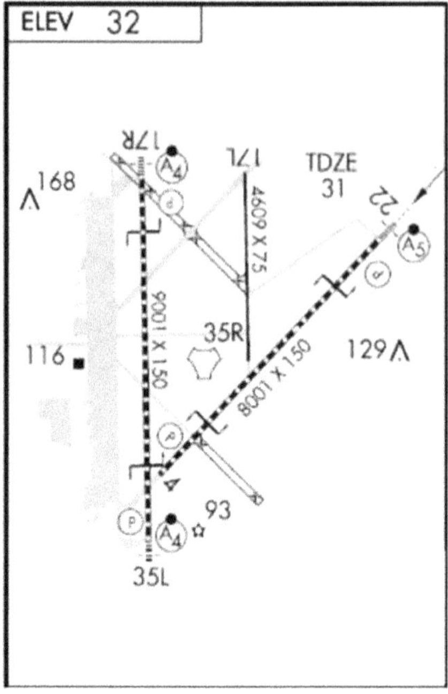

Figure 100: Runways (Source: U.S. AIB report).

Due to Channelized Attention on the mismatch between what he was seeing outside and what his instruments indicated, he allowed his airspeed to decrease well below a safe airspeed and descended at an insufficient rate, placing him well above a normal glidepath.

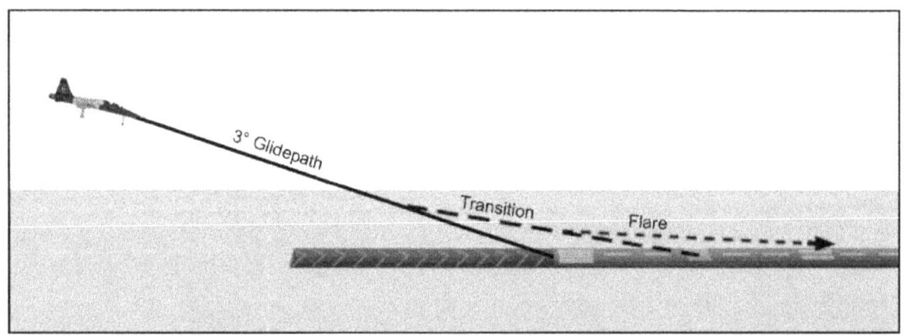

Figure 101: Side view of what the final approach to landing should look like (Source: U.S. AIB report).

See the accompanying graphic above for a side view of what the final approach to landing should look like.

In an attempt to fix his glidepath, he developed an excessive sink rate. He did not detect his slow airspeed or excessive sink rate in time to prevent a runway impact of sufficient force to cause catastrophic damage to the MA's landing gear and right wing.

The MP was unable to prevent the MA from departing the runway, incurring further damage. The MA came to rest 2,500 feet from the point of impact. The MP accomplished a safe ground egress.

Figure 102: MA aircraft (Source: U.S. AIB report).

The 50th Flying Training Squadron Commander originally approved the MP's cross-country plan to remain overnight at Charleston, South Carolina, to support a Reserve Officer Training Corps (ROTC) event he had organized for The Citadel. One week prior to the mishap, the commander changed his policy to require all cross-country pilots to remain overnight at Ellington. The commander informed the MP of the new policy; the MP could still support the Citadel event if his plan allowed him to stay at Ellington. The commander did not consider cancelling the MP's ROTC event. The MP still wanted to support the ROTC event and believed that his planned timeline, while aggressive, would allow him to safely arrive at Ellington. This policy change, combined with the MP's ROTC commitment, led to the MP flying a high-risk mission of a fourth sortie, solo, single-ship, for his first night arrival to Ellington.

Figure 103: MA aircraft after runway departure (Source: U.S. AIB report).

Human factors analysis

The AIB considered all human factors contained in the DoD HFACS guide and analyzed them to identify relevant factors in this mishap. After reviewing all the factual evidence and witness testimonies, factors that were found to be relevant to this mishap were identified using the taxonomy and definitions set forth in the DoD HFACS guide. In this mishap, the AIB determined many facts overlapped multiple human factor definitions and did not clearly fall into only one definition according to the taxonomy. Where this occurs, the human factors involved are first identified, then the facts relating to those human factors are discussed together.

A. Acts and Preconditions related to the MP

1. Excessive Motivation to Succeed

a. **Excessive Motivation to Succeed.** This is a factor when the individual is preoccupied with success to the exclusion of other mission factors leading to an unsafe situation.

b. **Task/Mission-In-Progress Re-Planning.** This is a factor when crew or team members fail to adequately reassess changes in their dynamic environment during mission execution and change their mission plan accordingly to ensure adequate management of risk.

c. **Discussion.** The MP originally planned a cross country to Charleston AFB to attend a ROTC event at his *alma mater*, The Citadel. On his original plan, the MP had planned two sorties to Charleston on Friday, 11 Feb 2011. He would then coordinate at The Citadel for the next day's events and remain overnight in Charleston, SC. On Saturday, 12 Feb 2011, the MP would make a presentation about pilot training and being a pilot in the Air Force to ROTC cadets at approximately 0800 Eastern Standard Time (EST). From there the MP and the cadets would proceed to Charleston AFB from approximately 1000 to 1200 EST to view the T-38, T-6 and T-1 aircraft that were being flown in on various cross-country sorties to Charleston AFB. After the AFROTC Day events were completed, the MP planned to fly out-and-back sorties from Charleston AFB. On Sunday, 13 Feb 2011, the MP would fly two sorties returning to Columbus AFB.

On Friday, 4 Feb 2011, the 50 FTS/CC (Flying Training Squadron/CC) announced a squadron cross-country policy change regarding remain overnight location and directed the MP to change his plans. The 50FTS/CC now required the MP to remain overnight at Ellington Field both nights if he still wanted to go cross country. He also told the MP that he could still accomplish his obligations at The Citadel as part of the continuation training cross country.

Therefore, the MP now had two goals. The first goal was to fulfill his obligations at The Citadel. The second goal was to comply with 50 FTS/CC's directive to remain overnight at Ellington Field.

At no time did the MP consider opting out of the Citadel event. He developed and coordinated the event starting more than one month prior. As a result, he felt a professional obligation to follow through on the event.

The MP wanted to satisfy the mission requirement of remaining overnight at Ellington Field while incorporating the Citadel event. The MP knew the schedule for 11 Feb 2011 was going to be tight, "…when the plan had changed for me being able to go to Charleston with my formation, that week it was known that that was going to be a long day, regardless…" Despite knowing his FDP was going to be tight, he did not consider staying at Mobile Downtown Airport; "the jet was to be in Ellington. And I still had time on my duty day."

On the ground at Mobile Downtown Airport, the MP realized he needed a quick turn. When he arrived at Mobile Downtown Airport, around 1800, he had accumulated multiple delays totaling 1.5 hours from the planned arrival. The MP and JIMBO 62 "were looking at the next day's events, because [they] needed to have 12 hours…before the next day's events." Because it was night, the MP was forced to re-plan the last leg to split the formation into two single-ship entities. The MP confirmed the FBO personnel were going to service their aircraft quickly. At about 1820, he called new flight plans in for himself and JIMBO 62 for a planned departure in the 1840 to 1850 timeframe. With a planned 52 minutes enroute to Ellington Field, the MP expected to land 10 minutes prior to the end of his allowable FDP (which would end no later than 1945). The MP and JIMBO 62 briefed their plan and expected the MP to start before JIMBO 62.

The MP experienced further delays when attempting to start his jet at Mobile Downtown Airport. The T-38 requires an external source to provide air to start the two engines and the only start cart at Mobile

Downtown Airport was already connected to JIMBO 62's aircraft. As a result, the MP allowed JIMBO 62 to start first. Once the start cart was moved to his aircraft, one of the MA's engines failed to start on the first attempt. The MA's Mission Display Processor (MDP: the aircraft's central computer) was turned on at 1859. Even if it was possible to takeoff immediately after MDP power up, based on the MP's planned flight time of 52 minutes, it was no longer possible for the MP to arrive at Ellington Field within his allowed FDP. The MP actually departed at 1916. The MP had 17 minutes between MDP power-up and takeoff to realize he could no longer arrive at Ellington Field prior to the end of his FDP. The MP did not adequately monitor the time in relation to his FDP while at Mobile Downtown Airport.

The MP's excessive motivation to succeed in both goals led to him flying a fourth sortie, flown entirely at night, and attempting to land more than 30 minutes beyond the end of his FDP. This combination of factors may have led to fatigue, as discussed below.

2. Fatigue

a. **Fatigue – Physiological/Mental.** This is a factor when the individual's diminished physical or mental capability is due to an inadequate recovery, as a result of restricted or shortened sleep or physical or mental activity during prolonged wakefulness. Fatigue may additionally be described as acute, cumulative, or chronic.

b. **Discussion.** The MP testified that he had not had any problems with sleep or fatigue during the two weeks prior to the mishap. Cumulative and chronic fatigue were not factors in this mishap.

The MP did not specifically more fatigued than usual leaving Mobile Downtown Airport or in the air on his final sortie to Ellington Field. Additionally, JIMBO 62 did not identify concerns of fatigue in the morning or prior to the fourth sortie. However, when asked if he felt fatigued, the MP testified:

As it gets nighttime you're obviously going to be aware of your crosscheck and you know, I realized it was getting a little bit slower. Looking back on it, seeing that my instruments were not doing what I was expecting them to do and things like that, obviously I was, but at the time I did not notice any kind of effects or need or feel tired.

According to Operational Risk Management of Fatigue Effects by James C. Miller, Ph.D., states of wakefulness and sleepiness have direct effects on cognitive and physical performance effectiveness as individuals work across the day and night. "Fatigue in its many forms is often misrepresented as an unavoidable risk in military operations, and its severity is often underestimated by those affected." Potential fatigue-related effects include cognitive impairment, slowed response time, narrowed attention, loss of situational awareness, and reduced interpersonal communications among others. Based on the MP's testimony, in hindsight, he self-identified several cognitive effects consistent with fatigue.

3. In-flight Procedures and Decision Making

a. **Procedural.** This is a factor when a procedure is accomplished in the wrong sequence or using the wrong technique or when the wrong control or switch is used. This also captures errors in navigation, calculation or operation of automated systems.

b. **Risk Assessment – During Operation.** This is a factor when the individual fails to adequately evaluate the risks associated with a particular course of action and this faulty evaluation leads to inappropriate decision and subsequent unsafe situation. This failure occurs in real-time when formal risk-assessment procedures are not possible.

c. **Decision-Making during Operation.** This is a factor when the individual through faulty logic selects the wrong course of action in a time-constrained environment.

d. **Task/Mission-In-Progress Re-Planning.** This is a factor when crew or team members fail to adequately reassess changes in their dynamic environment during mission execution and change their mission plan accordingly to ensure adequate management of risk.

e. **Discussion.** The MP filed a flight plan departing Mobile Downtown Airport to Ellington Field via Lake Charles, LA. The MP and JIMBO 62 had planned and briefed an ILS approach (a precision approach) to runway 35L at Ellington Field. The MP did not have a copy of the book that contains the Ellington Field instrument approach plates. He obtained the ILS instrument approach plate for runway 17R, but only had a TACAN instrument approach plate for runway 22, as a backup. After leaving Mobile Downtown Airport with a night takeoff, the two aircraft proceeded separately direct to Lake Charles and then via ATC vectors to Ellington Field. The two pilots learned from the Ellington Field Automated Terminal Information System (ATIS) the active runway was 17 Right, not 35 Left as originally planned.

JIMBO 62 decided to fly a visual approach into Ellington Field due to an aircraft malfunction and his belief that a visual approach would enable him to land sooner. The MP elected to mimic JIMBO 62 and perform a visual approach. He reported that there were communications issues due to the number of JIMBOs on frequency and radio transmissions that were missed or incorrectly responded to, so he wanted to minimize the number of vectors he would receive by accomplishing the visual approach. A thorough review of the transcripts and the audio recordings from both Houston Approach sectors does not reveal any evidence of aircraft missing radio calls nor responding incorrectly, except by the MP. In addition, based on the transcripts, the MP had already decided to fly a visual approach prior to his first contact with Houston Approach Control. The MP felt comfortable flying a night visual approach because he had recently flown night visual approaches at Columbus AFB. He assessed only the benefits of the visual approach and weighed this against what is allowed by the AFIs. In his testimony, the MP did not report attempting to assess the risks of flying a visual approach into Ellington Field prior to making his decision. Yet, the MP knew flying into Ellington Field was difficult, especially at night. "It's a dangerous place. If you've never flown into there, it's a dangerous place flying, at night, just because of the environmental [lights]."

According to the AFI 11-2T-38, Volume 3, AETC Supplement 1, the "preferred" night landing approach procedure is a precision approach (such as ILS). The visual approach falls below precision approach and non-precision approach in the preferential order. Additionally, this instruction states ILS glide slope will be used if available. The MP did not intend to use ILS glide slope guidance. Multiple IPs in the 50 FTS, including the 50 FTS/CC, testified they believe they must choose the most precise approach available, i.e. fly ILS approach if available.

Furthermore, they would not choose to fly a visual approach on their first night arrival into a given airfield. The MP chose an approach procedure that other 50 FTS IPs would not have chosen when in the same situation.

The MP did not utilize an ILS to guide his approach into Ellington Field. The MP selected the Ellington TACAN as his Primary Navigation Source and set the final approach course for the ILS to 17R in his course window to help give an overall global picture of his location and to aid his approach into Ellington Field. The MP turned toward the first runway he saw without realizing it was runway 22. However, the MP was unsure since the runway did not look like what he expected. Specifically, he expected to see ramp lights to the right of the runway, but they were not there. In addition, the MP was comparing what he was seeing to his navigational instruments. He reported that, "the instruments and what I was seeing was not making too much sense." Despite these discrepancies, he did not consider executing a go around.

4. Disorientation

a. **Geographic Misorientation.** This is a factor when the individual is at a latitude and/or longitude different from where he believes he is or at a lat/long unknown to the individual and this creates an unsafe situation.

b. Spatial Disorientation (Type 1) Unrecognized. This is a failure to correctly sense a position, motion or attitude of the aircraft or of oneself within the fixed coordinate system provided by the surface of the earth and the gravitational vertical. Spatial Disorientation (Type 1) Unrecognized is a factor when a person's cognitive awareness of one or more of the following varies from reality: attitude; position; velocity; direction of motion or acceleration. Proper control inputs are not made because the need is unknown.

c. Spatial Disorientation (Type 2) Recognized. This is a failure to correctly sense a position, motion or attitude of the aircraft or of oneself within the fixed coordinate system provided by the surface of the earth and the gravitational vertical. Spatial Disorientation (Type 2) is a factor when recognized perceptual confusion is induced through one or more of the following senses: visual; vestibular; auditory; tactile; proprioception or kinesthetic. Proper control inputs are still possible.

d. Misinterpreted/Misread Instrument. This is a factor when the individual is presented with a correct instrument reading but its significance is not recognized, it is misread or is misinterpreted.

e. Discussion. As stated above, the MP departed Mobile Downtown Airport, travelled directly to Lake Charles, and then to Ellington Field via radar vectors. The MP selected the Ellington TACAN as his Primary Navigation Source and set the final approach course for the ILS to 17R as his final approach course to help give him overall situational awareness of his position and direction of travel relative to the runway. During the approach into Ellington Field, he felt as if he was on a base leg (approximately perpendicular to final approach) for about a 5 NM final approach to runway 17R. Once the MP visually acquired a runway (in fact runway 22), the position of the runway was consistent with where he expected to find runway 17R. When asked if he felt he was on a base leg to runway 22, the MP testified, "When I picked up 22 I felt that was Runway 17... I was on base, you know, and I'm turning towards a dogleg here that's got to be it." However, he noticed his navigation instruments and the airfield lighting were inconsistent with what he expected and he did not believe his instruments. This is consistent with Misinterpreted/Misread Instruments. The MP had lost situational awareness and was, in fact, geographically misoriented. The MP realized his error only after the Ellington Tower controller communicated that he was approaching runway 22:

Tower then informed me that it looked like I was lining up with Runway 22. That's about the time that my situational awareness got back to where it needed to be and that's why it was not looking correct outside, and why my instruments--they weren't lying to me. They were telling the truth as to [the] way I was lined up.

While the MP had regained situational awareness in relation to his heading, he was still geographically misoriented in relation to his distance from the runway. As the MP was establishing himself on final approach and receiving the radio call notifying him that he was landing on runway 22, he thought he was 3 to 4 NM from the runway. In fact, he was much closer (approximately 1 NM from the runway).

The MP knew he was steep and used the PAPI and his Heads-Up Display flight path marker to aid in his descent as he approached the runway. He believed the PAPI was telling him he was approaching with a normal glidepath (In fact, he never would have received any PAPI indications other than "high"). The MP had an excessive vertical velocity but did not realize this because he did not monitor his Vertical Velocity Indicator (VVI). The MP did not sufficiently monitor his airspeed and did not realize that it had decayed to 23 knots below FAS over the 18 seconds prior to impact. Both of these failures are consistent with Unrecognized Spatial Disorientation.

5. Channelized Attention

a. **Channelized Attention.** This is a factor when the individual is focusing all conscious attention on a limited number of environmental cues to the exclusion of others of a subjectively equal or higher or more immediate priority, leading to an unsafe situation. May be described as a tight focus of attention that leads to the exclusion of comprehensive situational information.

b. **Discussion.** There is evidence of three distinct instances of Channelized Attention in this mishap: finding the runway, determining why the runway looked wrong, and fixing his glidepath.

First, the MP reported he was overly focused on "finding the field." At this point, other IPs reported that they would be attempting to line up on a 3 to 5 NM final. This may have led to the Geographic Misorientation discussed in this section.

Second, when he was cleared to land on runway 17R and visually acquired a runway (in fact, it was runway 22), the MP focused his attention upon determining why his visual cues did not match his expectations. He did not see the ramp lights which he expected to see to the right of the runway. The MP also noted that his navigational instruments did not display what he should have seen if he was lining up on runway 17R. He became focused on looking for the ramp lights and his instrument approach plate trying to reconcile what he actually saw with his expectations. This led to the MP failing to achieve an appropriate glidepath.

Third, once he was informed he was lined up on runway 22, the MP became channelized on establishing an appropriate glidepath. He did not monitor his airspeed, allowing it to decay to 23 knots below FAS over the 18 seconds prior to impact. The MP's failure to recognize his slow airspeed is consistent with Channelized Attention.

6. Visual Scan

a. **Breakdown in Visual Scan.** This is a factor when the individual fails to effectively execute learned/practiced internal or external visual scan patterns leading to unsafe situation.

b. **Discussion.** Ellington Field can be difficult to locate at night due to the dim lighting of the runway when contrasted with the intense cultural lighting of Houston and the bright lights of nearby industrial facilities. On approach to Ellington Field, the MP was cleared for the visual approach and instructed to contact the tower. At that time, he had visually acquired the "void" which he had identified as the airfield, but he did not have the runway lights in sight.

The MP was cleared to land by Ellington Tower but the visual cues did not seem to line up with the MP's expectations based upon his navigational aids. The MP then focused his attention on the visual scan outside of the cockpit and to his instrument approach plate for runway 17R on his kneeboard to provide better situational awareness. He was initially monitoring his airspeed to determine when to lower his gear and flaps. The MP stated, "I felt like had gotten back onto and captured a green speed [FAS] at short final." However, the MA's airspeed decayed below the appropriate FAS over the 18 seconds prior to impact. This discrepancy is consistent with a breakdown in visual scan.

Figure 104: MA aircraft after runway departure (Source: U.S. AIB report).

7. In-flight Perception

a. **Error due to Misperception.** This is a factor when an individual acts or fails to act based on an illusion; misperception or disorientation state and this act or failure to act creates an unsafe situation.

b. Overconfidence. This is a factor when the individual overvalues or overestimates personal capability, the capability of others or the capability of aircraft/vehicles or equipment and this creates an unsafe situation.

c. Misperception of operable conditions. This is a factor when an individual misperceives or misjudges altitude, separation, speed, closure rate, road/sea conditions, aircraft/vehicle location within the performance envelope or other operational conditions and this leads to an unsafe situation.

d. Discussion. The MP first picked up the runway environment, the "black hole where you would expect Ellington to be," about 10 NM from Ellington Field. At a perceived 5 NM he could see runway lights but was not lined up with the runway. When he thought he was still 3 NM from the runway, he did not have full situational awareness of the runway; he expected to see the ramp lights on the right side of the runway and they were absent. Additionally, his navigational instruments did not correlate with what he saw. The MP would have wanted a final approach of 5 to 6 NM but once he turned to his final approach, the runway came upon him quicker than expected. Yet, he felt he was capable of landing the MA.

As the MP was establishing himself on final approach and receiving the radio call notifying him that he was landing on runway 22, he thought he was 3 to 4 NM from the runway. In fact, he was approximately 1 NM from the runway. During this timeframe, he relied on how the jet felt when maneuvering to determine his airspeed. He felt he had not slowed down because the jet "will start to fly sloppy around final turn speeds…the jet still responded pretty well." In fact, based upon the MDP data, during the radio call he was slowing through 161 KCAS (1 knot below final turn speed). This misperception of his airspeed and overconfidence that he could determine his airspeed based solely upon the characteristics of flight led to a false sense of security; he did not monitor his airspeed which led to an unsafe situation.

8. Negative Transfer

a. **Negative Transfer.** This is a factor when the individual reverts to a highly learned behavior used in a previous system or situation and that response is inappropriate or degrades mission performance.

b. **Discussion.** The MP chose to land with full flaps at Ellington Field. IPs have the option to land continuation training sorties with full or 60% flaps. However, Flight Crew Information File (FCIF) 10-019 part B which was published on 16 Apr 2010 at Columbus AFB required student sorties to land with 60% flaps, selecting full flaps when landing is assured on full stop landings.

Since he regularly flew with students at Columbus AFB, the MP routinely used 60% flaps for landings. When flying solo, the MP preferred to land full stop with full flaps because he believes this helps decrease the chance of landing fast or ballooning (climbing during the flare). At Ellington Field, the MP decided to land with full flaps, consistent with his stated preference. A full-flap final approach requires more thrust to maintain adequate airspeed. While the MP was generally unaware of his airspeed (See Channelized Attention discussion), when he did make power corrections, they were more consistent with a 60% flap final approach, which exacerbated his airspeed decay.

9. Undercontrol

a. **Overcontrol/Undercontrol.** This is a factor when an individual responds inappropriately to conditions by either overcontroling or undercontroling the aircraft/vehicle/system. The error may be a result of preconditions or a temporary failure of coordination.

b. **Discussion.** The MP felt his approach was high and fast and, therefore, decreased the throttle. He thought this correction put him back on normal approach speed at approximately one half mile to the end of runway and he increased the power to maintain his approach speed. At the threshold of the runway, he performed his normal approach procedure by pulling power back to idle and started to flare the aircraft. However, as discussed in section 4 of this report, he was below the appropriate FAS for 18 seconds prior to impact. By three seconds prior to impact, the MP had allowed the MA to slow to 23 knots below his FAS. Therefore, he undercontroled the aircraft on his approach into Ellington Field.

Human Factors Related to Supervision

Supervision is a factor in a mishap if the methods, decisions or policies of the supervisory chain of command directly affect practices, conditions, or actions of individuals and result in human error or unsafe situation.

1. **Oversight**

    a. **Leadership/Supervision/Oversight Inadequate.** This is a factor when the availability, competency, quality or timeliness of leadership, supervision or oversight does not meet task demands and creates an unsafe situation. Inappropriate supervisory pressures are also captured under this code.

    b. **Discussion.** The 50 FTS/CC established the date for the cross country more than a month in advance. The 50 FTS/DO, in coordination with the 50 FTS/CC, originally approved the MP's six-sortie cross-country plan to remain overnight at Charleston AFB on a cross-country coordination worksheet dated 18 Jan 2011. The 50 FTS/CC subsequently changed his approval on 4 Feb 2011 in conjunction with his change in policy that all CT cross-country missions for the weekend must remain overnight at Ellington Field. For this cross country, the 50 FTS/DO was not aware of many of the changes that had occurred to the overall squadron cross-country plan after he signed the coordination worksheet. He couldn't say for certain who was aware of the complete plan, but thought that the 50 FTS/CC was aware. The fact that the squadron commander did not actively keep the squadron operations officer aware of the full plan is an indication of inadequate oversight of the mission.

2. Supervision and Risk Assessment

a. **Supervision – Policy.** This is a factor when policy or guidance or lack of a policy or guidance leads to an unsafe situation.

b. **Risk Assessment – Formal.** This is a factor when supervision does not adequately evaluate the risks associated with a mission or when pre-mission risk assessment tools or risk assessment programs are inadequate. c. Authorized Unnecessary Hazard. This is a factor when supervision authorizes a mission or mission element that is unnecessarily hazardous without sufficient cause or need. Includes intentionally scheduling personnel for mission or operation that they are not qualified to perform.

c. **Unit/Organizational Values/Culture.** This is a factor when explicit/implicit actions, statements or attitudes of unit leadership set unit/organizational values (culture) that allow an environment where unsafe mission demands or pressures exist. AIB Note: This human factor is categorized under Organizational Influences of the DOD HFACS, but applies here when discussed at the unit (squadron) level.

d. **Discussion.** The 50 FTS/CC had a limited TDY budget. Additionally, his student load had increased steadily since FY09. This increased student load, combined with his desire to send each student cross country, reduced the portion of his TDY budget available for IPs to go on CT cross-country trips. Therefore, the 50 FTS/CC wanted to minimize the cost of each CT cross country in order to maximize the number of IPs who could go on a CT cross country. At the same time, he wanted to maximize the training his IPs received while cross country. To achieve this goal, the 50 FTS/CC developed his CT cross-country weekend concept. The stated goal of these CT cross-country weekends was to complete CT requirements and/or gain proficiency in the aircraft. The CT cross-country weekend concept called for flying four times on Friday, four times on Saturday, and then two times on Sunday. A squadron CT cross-country weekend was accomplished under this guidance on 3-5 Dec 2010. Sixteen IPs logged more than 100 CT requirements. Four recent pilot training graduates accompanied the IPs and received training. The 50 FTS/CC perceived the December 2010 cross country as very successful and highlighted the CT cross-country weekends as a squadron priority for 2011.

However, outside of the CT cross-country weekends, flying four sorties in a day was rare in this squadron unless there was an extenuating circumstance such as retrieving an off-station aircraft. Furthermore, given the already high OPTEMPO and long work days, multiple IPs chose not to participate in these CT weekends. In fact, several IPs felt that the risk of this mission outweighed the benefits. Specifically, one IP said, "For me as an experienced T-38 instructor pilot, I did not feel that the benefit of flying four sorties in a day outweighed the risks of flying four sorties in a day." Lt Col Grizzard, the Air Force Reserve flight commander associated with 50 FTS, stated:

"[Flying four sorties] on back to back days, the first and second day of a cross country, it's going to ultimately lead to fatigue and the possibility of mistakes. To that end, these cross countries were never advertised to reservists, specifically the traditional reservists that I supervised."

Finally, Lt Rabell testified that the 50 FTS/CC told IPs during the mass cross country briefing they would probably not want to go anywhere after flying four times since they would be tired.

The 50 FTS/CC saw the benefits of these cross-country weekends to be: completing continuation training requirements, pilot proficiency, hours for inexperienced IPs and making progress toward completing the Flying Hour Program. Yet, one IP testified, "And for me as an instructor pilot with a lot of experience in the T-38, I don't think that flying a third or fourth sortie in a day or in a night or a tenth sortie on a weekend is going to make me a better pilot or instructor pilot." During the February 2011 CT cross-country weekend, numerous IPs were flying solo which required flying from the front cockpit. AETC does not require any front cockpit training at all. The 50 FTS/CC believed flying solo helped "[e]nsure pilot proficiency, front seat … gave me more instructional skills to be able to talk to references in HUD cross checks from the front seat that are difficult to keep fresh in your mind when you always fly in the back seat." The AETC guidance for CT and ID states, "Since the focus is on instructor development, ID sorties will be scheduled and flown dual to the absolute maximum possible." Only one of 15 sorties that logged instructor development (ID) sorties was flown dual.

An analysis of the risk versus benefit of the February 2011 cross country was never accomplished. When asked if they had weighed risks versus benefits, the 50 FTS/DO stated, "I'm not sure we ever specifically sat down and discussed the virtue versus vice, if you will, on that subject." When asked if any concerns over the risk of the 10-sortie weekends had reached his level, the 50 FTS/CC stated, "No, sir. We had talked about that in November for that type of plan and once we executed the plan and saw that in that particular instance a very successful execution. At that point … we had stopped addressing risk associated with it". Additional risk factors were present in February 2011 that had not been present in December 2010. The first additional risk factor was the higher number of aircraft flown solo. The plan called for 11 pilots (of which 3 were students) to depart Columbus in 10 aircraft, with 2 additional IPs scheduled to join the cross country on Saturday. The second additional risk factor was later arrivals at Ellington Field driven by the initial departure time being moved from early in the day to the afternoon. While he was aware of these differences, the 50 FTS/CC did not see a need to take risk mitigation measures. As mentioned previously, the 50 FTS/CC and 50 FTS/DO had approved the MP's original plan to remain overnight at Charleston AFB. However, once the squadron's policies changed, the 50 FTS/CC changed the MP's plans. The MP was now required to remain overnight at Ellington Field if he still wanted to go cross country. The MP discussed the change with the 50 FTS/CC and stated he still wanted to support the Citadel ROTC event. The 50 FTS/CC did not consider cancelling the MP's Citadel activities. The 50 FTS/CC discussed the MP's plan with him, including servicing locations for his aircraft, and felt that the MP's plan would work, but did not ask what time the MP needed to be at The Citadel each day. The 50 FTS/CC "considered [the MP's] Saturday plan as aggressive" but agreed to continue to support the MP's Citadel events as long as the weather was not going to be a factor.

The night before the mishap, the 11 Feb 2011 schedule changed and the MP was scheduled for a student instructional sortie at 0900, the first 50 FTS takeoff time that day. As a result, the MP's new plan would now lead to his flight into Ellington Field being his fourth sortie of the day. The 50 FTS/CC and 50 FTS/DO were not aware the MP was going to be flying four sorties the day of the mishap. Yet, the MP had never flown four sorties in a day. On the day of the mishap, Lt Col Gordon Kimpel, another 50 FTS IP, was concerned regarding the expected length of the MP's day. He expressed his concern to an assistant operations officer (ADO). The ADO told him it could be done if it was planned correctly and chose not to elevate the concern to a higher level. Finally, the operations supervisor that gave the MP his step briefing from Columbus AFB was aware that the MP was flying four sorties that day. However, their ORM discussion only covered the first sortie of the MP's cross country.

Before each of these cross-country missions, each IP has to fill out an ORM chit based on the 50 FTS ORM Assessment worksheet. When starting a CT cross country, many IPs fill out the chit for the entire day. However, both the MP and the operations supervisor on duty were under the impression that the MP needed to fill out the ORM chit for only the sortie leaving Columbus AFB. There was no written guidance on what was expected.

The MP assessed his ORM at Mobile Downtown Airport before his flight to Ellington Field and it did not require operations supervisor approval. The AIB confirmed that a properly assessed ORM worksheet for the profile for the MP's last sortie would only require aircraft commander approval. No discussion with the operations supervisor or higher supervision was necessary. The worksheet only accounted for these hazards on the mishap sortie: fourth sortie of the day, night, and off-station sortie. The ORM worksheet does not take into account the following hazards that were present in this mishap: first night arrival into a given airfield, extended time into FDP, and the combination of solo and single-ship. The Vice-Wing Commander, Operations Group Commander, and Deputy Operations Group Commander all believe a sortie with this combination of hazards present should require supervisory approval. In fact, the Vice-Wing Commander stated, "My opinion is that a fourth sortie at night needs to have squadron supervision for approval." Furthermore, there is no mechanism present in the ORM matrix, other than total score, that elevates approval to a higher supervisory level.

Finally, there was a culture of risk tolerance related to CT among squadron supervision at the time of the mishap. The AIB found four specific examples that highlight this.

First, the 50 FTS/CC believed flying four CT sorties on back-to-back days was low risk. He stated, "the particular task loading in this airplane for going cross country—I believe there's a small factor for the fourth sortie." There was also a mindset among supervision that a day consisting of four CT sorties was less risky than a day consisting of three student pilot instructional sorties. Major Jeffrey Isgett, a squadron assistant operations officer, stated, "...instructor pilots under reasonable circumstances can manage four sorties in a day without a real increase—without any increase in risk over three sorties a day with students. We accept the risk of flying student sorties, with three students, on a daily basis."

Second, as already discussed in this section, the successful execution of a similar cross country plan in December 2010 also led to a sense of reduced risk for the overall plan for the February 2011 cross country for the 50 FTS/CC.

Third, the ORM matrix rarely drove the mission decision authority above the aircraft commander for CT sorties. This may have led to a sense among squadron IPs that CT is always low risk.

Finally, there was frequent approval for solo, single-ship CT sorties and, at the time, there was blanket approval for solo aircraft on this cross country. Captain Matthew Eldredge, a flight commander in the 50 FTS, stated, "There is a blanket waiver that the [50 FTS/DO] threw down with that said that if there is a jet available for a solo IP--or solo instructor pilot, you were cleared to take that and do your instructor development from there." This automatic approval may have led to a sense that a lack of mutual support does not impact risk.

Human Factors related to Organizational Influences

Organizational Influences are factors in a mishap if communications, actions, policies or significant omissions by upper-level management directly or indirectly affect supervisory unsafe situation.

1. **Procedural Guidance**

    a. **Procedural Guidance/Publications.** This is a factor when written direction, checklists, graphic depictions, tables, charts or other published guidance is inadequate, misleading or inappropriate and this creates an unsafe situation.

    b. **Discussion.** According to paragraph 3.21.7 of AETC Supplement 1 to AFI 11-2T-38 Volume 3, as well as paragraph 5.12.4 of AETC Supplement 1 to AFI 11-202, Volume 3, the preferred method for night approach in descending order is precision, non-precision with an associated visual descent path indicator, VFR straight-in, and VFR rectangular pattern. The same guidance also states, "Also use the instrument landing system (ILS) glide slope if available." (For the full text of paragraph 3.21.7 of AETC Supplement 1 to AFI 11-2T-38 Volume 3, see section 4 of this report.) The use of the word "preferred" leads to inconsistent interpretations of the guidance. For example, the MP and other IPs believe ILS approach at night, if available, is only preferred and not required. However, other IPs believe an ILS approach is required if available.

25 F-16C Midair Collision

Figure 105: F-16C (Source: U.S. AIB report).

The United States Air Force Aircraft Accident Investigation Board (AIB) describes in their report that:

On 1 August 2013, at 22:23:56 local time (L), an F-16C, tail number (T/N) 87-0314, collided mid-air into an F-16C, T/N 86-0357, while participating in night tactical air intercept training over the Atlantic Ocean, off the coast of Maryland.

The right wing of the first mishap aircraft, F-16C, T/N 87-0314 (hereinafter referred to as MA1) struck the left stabilator of the second mishap aircraft, F-16 C, T/N 86-0357 (hereinafter referred to as MA2). The MA1 suffered significant structural damage to its right wing, but the mishap pilot (MP1) was able to recover the aircraft. The MA2 experienced debilitating structural damage causing the aircraft to be uncontrollable. The mishap pilot two (MP2) successfully ejected, sustained non-life threatening injuries, and was recovered by search and rescue (SAR) forces. The MA1 suffered damage .The MA2 was destroyed upon impact with the water.

According to the AIB report, the MA1 and the MA2 departed Joint Base Andrews (JBA), as part of a three-ship F-16C formation to complete a Mission Qualification Training (MQT) Aerospace Control Alert (ACA) night intercept upgrade.

The MP1 was the Instructor Pilot, and the MP2 was number three in the formation as the nonmaneuvering adversary training aid. During the upgrade, the MP1 elected to lead an intercept for a demonstration of intercept geometry and ACA pacing. During the intercept, the MP1 rolled out at 3900 feet behind the MA2 then proceeded to close on the MA2's position to demonstrate an ACA inspect procedure, i.e. fly close enough to allow inspection into a target of interest cockpit. During this phase, the MP1 failed to process the accurate range, airspeed, and closing velocity cues displayed by his aircraft, and attempted to close visually (not monitoring radar cues) under low-illumination/dark night conditions. At 500 feet directly behind the MA2, and at the same altitude, the MP1's airspeed had increased to 412 knots, with 100 knots of closing velocity. His closing velocity should have been less than 5 knots at that range, with an offset, both in horizontal and in vertical altitude, until sufficient visual references were available to close for the inspect procedure. Three seconds later, the MP1 collided into the back of the MA2.

Accident cause

The Board President (BP) found by clear and convincing evidence the cause of this mishap was failure of the MP1 to maintain flight path deconfliction between himself and the MA2 due to three human factors causal to the mishap: Misperception of Operational Conditions, Channelized Attention, and Task Misprioritization. By a preponderance of the evidence, the BP found four human factors substantially contributed to the mishap: Overconfidence, Inadequate Crew Rest, Fatigue Physiological/Mental, and Violation Lack of Discipline.

Accident summary

The AIB report describes the accident as follows: The MF taxi, takeoff, departure, and airspace entry were uneventful. The MP1 elected to lead an intercept with the

Upgrade Pilot (UP) in trail behind him, for a demonstration of proper intercept mechanics and ACA.

The MP1's demonstration intercept included real-time verbal instruction to the Upgrade Pilot (UP) and radio inputs, as the MP1 was not only instructing, but also acting as both lead and the ACA controlling agencies.

The AIB explains that at the beginning of the intercept, the MP1 directed the MP2 to turn off all external lighting.

During the intercept, the MP2 flew in a straight line back and forth across the airspace at 310 knots, and 11,180 feet mean sea level (MSL).

The MP1 proceeded to circle around the MA2 and fly within 3900 feet behind the MP1 at 335 knots with 0 knots of closing velocity. The MP1, playing both the role of the ACA controlling agencies and the intercepting pilot, directed himself to perform an ACA inspect of the MA2. An ACA inspect is a directive to look at and gather data from the cockpit of the target of interest and implies flying within 500 feet to the side of the target.

Ten seconds later, the MP1 was 3,000 feet behind the MA2, at the same altitude, with an airspeed of 386 knots and 60 knots of closing velocity. At 500 feet behind the MA2, the MP1's airspeed had increased to 412 knots with 100 knots of closing velocity; a "break-X" appeared in the MP1's head-up display (HUD). A break-X displays in the HUD under these circumstances as a warning indicating that the pilot should maneuver to ensure safe distance from another aircraft. The MP1 did not see the break-X that appeared in the HUD of the MA1. Three seconds later, the MP1 collided into the back of the MA2.

Figure 106: Impact (Source: U.S. AIB report).

The AIB explains that the MA1's right wing suffered significant structural damage, to include having part of the left stabilator from the MA2 embedded in its wing, but the MP1 was able to recover the aircraft to JBA .The MA2 experienced significant structural damage, to include the likely loss of its left stabilator, causing the aircraft to be uncontrollable. The MP2 successfully ejected and sustained non-life threatening injuries before recovery by SAR forces.

Just after the mid-air collision, the MA2 began a slow barrel roll to the left, did not respond to the MP2's control inputs, and continued rolling. The MP2 made a prudent decision to eject and did so once he ensured the MA2 cockpit was pointed upright. The MP2 pulled the ejection handle and the force of the ejection caused the MP2 to be "thrown around like a ragdoll" for five to seven seconds. The parachute successfully opened, and the MP2 descended to the ocean. The MP2 hit the water, popped back up from the water as his life preserver unit inflated, disconnected the parachute, and located his life raft, which had fully inflated.

The MP2 sustained injuries to both legs during the ejection and had difficulty getting into the life raft. Approximately 40 minutes after ejecting, the MP2 had boarded the life raft, located the survival kit radio, and contacted the on-scene commander (OSC) on the military Guard frequency. The OSC advised the MP2 that the Coast Guard was on the way.

The AIB report describes the Search and Rescue (SAR) as follows:

Approximately 10 seconds after the midair collision. The MA2's emergency locator transmitter (ELT) sounded through the MP1' s and the UP's communications systems. Within a minute of the midair collision, the MP1 communicated the collision to the W-386 controlling agency and passed approximate GPS coordinates of the mid-air collision. The controlling agency responded that SAR forces would be launched. One of the mission sortie pilots assumed OSC duties and attempted for 40 minutes to contact the MP2 via military guard frequency.

Approximately 40 minutes after ejecting, the MP2 boarded his survival liferaft and contacted the OSC via radio. The MP2 communicated his location to the OSC who relayed the information to the Coast Guard. A HH-60G helicopter and a Navy Ship with a helipad were sent to recover the MP2.

The MP2 utilized flares and verbal directions to guide the helicopter to his location. Within two hours of impact, and without any difficulties, a Coast Guard rescue diver deployed into the water, successfully strapped the MP2 to a floating litter, and lifted the MP2 out of the water and into the helicopter. The helicopter transported the MP2 to JBA uneventfully.

Human factors analysis

The AIB evaluated human factors relevant to the mishap using the analysis and classification system model established by the Department of Defense Human Factors Analysis and Classification System (DoD HFACS) guide, implemented by AFI 91-204, USAF Safety Investigations and Reports, and the relevant Human Factors are defined below:

1. Misperception of Operational Conditions

Misperception of Operational Conditions is a factor when an individual misperceives or misjudges altitude, separation, speed, closure rate, road/sea conditions, aircraft/vehicle location within the performance envelope or other operational conditions and this leads to an unsafe situation.

According to the report, Misperception of Operational Conditions occurred in the final phase of the mishap intercept. To begin the intercept, the MP1 proceeded to roll out and fly within 3900 feet directly behind the MA2 at 335 knots and 0 knots of closing velocity. Night illumination was low over the water, and the MA2 had all of its lights out, as directed by the MP1. The MP1 flew closer to the MA2 in order to inspect the target as a part of the ACA demonstration intercept for the UP. Despite being at 1000 feet, 80 knots of closure, and 0 degrees aspect, the MP1 called over the radio that he was at 3000 feet behind the MA2. Within seconds, at 100 knots of closure on the MA2 and flying at the same altitude, the MA1 collided into the MA2. Accurate range, speed, and closure were available from the radar target track and displayed in the HUD, yet the MP1 failed to look at and/or process this data as he attempted to complete the inspect of the MA2.

In addition, during the low-illumination mishap intercept, the MP1 directed the MP2 to turn off all external lighting, which is an acceptable objective for an MQT ACA qualified pilot. However, by turning off all external lighting, the MP1's primary visual reference was the MA2's exhaust plume, until just prior to impact, when he picked up visual line of sight and closure details in his Night Vision Goggles (NVGs), thus adding to the misperception of operational conditions.

2. Channelized Attention

Channelized Attention is a factor when the individual is focusing all conscious attention on a limited number of environmental cues to the exclusion of others of a subjectively equal or higher or more immediate priority, leading to an unsafe situation. It may be described as a tight focus of attention that leads to the exclusion of comprehensive situational information.

According to the report, the MP1 was not monitoring available range, airspeed, and closure rates available from the radar target track and displayed in the HUD during the critical final phase of the intercept leading up to the mishap, and he failed to maintain flight path deconfliction, i.e, flying with enough distance between him and another aircraft. His attention was channelized elsewhere. The MP1's testimony was that he:

> (1) either focused his attention completely on maintaining his visual of the MA2's exhaust plume; or

> (2) he was focused inside his cockpit; either one to his exclusion of available and accurate target conditions provided by the radar.

The MP1 also testified that his only visual reference of MA2 until just prior to impact was the hot exhaust seen through his NVGs. The MP1 channelized on the limited visual references available from the MA2 to discern sufficient cues to complete his attempt at a night visual rejoin to an inspect position. The MP1's channelized attention led to his exclusion of accurate target information provided by his aircraft, and resulted in the MA1 colliding into the MA2.

3. Task Misprioritization

Task Misprioritization is a factor when the individual does not organize, based on accepted prioritization techniques, the tasks needed to manage the immediate situation.

According to the report, the MP1 failed to prioritize the tasks of "*aviate, navigate, and communicate*" in the final portion of the mishap intercept. As indicated in AFTTP 3-3.F-16, paragraph 9.3.4.1, when one aircraft approaches another from behind, the pilot must first ensure flight path deconfliction, i.e. he must aviate. The MP1 failed to effectively prioritize the acceptable tasks required to complete a safe intercept and rejoin, and instead focused on ACA-simulated radio calls and verbal instruction to the upgrade pilot. The MP1 attempted to lead the intercept/inspect while making anticipated radio calls as both the intercepting pilot and the simulated controlling agencies, while also providing real-time verbal feedback to the UP. The MP1 stated, "*I felt that I was failing my student at the time, and I began to obsessively focus on instruction*". Rather than prioritizing the monitoring of available and accurate target range, closure, aspect, and altitude readily displayed to him by his radar or following accepted Tactical Intercept (TIPs) to maintain flight path deconfliction, the MP1 prioritized instruction and communications.

So the MP1's stated priority was on instruction immediately prior to his collision into the MA2. This misprioritization led to the MP1's failure to monitor and react to the available and accurate target information readily displayed to him, and his failure to follow established TTPs for controlling closure and maintaining flight path deconfliction.

4. Overconfidence

Overconfidence is a factor when the individual overvalues or overestimates personal capability, the capability of others or the capability of aircraft/vehicles or equipment and this creates an unsafe situation.

According to the report, during the week of the mishap sortie, the MP1 overestimated his personal capabilities and underestimated the effects fatigue would have on him the night of the mishap. The MP1 stated, "*Through learned behaviors and prior success managing long work schedules, I had been accustomed to working long and demanding days. Even so, had I exhibited better judgment I would have managed my workday more prudently to ensure I was sufficiently rested for this lengthy and somewhat demanding mission*". Furthermore, overconfidence led to an inaccurate self-assessment prior to the mishap sortie. The MP1 stated, "*One of my obligations as a pilot is to assess whether I'm fit to fly prior to each sortie. At the time that day, I believed that I was fit to fly. I was obviously wrong in the self-assessment as evidence by my monumental mistake the night of the mishap sortie*".

The MP1 overestimated his ability to manage both civilian employment and Air National Guard duties during the week of the mishap. The MP1 stated, "*I also believed that I could handle the combination of civilian employment and Air National Guard duties for the week as long as I reduced my social commitments. I admit that I was grossly mistaken in this assessment and did not demonstrate sound judgment*".

The MP1 summarized, "*Overconfidence in my own abilities was firmly rooted in my previous work habits which had time and again proven successful for me. This misplaced confidence in my ability to overcome the need for reasonable rest in my opinion was a root cause of the accident*".

Furthermore, the MP 1 overestimated his personal capability during the mishap intercept by juggling multiple roles and providing verbal instruction immediately prior to impact, which contributed to the collision.

5. Inadequate Rest

Inadequate rest is a factor when the opportunity for rest was provided but the individual failed to take the opportunity to rest.

According to the report, the MP1 had 4.5 hours of sleep the day of the mishap and 4 hours the previous day. Further the MP1 had been awake for a continuous period of 15.92 hours before the mishap.

His inadequate rest history is a direct result of the MP1' s attendance during the day at his civilian job while flying nights with his unit resulted in his inadequate rest and subsequent fatigue.

6. Fatigue - Physiological/Mental

Fatigue - Physiological/Mental is a factor when the individual's diminished physical or mental capability is due to an inadequate recovery, as a result of restricted or shortened sleep or physical or mental activity during prolonged wakefulness.

According to the report, by his own admission, the MP1 felt tired prior to the mishap flight. By a preponderance of the evidence, the MP1's fatigue directly contributed to his loss of situational awareness during the mishap intercept and exacerbated his Misperception of Operational Conditions, Channelized Attention, and Task Misprioritization, which caused the mishap.

The level of fatigue that MP1 has at the flight moment was associated with the following predictable effects: impaired judgment, lowered alertness, reduced coordination, reduced ability to track moving objects, difficulty steering, and reduced response to emergency driving situations.

7. Violation - Lack of Discipline

Violation - Lack of Discipline is a factor when an individual, crew or team intentionally violates procedures or policies without cause or need. These violations are unusual or isolated to specific individuals rather than larger groups. There is no evidence of these violations being condoned by leadership.

According to the report, the MP1 began the mishap sortie without adequate crew rest, the MP1 knowingly and intentionally began the flight after violating Air Force crew rest minimum requirements, both the night of the mishap and the night prior.

26 A-10 Distraction and Decision-Making

Figure 107: A-10C (Source: U.S. AIB report).

The United States Air Force Aircraft Accident Investigation Board (AIB) describes in their report that:

On 10 May 2010 at 1655 local time, A-10C, tail number 79-0141, assigned to the 75th Fighter Squadron, 23rd Wing, Moody Air Force Base (AFB), Georgia, departed the right edge of runway 18L when the mishap pilot (MP) did not successfully stop the aircraft during an aborted takeoff. As the mishap aircraft (MA) departed the runway, the MP ejected sustaining minor injuries. The MA continued traveling over soft uneven grassland until the nose gear collapsed and the right main landing gear and MA nose became lodged into the ground causing a catastrophic fuselage failure just forward of the right wing's leading edge. The MA stopped approximately 500 feet into the grassland at a 45° angle off the end of the runway.

Minutes later, the MA was engulfed in fire due to the ruptured forward main fuel tank. The MA was destroyed.

As the wingman in the two-ship formation, the MP was briefed to takeoff 20 seconds behind his flight lead. After his flight lead began his takeoff roll, but prior to the MA brake release, the MP realized he had not put on his prescription glasses.

The MP released brakes at the 20 second mark; however donning his glasses distracted him from immediately advancing the throttles to their takeoff setting. The MP noted a lower than calculated airspeed at the required airspeed check point 1000 feet down the runway and attributed it to his late application of power, so he continued the takeoff. The MP checked his speed again at 1500-2000 feet and the indicator showed negligible to no change. At 3500 feet, the MP correctly diagnosed a pitot-static issue but elected to continue with the takeoff versus executing an abort. Approaching the calculated takeoff distance, the MP rechecked the airspeed indicator and noted an unexpected airspeed rise to 90-100 knots indicated airspeed (KIAS). At the same time, the MP had a visual misperception that the MA was no longer accelerating. The MP concluded that the airspeed indicator was working properly and for an unknown reason the MA was unable to attain the takeoff speed of 136 KIAS. The MP aborted the aircraft with approximately 3500 feet of runway remaining.

Evidence supports that the MA was traveling 160-170 KIAS at the time the abort commenced.

Due to his perceived lower airspeed, the MP did not apply the required maximum braking. In a final attempt to stop the MA on a prepared surface, the MP attempted a ninety degree right turn onto the last taxiway at the end of the runway. The MP recognized the MA was traveling too fast to complete the turn and subsequently ejected as the MA departed the prepared surface.

Accident cause

The accident investigation board (AIB) president found clear and convincing evidence that the cause of the mishap was human factor error. Specifically, the

MP's initial decision not to abort the takeoff, and then once the decision to abort was made, the MP applying an inappropriate braking procedure that was based on his perception of being at a lower airspeed.

Additionally, the AIB president found by a preponderance of the evidence, that the pitot-static system blockage, task misprioritization, distraction, and procedural error were substantially contributing factors to the mishap.

Accident summary

The MF taxied into position to hold on Runway 18L. Runway 18L is 9300 feet long. Moody Tower cleared the MF for takeoff.

The briefed takeoff was a 20 second interval takeoff. The MF ran their engines up to 90% rpm, standing up the throttles to a vertical position, and completed final pre-takeoff checks. The MFL released brakes and executed a normal single ship takeoff. As the MFL released brakes, the MP started a timer in his cockpit to execute the planned 20 second interval takeoff.

At that time, the MP realized that he was not wearing his prescription glasses. The MP grabbed the glasses case out of the saddlebag located on the MA's glare shield, pulled the glasses out of the case, put them on, and returned the case to the saddlebag. As the MP put the glasses on, he noticed the timer reach 19 seconds. The MP released brakes at 20 seconds as briefed, finished putting the glasses on, lowered the visor on his helmet, and placed his hands back on the throttles and stick.

As the MP placed his hand back on the throttles, approximately 250-500 feet into the takeoff roll, he realized that he had not, per normal procedures, pushed the throttles to maximum (max) power after brake release. The MP pushed the throttles to max and continued the takeoff roll.

At 1000 feet down the runway, the MP looked at the airspeed indicator to verify that the MA had met the required acceleration check speed. Providing the throttles are advanced to max at brake release, acceleration check speed is a minimum speed for a given distance during takeoff which validates that the engines are producing the expected thrust. For the A-10C, if the acceleration check speed is not met at 1000 feet, a system malfunction is indicated and the takeoff should be aborted. The acceleration check speed indicated on the MF's line up card was 80 KIAS. When the MP checked at 1000 feet down the runway, he noted the airspeed indicated between 50-60 KIAS. However, due to the late push of the throttles to max power, the MP elected to continue the takeoff and check the airspeed again further down the runway.

Between 1500-2000 feet down the runway, the MP rechecked the airspeed indicator and noted 60-70 KIAS. The MP looked in the head up display (HUD) to verify the airspeed, but for an undetermined reason he did not see the digital airspeed readout. At this point, the MP suspected a pitot-static system failure. The pitot-static system takes air pressure readings from different areas on the aircraft to determine and display the airspeed.

The MP believed the aircraft was traveling —a lot faster than indicated and chose to continue the takeoff roll with the intent of rotating just past the predicted takeoff distance and rejoin with the MFL rather than attempt a high speed abort —and have hot brakes and possibly do some damage to the airplane. During this decision making process, the MP either stood the throttles up or pulled them to idle for —a second or less to start an abort, but pushed them back to max once the decision to continue was made.

Approaching the takeoff distance, approximately 4000-4500 feet down the runway, the MP checked the airspeed indicator again and saw a reading of 90-100 KIAS. The MP expected the airspeed to remain at 60-70 KIAS throughout the takeoff due to the pitot-static failure. Despite the indicated airspeed rise, at the same time, the MP had a contradictory visual perception that the MA was no longer accelerating.

The MP concluded that the airspeed indicator was working properly and for an unknown reason the MA was unable to attain takeoff speed. At this point, with 3000-4000 feet of runway remaining and a perceived 100 KIAS, the MP decided to abort the aircraft. Air Traffic Controllers (ATC) and the Supervisor of Flying (SOF) who witnessed the mishap stated that the MA abort started with 3000-4000 feet remaining, but that the aircraft was —carrying a lot of speed and —looked as if he could still probably lift off.

An airfield surveillance camera captured the second half of the MF's takeoff/abort sequence.

Analysis of the video shows the MA traveling on the runway at approximately the same speed as the MFL when reaching approximately 3000-3500 feet runway remaining. Using airfield references on the video, visual comparison of MFL and MP, and simulator modeling of the MFL's speeds after liftoff, the MA's groundspeed at the beginning of the abort was calculated at approximately 160-170 KIAS.

The MP applied the abort procedure for the perceived airspeed of 100 KIAS, bringing the throttles to idle, extending the speed brakes fully, and applying wheel brakes for 3-4 seconds.

The MP felt —good deceleration and came off the brakes for 1-2 seconds to avoid overheating them. If the MA was actually travelling at 100 KIAS then these procedures would have been enough to bring the aircraft under control and stopped within the remaining runway with minimal braking required.

If maximum braking is deemed required, minimum stopping distance is achieved with speed brakes open, throttles at idle, and wheel brakes applied with a firm continuous force sufficient to feel anti-skid cycling. With a speed of 160-170 knots, the MA, utilizing maximum braking procedures, required 2540–2790 feet to stop. Maximum braking would have stopped the MA 800-1000 feet' short of the end of the Runway 18L, without use of the 1000 foot overrun.

The MP reapplied the wheel brakes with 1500-2000 feet remaining on the runway, but did not feel the deceleration he expected. Despite maintaining brake pressure throughout the remainder of the abort roll, the MP never applied enough force to feel the anti-skid cycle and in fact indicated that —...I was wanting to let off the brakes because I didn't want it to get to that cycling.

Approaching 500 feet of runway remaining, the MP determined that the MA would not come to a stop prior to the end of the runway. While maintaining brake pressure, the MP attempted a ninety-degree right turn using nose wheel steering in an effort to utilize the additional prepared surface of Taxiway Alpha and the Alpha Pad. Taxiway A is the perpendicular taxiway at the end of the runway and Alpha Pad its accompanying aircraft parking area. About 30 degrees through the turn, the MP realized that the MA ground speed was too fast to successfully complete the turn. The MP centered the nose wheel steering and evened out the brake pressure as the MA departed the runway. As the MA left the prepared surface, the MP ejected from the aircraft. The MA continued traveling over soft uneven grassland until the nose gear collapsed and the right main landing gear and MA nose became lodged into the ground. The lateral forces applied to the aircraft during the abrupt stop caused a catastrophic fuselage failure just forward of the right wing's leading edge. The MA stopped approximately 500 feet into the grassland at a 45 degree angle off the end of the runway. Within minutes, the MA was engulfed in fire due to the ruptured forward main fuel tank and was destroyed.

Impact

All wreckage from the fire and subsequent clean-up was contained on Moody AFB, GA. There was no evidence of damage to civilian property.

Pitot-Static Probe

The Pitot-Static Probe is located at the tip of a four foot boom on the right wing. Its purpose is to provide pitot and static pressures for airspeed, altimeter, and vertical velocity indicators, central air data computer (CADC), altitude and air speed switches, alpha mach computer, and differential pressure switches. The probe was found intact and appeared to be in normal condition. The boom was removed from the aircraft at the wing. The probe was then removed from the boom by cutting the boom from the probe. Low pressure air was applied to the pressure port and confirmed a blockage. A borescope inspection was performed which validated foreign object intrusion four inches from the port opening. The inspection revealed the foreign object to be comprised of a light brown, granular composition resembling soil.

Figure 108: Exterior view of pitot probe from MA (Source: U.S. AIB report).

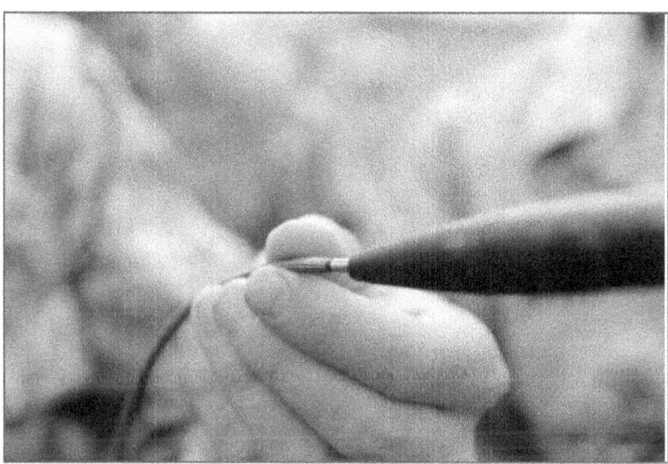

Figure 109: Borescope inspection being accomplished (Source: U.S. AIB report).

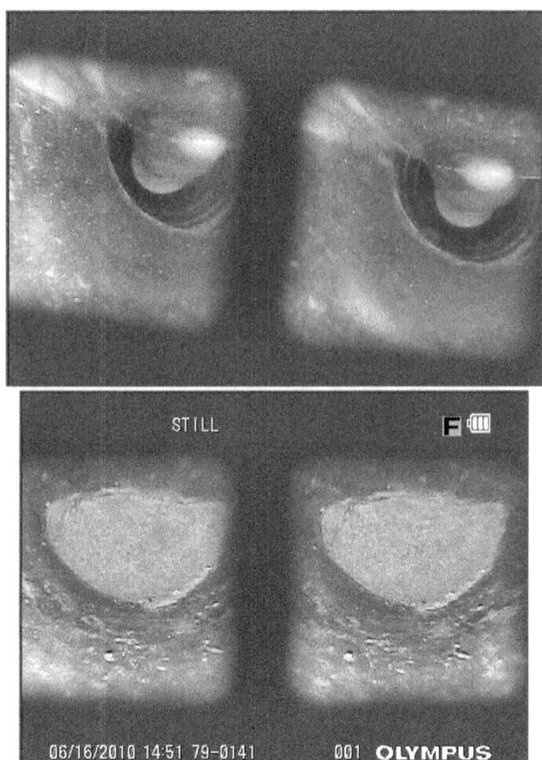

Figure 110: New pitot tube (left) compared with blocked pitot tube from MA (right) (Source: U.S. AIB report).

If the foreign object allows absolutely zero air to pass through the pitot port on the probe, then the air speed indications would not move from the baseline. If the blockage has some fraction of permeability, then the pressure from the aft side of the blockage will eventually equalize and an airspeed will be indicated.

The MA returned from Nellis AFB on Friday, 7 May 2010. Aircraft covers (-21) were installed on 7 May 2010. The Sunday mid-shift supervisor testimony states that the pitot tube cover was already in place when his shift began. The -21 covers were removed while servicing the aircraft during mid-shift prior to the mishap. The launch crew chief came in on day-shift on the day of the mishap. When he arrived at the mishap aircraft the pitot tube cover had already been removed.

Human factors analysis

The Department of Defense Human Factors Analysis and Classification System (DoD-HFACS) is comprised of a list of potential human factors that can be contributory or causal to a mishap. A total of five human factors were identified and described below for this mishap: decision making during operation, misperception of operational conditions, task misprioritization, distraction, and procedural error.

1. Decision-Making During Operation

Decision-Making During Operation is a factor when the individual, through faulty logic, selects the wrong course of action in a time-constrained environment.

(a) Decision to continue takeoff without acceleration check speed met

The MF's line-up card shows that 80 KIAS was the calculated speed necessary to achieve as the aircraft arrives at 1000 feet down the runway. If the check speed is not met, the procedure is to abort the takeoff. The MP noted that, —At 1000 feet I checked the airspeed which is the procedure where you check our acceleration speed. The airspeed indicator indicated between 50 and 60 knots. I thought to myself, ok, this is because you failed to push the throttles all the way to max at first. Check it again when you get down a little bit further . The decision to continue the takeoff roll with a new non-standard check speed distance is not in accordance with established procedure.

(b) Decision to continue takeoff with suspected pitot-static failure

The MP suspected pitot-static failure 2000-3500 feet down the runway. At this point, the MP rationalized that he would rather not abort and —...have hot brakes and possibly do some damage to the airplane. With this perception, the MP continued with the takeoff. During his decision making process, the MP either stood the throttles up or pulled them to idle for —a second or less to start an abort, but pushed them back to max once the decision to continue was made. This decision to continue ultimately resulted in the MA traveling down the runway at an estimated 160-170 knots without the MP having definitive airspeed data available to him.

2. Misperception of Operational Conditions

Misperception of Operational Conditions is a factor when an individual misperceives or misjudges altitude, separation, speed, closure rate, road/sea conditions, aircraft/vehicle location within the performance envelope or other operational conditions and this leads to an unsafe situation.

According to the report, approaching the takeoff distance, about 4000 feet down the runway, the MP rechecked the airspeed indicator and saw a reading of 90-100 KIAS. Despite the indicated airspeed rise, at the same time, the MP had a contradictory visual perception that the MA was no longer accelerating. The MP concluded that the airspeed indicator was working properly and for an unknown reason the MA was unable to attain takeoff speed.

With 3000-4000 feet of runway remaining and a perceived 100 KIAS, the MP decided to abort the aircraft. As noted previously, the MA's actual speed at this time was approximately 160-170 knots. The MP's underestimation of the MA's actual airspeed led to the MP applying insufficient braking for the actual conditions.

3. Task Misprioritization

Task Misprioritization is a factor when the individual does not organize, based on accepted prioritization techniques, the tasks needed to manage the immediate situation.

According to the report, the briefed takeoff interval was 20 seconds. The MP realized that he forgot to don his glasses after the MFL initiated his takeoff roll. By the time the MP retrieved his glasses from the saddlebag he noticed the time was 19 seconds. The MP then misprioritized the need to proceed with his brake release precisely at 20 seconds instead of taking additional time to fully complete the immediate task of putting on his glasses. In retrospect, the MP stated, ―In my mind, if I had my glasses on when they should have been on this never would have happened. I would have realized at 1000 feet that I didn't have the airspeed indicator and I would have aborted right there.

4. Distraction

Distraction is a factor when the individual has an interruption of attention and/or inappropriate redirection of attention by an environmental cue or mental process that degrades performance.

According to the report, the MP's task of donning his glasses at an atypical time in the pre-takeoff routine contributed to the MP's inappropriate redirection of attention from the required task of advancing the throttles to max at brake release.

5. Procedural Error

Procedural Error is a factor when a procedure is accomplished in the wrong sequence or using the wrong technique or when the wrong control or switch is used. This also captures errors in navigation, calculation or operation of automated systems.

In accordance with A-10C procedure, if maximum braking is required during an abort, minimum stopping distance can be achieved in a three-point attitude, throttles idle, speed brakes full open, and wheel brakes applied with a firm continuous force sufficient to feel anti-skid cycling.

According to MP testimony, with 1500-2000 feet runway remaining he felt that the MA braking action was insufficient and that stopping distance was critical. He stated that —as I got back on the brakes. I didn't feel a good deceleration like I had before. In fact I felt very minimal to none if any at all. Approaching 500 feet remaining the MP realized that, —...I'm not going to get it stopped even by the end of the overrun.

When the MP was asked about whether he recalled feeling anti-skid cycling during the abort he stated, —No, I did not. When asked what gave the MP the impression that the antiskid had not cycled he further elaborated, —I felt it cycle before on other aborts, not necessarily a high speed abort, but I have had to abort on takeoff rolls before and I felt it cycle. I used to be a functional check flight pilot, FCF pilot, and I've felt that before. I don't recall feeling it cycling on this. Since I was doing the abort, I was feeling that and I was wanting to let off the brakes because I didn't want it to get to that cycling. Pilot-Static System Blockage

The pitot-static system blockage directly contributed to the MP's decision-making process and misperception of airspeed at the time of the abort. In particular, the unexpected airspeed rise between the decision to continue the takeoff and the decision to abort weighed heavily into his perception that the airspeed indicator was correct.

27 C-130J-Jalalabad Afghanistan crashed after takeoff

Figure 111: C-130J (Source: U.S. AIB report).

The United States Air Force Aircraft Accident Investigation Board (AIB) describes in their report that:

On 2 October 2015, at approximately 0016 hours local time (L), a C-130J, Tail Number (T/N) 08-3174, crashed after takeoff from Runway 31, Jalalabad Airfield (JAF), on the second scheduled leg of a contingency airlift mission. The mishap aircraft (MA) was assigned to the 455th Air Expeditionary Wing at Bagram Airfield, Afghanistan. The mishap crew (MC) was from the 774th Expeditionary Airlift Squadron. The MC consisted of the mishap pilot (MP), the mishap copilot (MCP), and two mishap loadmasters. Also onboard were two fly-away security team (FAST) members and five contractors travelling as passengers. Upon impact, all eleven individuals onboard the aircraft died instantly. The aircraft struck a guard tower manned by three Afghan Special Reaction Force (ASRF) members, whom also died. The MA and cargo load were destroyed, and a perimeter wall and guard tower were damaged.

On 1 October 2015, at approximately 2313L, the MA landed at JAF following the first scheduled leg of a contingency airlift mission.

While on the ground, the MP placed a hard-shell night vision goggle (NVG) case forward of the yoke during Engine Running Onload/Offload (ERO) operations to maintain the MA elevator in an up position to accommodate loading operations of tall cargo.

In the 50 minutes that followed prior to take-off at 0015L, neither the MP nor the MCP removed the case. During the takeoff roll, with the MCP at the controls, the MA rotated early and lifted off the ground approximately three knots below the anticipated takeoff speed. The MA's pitch angle continued to increase due to the hard-shell NVG case blocking the flight controls, thus preventing the MCP from pushing the yoke forward to decrease the pitch angle.

The MCP misidentified the ensuing flight control problem as a trim malfunction resulting in improper recovery techniques being applied by both mishap pilots. The rapid increase in pitch angle resulted in a stall that the mishap pilots were unable to recover. The MA impacted approximately 28 seconds after liftoff, right of the runway, within the confines of JAF.

Accident cause

The Accident Investigation Board (AIB) president found by a preponderance of the evidence that the causes of the mishap were the MP's placement of the hard-shell NVG case in front of the yoke blocking forward movement of the flight controls, the distractions experienced by the MP and MCP during the course of the ERO, and the misidentification of the malfunction once airborne.

The AIB president also found by a preponderance of the evidence that environmental conditions, inaccurate expectations, and fixation substantially contributed to the mishap.

Accident summary

The AIB report describes the accident as follows:

The first sortie flown by the MC on 1 October 2015 was a planned flight from BAF to JAF. The MA took off as scheduled at 2136L. After takeoff, the MA experienced a bird strike and returned to Bagram Airfield (BAF) to allow maintenance personnel to inspect the MA before continuing the mission. The MC landed at 2155L, taxied to park, and returned the MA to maintenance for inspection. At this time, the MP and MCP returned to the operations building. They informed the Assistant Director of Operations (ADO) of the bird strike and their plans to continue the mission. The MP and MCP did not seem concerned by the event; once cleared by maintenance, they returned to the MA to continue the mission as planned.

The AIB report then explains, the MC took off for JAF at approximately 2253L. The sortie was uneventful and the MA landed safely at JAF at approximately 2313L. The MP and MCP noted fireworks during the approach into JAF, but did not consider it enemy action and did not execute evasive maneuvers. The MCP relayed this information back to unit leadership.

After landing Loading & Ground Operations started.

The MP taxied to Alpha Ramp to begin Engine Running Onload/Offload (ERO) procedures at 2316L. The MC followed the ERO checklist in accordance with the planned mission. The FAST members took their position outside the MA prior to the cargo offload. During the cargo offload sequence, ML1 requested that the MP raise the elevator on the MA to provide more clearance for offloading the high-profile (tall) cargo.

Raising the elevator lifts the control surface above horizontal and is accomplished by pulling the yoke aft (toward the pilot).

According to the AIB report and this is very important to understand the root cause of this accident: This request was not considered an unusual request by the MP who complied it. For the next six minutes, there were changes in the elevator deflection, indicating that the MP was holding the yoke back to maintain between positive 6 and positive 13 degrees of elevator deflection. After that the elevator position increased to positive 20 degrees deflection momentarily before settling to a position between six to eight degrees positive deflection. This occurred immediately before the MP told the MCP, "My NVG case is holding...the elevator" as demonstrated in following figures.

This is main cause of the accident:

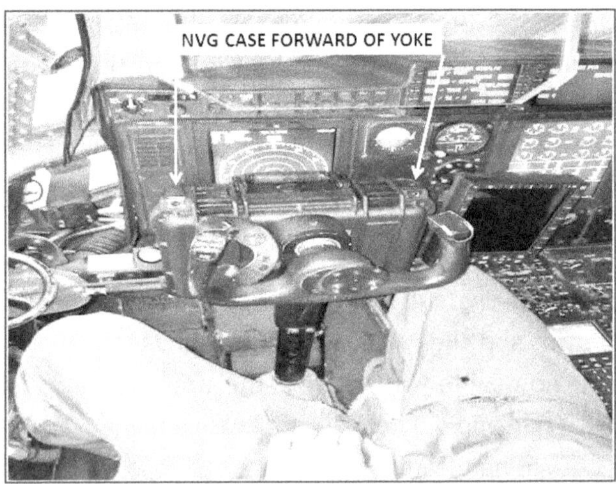

Figure 112: Case Forward of Yoke (Daytime) (Source: U.S. AIB report).

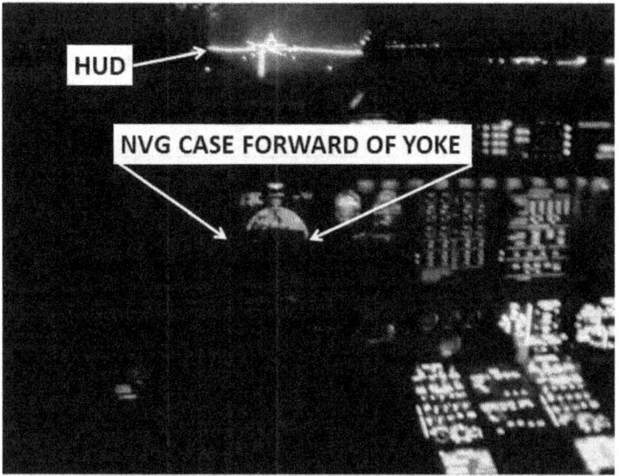

Figure 113: Case Forward of Yoke (Nighttime) (Source: U.S. AIB report).

The natural resting state of the elevator during ground loading operations is approximately negative 15 degrees deflection, as demonstrated in following figure.

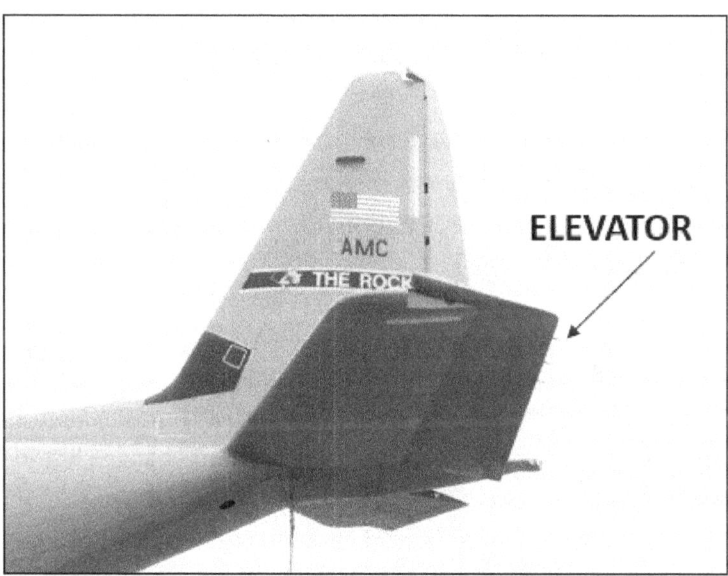

Figure 114: Elevator Without Case Forward of Yoke (Source: U.S. AIB report).

On the MA, the elevator position remained between six to eight degrees positive deflection while loading operations continued, as demonstrated in following figure.

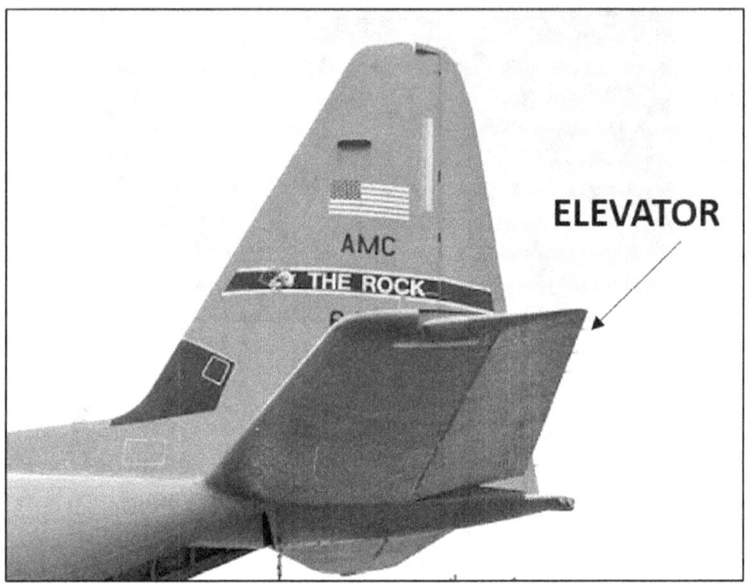

Figure 115: Elevator With Case Forward of Yoke (Source: U.S. AIB report).

This positive elevator deflection was collaborated by video evidence of the MA loading operations. Approximately ten minutes after the hard-shell NVG case was placed forward of the yoke, the MCP got out of the right seat to assist with loading operations in the back of the MA.

The MLs were tasked with onloading five pallets utilizing ERO procedures. The onload also included five passengers not included in the original load plan, prompting a decision by the MLs to move the forward-most pallet aft to pallet position three rather than pallet position two. This load change shifted the center of gravity (CG) to 28.6% of Mean Aerodynamic Chord (MAC) for takeoff. The total load weight was 40,300 pounds (including the passengers) and the calculated aircraft gross weight for takeoff was 153,200 pounds. According to the AIB report, the cargo weight and CG computed based on the new load plan was within flight limits and met all requirements for safe flight.

During cargo loading operations, the MP was in the left pilot seat determining if the MA's performance would be sufficient to takeoff from JAF. The MP initially expected the MC would need to perform an Adjusted Maximum Effort (AMAX) takeoff instead of a normal takeoff, which would allow the MA to takeoff in a shorter runway distance and at a lower takeoff speed.

The MP then verified that the load weight was 40,300 pounds. After running the Takeoff and Landing Data (TOLD) calculations, the MP acknowledged that they had 750 feet of runway available beyond what was required for takeoff. AIB calculations show this matches the distance required to perform a normal takeoff. The MCP returned to the right seat and the MP confirmed that they would perform an AMAX takeoff, with an expected liftoff speed of 111 knots. The AIB calculated the normal takeoff speed for the MA would have been 122 knots.

The AIB report then explains that throughout the remainder of the ground operations, the mishap pilots did not discuss the hardshell NVG case holding the elevator in a raised position; video and DFDR data confirmed that the elevator remained in its raised position until the takeoff roll.

The investigation revealed that the blocking of flight controls during loading operations was a nonstandard procedure and there was no regulatory guidance to accompany the proper placement and removal of an object blocking the controls. The ERO checklist did not include a step requiring the pilots to check the flight controls prior to departure; therefore, it was incumbent on the MP and the MCP to remember to remove the hard-shell NVG case. To check the flight control, the MP or MCP would move the yoke forward and aft to confirm full range of motion. When accomplished, all flight control checks occur solely within the flight deck; no external check would have been accomplished that may have alerted the MP or MCP to the raised elevator position. The AIB could not determine whether a flight control check would have alerted the MP or MCP to the hard-shell NVG case forward of the yoke.

The report continues, after the completion of the ERO, the MC taxied to the active runway and back-taxied for takeoff on Runway 31. The MP and MCP were wearing NVGs for the takeoff. Tower called the winds at three knots from 220 degrees.

There was no elevator movement up to this point, indicating that the MP and MCP had not removed the hardshell NVG case from forward of the MP's control yoke.

The MCP conducted the takeoff from the right seat and began the takeoff roll. Normally during a takeoff roll, the pilot keeps the elevator deflected down until the aircraft reaches rotation speed, at which point the pilot pulls the yoke aft, which raises the elevator, and the aircraft becomes airborne. During the MA's takeoff roll, the elevator deflection decreased from positive six to eight degrees to positive three to five degrees. This slight change is consistent with aerodynamic forces across the elevator surface. The MA passed the briefed acceleration time check and the MP called rotate. The MA became airborne at an indicated airspeed of 107.5 knots.

After the MP called "Rotate", the MCP responded that the MA was "going off on its own". The MCP became aware of a problem when he stated, "Ahh," and verbalized a trim failure two seconds later as the MA reached its top airspeed of 117 knots. The MCP applied full nose-down trim in an attempt to help move the yoke forward. The trim reached full negative deflection in three seconds, indicating that the trim system was operating normally. The MA continued to pitch up as the mishap pilots attempted to remedy the perceived trim malfunction. Three seconds after the MCP verbalized a trim malfunction, the first stall warning occurred.

The MA was at greater than 20 degrees nose-up pitch, wings level, and an airspeed of 115 knots.

The AIB report says when the MA was at 25 degrees of positive pitch, the MP, already in control of the MA, applied right aileron, and began rolling the MA to the right. This input is consistent with the MP attempting to maintain controlled flight. The MA entered a stall and, except for a brief period just prior to impact, remained stalled throughout the remainder of the MS. The MA issued a second stall warning as the MA's pitch continued to increase through 35 degrees nose-up.

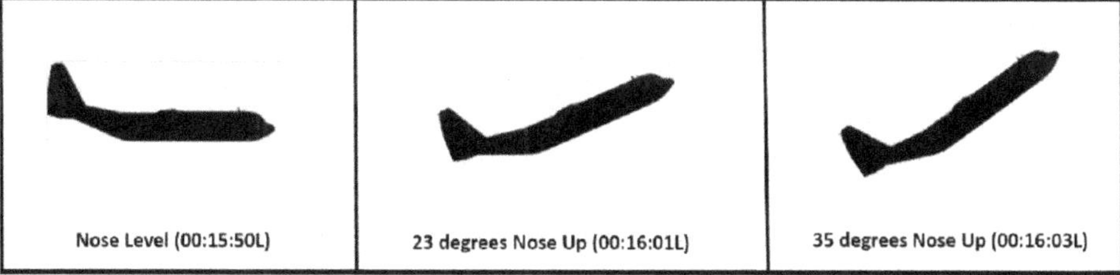

Figure 116: Pitch Angles of MA w/ Time Stamps (Source: U.S. AIB report).

The stick pusher, a device that applies approximately 49 to 71 pounds of forward column force to the yoke to reduce the angle of attack (AOA), activated just prior to the second stall warning. During AIB simulations with the hard-shell NVG case behind the yoke, the stick pusher activated but was ineffective because of the blocked controls. The MP confirmed he had control of the MA and directed the MCP to select emergency trim, an alternate to the normal trim system. The MCP confirmed he had selected emergency trim; however, the DFDR shows the trim system functioned properly in the normal position and the MCP switching to emergency trim had no additional effect. The pitch and roll continued to increase until the MA reached a maximum positive pitch of 42 degrees.

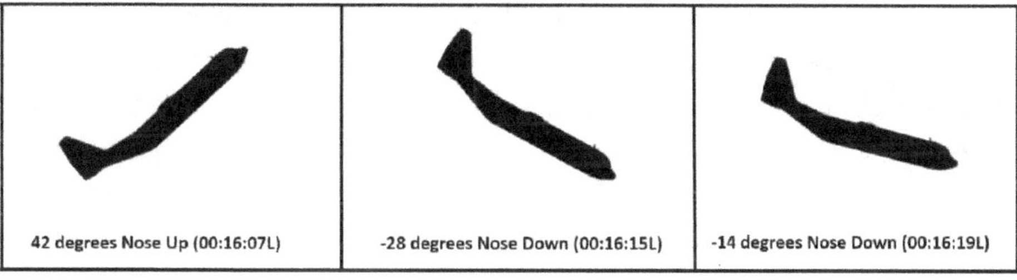

Figure 117: Pitch Angles of MA w/ Time Stamps (Source: U.S. AIB report).

The MA issued a third stall warning. The roll continued to increase through the stall and the MA's nose dropped. The MP input left aileron to correct the roll but due to the stalled condition, the right roll continued to increase. The MA reached a maximum right bank of 75 degrees.

Data indicated that the MA began to roll to the left. The MA's nose continued to drop, eventually reaching negative 28 degrees pitch. Short after the MP stated,

"We're going down," a statement he repeated three consecutive times. The nose-down pitch angle was arrested as the MA nose started to rise.

The AIB investigators say in their report that the Impact was as follows:

With a descent rate in excess of 8,000 feet per minute, the MA impacted the terrain, a perimeter wall to the right of the runway, and a guard tower at a force from 40g to more than 97g. The MA impacted at 14 degrees nose-down, 28 degrees of right bank, airspeed of 111.5 knots, and approximately 50% flaps, 28 seconds after becoming airborne. The MA exploded upon impact and was destroyed.

Human factors analysis

That AIB report explains the DoD Human Factors Analysis and Classification System (HFACS) version 7.0 lists potential human factors that can play a role in mishaps. It is designed for use by an investigation board in order to accurately record all aspects of human performance associated with an individual and the mishap event. DoD HFACS helps investigators perform a more complete investigation, classify particular actions (or inactions) that sustained the mishap sequence, and contribute to a safety database as a repository for detecting mishap trends and preventing future mishaps. The discussion below lists the human factors directly involved in this mishap.

1. Inadequate Real-Time Risk Assessment

Inadequate Real-Time Assessment is a factor when an individual fails to adequately evaluate the risks associated with a particular course of action, and this faulty evaluation leads to inappropriate decision-making and subsequent unsafe situations.

According to the report, the MP placed a hard-shell NVG case forward of the left seat control yoke during the ERO. The ERO continued for approximately 50 minutes after the elevator was blocked. The blocking of flight controls during loading operations was a nonstandard procedure and there was no regulatory guidance to accompany the proper placement and removal of an object blocking the controls. The ERO checklist did not include a step requiring the pilots to check the flight controls prior to departure and therefore, it was incumbent on the MP and the MCP to remember to remove the hard-shell NVG case. The MP did not adequately evaluate the risk associated with blocking the elevator controls with the hard-shell NVG case.

2. Distraction

Distraction is a factor when the individual has an interruption of attention and/or inappropriate redirection of attention by an environmental cue or mental process.

According to the report, the MC landed at JAF at 2313L and began the ERO at 2316L. During the cargo offload, ML1 requested that the MP raise the elevator to provide more clearance for the high-profile cargo during ERO operations. For the next six minutes, there were changes in the elevator deflection between the range of positive 6 and positive 13 degrees of deflection. At 23:26:06L (DFDR time 5087) the elevator position increased to positive 20 degrees deflection momentarily before settling to a position between six to eight degrees positive deflection. This occurred immediately before the MP told the MCP that the "NVG case is holding...the elevator". The elevator position remained steady between six to eight degrees positive deflection until the takeoff roll.

During the 50 minutes after the MP placed the case forward of the yoke, the MP's and MCP's attention was redirected towards discussing loading operations, aircraft gross weight, climb-out procedures, and TOLD. Neither the MP nor the MCP referenced the case again.

3. Wrong Choice of Action During an Operation

Wrong choice of action during an operation is a factor when the individual, through faulty logic or erroneous expectations, selects the wrong course of action.

According to the report, during the takeoff sequence, the MA lifted off the ground greater than three knots below the calculated AMAX takeoff speed. The MCP, who was performing the takeoff, recognized a control problem identified on the CVR. Two seconds later, the MCP incorrectly identified the flight control malfunction by stating "Trim failure". The first stall warning indication occurred three seconds after the verbal misidentification of a trim malfunction. Due to the rapid progression of the nose-up pitch attitude, the mishap pilots had eleven seconds from MA liftoff until the first stall warning indication to identify and correct the malfunction.

4. Environmental Conditions Affecting Vision

Environmental Conditions Affecting Vision is a factor that includes obscured windows; weather, fog, haze, darkness; smoke, etc.; brownout/whiteout (dust, snow, water, ash or other particulates); or when exposure to windblast affects the individual's ability to perform required duties.

According to the report, three inter-related environmental conditions affecting vision were factors in this mishap: nighttime operations, use of NVGs, and reliance on the HUD in conjunction with the Advisory, Caution, and Warning System (ACAWS) notifications.

The MA landed at JAF at 2313L. The weather was VMC with 9,000 meters visibility. The predicted lunar illumination at takeoff was approximately 81 percent. Due to the operations occurring at night, the MC wore NVGs. It was standard operating procedure for aircrews operating on NVGs to dim the cockpit lights and increase the brightness of the HUD.

NVGs permit aircrews to operate more effectively in low-illumination environments. The field of view (FOV) the NVGs provide is less than the eye's natural FOV, particularly in peripheral vision. Therefore, a person must constantly process two input components to his visual system. The two components are focal vision, which is primarily responsible for object recognition, and ambient vision, which is responsible for spatial orientation. This reliance on focal vision increases the aviator's workload and ultimately decreases the recognition of peripheral cues.

The information provided by the HUD, combined with the ACAWS, allowed aircrews to maintain their visual scan external to the aircraft with only occasional crosschecks of the HDD to monitor aircraft systems. Due to the Head Down Display (HDD) design, internal crosschecks of aircraft systems were normally done without the aid of NVGs. Prior to the takeoff roll, the MCP and MP checked the horsepower setting. After this, all information required to perform the takeoff was available in the HUD.

During the AIB's simulations at Little Rock Air Force Base, the AIB Pilot Member (AIB/PM) dimmed flight deck lighting to replicate nighttime operations. The hard-shell NVG case placed forward of the yoke became inconspicuous to all three AIB pilots during the course of multiple takeoff sequences.

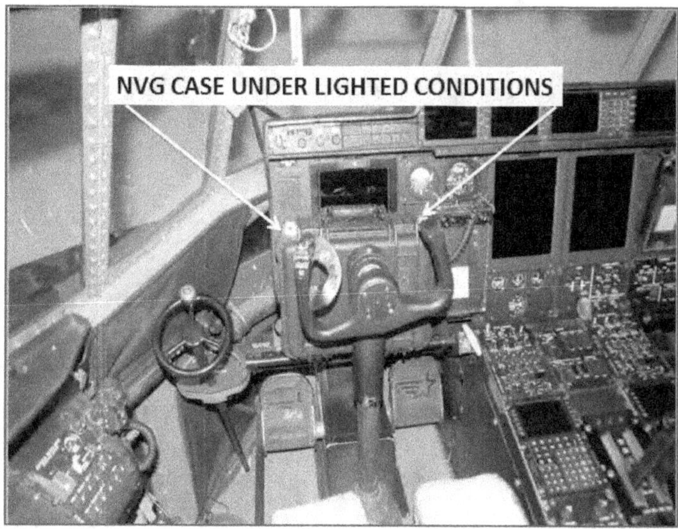

Figure 118: View of HDDs w/ Light (Source: U.S. AIB report).

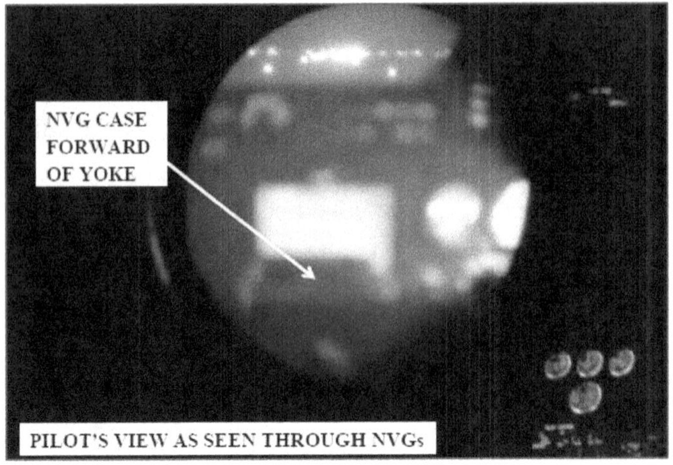

Figure 119: View of HDDs through NVGs (Source: U.S. AIB report).

5. Inaccurate Expectation

Inaccurate Expectation is a factor when the individual expects to perceive a certain reality and those expectations are strong enough to create a false perception of the expectation.

According to the report, the MP initially expected the MC would need to perform an AMAX takeoff instead of a normal takeoff. The MP then verified that the load weight was 40,300 pounds. After running the TOLD calculations, the MP acknowledged that they had 750 feet of runway available beyond what was required for takeoff. AIB calculations showed this matched the distance required to perform a normal takeoff. When later asked by the MCP, the MP confirmed that they would perform an AMAX takeoff.

The decision to perform an AMAX takeoff resulted in a planned rotation speed of 111 knots instead of 122 knots associated with a normal takeoff. During the MS, the MA lifted off at 107.5 knots, only a few knots below the planned rotation speed. For a normal takeoff, had the MA lifted off at 107.5 knots instead of 122 knots, it may have provided a more pronounced alert of the problem to the mishap pilots, allowing them to abort the takeoff. The MP's inaccurate expectation that an AMAX takeoff was required led to an unnecessary AMAX takeoff.

6. Fixation

Fixation is a factor when the individual is focusing all conscious attention on a limited number of environmental cues to the exclusion of others.

According to the report, at liftoff, the MP reported "You're a little early;" the MCP replied "It's going off on its own". Six seconds after liftoff, the MCP became aware of a problem with the MA.

He then misidentified the problem as trim failure and the MP instructed him to "Go emergency". During the five seconds from when the MCP first realized something was wrong to the first ACAWS stall warning, both MP and MCP focused their attention on a trim failure problem. The mishap pilots neither verbalized a different flight control problem nor attempted to reduce power to control the increasing aircraft pitch.

28 F-16C Midair Collision

Figure 120: F-16Cs (Source: U.S. AIB report).

The United States Air Force Aircraft Accident Investigation Board (AIB) describes in their report that:

On 7 June 2016, at approximately 2114 local, two F-16C Block 52 aircraft collided head-on during a training mission in the Bulldog Military Operating Area near Louisville, Georgia (GA).

Following the collision, both pilots ejected safely, suffering minor injuries. Mishap Pilot 1 (MP1) is assigned to the 316th Fighter Squadron, 169th Fighter Wing, McEntire Joint National Guard Base (JNGB), South Carolina (SC).

Mishap Pilot 2 (MP2) is assigned to the 157th Fighter Squadron, 169th Fighter Wing, McEntire JNGB, SC.

Mishap Aircraft 1 (MA1, tail number 92- 3899) and Mishap Aircraft 2 (MA2, tail number 93-0531) are assigned to the 157th Fighter Squadron, 169th Fighter Wing, McEntire JNGB, SC.

Both aircraft were destroyed after impacting the ground in a rural area of approximately four square miles, with damage to private property (timber).

MP1, a recently assigned, active duty, experienced F-16C instructor pilot, was the flight leader undergoing an additional 169th Fighter Wing instructor pilot qualification program.

MP2, also an experienced F-16C instructor pilot, was responsible for administering the upgrade while flying in a visual (wedge) formation several miles behind MA1.

The mishap occurred 10 minutes after civil twilight, in the latter phase of a training mission. After MP2 issued a low fuel (Bingo) call, MP1 executed a sharp left turn at an altitude of 15,000 feet mean sea level (MSL) (MP1's assigned sanctuary altitude).

Note: "*Bingo*" is a pre-briefed fuel state that, when reached, requires termination of tactical maneuvering and return to base with normal recovery fuel.

MP2, approximately 4 nautical miles (nm) behind at 16,000 MSL (MP2's sanctuary altitude) turned to follow MA1's external lights visually, but did not cross-check available sensors to confirm MA1's position.

MP2 did not realize MA1 had executed a complete turn and was headed towards him. MP2 pointed directly at MA1's external lights in an attempt to acquire a visual mode radar lock on MA1. During this time, the distance between aircraft decreased rapidly and MP2 descended from his sanctuary altitude of 16,000 MSL without the requisite situational awareness.

MP2 acquired radar lock at 2,500 feet separation but failed to recognize the conflict. At the last moment, both aircraft initiated a left bank away from the other, but their high right wings impacted. Neither MP1 nor MP2 were able to regain control of their aircraft, with both pilots ejecting shortly after impact.

Accident cause

The Accident Investigation Board (AIB) President found by a preponderance of the evidence that the cause of the mishap was MP2's failure to fulfill his primary responsibility to ensure flight path deconfliction and separation of aircraft.

Additionally, the AIB President found by a preponderance of the evidence that there were two substantially contributing factors to the mishap:

(1) MP1 did not terminate tactical maneuvering following MP2's "*Bingo*" fuel call and

(2) MP1 and MP2 overly relied on visual cues from external aircraft lighting to judge critical flight parameters.

Figure 121: F-16C (Source: U.S. AIB report).

Accident summary

Prior to Scenario

Engine start, taxi, and arming the aircraft were all uneventful for both MF (Mishap Flight) and RF (Red Flight). MF performed afterburner takeoffs at 2015L with 15-second spacing between aircraft and rejoined to a 2+2 formation with one nm spacing between elements. RF performed the same takeoff sequence and performed a visual rejoin to wedge formation. There was nothing of note with Air Traffic Control (ATC) instructions, routing, or weather during the departure to the MOA (Military Operating Area) for either MF or RF.

MF entered Bulldog MOA, followed by RF. MF and RF performed separate G-awareness (a turning exercise to determine the pilots' tolerance of gravitational forces) exercises prior to beginning the first scenario. Following G-awareness maneuvers, MP1 directed MP2 and ME4 to fly fighting wing formation off flight leads and directed ME3 (Mishap Element) to one nautical mile trail formation.

1. First Scenario

The first scenario began at 20:35:12L. It lasted approximately twenty minutes and included multiple air-to-air engagements as well as multiple Surface-to-Air Missile (SAM) engagements. The first scenario was uneventful with the exception of MP2 calling blind (lost visual contact). No training rule violations were noted. The first scenario ended with the accomplishment of established DLOs (Desired Learning Objectives) and a "Knock it off" call by MP1.

2. Second (Mishap) Scenario

The second scenario began at approximately 21:00:00L. MF executed the scenario in a spread four formation and the SEAD (Suppression of Enemy Air Defenses) engagement with MP2 and ME4 in a visual wedge formation. MF prosecuted multiple red air presentations and SAM engagements prior to the mishap.

MF began a SAM engagement requiring numerous threat avoidance maneuvers, resulting in MP1 and MP2 exceeding the planned visual wedge formation.

MP2 lost visual contact with MA1 and called blind ("One, say your bullseye, two's blind").

MP1 responded with heading information ("One's at 15, bullseye 209 for 27").

MP2 made another blind call ("Two's still blind at sixteen one, give me a flare") and 5.2 nm separation.

Following MP2's visual acquisition of MP1's flare, MP2 acknowledged ("One press"), and MP1 relayed heading information for his next SAM engagement ("One's engaged, One's heading three zero zero").

The distance range between MA1 and MA2 decreased to 3.2 nm.

ME3 and ME4 had communicated their impending attack on a SAM.

MP2 made a "Bingo" fuel call ("Two's Bingo").

Four seconds later, MP1 acknowledged the call ("Copy Bingo") and began a sharp left turn at 15,200 MSL.

MP1 did not communicate the left turn.

MP2's aircraft position was 3.8 nm behind MP1 at 15,640 MSL.

MP1 intended a communication for MP2, but incorrectly stated, "Four, you can continue north", to which ME4 confirmed that he was attacking a northern SAM.

Approximately five seconds later, MP2 began attempts (the first of nine attempts) to obtain a fire control radar (FCR) boresight lock on MA1. The FCR boresight lock is utilized for targeting but would provide limited information on the other aircraft, including bearing and altitude.

MP1 continued his sharp left turn and corrected his incorrect call ("Sorry, two continue north"), which MP2 acknowledged ("Copy that").

MP2 continued maneuvering visually with MA1 in a southwest direction.

MP2 assessed MA1's line of sight from right to left, incorrectly perceiving that MA1 was in a slight left turn, heading away from MP2.

MP2 believed the MF would eventually turn north together.

MP1 had completed his turn, was heading northeast at 15,290 MSL, and attempted an FCR boresight lock on MA2.

At six seconds to impact, MP2 achieved a boresight lock on MA1, as confirmed by removable media cartridges, but MP2 did not recall intentionally taking a boresight lock. The boresight lock indicated an initial range of 2,500 feet that decreased almost immediately to 1,400 feet between aircraft. The heads up display (HUD) provided "Break-X symbology", indicating that the two aircraft were approaching head-on.

Prior to impact, MP2's last assessed heading was 234 degrees (southwest) and 15,300 MSL.

At five seconds to impact, MP1 achieved a boresight lock on MA2, which indicated an initial range of 5,700 feet that decreased almost immediately to 3,700 feet between aircraft, with Break-X symbology in the HUD. MP1's last recorded HUD data indicated a heading of 054 degrees, 15,290 MSL, and a range of 1,300 feet between aircraft with Break-X symbology in the HUD.

MA1 and MA2 flight controls first revealed significant control inputs approximately one second prior to the mishap.

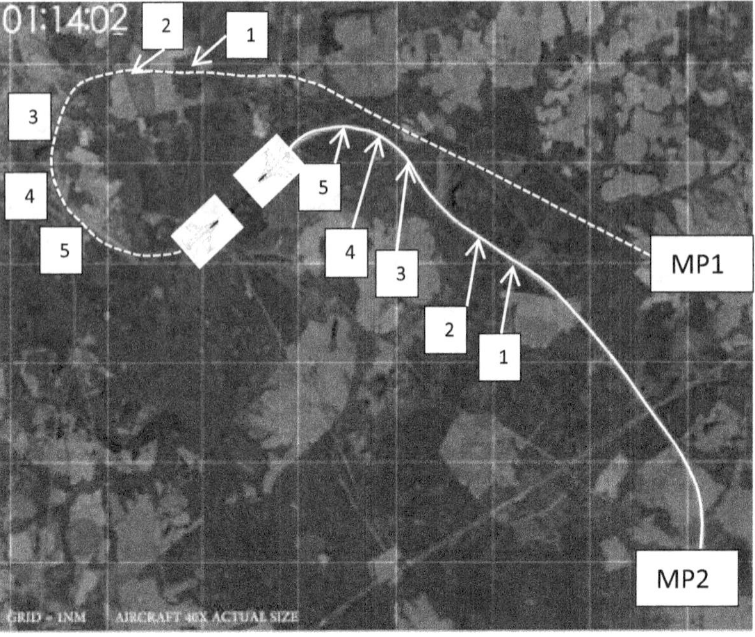

Figure 122: Time Sequence of events from 21:13:23 (MP2 *"Bingo"* call) to 21:13:48 (Source: U.S. AIB report).

(1) MP2: "Two is bingo"
ME4: "Mace four is attacking twenty-six"
ME3: "Four cleared"
(2) MP1: "Copy bingo"
RF1: "Elevator in the north, regen."
MP1: "Cleared"
ME4: "Mace four, magnum the south twenty-six, bullseye one-eight-two, thirty-four; shutdown."
ME3: "Three and four cold left"
(3) MP1: "Four, you can continue north".
ME4: "Four's attacking the north twenty-six"
(4) MP2: First attempt to acquire FCR visual boresight lock".
ME3: "HARM inbound"
(5) MP1: "Sorry, two you can continue tracking north"
MP2: "Copy that"

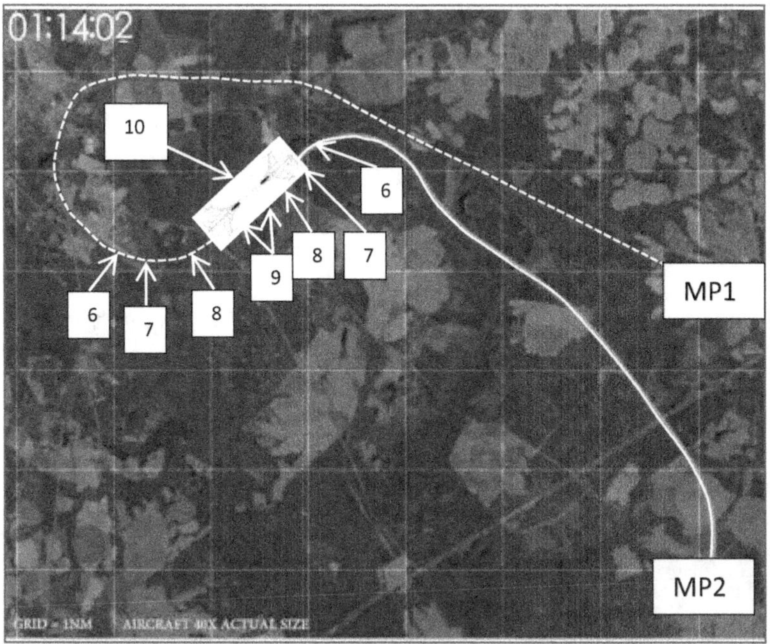

Figure 123: Time sequence of events from 21:13:49 to 21:14:03 (Impact) (Source: U.S. AIB report).

(6)MP1:"First attempt to acquire FCR visual boresight lock".

ME3: "Three and four cold"

(7)MP1: "boresight lock successful, HUD indicates range at 1.5 nm."

(8)MP2: -Last data prior to impact- boresight lock successful, HUD indicates range decreasing rapidly from 2500 feet to 1400 feet and break X symbology with MA1 in centre of HUD.

RF(1): "Mace, Darkstar, single group, bullseye two-five-one, thrirty-two, ten thousand, hostile".

MP1: boresight lock successful, HUD indicates range decreasing to 1400 feet and Break-x symbology.

(9)MP1: Last data prior to impact, HUD indicates range decreasing to 1300 feet and Break-X symbology.

(10)Impact

Impact

At 21:14:03L, MP1 and MP2 collided approximately 110 nm southwest of McEntire JNGB, SC, and east of Louisville, GA, in the Bulldog MOA. At impact, MP1's aircraft was heading 054 degrees, 20.4 degrees left wing down, 7.4 degrees nose up, and 327 knots calibrated air speed (KCAS). MP2's aircraft was heading 234 degrees, 11.9 degrees left wing down, 5.0 degrees nose up, and 257 KCAS.

There were two primary crash sites located approximately 1.7 nm apart with the majority of aircraft debris contained at the individual crash sites. Crash recovery teams located debris over an approximately four square mile area.

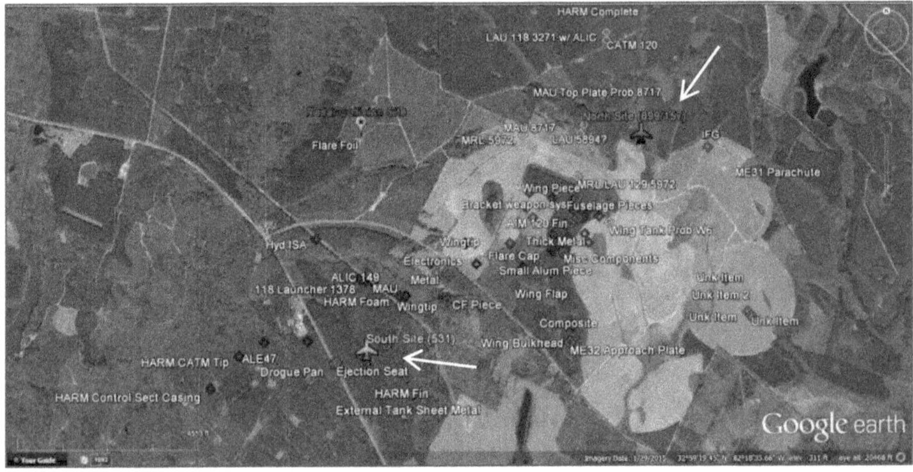

Figure 124: MA1 and MA2 crash sites and debris field (Source: U.S. AIB report).

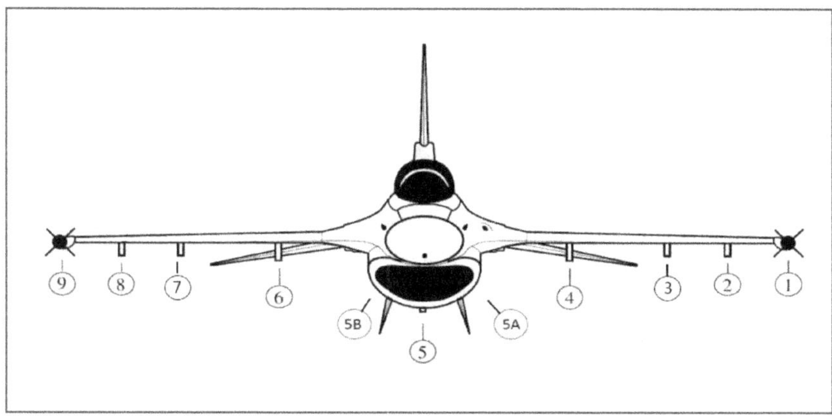

Figure 125: MA1's and MA2's mishap sortie configuration: MA1 impact near Station 7; MA2 impact undetermined (Source: U.S. AIB report).

The leading edge of MA2's right wing exhibited a blunt force indentation in an upward direction near station seven. There was insufficient physical evidence to conclusively d MP1 and MP2's aircraft were similarly configured. For reference, the numbers in Figure above correspond to the following station numbers:

- Station 1: AIM-120B
- Station 2: ACMI Pod Station 3: AGM-88C
- Station 4: 370 Gallon Fuel Tank and 16S1300 Pylon Station 5A: HARM Targeting System
- Station 5: Empty
- Station 5B: Sniper Pod
- Station 6: 370 Gallon Fuel Tank and 16S1300 Pylon Station 7: AGM-88C
- Station 8: AIM-9X Station 9: AIM-120Cetermine impact geometry on MA1 (Tab Z-34).

Figure 126: MA2's right wingtip with upward blunt force indentation (Source: U.S. AIB report).

Human factors analysis

The Department of Defense Human Factors Analysis and Classification System (DoD-HFACS) is comprised of a list of potential human factors that can be contributory or causal to a mishap.

1. Inaccurate Expectation

"Inaccurate Expectation" is when an individual expects to perceive a certain reality and those expectations are strong enough to create a false perception of the expectation IAW DoD Human Factors Analysis and Classification System (HFACS) version 7.0.

According to the report, both MP1 and MP2 inaccurately judged their positions relative to each other following MP2's "Bingo" call. Both had the mental model of pursuing the other aircraft following MP1's final left turn. When presented with new data that conflicted with their expectations, each pilot was unable to process and translate the data into timely actions necessary to avoid the mishap.

Six seconds prior to the collision, MP1 was presented with HUD radar data showing MA1 and MA2 pointing directly at each other with only 1.5 nm of separation. MP1 had expected MA2 to be six miles away headed north. His expectation that MP2 was headed away from him was so strong that he ignored that data and switched to an air-to-ground priority mode for SEAD operations. This action removed critical information, which would have warned MP1 of imminently collapsing distance.

During MP1's final left turn, MP2 visually tracked MA1's light moving from right to left on the horizon. Per his testimony, MP2's last recalled distance from MA1 just prior to his left turn was *"three-ish"* nm, later verified as 3.8 nm by his A/A TACAN display.

Based on an expectation that MA1 was continuing with a southern heading, MP2 was unaware that MA1 had in fact reversed direction and was headed toward him.

Over the next 14 seconds, MP2 attempted to acquire a visual boresight lock on MA1, did not attempt to clarify an earlier ambiguous radio call from MP1 to *"track north"*, or cross check distance with his A/A TACAN.

Although data reflected a descent from the sanctuary altitude, MP2 stated that he did not know if he was or was not descending during his boresight lock attempts. When he achieved the desired radar lock approximately six seconds before collision at a range of 2,500 feet separation, MP2 was presented with an immediate *"Break X"* symbol in his HUD. MP2 did not process the immediate peril due to his expectation that MA1 was moving away from him.

Each pilot's expectation that the other was moving away hampered timely evasive maneuvering. Lockheed Martin analysis of the flight controls showed no significant control inputs by either pilot until less than one second prior to the collision.

2. Fixation

"Fixation" is a factor when the individual is focusing all conscious attention on a limited number of environmental cues to the exclusion of others IAW DoD HFACS version 7.0.

According to the report, MP2 was flying in a night visual wedge formation, which requires use of all available tools to ensure aircraft separation and deconfliction.

Night flying is challenging as there is degradation of both visibility and depth perception. MP2 had A/A TACAN and A/A FCR available to him as positional aides.

As MP2 tracked MA1, he descended from his sanctuary altitude while maintaining visual contact. MP2 maneuvered to place MA1's lights in the center of his HUD, maintaining a pure pursuit course, never referencing his A/A TACAN.

During this 14-second block of time, MP2 made at least nine switch actuations in an attempt to acquire an FCR visual mode boresight lock on MA1. He was unaware of MA1's turn to the northeast due to fact that he exclusively relied on visual cues, and did not confirm MA1's maneuver with available sensors.

MP1 similarly over relied on visual cues and did not confirm closing distance with A/A TACAN following his unannounced left turn. MP1 immediately identified MA2 by the sequenced flashing lights and acquired a visual boresight lock on MA2.

MP1 relied on an inaccurate mental perception of MA2's relative position and did not crosscheck his A/A TACAN, confirm his radar data or clarify MA2's position on the radio. Unlike MP2 however, MP1 maintained his briefed sanctuary altitude.

3. Failure to Prioritize Task Adequately

"Failure to Prioritize Task Adequately" is a factor when the individual does not organize, based on accepted prioritization techniques, the tasks needed to manage the immediate situation IAW DoD HFACS version 7.0.

According to the report, MP1 did not call *"Knock it off"* following MP2's "*Bingo*" call.

Per AFI 11-214, an immediate "Knock it off" or "Terminate" radio transmission was required to have been called by the flight lead (MP1) to unequivocally cease tactical maneuvering and allow the mishap flight to begin administrative maneuvering back to base.

MP1's failure to call *"Knock it off"* created a misprioritization between tactical and administrative maneuvering. Without a *"Knock It Off"* call, MF continued tactical operations, further degrading radio communication between MP1 and MP2.

At the point MP2 called *"Bingo"*, the overall mission objective of an Instructor Pilot Upgrade sortie for MP1 had already been met.

No other member of the MF had training requirements. MP1 acknowledged that the training rules required termination. Nevertheless, MP1 assessed that he *"wanted them to have that quick opportunity before I knock(ed) off the fight"*. The delay in a *"Knock it off"* call was secondary to MP1's desire to continue tactical maneuvering for the MF so that additional training could be achieved. MP1 prioritized unnecessary training over a timely "Knock it off" call as required by AFI 11-214.

4. Failure to Effectively Communicate

"Failure to Effectively Communicate" is a factor when communication is not understood or misinterpreted as the result of behavior of either sender or receiver. Communication failed to include backing up, supportive feedback or acknowledgement to ensure that personnel correctly understood announcements or directives in accordance with DoD HFACS version 7.0.

According to the report, approximately 17 seconds prior to impact, after MP1 had nearly completed his left turn, transcripts show that MP1 made an unclear radio call (*"Sorry, two, you can continue tracking north"*. Although MP1's communication was delayed, he believed MP2 would have turned north and would still be approximately six miles away from MA1. MP2 acknowledged the call five seconds later (*"Copy that"*). MP2 believed that *"tracking north"* was not a directive to change heading, but instead meant the mishap element would eventually flow north together in a visual wedge formation. The other pilots interviewed also agreed that a *"track north"* instruction was ambiguous and would have merited further clarification. Neither MP attempted to make a clarifying radio call.

5. Complacency

"Complacency" is a factor when the individual has a false sense of security, is unaware of, or ignores hazards and is inattentive to risks IAW DoD HFACS version 7.0.

According to the report, Cross-checking visual cues with other sensor data, altitude separation, and informative radio calls are required to ensure aircraft deconfliction as both depth perception and visibility are degraded during night operations. Prior to the mishap, MP2 stated he was flying a night visual wedge formation and that his intent was to flow south with MP1. Both MP1 and MP2 testified that they were in a visual wedge formation. MP2 stated that, because he was in a visual formation, he did not need to adhere to his sanctuary altitude, believing instead that the sanctuary altitude was only for sensor formations. MP2 observed MA1's external lights moving from right to left on the horizon but did not monitor with A/A TACAN or FCR to confirm MA1's maneuver.

Review of HUD video, showing MP2's attempted boresight lock indicated that the member was complacent in relying on visual cues as his primary means of deconfliction.

MP2 did not crosscheck his visual perception against his available sensor data or attempt to clarify on the radio. MP2's statement that he did not need to utilize his sanctuary altitude and decision not to crosscheck his visual observations against available instrumentation during night visual wedge formation led to a false sense of security, ignoring hazards, and was inattentive to risks.

29 A-10 Nellis Midair Collision

Figure 127: A-10C (Source: U.S. AIB report).

On 6 September 2017, at 19:44 local time (L), two A-10C aircraft, tail number 79-0204 (Mishap Aircraft 1 [MA1]) and tail number 78-0657 (Mishap Aircraft 2 [MA2]), assigned to the 66th Weapons Squadron, 57th Wing, Nellis Air Force Base (AFB), Nevada, collided over Range 65C on the Nevada Test and Training Range (NTTR), 55 miles northwest of Nellis AFB. The midair collision rendered both MA1 and MA2 uncontrollable and both pilots (Mishap Pilot 1 [MP1] and Mishap Pilot 2 [MP2]) ejected. Military search and rescue forces rapidly located MP1 and MP2. MP1 and MP2 suffered only minor injuries during the ejection or parachute landing. Both MA1 and MA2 were destroyed when they crashed on the NTTR. This resulted in the loss of aircraft.

The accident occurred during a night mission conducting close air support as part of the Weapons Instructor Course for MP1, with MP2 as the instructor of record.

MP1 was the flight lead and briefed 1,000-foot (ft) altitude separation as the method to procedurally deconflict the mishap flight (MF), both within the formation and from other aircraft. This separation is in accordance with Air Force guidance for night operations.

MP1 and MP2 both acknowledged the correct altimeter setting for the area of operations and flew at the correct altitudes from takeoff. Although night vision googles were worn and the MF was clear of clouds, mission tasks and environmental conditions did not allow the use of visual deconfliction procedures.

As briefed, MP1 directed an altitude deconfliction plan for the MF with a 1,000-ft buffer zone between altitude blocks. MP1 directed MA1 would maintain below 10,000 ft Mean Sea Level (MSL) and MA2 would maintain 11,000 -12,000 ft MSL.

As the sortie progressed, increased radio communications, coordination with other participants and tasks related to weapons delivery diverted MP1's time and attention from effectively crosschecking aircraft altitude. MP1 stated he did not hear an audible notification indicating MA1 had climbed above the directed altitude and into the buffer zone established to separate MA1 and MA2. MA1 progressively climbed 1,400 ft above the directed altitude block. MP1 and MP2 were unaware they were flying co-altitude at approximately 11,400 ft MSL. At 19:44:09L, while making final preparations to attack a Range 65C target, MA1 and MA2 collided.

Accident cause

The Accident Board President found by a preponderance of the evidence the cause of the accident was an unintentional failure to adhere to established altitude deconfliction procedures. Substantially contributing factors include task oversaturation, misperception of changing environment, breakdown in visual scan, and environmental conditions affecting vision.

Accident summary

The MF requested to taxi at 18:26L and was cleared for takeoff at 18:46L. The takeoff and enroute portions of the sortie were uneventful.

The MF entered the NTTR with the correct altimeter setting of 29.85 inches of mercury (") and climbed to the planned altitude of 15,000 - 17,000 ft MSL. The MF began communicating with the JTAC (Joint Terminal Attack Controller).

The MF entered the western AO (Area of Operations) and requested approval from the JTAC to descend below a thin layer of clouds, located at 16,000 ft MSL, which was obstructing views of the target area. The JTAC approved the MF to descend to 8,000 - 12,000 ft MSL.

MP1 established altitude deconfliction from MP2 by directing separate altitude blocks within the MF; the assigned altitude block for MP2 was 11,000 - 12,000 ft MSL, and the assigned altitude block for MP1 was 8,000 - 10,000 ft MSL .

Both MP1 and MP2 reached their assigned altitude blocks . External lighting for the MF was off, and MP1 and MP2 wore NVGs to facilitate target attacks. The pilots noted illumination levels were high, but environmental conditions negatively impacted NVG use in some viewing directions; specifically, light from the setting sun made it difficult to distinguish detail when looking west.

MP1 established the MF in a north/south holding pattern west of the planned target area . MP1 directed MP2 to begin looking for targets along the JTAC's planned route while MP1 provided observation of the JTAC's current position. MP2 used the TGP (Targeting Pod) to find enemy vehicles and then passed this information to MP1. MP1 then relayed the enemy coordinates to the JTAC.

While in the holding pattern west of the target area, MP1 climbed above the 10,000 ft MSL ceiling of the altitude block for MA1 and continued a slow climb of approximately 100 feet per minute, reaching 10,500 ft MSL.

Shark 41 flight requested entry into the western AO. MP1 directed Shark 41 flight to enter above 13,000 ft MSL. MP2 verified Shark 41 flight had the correct altimeter setting of 29.85", and verified Shark 41 flight understood their altitude assignment was 13,000 ft MSL and above. MP2 then transmitted a situation update to Shark 41 flight providing known friendly and enemy locations. The JTAC gave a target attack briefing, or "nine-line," to the MF and Shark 41 flight. The JTAC then requested the A-10Cs to attack the targets.

The MF continued to operate in the holding pattern west of the target area with less than the directed 1,000 ft vertical separation between directed altitude blocks. Radar and AIS (Advanced Instrumentation System) data shows MA1 was at approximately 10,800 ft MSL and MA2 was at approximately 11,500 ft MSL.

Both the MF and Shark 41 flight had completed required read-backs to the JTAC and were preparing to attack the targets. The mission required MP1 to develop a plan that enabled both the MF and other aircraft to attack a target area. MP1 developed a coordinated attack plan and then informed the JTAC the A-10Cs would strafe the targets.

The JTAC transmitted the A-10Cs needed to conduct attacks immediately. The JTAC emphasized the need for an attack by transmitting the enemy was in close proximity to friendly forces.

MP1 informed MP2 the MF would attack targets from a 20 degree dive attacked called 20 High Angle Strafe (20 HAS). MP2 recommended to MP1 the attack should instead be a 30 HAS delivery.

MP1 started to climb above 10,800 ft MSL; **this soon resulted in MP1 and MP2 operating at or near the same altitude** but still not visual with each other.

Both aircraft were flying at approximately 11,400 ft MSL with 1.7 miles horizontal separation and proceeding southbound in the holding pattern.

MP2 directed Shark 41 flight to proceed to the southwest of the target area and to report upon arrival. MP2 then passed a plan for the MF to sequentially attack the targets from the west and then fly to the northwest. Once the MF was established northwest of the target, Shark 41 flight would attack the targets.

While still transmitting this attack plan, MP2 began a 60-degree right bank turn towards the west to setup for the MF attack. MP1 was co-altitude and offset 1 mile to the northwest of MP2. MA1 was in a slight right bank on a southbound heading. 17 seconds later the flight paths of MA1 and MA2 converged.

MA1 (heading 200 degrees in a 10-degree right bank) and MA2 (heading 300 degrees in a 60-degree right bank) collided at approximately 11,400 ft MSL.

Following the midair collision, MP1 observed fire on the left side of MA1. To counter the rolling motion, MP1 applied control inputs, but these were ineffective at stopping the roll.

Figure 128: MF simulation (viewed from the north) 0.2 seconds prior to collision.

Figure 129: MF simulation (viewed from above) 0.1 seconds prior to collision.

Unable to control the aircraft, MP1 made the decision to eject. MA1 transmitted an emergency radar code signifying ejection had occurred.

Immediately following the midair collision, MA2 began an uncommanded descent towards the northwest. MP2 applied control inputs that helped counter, but did not stop the descent. Because of the continued descent of MA2 towards high terrain, MP2 made a decision to eject. MP2 made a radio call of "*[callsign] bailing out*". Immediately following this radio call, MP2 commanded an ejection.

Impact

Wreckage from the collision of MA1 and MA2 landed in a mixed debris field near the midair collision location (between the two crash sites). MA1 crashed into the ground 1 mile southwest of the midair collision location. Based upon an inspection of the crash site, MA1 crashed in a left-wing-low orientation. At the time of the crash, MA1 was carrying training munitions.

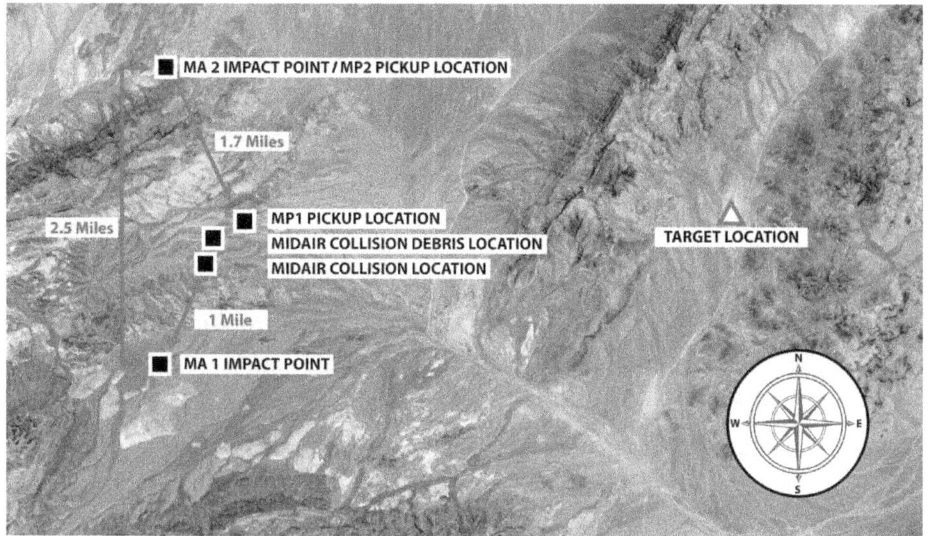

Figure 130: Map of crash and recovery sites

Human factors analysis

The AIB identified four human factors relevant to this accident: (1) Task Over-saturation; (2) Misperception of Changing Environment; (3) Breakdown in Visual Scan; and (4) Environmental Conditions Affecting Vision.

1. Task Over-saturation

Task Over-Saturation is a factor when the quantity of information an individual must process exceeds their mental resources in the amount of time available to process the information.

According to the report, at the time of the accident MP1 was planning multi-flight attacks in close proximity to friendly forces, receiving and sending frequent radio communications, recalculating weapons delivery parameters, and flying an upgrade mission. MP1 did not recall hearing an audible notification when MA1 climbed above 10,000 ft MSL. Task over-saturation is evident based upon not perceiving the aircraft altitude information available within the cockpit, missing an audible notification when exceeding the directed altitude, as well as pauses in communication and lags in replying to radio calls.

MP1 was an upgrading pilot in the Weapons Instructor Course. The sortie was a night Close Air Support mission, which required MP1 to coordinate target attacks with other aircraft and ground parties.

MP1 likely set altitude alerts to cause an audible notification if MA1 climbed above 10,000 ft MSL. However, because of communications on multiple radios and the number of tasks being conducted, MP1 did not hear or comprehend this one-time audible notification. Over the next 15 minutes, the training scenario further intensified. Just prior to the midair collision, MP1 was developing a coordinated attack plan for the two flights of aircraft, communicating with the Joint Terminal Attack Controller as well as the instructor pilot, and calculating revised weapons delivery parameters. MP1 task over-saturation was evident based upon a failure to identify or correct the large altitude deviation, not hearing the audible alert, and lengthy pauses and lags in radio communication.

2. Misperception of Changing Environment

Misperception of Changing Environment is a factor when an individual misperceives or misjudges altitude, separation, speed, closure rate, road/sea conditions, aircraft/vehicle location within the performance envelope or other operational conditions.

According to the report, MP1 stated he was flying between 8,000 - 10,000 ft MSL. MP1 never gave a radio call or took corrective actions required by pilots who fly outside of an assigned altitude block. There is no evidence that MP1 was aware MA1 had climbed above the directed 10,000 ft MSL altitude ceiling for MA1 and then continued to climb to 11,400 ft MSL. MP2 did not detect the reducing altitude separation between MA1 and MA2 that would have been displayed on the TAD (Tactical Awareness Display).

According to the report, the primary means of determining altitude and ensuring deconfliction from other aircraft at night is by use of the cockpit altimeter. The pilot must check the altimeter against a known elevation while on the ground, set the local atmospheric pressure correction using the baroset knob on the face of the altimeter, and verify the altimeter does not have a warning flag displayed.

A pilot can also read aircraft altitude from other displays within the cockpit. Pilots can set the Heads Up Display (HUD) to depict the same altitude source as the cockpit altimeter or a True Altitude/Global Positioning System altitude. The Attitude Reference System (ARS) located at the bottom of the Multi-Function Color Display depicts altitude in three digits, representing ten thousands, thousands, and hundreds of feet. Additionally, the Tactical Awareness Display (TAD) provides pilots with awareness of altitudes (rounded to the nearest thousand feet) for aircraft operating on the datalink. The evidence collected by the AIB suggests each of these systems was working for MA1 and MA2.

3. Breakdown in Visual Scan

Breakdown in Visual Scan is a factor when the individual fails to effectively execute visual scan patterns.

According to the report, aircraft altitude is displayed in multiple locations in the cockpit in addition to the Altimeter (Heads Up Display, TAD, and Attitude Reference System). A proper visual scan of instruments is required to accurately assess aircraft parameters and identify deviations. However, MP1 flew for an extended period of time above the directed altitude block.

4. Environmental Conditions Affecting Vision

Environmental Conditions Affecting Vision is a factor that includes obscured windows; weather, fog, haze, darkness, smoke, etc.; brownout/whiteout (dust, snow, water, ash or other particulates); or when exposure to windblast affects the individual's ability to perform required duties.

According to the report, MP1 and MP2 stated they were unable to effectively use visual observation as an additional method to maintain aircraft separation because the accident occurred at night and external lights were off. NVG use was negatively impacted by environmental conditions, in particular light interference made it difficult to distinguish detail when looking west.

30 A-29B crash during training close air attack

Figure 131: A-29B (Source: U.S. AIB report).

On 6 March 2017, at approximately 1432 hours local time, the Mishap Aircraft (MA), an A-29B, T/N 13-2015, assigned to the 81st Fighter Squadron, 14th Flying Training Wing, Moody Air Force Base, Georgia, crashed during a close air attack (CAA) student flight and impacted the ground approximately 1.5 nautical miles (NM) northwest of the Homerville Airport. The Mishap Instructor Pilot (MIP) and Mishap Student Pilot (MSP) ejected safely, with the MIP sustaining injury during the ejection. The MA was destroyed on impact.

The mishap occurred during a CAA syllabus sortie (flight) as part of the Afghan A-29B training course. The MA was number two of a two-ship formation with the MSP in the front seat and the MIP in the back seat. The MA experienced a Power Management System (PMS) fault early in the sortie profile, and after consultation with Top-3 leadership, the mission proceeded.

Approximately one hour later, the propulsion system suddenly malfunctioned, significantly reducing propeller speed (Np), driving the propeller blades toward the feathered position, and increasing engine torque above limits. The MIP immediately initiated the Compressor Stall checklist; however, he exited that checklist after he established aircraft control and assessed the engine was not stalled.

The MIP then took action to trouble shoot the propulsion system malfunction and restore normal operation; cycling the PMS system from Auto to Manual, then back to Auto, and later placing it in Manual for the remainder of the flight without any apparent effect on aircraft performance.

The MIP quickly decided to divert to the nearest field at Homerville in an attempt to make a straight-in landing. The MIP continued to balance throttle inputs with engine limits seeking maximum performance from the aircraft until he commanded ejection at approximately 300 feet above ground level. The MA crashed approximately 1.5 NM from the Homerville airport, 5 minutes and 26 seconds after the propulsion system malfunction.

Accident cause

The Accident Investigation Board (AIB) found by a preponderance of the evidence the MA loss was caused by a propulsion system malfunction that dramatically reduced thrust. The MA retained some degree of thrust, but was incapable of sustaining level flight.

It additionally found visibility restrictions from the rear cockpit and task oversaturation to be substantially contributing factors. The initial heading flown to allow the MIP to visually acquire Homerville and the ensuing task saturation resulted in a longer ground track than intended.

Although analysis of recorded flight data and subsequent flight simulation is not conclusive, it suggests it was possible to reach the field for a very limited period of time if the aircraft flew on a straight line to Homerville.

Accident summary

Taxi, Takeoff, Departure, and Training Set-up

The MF's taxi, takeoff, and departure were all uneventful and IAW local standards, procedures, and requirements. Upon entering the airspace, the MFL directed the formation to "FENCE-in" and initiated the simulated CAA scenario. Shortly after checking into the airspace and while the MFL was still doing the simulated coordination for the CAA scenario, the MA received a Pilot Fault List (PFL) code "ENG_PMS 001" in the cockpit, indicating the "PMU accommodates a detected fault and retains control of the engine".

After discussing the indications within the formation and with the Top-3, the MF elected to continue the mission, at which point the MFL resumed coordination for the simulated CAA scenario.

Close Air Attack (CAA) Scenario

During the CAA scenario, the MF was operating in the Moody 2 North MOA, which lies just north east of MAFB. The Moody 2 North MOA confines extend east/west approximately 19 nautical miles (NM) and north/south approximately 21 NM. The vertical portion of the MOA being used extended from 500' above ground level (AGL) to up to but not including 8,000' mean sea level (MSL).

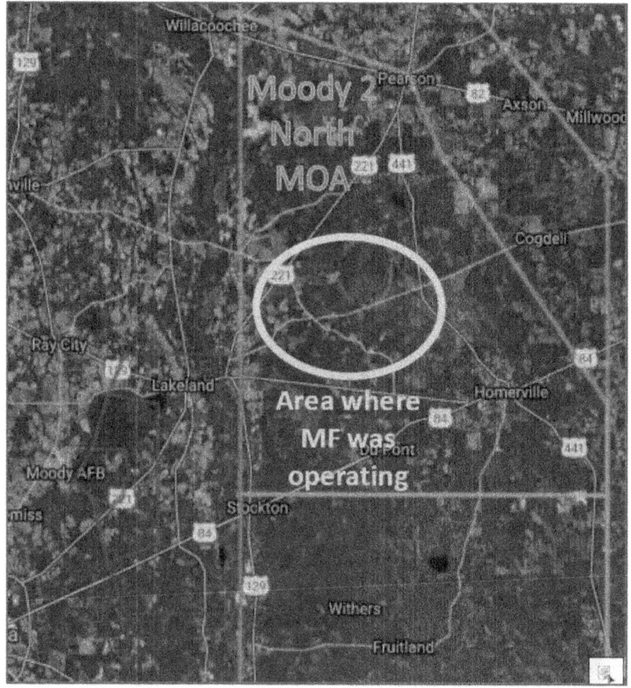

Figure 132: Close Air Attack (CAA) Scenario (Source: U.S. AIB report).

The CAA scenario involved the MFL coordinating with a simulated Terminal Attack Controller on the ground to engage targets in the vicinity. Two-ship tactics employed by the A-29B routinely involve the flight lead and the wingman operating "detached" from one another in separate altitude blocks. Initially, the MFL directed the MA into the "high block" while the MFL stayed in the "low block". This put the MA above the MFL separated by a 1,000' altitude block for deconfliction.

The weather forecast on 6 March 2017 predicted broken clouds from 5,000' to 6,000'. This weather was initially not a factor, and the MSP was able to conduct a simulated bomb attack on the first target from 7,000'. Following the MSP's attack from 7,000', the clouds became a factor, which required the MFL and MA to swap altitude blocks so the MSP could tactically maneuver as required. The MA was now in the "low block" (6,000' and below) with the MFL in the "high block" (7,000' and above).

The MFL continued the training scenario and guided the MSP's eyes onto the next target. The MSP located the new target and maneuvered the MA to attack the target from a 5,000' bomb pass. The MSP made two bomb passes on the new target but was unable to "drop" simulated ordinance on either due to not being within +/- 5° of the desired dive angle as required. The MSP transmitted he was "off dry" (indicating no simulated ordinance was released) on each of these two passes and started a climb back up to 5,000' to re-attack the target.

Propulsion System Malfunction and Divert

Note: (0+00) Represents the moment the propulsion system malfunction occurred (Min+Sec). All subsequent times represent the elapsed time from that moment. Zulu (Z) time is Greenwich Mean Time (GMT).

At 19:27:22Z (0+00), approximately 1427L, while the MSP maneuvered the aircraft to initiate the next attack, the MA experienced a decrease in thrust and a noticeable change in engine noise.

The MIP initially perceived the decrease in thrust and change in engine noise as a compressor stall, immediately taking control of the aircraft from the MSP and performing the initial steps of the Compressor Stall emergency procedure checklist while simultaneously starting a left hand 30° bank turn.

As the MIP analyzed the situation, he determined the malfunction was not a compressor stall and discontinued that checklist. The MIP spent the remainder of the sortie analyzing the emergency while continuously manipulating the throttle to obtain maximum thrust without exceeding engine limitations. At the moment the MA experienced the propulsion system malfunction, the MA was at 162 knots calibrated airspeed (KCAS), 5,209' MSL (4,995' AGL), on a heading of 334°, 7 NM west of Homerville Airport (KHOE) and 15 NM east northeast of MAFB.

At 19:27:45Z (0+23), the MIP initiated a knock-it-off (KIO) call over the radio and told the MFL *"I think we've got an engine issue here"*. The MFL then asked if the MIP planned to recover the MA to *"Homer or home"*. *"Homer"* referenced Homerville Airport (KHOE) with a single runway oriented 140° / 320°, and *"Home"* referenced MAFB. At 19:28:09Z (0+47), the MIP stated "snapping towards

Homerville" on the radio while still in a left turn passing through heading 154° and descending through 4,584' MSL (4,393' AGL).

During the entire mishap, the MFL was not visual with the MA. Once the MIP stated the intention to land at Homerville, the MFL began coordinating on the Common Traffic Advisory Frequency (CTAF) for the MA's arrival in the Homerville traffic pattern.

The MIP said *"I'm gonna go PMU Man"* to the MSP, indicating the intent to switch the Power Management Unit (PMU) from the AUTO (Automatic) mode to MAN (Manual) mode. The PMU is responsible for the main functions of the Power Management System and receives signals from sensors on the engine and the airframe for the automatic control of the engine and propeller. In switching the PMU to the manual mode, the MIP's intent was to reset the engine or get more thrust.

However, according to the MIP aircraft performance did not improve and the MIP stated over the intercom *"Reset back to AUTO here"* indicating the PMU switch was moved back to the AUTO position.

At this time, the MA rolled out of the left hand turn on an approximate heading of 052°, bearing 280° and approximately 6.7 NM from Homerville Airport. This heading allowed the MIP to keep KHOE in sight as he analyzed the malfunction.

The MIP began a conversation with the MFL and described the MA's engine parameters, stating, *"We're getting a little bit of thrust"*.

The MFL requested the MA switch to Homerville's frequency of 122.9 and then soon thereafter told the MA to "Squawk emergency". The MIP began to read the Engine Limits Exceeded checklist over the intercom turn passing through a heading of 065°, on a 300° bearing approximately 6 NM from KHOE.

Shortly after starting to read this checklist aloud, the MIP said, *"Go back to MAN"* to the MSP.

10 seconds after beginning to read the Engine Limits Exceeded checklist, the MIP said, *"I'm going to go ahead and jettison..."* while the MSP simultaneously said

"You're in MAN" indicating the PMU was switched to the Manual mode where it stayed the rest of the flight.

The MIP stated, *"We've got a stagnated engine here"*, and 14 seconds later, the MFL said, *"Two, are you up 122.9?"*. The MIP responded, *"We are up 122.9"*.

The MIP stated *"All right. So far, I have not jettisoned my tanks yet. I still got a decent amount of thrust. I'm not going to configure until the last minute."*.

The MFL said, *"Two, are you going to land this?"* to which the MIP responded, *"Yeah, I'm showing the winds at 15. Landing pointed towards the south, so..."*.

The MFL asked 30 seconds later, *"How you doing, two?"* however, the MIP did not respond.

At that point, the MA was at 104 KCAS, 1,054' MSL (833' AGL), on a heading of 137° approximately 2.5 NM from KHOE.

The MIP stated *"Might have to jettison the tanks here"* while the MFL simultaneously asked *"Two, how are you doing?"*.

Then, at 19:32:43Z (5+21), the MIP stated *"All right, we're going to have to eject"* and 1 second later, the MIP commanded, *"Eject, Eject"*. At ejection, the MA was at 95 KCAS, 518' MSL (215'AGL), with the vertical velocity indicator (VVI) showing a 2,334 feet per minute (FPM) descent on a 138 heading approximately 1.5 NM from KHOE.

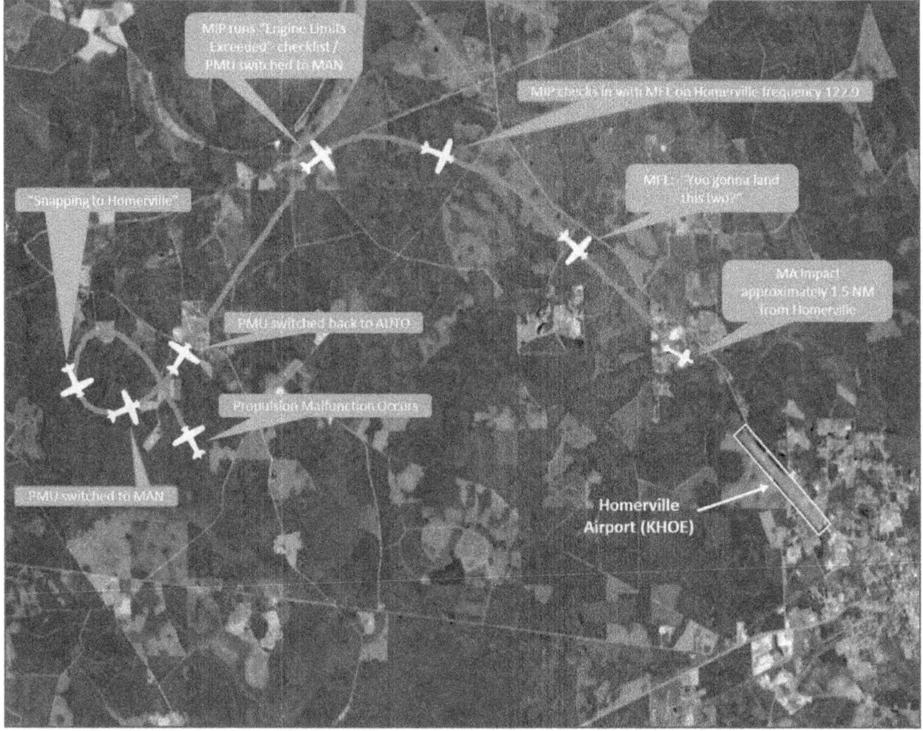

Figure 133: Flight view (Source: U.S. AIB report).

Impact

At 19:32:48Z, the MA crashed approximately 1.5 miles northwest of KHOE at an elevation of approximately 200 feet MSL. The MA was configured with two external fuel tanks on stations two and four. The MA struck trees on the way down and impacted the ground at an approximate 133° magnetic heading. The MA struck the ground in approximately 60° of left bank, with a pitch attitude 30° nose low at 100 KCAS. The MA came to rest after striking a tree approximately 75 feet from the impact site and was mostly intact with the exception of the tail section and a portion of the right wing, both of which separated from the main aircraft during its descent and impact.

Figure 134: Impact photos (Source: U.S. AIB report).

Egress and Aircrew Flight Equipment (AFE)

At 19:32:44Z, the MIP and MSP initiated ejection. Both parachutes opened successfully, and each crewmember recalls approximately two swings under the parachute prior to landing in trees. The ejection seats were recovered mostly intact, but one was severely damaged by ground impact. Post ejection analysis determined both ejection seat subsystems functioned as intended.

A post-ejection analysis of both MIP and MSP Aircrew Flight Equipment (AFE) gear showed they were in serviceable condition, except for the parachute fabric and suspension line cords, which had been damaged upon tree entanglement.

The MIP and MSP were current for AFE Continuation Training requirements. There were no overdue inspections or time changes due on the AFE equipment.

Figure 135: Impact (Source: U.S. AIB report).

Figure 136: Impact Zone (Source: U.S. AIB report).

Human factors analysis

Human factors relevant to the mishap were evaluated using the analysis and classification model established by the DoD Human Factors Analysis and Classification System (DoD HFACS) Version 7.0, implemented by AFI 91-204, USAF Safety Investigations and Reports, dated 10 April 2014. A factor is any deviation, out-of-the-ordinary or deficient action, or condition discovered in the course of a mishap investigation that in the board's opinion contributed to the eventual outcome. Multiple sources of data were reviewed, including but not limited to: witness testimony, medical records, toxicology results, audio and video recordings, and flight reconstructions.

The human factors relevant to this mishap are described below:

1. Visibility Restrictions (not weather related)

Visibility restrictions are a factor when the lighting system, windshield/windscreen/canopy design, or other obstructions prevent necessary visibility; this includes glare or reflections on the windshield/windscreen/canopy.

According to the report, the MIP was positioned in the back seat of the MA during the flight, limiting forward field of view. As a result, the MIP's ability to visually acquire Homerville for the emergency divert landing was degraded.

Although VADR analysis and subsequent flight simulation is not conclusive, it supports the assertion the propulsion system was producing some thrust after the malfunction occurred.

Analysis of the MA ground track also suggests it was possible to reach Homerville for a very limited amount of time if the aircraft flew on a straight line to the field from the point where the MIP made the decision to land there.

Although the MIP's intent was to fly directly to Homerville, cockpit visibility restrictions from the back seat caused him to initially fly a northeasterly heading as he visually acquired Homerville in the right hand side of his canopy.

The MIP maintained this general heading for approximately 90 seconds before turning direct to Homerville. The fact the propulsion system was producing some thrust and the early appearance from the cockpit of a normal glide path angle initially masked the negative impact of the extra distance traveled as the aircraft maneuvered to a five-mile final approach position.

From this position, the aircraft energy state and the available thrust from the propulsion system was insufficient to land successfully at Homerville. Flight simulation also revealed the decision to retain the external tanks did not have a significant impact on the aircraft's performance, and alone would not have changed the outcome.

2. Task Oversaturation

Task over-saturation is a factor when the quantity of information an individual must process exceeds their mental resources in the amount of time available to process the information.

According to the report, the MIP assumed control of the aircraft, analyzed the situation, took the actions perceived as necessary, and attempted to land as soon as conditions permitted. The MIP encountered challenges initially establishing a direct heading to Homerville, which was in part related to the visibility restrictions, but additionally compounded by numerous factors (e.g., instrument crosscheck, communication, coordination) significantly increasing cognitive workload, contributing to task over-saturation.

The low altitude and time-compressed nature of this emergency afforded the MA crew very little time to react in a manner that could have produced a successful outcome.

Task oversaturation in the minutes that followed compounded the emergency. Due to wind conditions at the time of the propulsion system malfunction, it was not possible to glide safely to Homerville. Given the extremely limited thrust, it is estimated the MA would have needed to make a divert decision within the first minute of the emergency and then fly directly to the field in order to land safely at Homerville.

The MIP quickly made the decision to proceed to Homerville 47 seconds after the propulsion system malfunction occurred.

However, visibility restrictions previously discussed caused the MIP to initially fly a northeasterly heading in order to visually acquire Homerville.

Ensuing task oversaturation kept the MIP from changing the heading for approximately 90 seconds before correcting course direct to Homerville. During this time, the MIP attempted to maintain aircraft control and best range airspeed, coordinate actions with the MSP, trouble shoot the propulsion system malfunction by cycling the PMU, assess throttle inputs and manage engine parameters while seeking to obtain maximum aircraft performance, initiate and complete the Engine

Limits Exceeded emergency checklist, navigate the aircraft, set the aircraft squawk to emergency, communicate and coordinate intentions with flight lead, switch radios to Homerville Common Traffic Advisory Frequency, and determine whether to jettison the external tanks.

Although the MA only deviated heading for 90 seconds, the scenario did not afford any deviation tolerance.

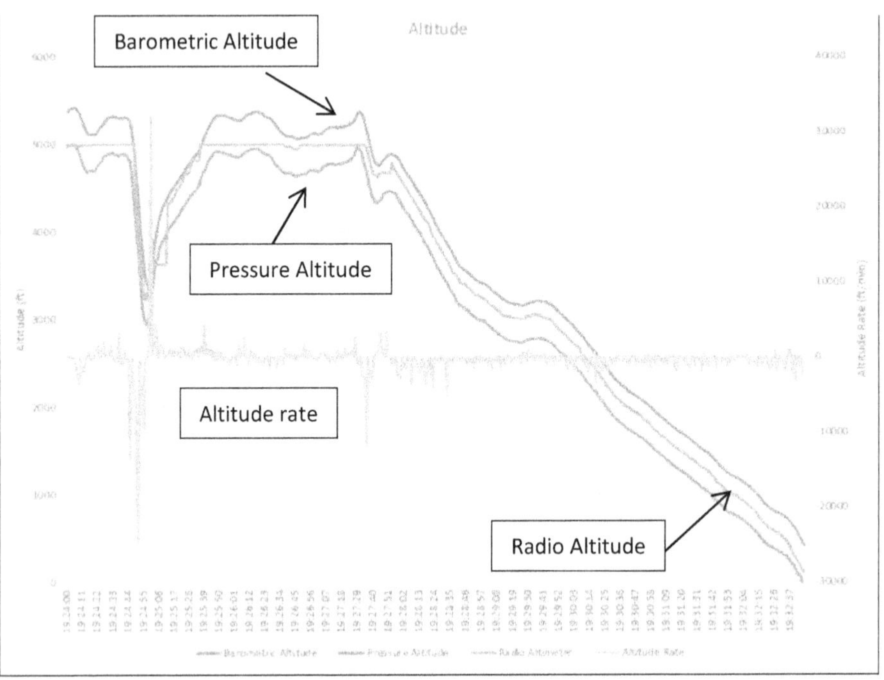

Figure 137: Flight Parameters (Source: U.S. AIB report).

31 F-16C collided on runway

Figure 138: F-16C (Source: U.S. AIB report).

The United States Air Force Aircraft Accident Investigation Board (AIB) describes in their report that:

On 15 August 2015 at 1102 hours local time two F-16Cs collided on a runway at Nellis Air Force Base, Nevada. Mishap Aircraft 2 (MA2) impacted the back portion of Mishap Aircraft 1 (MA1) conjoining them. Mishap Pilot 1 (MP1) suffered no injuries and Mishap Pilot 2 (MP2) suffered life-threatening injuries. MA1, tail number 85-01546 and MA2, tail number 85-01549, are assigned to the 457th Fighter Squadron, 30lst Fighter Wing, Naval Air Station Fort Worth Joint Reserve Base, Texas.

The mishap occurred as part of a local area orientation sortie for Red Flag 15-4, a large force training exercise. The mission was uneventful until landing when MA2 impacted MA1 slightly left of centerline with 2512 feet remaining on Runway 21 Right. MP1's landing, aerobrake, and initial landing rollout were uneventful. However, during deceleration after rollout, he did not clear to the cold (exit) side of the runway. MP2 configured for landing without opening his speedbrakes (flight control surfaces that slow the aircraft). While MP2 landed with proper spacing, he landed too fast, touched down long, and had the engine above idle power.

Additionally, MP2 did not aerobrake within prescribed limits. Combined, these actions created a substantial closing velocity between the aircraft. MP2 did not immediately perceive this closure.

As MP2 recognized this closure, he saw MA1 still on the hot (landing) side of the runway. MP2 then applied heavy braking pressure and directed MP1 to "clear to the right" (runway exit/cold side). MP1 let his aircraft continue drifting left as he mentally processed this directive radio call.

On hearing MP2's second directive radio call, MP1 braked and maneuvered hard right toward the cold side. Simultaneously, MP2 applied maximum braking (minus extended speedbrakes) and abandoned normal runway deconfliction with a hard right maneuver in an attempt to pass MA1 on the right.

MP1 's hard right maneuver coincided with MP2's right maneuver resulting in ground collision. The force of this collision conjoined the aircraft, pinned MP2 under MA1 's right wing, fired MP2's ejection seat, and drove them off the runway. When the conjoined aircraft came to a stop, MP 1 ground egressed. MP2 sustained life-threatening injuries and was lodged in his aircraft, which promptly caught on fire engulfing MA2 in flames. Nellis AFB first responders were on scene fighting this fire in 68 seconds, and subsequently removed MP2 from the wreckage. MP2 was transported to the Nellis AFB Hospital where medical personnel initiated critical life-saving measures.

Accident cause

The Accident Investigation Board President found by a preponderance of evidence the causes of the mishap were MP2's landing, lack of comprehensive braking and flight path deconfliction, combined with MP1's delayed transition to the cold side of the runway.

Accident summary

Stepping to the aircraft, taxi, take off, and travel out to airspace were all uneventful. MA1 and MA2 took off followed by Bleed 3 and Bleed 4 who were not involved in the mishap sequence. The flight back to Nellis AFB, and the air traffic pattern were uneventful.

As flight lead, MP1 made the first landing approach to Runway 21 Right.

MP1's configuration for landing was in accordance with Technical Order (TO) 1F-16C-1 landing gear down with speedbrakes (flight control surfaces that slow the aircraft) open. MP1's landing, aerobrake and initial landing rollout were unremarkable. MP1 landed approximately 750 feet down the runway, aerobraked, and applied wheel brakes.

In accordance with AFI 11-2F-16 Volume 3, F-16-Operations Procedures, each F-16 is required to land on the centerline, decelerate until at a safe speed, and then maneuver to the cold side of the runway (the side the aircraft will exit the runway). MP1 landed on the centerline of the runway and continued decelerating through 60 knots airspeed (indicated by "000" on the left side of figure).

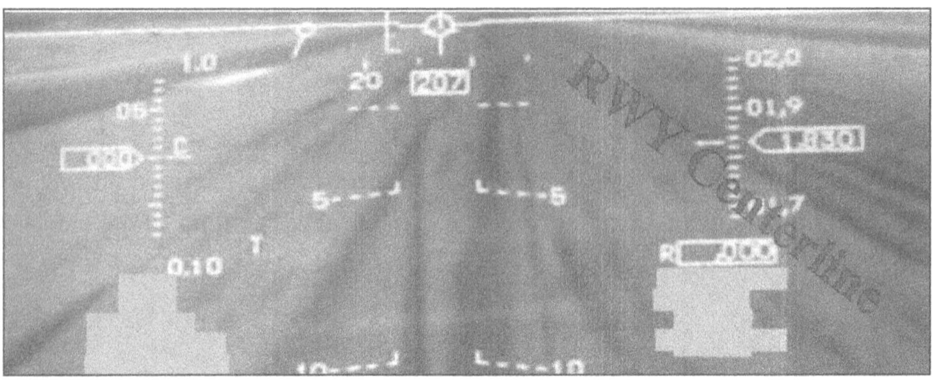

Figure 139: An image of the Head-Up Display from MA1, 10 seconds before impact, MA1 on hot side of runway (HUD) (Source: U.S. AIB report).

However, during deceleration, MA1 stayed on the hot (landing) side of the runway.

MP2's final approach to land was uneventful. MP2 configured for landing without opening speedbrakes (not in accordance with TO 1F-16C-1). The heat deformation on the speedbrakes, the position of the speedbrake switch, and Lockheed Martin Aerodynamics (LM Aero) advanced fluid dynamic modeling show MP2 configured for landing without opening speedbrakes.

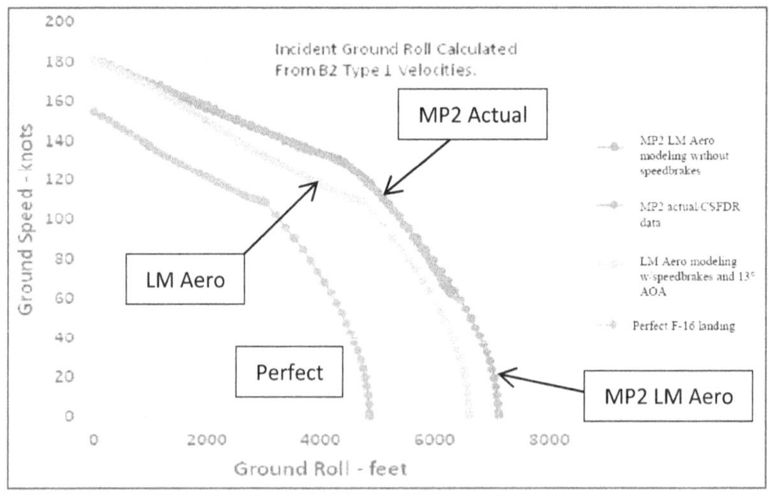

Figure 140: LM Aero data graph modeling (Source: U.S. AIB report).

MP2 landed 15 seconds after MP1 and approximately 3052 feet behind MP1, which is standard practice for F-16 landings. MP2's landing was approximately 1192 feet down the runway, compared to MP1's landing at approximately 750 feet down the runway.

AFI 11-2F-16 Volume 3 requires landing between 150-1000 feet down the runway. MP2 landed at a speed of 181 knots ground speed (as) versus MP1's landing speed of 163 knots as. MP2 pulled his throttle to the idle position at touchdown, whereas MP1 pulled his throttle to idle position two seconds before touchdown.

Additionally, MP2 maintained an aerobrake of 10 degrees Angle of Attack (AOA) or less after landing. Aerodynamic braking, also known as aerobraking, is a braking procedure required for F-16 landings. A proper aerobrake consists of maintaining a 13-degree AOA after touchdown, which increases drag.

Figure 141: F-16C aerobraking (Source: U.S. AIB report).

For F-16C aircraft configured like MA1 and MA2, an AOA of 13 degrees should be maintained until airspeed reaches approximately 100 knots.

After MA2's weight settled on the main landing gear, MP2 maintained an AOA of less than 10 degrees. MP2's AOA allowed less nose authority (aerodynamic lift) to maintain the aerobrake causing it to end prematurely at 116 knots GS.

MP2 did not open his speedbrakes in accordance with TO 1F-16C-1, and according to the LM Aero report he did not apply his wheel brakes sufficiently, thus creating a substantial closing velocity between MA1 and MA2.

MP2 recognized the excessive closure and saw MA1 still on the hot (left) side of the runway. MP2 applied heavy braking pressure and directed MP1 to "clear to the right (cold side of the runway)". MP1 let his aircraft continue drifting left as he mentally processed this directive radio call. See Figure 142, an image from the MA1 HUD two seconds before impact.

Figure 142: MA2 perspective: Far left side of runway (runway centerline not visible) (Source: U.S. AIB report).

After MP2's second directive radio call, MP1 braked and began a hard right maneuver toward the cold (exit) side of the runway. Simultaneously, MP2 perceived MP1 staying on the left side of the runway and abandoned normal runway deconfliction. MP2 maneuvered hard right to pass MA1 on the right. It appears MP2 maneuvered right, believing MP1 was not moving right fast enough.

In accordance with AFI 11-2F-16 Volume 3, normal runway deconfliction requires landing on the centerline and maneuvering to the cold side of the runway when speed/conditions permit. See following Figure 143, an image from the MA2 HUD one second before impact as MA1 begins a maneuver right.

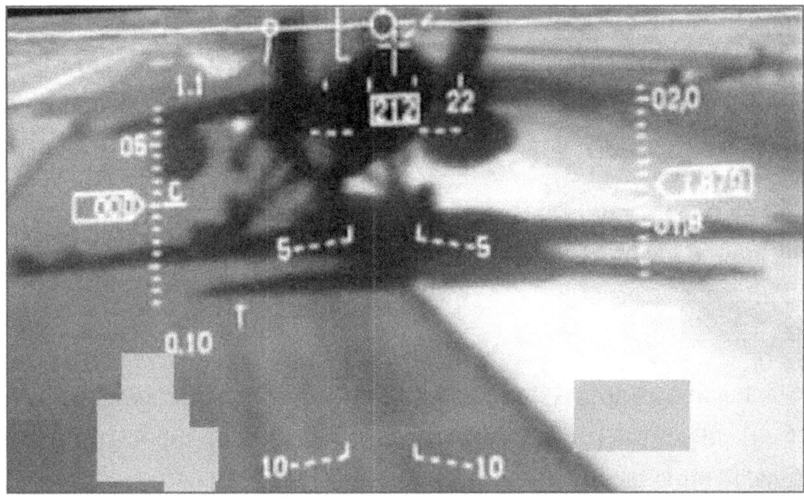

Figure 143: MA2 perspective: MA2 in a hard right tum to pass MA1 on right (runway centerline not visible) (Source: U.S. AIB report).

MP1's hard right maneuver coincided with MP2's maneuver to the right resulting in the collision. See following Figure 144, an image from the MA2 HUD at impact.

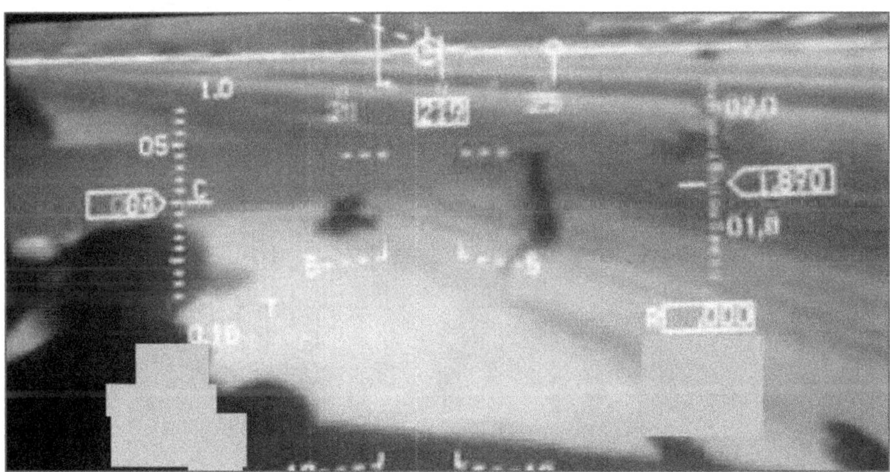

Figure 144: MA2 perspective: MA1 turns hard right, while MA2 attempts to pass on the right (Source: U.S. AIB report).

The force of this collision conjoined MA1 and MA2 and resulted in a left vector off the runway. As the conjoined aircraft traveled to the infield, MP2 was pinned under the right wing of MA1. The force of the impact broke the nose off of MA2. During the collision, the trailing edge of MA1's right wing: (1) forced MP2's panel against the ejection seat lever, (2) executed MP2's ejection seat sequence, and (3) pinned MP2 forcefully against the back of his ejection seat.

During this ejection sequence, the canopy and drogue parachute departed, but the right wing jammed MP2 in the cockpit while the ejection seat fired.

Impact

MA2 (traveling at 60 knots GS) impacted MA1 (traveling at 30 knots GS) 37 feet to the left (hot) side of the runway centerline. At the point of impact, there was 2500 feet of runway remaining.

See below Figure 145, picture of tire marks and debris showing point of impact.

Figure 145: Point of impact left of centerline (Source: U.S. AIB report).

MA2 struck the engine nozzle, right horizontal tail, and right wing of MA1, resulting in the forward cockpit section of MA2 resting beneath the right flaperon of MA1. The MA2 radome separated during impact. The conjoined aircraft departed the east (left) side of the runway approximately 350 feet from the point of impact and a post-impact fire erupted below the aft (rear) section of MA2.

Debris was scattered along the runway from the impact point to the runway departure point. Furthermore, debris was scattered in the infield from the runway departure point to the mishap aircraft stopping point. The conjoined aircraft came to rest upright with MA2 rotated counterclockwise from the orientation of MA1.

Immediately after the conjoined aircraft came to a stop, the left fuel tank (station 4 of MA2) exploded. At this point, MA2 was engulfed in flames. Subsequently, the right fuel tank (station 6 ofMA2) burst as MA2 continued to bum. The left side of the MA1 fuselage burned beyond repair and MA2 was a total loss.

Figure 146: Mishap site post-crash recovery (Source: U.S. AIB report).

Egress and Aircrew Flight Equipment (AFE)

MP1 was not injured. After the conjoined aircraft came to rest, MP1 ground egressed from MA1. At this same time, MA1 caught fire and MP2 could not egress because he was pinned in his seat by MA1's right wing.

MP2 did not pull the ejection handle. Data from the Crash Survivable Flight Data Recorder (CSFDR) showed active control inputs (hand on stick and throttle) at the time of collision indicating MP2 could not have pulled the ejection handle. However, during initial impact MA1's right rear stabilizer dislodged the forward instrument panel of MA2 thereby initiating MA2's ejection sequence. The MA2 canopy jettisoned and all ejection sequence steps functioned. The seat traveled up the seat rails but did not leave the aircraft because the impact wedged the lower right leg guard behind a section of cockpit panel. After firing, the seat settled in a canted (angled) position. Before first responders extracted MP2, he sustained life threatening blunt force, burn, and crush-type injuries.

Recorded data, impact marks on the front of the canopy, and marks on the aft transparency all indicate the canopy was in place at the time of collision. MP1's and MP2's aircrew flight equipment records show all inspections were current.

Human factors analysis

The AIB considered all human factors as prescribed in the Department of Defense Human Factors Analysis and Classification System 7.0.

The AIB identified four human factors relevant to the mishap: (1) Procedure Not Followed Correctly; (2) Misperception of Changing Environment; (3) Interference/Interruption; and (4) Rushed or Delayed a Necessary Action.

1. Procedure Not Followed Correctly:

The definition of ' Procedure Not Followed Correctly' is when a procedure is performed incorrectly or accomplished in the wrong sequence in accordance with 000 HFACS version 7.0.

According to the report, MP2 did not follow procedures correctly for landing configuration, landing distance, and aerobrake.

MP2 configured for landing without opening his speedbrakes.

Procedure requires pilots to open the speedbrakes on fmal approach. MP2's speedbrakes remained closed throughout the mishap sequence.

Procedure dictates landing within the first 150-1000' of the runway, however MP2 landed 1192' down the runway.

MP2 did not properly aerobrake after landing. Procedure directs the pilot to maintain a nose high attitude of 11-13 degrees until approximately 80 knots in order to accomplish a proper aerobrake. During landing, MP2 maintained a nose high attitude of approximately 9 degrees until 116 knots as.

2. Misperception of Changing Environment:

The definition of 'Misperception of Changing Environment' is when an individual misperceives or misjudges altitude, separation, speed, closure rate, road/sea conditions, aircraft/vehicle location within the performance envelope or other operational conditions.

According to the report, upon landing, MP1 and MP2 were flying similarly loaded aircraft (gas, configuration, and stores). However, MP2's misperception of his energy state led him to land faster, touch down longer, and reduce the throttle to idle later in the landing sequence than MP1. Combined, these actions created substantial closing velocity between the aircraft.

MP2 misperceived closure with MP1 as his nose-wheel lowered and MP2 applied moderate braking for 8 seconds while the distance between the aircraft further reduced.

MP2 applied maximum braking pressure with approximately 220 feet to impact.

MA2 could have passed MA1 on the left and remained on paved surface.

This passing may have caused MA2 to go slightly outside the painted edge of the runway (still on paved surface). MP2 misperceived the ability to overtake MP1 safely on the left. This misperception led MP2 to abandon normal runway deconfliction procedures. MP2 turned hard right to pass MA1 on the right. MP2's hard right maneuver coincided with MP1's maneuver to the right resulting in ground collision.

3. Interference/Interruption:

The definition of 'Interference/Interruption' is when an individual is performing a highly automated/learned task and is distracted by another cue/event resulting in the interruption and subsequent failure to complete the original task or results in skipping steps in the original task.

According to the report, MP1 initially drifted to the hot (left) side of the runway on landing rollout. When MP2 made an ambiguous radio call for "one, [to] clear to the right," MP1 processed the call only as " ... right". This led MP1 to believe MP2 was advising him to look rightward for a problem or an aircraft passing him on the right side. MP1 thus continued leftward toward the hot side of the runway.

Following MP2's repeated radio calls of "One, clear to the right," MP1 correctly understood MP2's verbal directives to clear right. MPI then turned sharply rightward utilizing brake input and nose-wheel steering.

However, MP2 simultaneously turned rightward thus impacting MA1.

4. Rushed or Delayed a Necessary Action:

The definition of 'Rushed or Delayed a Necessary Action' is when an individual takes the necessary action as dictated by the situation but performs these actions too quickly or too slowly in accordance with 000 HFACS version 7.0.

According to the report, MP1 initially drifted to the hot (left) side of the runway on landing rollout. MPI delayed clearing to the cold side of the runway longer than was necessary.

32 DoD (Department of Defense) Human Factors Analysis and Classification System (HFACS)

As explained in: USA Department of Defense, (19th January 2018). Air Force Guidance Memorandum to AFI 91-204, Safety Investigations and Reports, ref.: AFI91-204_AFGM2018-04., DoD (Department of Defense) HFACS implements portions of DoDI (Department of Defense Instruction) 6055.07 which directs DoD components to **"Establish procedures to provide for the cross-feed of human error data using a common human error categorization system that involves human factors taxonomy accepted among the DoD Components and U.S. Coast Guard."**

All investigators who report and analyze DoD mishaps will use DoD HFACS and use the applicable HFACS nanocodes for all findings in the mishap sequence. Human Factors is not just about humans but about how features of people's tools, tasks and working environment systemically influence human performance. This model is designed to present a systematic, multidimensional approach to error analysis.

A thorough mishap investigation is absolutely necessary to determine the cascading events causal to a mishap, and to recommend corrective actions to prevent recurrence. Mishaps are rarely attributed to a single cause, or in most instances, even a single individual. The goal of a mishap or event investigation is to identify these failures and conditions in order to understand why the mishap occurred and how it might be prevented from happening again.

Reason's model

DoD HFACS is based on the Reason's "Swiss Cheese" model which describes the levels at which active failures and latent failures/conditions may occur within complex operations (see following Figure).

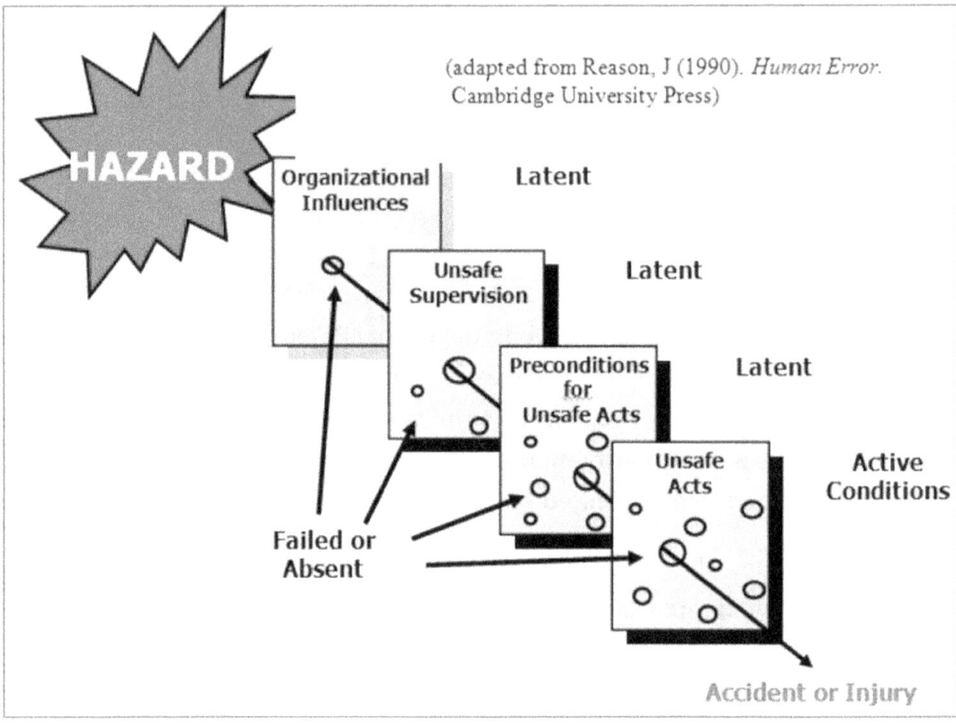

Figure 147: The Swiss Cheese Model

As explained in Organizations implement controls to mitigate hazards. Dr. Reason philosophized four layers of controls in an organization:

- Working backward from the mishap, the first level of Reason's model depicts those Unsafe Acts of Operators (operator, maintainers, facility personnel, etc.) that ultimately lead to a mishap. Traditionally, this is where most mishap investigations have focused their examination of human error, and consequently where most causal factors are uncovered. After all, it is typically the actions or inactions of individuals that can be directly linked to the mishap. What makes Reason's model particularly useful in mishap investigation is it forces investigators to address latent failures and conditions within the causal sequence of events.

- Latent failures or conditions such as fatigue, complacency, illness, and the physical/technological environment all affect individual performance, but can be overlooked by investigators with even the best of intentions. These particular latent failures and conditions are described within the context of Reason's model as Preconditions for Unsafe Acts.
- Likewise, Supervision can promote unsafe conditions of operators and ultimately unsafe acts will occur. For example, if an Operations Officer were to pair a below average team leader with a very junior/inexperienced crew, the result is increased risk of mission failure.
- Reason's model does not stop at supervision; it also considers Organizational Influences that can impact performance at all levels. For instance, in times of fiscal constraints, funding may be short and may lead to limited training opportunities."

Acts

Acts are those factors that are most closely tied to the mishap, and can be described as active failures or actions committed by the operator that result in human error or unsafe situation.

Errors are factors in a mishap when mental or physical activities of the operator fail to achieve their intended outcome as a result of skill-based, perceptual, or judgment and decision making errors leading to an unsafe situation. Errors are unintended.

As showed in the next figure, unsafe acts can be classified in the following groups:

- Errors: Factors in a mishap when mental or physical activities of the operator fail to achieve their intended outcome as a result of skill-based, perceptual, or judgment and decision making errors leading to an unsafe situation. Errors are unintended.

- Skill-Based Errors: Factors in a mishap when errors occur in the operator's execution of a routine, highly practiced task relating to procedure, training or proficiency and result in an unsafe situation.
- Judgment and Decision-Making Errors: Factors in a mishap when behavior or actions of the individual proceed as intended yet the chosen plan proves inadequate to achieve the desired end-state and results in an unsafe situation.
- Perception Errors: Factors in a mishap when misperception of an object, threat or situation, (such as visual, auditory, proprioceptive, or vestibular illusions, cognitive or attention failures, etc), results in human error.

• Violations: Factors in a mishap when the actions of the operator represent willful disregard for rules and instructions and lead to an unsafe situation. Violations are deliberate.

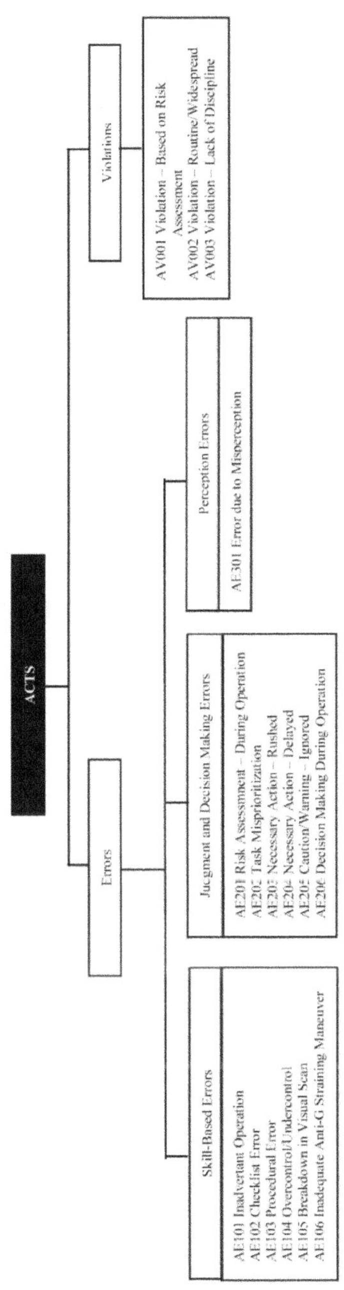

Figure 148: DoD HFACS – Acts.

Preconditions

Preconditions are factors in a mishap if active and/or latent preconditions such as conditions of the operators, environmental or personnel factors affect practices, conditions or actions of individuals and result in human error or an unsafe situation.

As showed in the next figure, preconditions can be classified in the following groups:

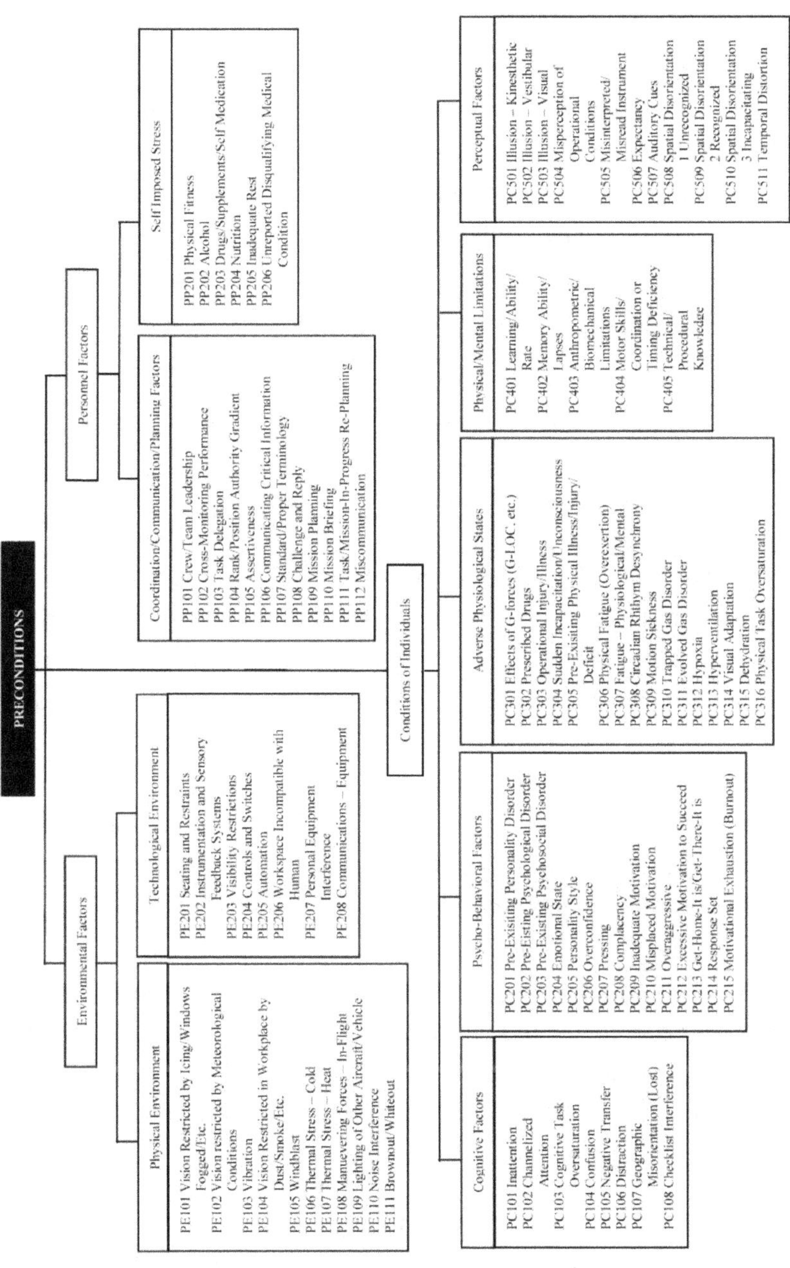

Figure 149: DoD HFACS – Preconditions.

- Environmental Factors: Factors in a mishap if physical or technological factors affect practices, conditions and actions of individual and result in human error or an unsafe situation.

  - Physical Environment: Factor in a mishap if environmental phenomena such as weather, climate, white-out or brown out conditions affect the actions of individuals and result in human error or an unsafe situation.
  - Technological Environment: Factor in a mishap when cockpit/vehicle/control station/workspace design factors or automation affect the actions of individuals and result in human error or an unsafe situation.

- Condition of Individuals: Factor in a mishap if cognitive, psycho-behavioral, adverse physical state, or physical/mental limitations affect practices, conditions or actions of individuals and result in human error or an unsafe situation.

  - Cognitive Factors: Factors in a mishap if cognitive or attention management conditions affect the perception or performance of individuals and result in human error or an unsafe situation.
  - Psycho-Behavioral Factors: Factors when an individual's personality traits, psychosocial problems, psychological disorders or inappropriate motivation creates an unsafe situation.
  - Adverse Physiological States: Factors when an individual experiences a physiologic event that compromises human performance and this decreases performance and results in an unsafe situation.
  - Physical/Mental Limitations: Factors in a mishap when an individual, temporarily or permanently lacks the physical or mental capabilities to cope with a situation and this insufficiency causes an unsafe situation.
  - Perceptual Factors: Factors in a mishap when misperception of an object, threat or situation, (visual, auditory, proprioceptive, or vestibular conditions) creates an unsafe situation.

- Personnel Factors: Factors in a mishap if self-imposed stressors or crew resource management affect practices, conditions or actions of individuals and result in human error or an unsafe situation.

- Coordination/Communication/Planning Factors: Interactions among individuals, crews, and teams involved with the preparation and execution of a mission that resulted in human error or an unsafe situation.
- Self-Imposed Stress: Factor in a mishap if the operator demonstrates disregard for rules and instructions that govern the individuals readiness to perform, or exhibits poor judgment when it comes to readiness and results in human error or an unsafe situation.

Supervision

Supervision is a factor in a mishap if the methods, decisions or policies of the supervisory chain of command directly affect practices, conditions, or individual actions and result in human error or an unsafe situation.

As showed in the next figure, supervision factors can be classified in the following groups:

• Inadequate Supervision: Factor in a mishap when supervision proves inappropriate or improper and fails to identify hazard, recognize and control risk, provide guidance, training and/or oversight and results in human error or an unsafe situation.

• Planned Inappropriate Operations: Factor in a mishap when supervision fails to adequately assess the hazards associated with an operation and allows for unnecessary risk. It is also a factor when supervision allows non-proficient or inexperienced personnel to attempt missions beyond their capability or when crew or flight makeup is inappropriate for the task or mission.

• Failure to Correct Known Problem: Factor in a mishap when supervision fails to correct known deficiencies in documents, processes or procedures, or fails to correct inappropriate or unsafe actions of individuals, and this lack of supervisory action creates an unsafe situation.

• Supervisory Violations: Factor in a mishap when supervision while managing organizational assets willfully disregards instructions, guidance, rules, or operating instructions and this lack of supervisory responsibility creates an unsafe situation.

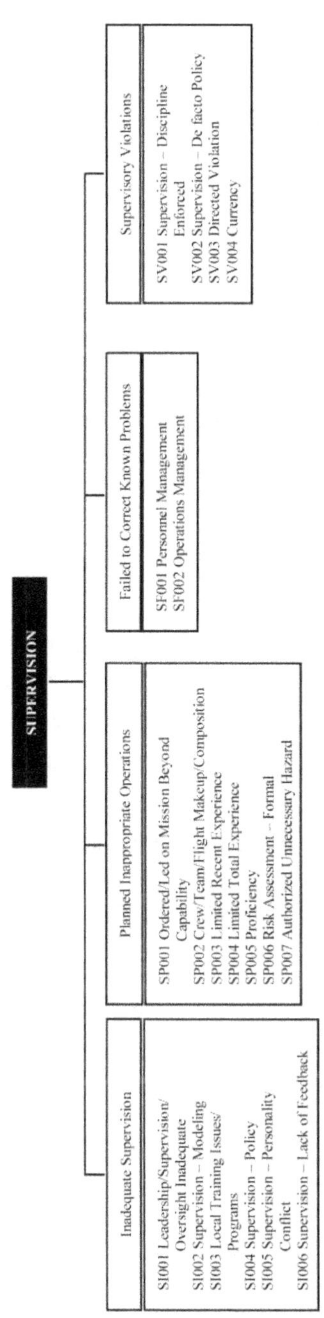

Figure 150: DoD HFACS – Supervision.

Organizational Influences

Organizational Influences are factors in a mishap if the communications, actions, omissions or policies of upper-level management directly or indirectly affect supervisory practices, conditions or actions of the operator(s) and result in system failure, human error or an unsafe situation.

As showed in the next figure, organizational influences can be classified in the following groups.

•	Resource/Acquisition Management: Factor in a mishap if resource management and/or acquisition processes or policies, directly or indirectly, influence system safety and results in poor error management or creates an unsafe situation.

•	Organizational Climate: Factor in a mishap if organizational variables including environment, structure, policies, and culture influence individual actions and results in human error or an unsafe situation.

•	Organizational Processes: Factor in a mishap if organizational processes such as operations, procedures, operational risk management and oversight negatively influence individual, supervisory, and/or organizational performance and results in unrecognized hazards and/or uncontrolled risk and leads to human error or an unsafe situation.

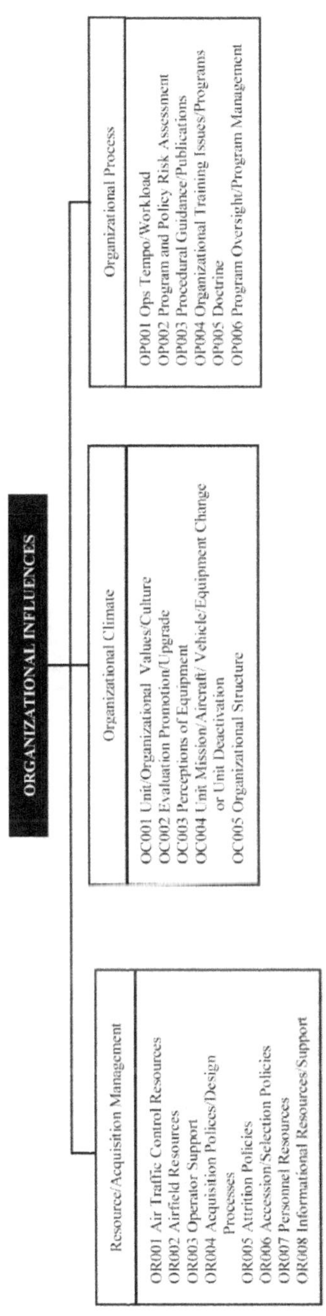

Figure 151: DoD HFACS – Organizational Influences